THE HUMANE SOCIETY
OF THE UNITED STATES

Complete Guide to Dog Care

Also by Marion S. Lane

The Yorkshire Terrier

Marion S. Lane
and the staff of The Humane Society of the United States

Photographs by Kathy Milani

THE HUMANE SOCIETY
OF THE UNITED STATES

Complete Guide to Dog Care

Little, Brown and Company   Boston New York Toronto London

First Edition

At least 6.3 percent of the catalog price of copies sold through commercial outlets at retail benefits The Humane Society of the United States.

A note on the photographs: with a few exceptions, the dogs pictured with their owners in this book have been adopted as strays or from shelters or rescue organizations.

LIBRARY OF CONGRESS CATALOGING-IN-PUBLICATION DATA

Lane, Marion.
    The Humane Society of the United States complete guide to dog care
/ Marion S. Lane and the staff of the Humane Society of the United
States. — 1st ed.
        p.   cm.
    Includes index.
    ISBN 0-316-51305-9 (hc)
    1. Dogs.   I. Humane Society of the United States.   II. Title.
SF427.L264   1998
636.7—dc21   97-44392

10 9 8 7 6 5 4 3 2 1

MV-NY

Book design by Julia Sedykh

Published simultaneously in Canada by Little, Brown & Company (Canada) Limited
Printed in the United States of America

Contents

Foreword

Dogs are, and have always been, part of our homes; more than 36 million other families in our country that have chosen to share their lives with more than 66 million of these special creatures. As we approach the new millennium and the United States continues the transition from a rural society to an urbanized one, dogs remain an important part of the structure of American households. Cats have taken the lead in absolute numbers, but dogs continue to be found in more homes.

It is because they are so familiar to us that people tend to lose sight of just how special they are. They have shared our lives longer than any other domesticated species. The earliest dogs were domesticated at least fourteen thousand years ago and the newest scientific evidence indicates this process may have started more than one hundred thousand years before that! From the beginning, the human–dog relationship has been a true partnership. Some have suggested that by acting as guards and sentinels and thus freeing humans from the constant need to be alert to the sounds and smells of danger, the dog freed those areas of our brains to further develop the capacity for higher reasoning and planning. As humans domesticated the dog, dogs may have helped shape humankind into its modern form.

The relationship between people and dogs provides the best opportunity most humans have to establish a dialogue with another intelligent species.

Other animals with which we share the planet may have greater abilities, but no other species is so committed to trying to understand us. They watch our actions, monitor our moods, and try to make sense of what we expect from them. They are often far better students of human behavior than many of us are of canine behavior. Unfortunately, many people do not bring as great a commitment to this relationship as do their dogs. Each year, millions of bonds between people and dogs are broken, often because people feel that their dogs no longer fit their picture of what that relationship should be like, or lack the resources or understanding to make this relationship work.

Sharing our lives with another person or companion animal, and building a lifelong, loving relationship, is a difficult process that inevitably creates problems under even the best circumstances. Our responsibility, as humane and caring individuals, is to solve those problems with understanding, compassion, and tolerance. That is what makes this book different from many other "dog books" you will find. This is not simply a "user's manual." In the preparation of every chapter, the guiding principle has been our overriding goal to produce a kinder, gentler, more compassionate world that respects animals as unique individuals who share the world with us. We urge readers to bring a real sense of empathy to their relationship with their dogs — to view the world and themselves through the animals' eyes and to better understand their needs and their actions. We hope this approach will help enrich that special relationship you have, or hope to have, with the canine members of your family. The Humane Society of the United States is committed to providing people with the best possible resources to preserve and enhance their relationships with the animals for which we care so deeply. I urge you to join with us in our efforts to create a truly humane society.

Paul G. Irwin, President
The Humane Society of the United States

Acknowledgments

This book has been a unique collaboration between a writer and the staff of an animal protection organization hundreds of miles apart, over almost three years. The contributors from The Humane Society of the United States, Deborah Salem, Randall Lockwood, Ph.D., Martha Armstrong, Geoffrey Handy, Kathy Milani, and Leslie Sinclair, D.V.M., wish to thank Paul G. Irwin, president of The HSUS, for his commitment to the project and his confidence in its completion; former HSUS staff members Rachel Lamb and Janet Hornreich, who were integrally involved in the project's early stages; Suzanne Hetts, Ph.D., who generously shared with us her materials on solving dog behavior problems, and Little, Brown's William D. Phillips, Jennifer Josephy, and Michael Mattil, who guided the manuscript through the publication process.

Notice

This book is intended to provide useful information regarding the care of dogs; however, a word of warning is in order:

Dogs sometimes behave unpredictably, especially when they are under stress. Caring for a dog inevitably involves some risk of injury to the dog, to other animals, to persons, or to property. Dogs sometimes have hidden health or psychological problems that may cause them to react unfavorably to treatment that would otherwise be considered proper. Laws regarding the treatment and disposition of animals vary from place to place, and lobbying and other forms of activism are regulated or may otherwise result in legal consequences.

The information provided in this book is not intended to substitute for veterinary, legal, or other professional advice. The information in this book should be used with caution, and you must rely on your own judgment in using this book or seek professional advice. Your use of this book expressly indicates your assumption of risk of injury or other consequences resulting from interacting with animals or using any products or procedures mentioned in this book. Neither the author nor The Humane Society of the United States assumes any liability for any injury to persons or property that may result from the use of this book.

THE HUMANE SOCIETY
OF THE UNITED STATES

Complete Guide to Dog Care

A dog contributes
companionship, love,
and loyalty. (Frank Loftus
and Sunshine)

All Things Considered

What Is a Dog?

To begin at the beginning: What *is* a dog, anyway?

This may seem like an odd question to ask someone who's holding a copy of *The Humane Society of the United States Complete Guide to Dog Care*, someone who probably just got a new dog or puppy, or is planning to get one soon.

The answer to the question seems obvious. D-o-g. You know — *Canis lupus familiaris*. Barks. Chases balls and sticks. Lassie and Snoopy. Faithful to the end — man's (or woman's) best friend.

Who on earth, you wonder, doesn't know what a dog is? And why on earth, if you didn't know, would you go out and get one?

Why indeed.

It's because you believe you *do* know, and of course in many ways, you do. Dogs *do* chase balls and sticks. They *do* bark. Dogs *are* Lassie and Snoopy — as well as your friend's cocker spaniel and the shepherd-mix down the street. They *are* faithful to the end.

Dogs are very *familiaris*. There are some fifty million of them in this country, and they are found in roughly 40 percent of all American homes. They live on farms, behind picket fences, in city high-rises. They look out at us from greeting cards, TV commercials, and calendars. In many ways we know dogs very well. They are so familiar, and so common, that it's easy to forget just how uncommon — how remarkable — they really are.

We've all known at least one dog who has bestowed on his owner those special gifts of companionship. (Kathy Milani and Brownie — Frank Loftus photo)

If pressed, most of us could come pretty close to a dictionary definition of the dog. We might leave out *carnivore* and we might forget the family name *Canidae*, but chances are we would remember the word *domesticated,* and we would remember the word *wolf.* What we've lost completely, however, is any sense of why this definition is important, what it actually means to you and me on that fine day we wake up and say, "You know, I think what I need is a dog. . . ." (In chapter 2 we will explore the importance of the dictionary definition, both in terms of living well and of living honorably with *Canis lupus familiaris.*)

There is no special mystery to the dog's tremendous appeal to us. We've all known at least one dog who's bestowed upon his or her owner those special gifts of companionship that we long to experience ourselves — either again or for the first time. We've witnessed the unique rapport that can exist between a person and a dog — maybe as they jog together in the park, walk amiably down the street, take a Sunday morning drive, or commiserate in front of Monday night football. Seeing these harmonious pairs together, our hearts are warmed, and we want what they have. In their presence, we believe it's possible. A skillful owner makes living with a dog look effortless.

The truth is that raising a dog isn't all that easy. Maybe it used to be, fifty years ago when even raising kids was easy, or at least easier, in those slower, simpler, safer times. But today there's a lot we have to teach a dog about living in our world, and how to communicate across the species barrier isn't obvious. How to care for a dog well and humanely is not self-evident. For every successful dog–owner relationship that you've known, how many others have you seen end in disappointment, frustration, and failure? Ever think about why that is? It's because what the successful owner knows, the rest of us must still discover: that the dog has special gifts to give us, but he also needs certain things in return. Not just food and water and a place to sleep. More than annual shots and a collar with an ID tag. Our dog needs us to understand what she *is* — a dog, first and forever — but also what she *isn't* — a four-legged human being with fur.

So maybe raising a dog isn't easy. But it's completely doable. And it's so well worth doing — you already know that. In this book, we'll give you all the information that you'll need in order to be one of the success stories, to have a happy, harmonious, humane, and lifelong relationship with your dog. To do so, we could jump right in to care, feeding, fun and games, but that would be skipping past the reasons why some people's doggy dreams come true and others become nightmares: the particular kinds of expectations that lie behind our decision to share our life with one of these special creatures.

Why a Dog?

If you ask the average person why he wants a dog, he can answer you in a few words:

- I just fell in love with the puppy in the window.
- A dog will keep my wife company when I'm on the road.
- I need something to get me out of the house.
- The kids keep begging for a pet and it's time they learned some responsibility.
- The house has been broken into twice in the past two years.
- A dog will keep animals away from the garden (the barn, the fields, the pasture, the coops).
- I've always wanted a dog. I just never had the space/time before.

Chances are these people think they've fully answered the question. Their reasons, however, don't explain why they specifically want a *dog*. For instance, what was it about a puppy that was so appealing? Why not a kitten or a gerbil? Why not a flowering houseplant? Likewise, couldn't a parakeet provide company for the woman whose husband travels a lot? Wouldn't a bicycle offer an equally good excuse to get out of the house? Wouldn't a state-of-the-art security system be a surer deterrent to burglars? Why a *dog*?

The dog has very special status in our culture. It resonates in the stories our parents read to us as children, it is in our nursery rhymes, it is depicted on our pajamas and cereal boxes. Between the dogs we met in our early literature, the real dogs we may have grown up with, and the dogs our family members remembered and talked about, few of us approach the decision to get a dog with no preconceptions. Much more likely, we bring to our decision a complex mixture of information and misinformation that both glorifies and devalues the dog. For instance, the dogs in our children's stories didn't piddle behind the curtains, or howl when left alone, or snap when they were brushed. The dogs our parents remember, or even the dogs we remember ourselves, didn't go to puppy kindergarten or to obedience school to be trained, but still knew how to be gentle with the neighborhood children and to walk calmly down the street at our side. For this reason, when we say *today* that we want a dog, it's a good idea to try to figure out what we mean.

The following scenarios give a little more information about why people really get dogs. In each case it should be clear that the potential dog owner has fairly specific hopes and expectations, which he probably has not examined closely and may not even be aware of. It's also clear that he tends to attach *general* characteristics of dogs and/or breeds of dogs to *specific* animals. As you read through this section, start thinking about what you might subconsciously be hoping for or expecting of your relationship with your dog. Look for ways in which you may be thinking in stereotypes that may not hold true for particular animals.

Why People Get Dogs

Rick and Susan recently bought a run-down property in the country. They have twelve rooms to restore, three acres of brush to untangle, and a century-old stone fence to repair. In Rick's mind's eye, their new home has a dog. It is a large mixed breed, a male they'll probably call King. Rick sees their dog quietly patrolling their property, barking to announce visitors, and keeping deer and raccoons away from the garden. Their dog "does his business" well away from the house and knows enough to stay on their property at all times. Rick met a dog named King several years ago when he stayed a few days at a bed-and-breakfast in rural Pennsylvania. Until King, Rick hadn't realized how great it would be to have a dog in the country.

Ellie has owned a succession of large dogs. Right now she has a Doberman named Destiny who's a great watch- and guard dog for the family. But for the past few months Ellie's been thinking she'd like to get a Yorkshire terrier. She likes the idea of a dog that she can take everywhere she goes — in the car, to restaurants, shopping at the mall, maybe even to work when she gets a new job. A few months ago she saw a woman in the city with a little doll-faced Yorkie peeking out of her purse, and the dog was perfectly content to stay inside the purse.

Noah is finally able to get a dog. He's completed his freshman year of college and will live off-campus in the fall. Growing up, Noah was never allowed to have a dog because his father didn't particularly like animals. All of Noah's childhood friends had had family dogs who slept in their rooms, and Noah never got over wanting that kind of buddy. So now, just as soon as he finds a place to rent, he's heading to the local shelter to get a dog.

When Jane had promised her son Charles that he could get a dog for his tenth birthday, she'd fully expected (and secretly hoped) that he'd change his mind long before the time came. Instead, Charles wants a dog more than ever, and a promise is a promise. Now Jane recalls that when she was a child, her parents had had a dog, a boxer named Tina, and that Tina had pretty much stayed in the utility room off the kitchen. Jane knows very well that just like in most households, she's probably the one who will end up having to take care of Charles's dog, so her plan is to look in the paper for some boxer puppies. Boxers have the additional advantage of short hair.

Mary and Don's visit has helped Cathy make up her mind. She's been leaning toward getting a dog for quite a while — ever since the last of her children left home. From television shows, she's seen what good company dogs can be for their owners, particularly older single adults like herself. Still, those are television dogs, whereas Mary and Don's Clementine is the real thing. Clem loves to ride in the car and is so calm and well-behaved that Mary and Don can even take her with them to stay with friends — like Cathy! To be honest, Cathy is concerned because she doesn't know the first thing about dogs; nevertheless, the idea of getting herself a dog like Clementine seems more appealing every day.

So, do you *really* want a dog? It's easy to identify with Rick's, or Ellie's, or Cathy's heartfelt desire for a dog. And it's easy to feel optimistic that they're making the right decision. A dog is just what they need! They're in for a wonderful time!

Maybe. But maybe not.

Potentially, a large mixed-breed named King could fit into Rick's rural dreamscape, and Ellie should have no trouble finding a Yorkie tiny enough to live inside her sleeve. Cathy's hope to fill her empty nest with a well-behaved dog like Clementine is not unrealistic. But will King automatically know and respect the boundaries of Rick's property? Will Ellie's Yorkie have the right kind of temperament to sleep all day on her desk? Will Cathy's dog be a happy traveler? What chance does *any* dog have of winning over Jane's reluctant heart or of finding a life-long home with Noah? In thinking about dogs, it's important to appreciate their potential to delight us in a thousand ways, but also to recognize that their potential — just like our own — may need work to become reality. We have to recognize, too, when circumstances simply may not be right for bringing a dog into our lives at all.

Dogs: Myths Versus Facts

Buried among all the notions we have about dogs, there may well be a number of myths that we mistake for gospel truth. If we believe the myths, we're likely to have unrealistic expectations of our dog and how he or she will behave. Then, if (or more probably when) the dog turns out to be quite different from what we'd imagined, we may feel disappointed, as if there's something defective about our dog.

To help you avoid the pitfall of unrealistic expectations, we've listed below some common myths about dogs. At first glance the myths may seem absurd; no one could seriously believe them. However, when we look at the actions of dog owners, including many of us who count ourselves dog lovers, we're left to conclude that we must partially believe the myth after all. Not surprisingly, believing in a myth can definitely lead to problems.

MYTH   Dogs are furry people. They have the same needs as humans.

FACT   Dogs are dogs and never will be people. They have some of the same basic needs as humans, but also others that are very different. It is up to us to meet all our dog's important needs in order to assure his health and well-being.

MYTH   Dogs are free spirits. They are self-reliant, can fend for themselves, and deserve to live as nature intended — unleashed and unconfined.

FACT   Today only those dogs who have been raised in the wild by generations of other wild dogs have the skills to survive independently.

For all practical purposes, dogs in this country cannot survive without human care and protection.

MYTH Dogs are furry appliances. They can be stored (in the pantry, the basement, the garage, the backyard) when we're preoccupied and they will suffer no ill effects. Like appliances, dogs come with a warranty, they are interchangeable, and they are easily transferred to new owners.

FACT Dogs are sensitive, social animals and do not do well in isolation. Dogs form strong bonds with their families and suffer considerable stress if removed from them. Acquiring and maintaining a dog involves substantial care.

MYTH Dogs may look different from one another but are all more or less the same. The idea of matching a dog to your lifestyle is silly.

FACT Although every dog has certain characteristics in common with every other dog, each dog is unique. Even within the same breed or same litter, no two dogs are alike. It is important to try to choose a dog who will fit into your family, home, and lifestyle. It is also important to realize that your lifestyle may have to change too, in order to accommodate your dog!

MYTH It is the nature of a dog to know what we are thinking and feeling and what we want him to do. Therefore, there is no real need to formally teach a dog. Also, dogs are common domestic animals who have lived with man for thousands of years. There can't really be a need to "study" dogs.

FACT Dogs and people communicate differently and learn differently. You do need to teach a dog what you expect of her, and in order to teach your dog, you first must learn how to communicate in her language.

Specifying What You're Looking For in a Dog

No matter what you may think of the "personals," those classified advertisements people write in order to find romantic partners through newspapers and magazines, the best of them do have one excellent feature. They encourage a sincere advertiser to be very specific and clear about what he or she is looking for. And since space in newspapers usually is charged for by the line or even by the word, most people writing personal ads seem to force themselves to get down to basics — not only about themselves and what they hope to find in another person, but also about what kind of relationship they have in mind. Against the backdrop of wariness that permeates so many of our interactions with others, the directness of many of these ads is almost startling, but if you're the one who is genuinely "in search of," it makes little sense to sabotage your own efforts by being less than clear and candid.

We'd like to encourage you to write a short personal ad for a dog (see In Search Of . . . , page 17). You may be surprised to find how much more you have to say about what you *really* want than you might have thought you did. Try to include the following points:

What Kind of Dog You're Looking For

Is it really just "a dog," or is it more like "a medium-size, calm, black-and-white dog" (you know, like old Shep)? Note: We're not suggesting that it's necessarily a good idea to be looking for a dog just like Shep; the purpose here is to zero in on what is truly in our own minds and hearts.

What You Hope or Plan to Do with the Dog

Is he to fit into your country setting, as Rick hopes King will do? Is she to be your jogging buddy, or to help you feel safe in the new neighborhood? To keep your other dog company while you're at work? To give to your boyfriend for his birthday? Take time to visualize all the different things you imagine doing with your dog. Once you've fleshed out this section, you may need to go back and revise some aspects of the kind of dog you're looking for. For example, if hiking is high on your list of Things to Do with a Dog, yet the physical image that comes to mind is *under five pounds*, some adjustments clearly are called for.

What You Bring to the Party

Most personal ads include what the advertiser considers his or her strong points — vital statistics, physical features, professional status, talents, interests, or other attributes that might persuade a potential partner to respond to the ad. Imagine for a moment that there are more homes than dogs instead of the other way around. What have you got that would impress a dog? Fenced-in yard for running around off-lead? Someone home all day with a strong arm for throwing balls? Precommitment to attending obedience class together? Enough financial security to provide quality care for a dozen or so years? This exercise will help you begin to realize that this human/companion-animal thing is a two-way street, that in a just world your dog would have a right to expect certain things from you, too.

What Kind of Relationship You're Looking For

What many personal ads lack and might do well to borrow from employment ads is a clear (if more gentle) statement of the relationship that the advertiser ultimately is offering. In a help-wanted ad, for example, an advertiser will state simply that he or she is looking for an assistant, or a manager, or a group v-p. In terms of a personal ad, equivalent descriptions might include friendship, romantic partner, traveling companion, someone to share interest in stamp collecting. Such frank admissions are really the bottom line in purposeful matchmaking. A lot of time, trouble, and upset could be saved by some old-fashioned soul-searching and straight talk.

When it comes to the possible relationship you might propose to a dog, however, the options are somewhat different. Even if you've already acquired your dog, it's not too late to rethink the kind of relationship you want to strive for. Here are several to consider:

Relationship Options

MASTER/SUBJECT   Politically incorrect as this immediately appears, it nevertheless is what many dog owners have in mind if they are honest with themselves. In truth, a dog could do worse than a wise and kind master. On the other hand, the mind-set of "master" can too easily lead to willful and arbitrary positions to which the dog may be expected to adapt. At worst, a master/subject relationship does not include the possibility that the dog may have a different point of view.

OWNER/PROPERTY   Worse than master/subject, this relationship does not even appreciate the dog as a living being with legitimate needs of his own. Nevertheless, it continues to be the legal relationship that is presumed to exist between human and dog in this country.

PARENT/CHILD   Dogs often are described as children who never grow up, and it is easy enough to fall into this way of relating to a dog. The sense of responsibility that a loving parent feels for his or her child is one of the positive aspects of this relationship. However, even a loving parent can confuse what she desires with what's "best" for a child. Also, if we think of our dogs as an intermediary stage of our own species, we are not likely to remember that they have at least some needs that are different from our own.

BUDDY/BUDDY   What could possibly be better than this? And, incidentally, how many dogs do you suppose are named Buddy or Pal? In its favor, the buddy/buddy concept does contain a reassuring sense of mutual affection and caring. What it lacks, however, or at least doesn't clearly include is a sense of human responsibility for the dog. But if you go back to our discussion of dog myths and facts, we humans, particularly in highly developed societies, really do need to accept this responsibility. In the high-voltage, four-lane, acid-rain world we've created, dogs can no longer be expected to fend for themselves.

PARTNER/PARTNER Rodgers and Hammerstein . . . Abbott and Costello . . . the cowboy and his horse . . . peanut butter and jelly . . . According to the American Heritage Dictionary, a partner is "one that is united or associated with another or others in an activity or a sphere of common interest. . . ." Partners are not necessarily equal in all respects: there are minor partners, silent partners, junior partners, limited partners. Partners may match one another's contributions dollar for dollar or deed for deed, or they may contribute very disproportionately to a joint enterprise. One partner may appear to be indispensable, while another seems easily replaced by any warm body. In essence, partners are partners by virtue of declaring that they are; partnership is as much a state of mind and intent as it is one of legal definition and assignment of liability.

What, then, of the partnership between a person and a dog? In the first place, this is not an equal partnership. On his side of the contract, the dog contributes companionship, his love, and loyalty. On ours, we accept the obligations of partnership with a dependent being, to care for the dog no matter what and to resolve any problems that develop rather than neglect or abandon our companion.

In actual practice, the human/companion-animal partnership can be as objective an arrangement as that of a vision-impaired person and her guide dog, or as subjective as that of the poet whose "muse" sleeps beneath her chair. The important thing about partnership is the first eight letters — p-a-r-t-n-e-r-s — two (or more) beings united in a common interest. For once we have recognized that dogs truly are our partners and companions rather than our property, we are that much more likely to realize that they are as entitled as we are to live in accordance with their basic nature. The unsuspected boon in all this is that in taking responsibility for our dog's health and well-being, we enable him to do even better what he does best: fill our lives with unconditional loyalty and love.

Why All the Fuss?

We've spent a lot of time in this chapter encouraging you to think differently about dogs than perhaps you ever have. We've asked you to recognize that through no fault of your own, you probably have accumulated too much myth and too few facts about what dogs really are "like." We hope we've persuaded you that this combination can lead to unrealistic expectations of your new companion.

A further word about expectations. No one could be more enthusiastic than we about the many joys and benefits of owning a dog. We firmly believe that even the rosiest scenarios involving the faithful family companion are not only possible but plausible. They're just not automatic. You *can* have a Hallmark-card kind of experience with a dog — as long as you're prepared to do some thinking and put in some effort where and when needed, particularly if problems come up down the line.

True and happy stories about dogs are abundant, and most of us know a beauty firsthand. But for every happy story we've heard about or witnessed, there are many more that end tragically. Tragic outcomes include ongoing misery for both humans and dog, as the unresolved questions of puppyhood grow into unmanageable adult problems; then, when resignation sets in, the dog is neglected. Neglected dogs live out hollow, shadowy lives on the end of a chain in the yard, in the basement or garage, or even in the utility room off the kitchen.

One of the worst of tragic outcomes is abandonment of the dog. No one knows how many of man's (or woman's) best friends meet this fate each year. But what we do know is that abandoned dogs starve to death, they eat or drink poison, they are hit by cars, they are shot by irate homeowners or neighbors, they contract diseases, they are injured — body, soul, and spirit — in a thousand unjust ways; the lucky ones are picked up by animal control personnel and rehabilitated and placed for adoption, while severely injured ones are euthanized. By and large, the former owners of these abandoned dogs are not evil, sadistic, unfeeling people. Instead, they are unsuspecting, ill prepared, and overwhelmed. They may lack the courage to take responsibility for their actions, but far from being unfeeling, many suffer guilt, remorse, and heartbreak when the dream becomes a nightmare. In the end, they still have no clear idea of what went wrong. Many will try and fail again with another dog.

More fortunate than their neglected and abandoned counterparts, somewhere between three and five million dogs a year are surrendered to the

A stray dog scrounges a meal on the street.

nation's animal shelters, most often because of unrealistic expectations on the part of their owners. Of these innocent casualties of failed human-animal relationships, 25 to 50 percent get a second chance at happiness by being adopted out of shelters. Unfortunately, that still leaves between one and a half and two and a half million to be euthanized.

Though tragic outcomes occur all too often, the good news is that the vast majority can be prevented if potential owners take time to assess their expectations, clarify what they're really looking for, and approach the whole subject more realistically. (Note: As in any relationship, some problems are bound to arise, and there needs to be a commitment to stay the course and work through those problems. For help resolving common problems, see Part Five of this book.)

In a make-believe world where there are roughly as many people looking for dogs as there are dogs looking for homes, the prospective dog owner might find herself writing an ad like the following to run in the Sunday edition of the *K-9 Chronicle*. Note that the advertisers place equal emphasis on what they want and what they have to offer.

IDYLLIC COUNTRY LIFESTYLE

Two-time successful dog owners in search of mellow male dog between two and three years of age to be all-around companion to responsible children aged seven and nine years. Dog should weigh between 40 and 60 pounds and enjoy vigorous outdoor play. Property contains small pond for swimming/retrieving and five fenced-in acres; extras include run-of-the-house privileges, at-home mom, and premium-quality diet. Breed not important, but short (no professional grooming!) all-weather coat a must. No short-legged or short-muzzled types, please. Must be neutered or willing to be.

2

The Canine Covenant

Can you remember the first dog you ever saw? Probably not — no more than you can remember the first car you ever saw. In this culture we grow up with dogs. If none lived at our house when we were children, chances are good that there was one next door or right across the street. The dog is so familiar to us that we take him or her for granted — just as we do the automobile. Yet imagine what it would be like if all dogs suddenly disappeared. Imagine that they were gone for, say, a whole year, then just as suddenly reappeared in all the old familiar ways and places. What fresh eyes of appreciation we would see them through! How remarkable they would appear to us, and how tenderly we'd cherish them. As well we should. . . .

The Uncommon Dog

In our hypothetical Year of No Dogs, we humans would have plenty of time to think about what we'd lost. High on the list would be the one being who's *always happy to see us,* whether we've been in Europe for a month or down at the corner grocery for fifteen minutes. Even more important would be the one being who *truly likes us just the way we are* — when we have a head cold and are cranky as well as when we've just gotten a raise or won a blue ribbon for our angel food cake. We'd lament the loss of someone it's *always all right to talk funny to,* someone we're *never afraid to show our feelings for,* someone who *lowers our blood pressure* when we stroke her, someone (maybe the only one) we grown-ups can *still be playful with,* someone who will *never stop needing us.*

If dogs weren't around for a whole year, when they came back we might look deeply into their eyes, perhaps for the first time, and see reflected there the many emotions that we have in common: contentment and joy, pleasure and pain, fury and fear. We might also see some qualities that we only wish we had in common with dogs, qualities such as emotional honesty, unconditional acceptance, and perfect loyalty, and about these we would marvel. After a year-long absence, for a while at least, dogs might not seem so common after all.

The Process of Domestication

Dictionaries define *dog* in a few phrases that invariably include *domesticated carnivore* and *relative of the wolf.* The definition seems to jibe pretty well with what we've always known about dogs. On second thought, though, do we really know what *domesticated* means? If we don't, how well can we understand the dog? How can we be sure we can offer one a good home?

According to the American Heritage Dictionary, to domesticate is "to train or adapt (an animal or a plant) to live in a human environment and be of use to human beings." Sounds simple enough, doesn't it? But again, are we sure we know what *adapt* means, and just as important, what it doesn't mean? For example, are we clear that the friendly dog, *a species* that is both related to but separate from the wolf, has been adapted over millennia to form a strong and permanent attachment to a human family, but that *in any individual dog* this attachment can be thwarted or aborted by mistreatment, mistakes, neglect, illness, and even genetic makeup? Do we really understand that the capability to be our best and loyal friend was built in eons ago, but we still must do our part to make it happen?

Experts disagree about where and when the dog came into being on the planet. Most do agree, however, with these general assumptions about *how* and *why:*

- Early humans occasionally killed adult wolves and captured and tamed wolf pups.

The wolf pack is the predecessor of the natural dog. (Kathy Milani's Sunshine)

- Some wolf pups remained tame as they grew older and some did not; the wild ones were probably killed or driven off, but the tamer ones remained around human settlements, where they began to show themselves useful to the humans in various ways.
- Over time, some of the tamed wolves bred with other tamed wolves, resulting in litters that contained a higher than average percentage of pups who would remain tame.
- Humans began deliberately to breed the tamest and most useful wolves to other tame wolves, so in time the influence of "wild" traits was lessened.
- Successive generations of pups from these tame-to-tame breedings began to look and behave differently than their ancestors had.
- Some of the new features were either appealing to humans or particularly useful to them, and they began further to control the breeding of animals with these characteristics.
- One of the most significant changes (adaptations) in behavior was that the adult animals, even if allowed to come and go as they pleased, chose to remain with or faithfully return to their human families, and their pups tended to be tame from birth, rather than needing to be tamed.
- The general time frame by which these results had been achieved was about fourteen thousand years ago (during the late Stone Age); and the new animal that had evolved from the first captured wolf pups was what we now call the dog.
- This process is called domestication; the first animal to be domesticated by man was the dog.

Selective Breeding

For most of the time they've lived on earth, wolves have been allowed to develop by the process Charles Darwin called *natural selection*. According to Darwin's theory, animals (or plants) who were best adapted to their environment were the ones who survived and reproduced. In this way, over time, the genes that would allow the species as a whole the best chance at survival were passed on to future generations, while those of individuals who were not as well adapted were diluted and eventually eliminated.

Up until the time that the wolf's path crossed with humans', natural selection saw to it that only well-adapted wolves who chose as their mates other well-adapted wolves were ultimately able to influence the future of the species through their offspring. But when early humans decided to keep those wolf pups who stayed tame and trainable even as they grew older, then later bred them to one another, they were inventing *selective breeding*, a technique that has become more and more prevalent through the ensuing centuries. Another name for this technique is *artificial* or even *unnatural* selection. Selective breeding meant that humans had begun to choose the traits *they* valued most, not necessarily the ones that nature might have favored.

Through the process of selective breeding, humans have been able to save or "fix" traits that most likely first arose by accident and would eventually have been eliminated — for example, the retention of puppy trustfulness into adulthood, which led some wolves to seek affection, approval, and leadership from another species (*Homo sapiens*). In doing so, humans altered the nature of selected wolves so substantially that in time a distinct species, the dog, had evolved alongside its wild ancestor. Furthermore, within the new species (dog), the continued use of selective breeding for particular features and abilities has given rise to the huge variety (some four hundred) of dog breeds in the world today. Some of these features, such as specialized hunting or herding skills, are considered very desirable to some owners; traits such as excessive barking or hyper-excitability or quarrelsomeness with other dogs are more problematic. The fact remains that once basic survival in nature was no longer the reality test, it was no longer possible to say that all changes in physical type or in temperament and behavior were in the ultimate best interest of the dog.

The Canine Covenant

On that red letter day in the Stone Age when a human brought home a litter of orphaned wolf pups and noticed that one in particular didn't want to leave his side, the destiny of what would evolve into the dog became inextricably linked to that of the human race. The long process of domesticating the dog, of "adapting it to live in a human environment," has literally made the dog unable to thrive or often even survive without the intervention of human beings. (Exceptions are the packs of so-called pariah [outcast] dogs that live mostly in underdeveloped countries, scavenging around human settlements largely without human intervention, much as it is believed all dogs did in the earliest days of their domestication.) It is clear that we who live in the Information Age have inherited from our Stone Age ancestors not only an uncommon companion animal, but a solemn responsibility toward that animal as well. The "deal" that *Homo sapiens* has struck with *Canis lupus familiaris* — a promise of care and protection in exchange for faithful service — is what we are calling the "canine covenant."

Granted, nothing is likely to be further from our minds as we happily make plans to get ourselves a nice family dog. But the canine covenant is bigger than you and I and your dog and mine. It is humanity's promise to the domestic dog and it is binding on all of us, whether or not we currently own a dog. However, for those of us who already have a dog or plan to add one to our lives, honoring the covenant that our ancestors made with *Canis lupus familiaris* is to be an active player on the evolutionary stage of the human/companion-animal bond. It is the right thing to do, the humane thing, the human thing. And remember: Humanity's relationship to the dog is not set in stone. It is a work in progress, and by our actions each of us can affect its outcome, however minutely — for good or for ill.

Broken Promises

Historically, we humans have repeatedly broken our promise to care for and protect the dog and to make sure her needs are met. In early times we fed dogs only when there was abundance. When food was scarce, we drove them off — or ate *them*. Dogs were welcome at the fireside as long as they were healthy; but let them contract a contagious illness, and again they were driven off or killed. Still, the early dog for the most part truly lived "the life of a dog" — before that expression came to mean a life of low quality! When dogs were kept primarily as workers and valued for the work they did, at least some owners took better care of them than do many owners today, who seem to view them as throw-away pets. Consider the following ways that humanity in general has let them down:

More Dogs Than Homes

When millions of sound, healthy dogs are euthanized every year because there are not enough homes to go around, there clearly is a pet overpopulation problem, which we humans have largely created and which we alone must take responsibility for solving (see Why You Should Not Breed Your Dog, page 27). When additional numbers are euthanized for "behavior problems," humans again must be held responsible — either for breeding dogs indiscriminately, for failing to socialize and provide early training, or for placing puppies carelessly into new homes. As owners, we often fail to acquire a new dog sensibly, we raise our puppy inconsistently, and then skimp on appropriate obedience training. As was discussed in chapter 1, many dogs don't even receive the benefit of euthanasia; they are simply turned out into the street to fend for themselves — which they cannot do.

Dogs with Defects

Many dogs are forced to live lives that are limited in one or more ways by genetic defects. An unavoidable consequence of selective breeding for desirable traits has been to inadvertently concentrate undesirable ones. (Responsible breeders are well aware of this by now, but many irresponsible or indiscriminate breeders ignore the risks in favor of trying to produce that one superior specimen or in favor of making money selling puppies; others lack the knowledge of genetics necessary to minimize risks.) There are more than three hundred genetic defects that plague dogs today, some relatively minor, such as allergies and skin conditions; many quite debilitating, such as blindness, deafness, and joint problems; and others life-threatening, notably defects of the heart, liver, kidneys, and digestive and circulatory systems.

Dogs Unable to Live the Normal Life of a Dog

Selective breeding has made it difficult or impossible for many dogs to live the life of a modern dog — which, remember, no longer means to survive in the wild, but just to run and jump and chase a ball and accompany their owners across terrain and in temperatures that reasonably should not be beyond the ability of any dog. Unfortunately, dogs with exaggerated physical features and/or disproportionate body types (most notably very large and heavy, very small and/or fragile, elongated bodies, short legs, very broad chests, very short muzzles, protruding eyes, long profuse coats, hairless, or very sparse coats) often are limited in the kinds of activities they can participate in.

For example, dogs who have flat, pushed-in faces and short nasal passages, such as the bulldog, the Pekingese, and the pug, have difficulty breathing during even mild exercise and particularly whenever the weather is hot and/or humid; these dogs are at increased risk of heatstroke in any situation where air does not circulate freely, such as in the cargo hold of an airplane. Dogs with large, round, prominent eyes, including the pug, the Pekingese, the shih tzu, the Maltese, and the Boston terrier, are in danger of injuring their eyes during normally rough play and even of having their eyeballs pop out of the sockets if they struggle with owners or veterinarians during handling and examination. Dogs who have been bred to have long hanging ears as well as heavy coats, such as cocker spaniels and poodles, often have so much thick hair growing in their ear canals that air cannot circulate, moisture collects, and chronic painful infections are the result. If these dogs are allowed to swim, which, ironically, they were bred to do, the problem is exaggerated.

In addition, many dogs are also limited by exaggerated temperamental or behavioral traits that make it difficult for them to live in today's chaotic world; such traits include excessive fearfulness, timidity, aggressiveness toward dogs or other animals, overprotectiveness, nonstop barking, and hypersensitivity to thunderstorms, fireworks, and other explosive sounds.

Dogs Forced to Live Isolated Lives

Through personal experience as well as through books, movies, and television, most of us realize how adaptable and agreeable dogs are, managing to fit happily into almost any kind of lifestyle as long as they are with their human families. How tragic, then, to see members of this highly social species forced to live almost without human contact, whether as breeding machines in the nation's puppy mills; as research subjects in biomedical, pharmaceutical, psychological, cosmetic, and other kinds of experiments; as racing machines on oval tracks; as nighttime guards of commercial property. Almost as sad are the many family dogs who spend their days and nights on the end of a chain in the yard, rarely exercised, trained, or played with, alternately ignored by their families and taunted by neighborhood children — living lives that may be safe and well fed but are nevertheless devoid of the kinds of social interactions that are so important to a dog.

Dogs Penalized for Owners' Irresponsible Actions

There seems to be no limit to the number of ways that we humans can make life harder for the dog. As the battle rages between the Haves and the Have-Nots (Have Dogs, Have-Not Dogs), it is the dog who suffers most. For example: A dog owner fails to sterilize his female dog. Neighbors complain about roaming, fighting, urine-marking males, and finally resort to throwing stones, shooting with pellet guns, or worse. Owners allow dogs to eliminate inside elevators, in stairwells and lobbies, on sidewalks and lawns around apartment buildings. Building owners and tenant associations insert "no pet" clauses into their leases. Owners leave dogs unattended in hotel/motel rooms, clog drains by bathing dogs in tubs, allow barking dogs to disturb other guests, and fail to use designated outdoor potty areas. More and more hotel chains proclaim "No Pets Allowed!" Dogs are bred/trained/encouraged to be vicious. Communities, cities, even whole states attempt to impose bans on specific breeds and breed-mixes thought to be untrustworthy around people and other pets.

Repairing the Covenant

If it weren't "broke" we wouldn't have to fix it. But it clearly is. Each and every dog owner can help. Here are some suggestions:

Think Long-Term

If you recognize up front that your commitment to a new dog needs to be lifelong, you will almost automatically avoid making the kinds of mistakes that can cause so much difficulty for dog and owner — possibly including getting a dog in the first place. Try approaching your decision to add a dog to your family with the same level of seriousness as if you were adopting a child who will never grow up — which in a way you are.

Educate Yourself about Dogs

The more you know about dogs — what they need, how they think and learn, what their natural behavior is, and how you can modify it to mesh with your lifestyle, and vice versa — the better your chances of choosing a good kind of dog for you and then making the relationship work.

Be Responsible

If you recognize that you are acquiring a companion who has no choice but to depend on you for everything, your responsibilities to him will be clear enough. But you have another responsibility too: to keep your dog from harming or becoming a nuisance to your neighbors, the public at large, other pets, and wildlife. Whenever you're tempted to minimize this responsibility, and you may well be when you notice that dog owners seem to be held to higher standards than other citizens, just remember that the negative opinions of others can and will make life harder for you and your dog as well as for all dog owners and all dogs.

Don't Be Part of the Problem

Of all the hardships that dogs can encounter within the human environment, the really catastrophic one is being born into a world where there just aren't enough homes to go around. Make sure you acquire your dog in such a way that you are not inadvertently encouraging the continued overproduction of dogs. How can you do this? By obtaining a puppy, whether purebred or mixed-breed, that has already been born, rather than placing an order from a future litter, or by adopting a puppy or dog from a shelter, which is not in the business of breeding more dogs.

Allowing our dog to have puppies feels like a human right almost as basic as having children of our own. Nevertheless, the fact that millions of dogs die each year for lack of homes is the most glaring breach of the canine covenant. A powerful personal step you can take to repair the damage is deciding *not* to breed your dog. (Note: You are just as much a breeder whether you decide to breed your dog or simply fail to have your dog sterilized and accidentally allow her to get pregnant or him to sire a litter.) In talking it over with yourself, or approaching others, here are some points to raise:

- There are already too many dogs. For every puppy you might place in a new home, another puppy or dog loses his chance to find one.
- Each female puppy you produce can go on to have puppies of her own, who in turn can give birth to an astonishing number of offspring (at two litters a year of six to ten pups each, the total over six years comes to 67,000!).
- There are significant health risks to dogs who are bred as well as to dogs who have not been sterilized, even if not bred. These include possible complications of pregnancy, including death, and loss of the very substantial health benefits that accompany sterilization (elimination of mammary cancer and infection of the uterus in females, and testicular cancer and prostatic disease in males).
- There is serious risk that some or all of your dog's puppies will suffer from genetic defects. Only the most dedicated, knowledgeable, and ethical breeders are able to reduce these risks to an acceptable level. Breeding sound, healthy puppies is best left to experts!
- If done "right," breeding dogs is a money-losing proposition for anyone who is not a professional breeder. Costs include prebreeding tests on both male and female dogs, special diets and supplements, veterinary care and maintenance of a litter of puppies for eight to twelve weeks, surgical expenses if a cesarean section is necessary, special equipment and supplies at home, advertising expenses, lost income, lost sleep, frazzled nerves.
- Breeding begets more breeding. If you breed your dog, your action advocates breeding to others: your friends and neighbors, your family members and children.

WHY YOU SHOULD NOT BREED YOUR DOG

3

A Good Dog for You

If you've gotten this far in our book, you already know more about dogs than the average person who goes out on any given day and gaily brings a dog home. You have a more realistic idea of the joys and benefits that await you, but you're also more aware of the responsibilities. Dogs, you've learned, are a lifetime commitment. You know that acquiring a dog has (or should have!) more in common with adopting a child than buying an entertainment system or a spiffy new piece of fitness equipment.

But you're up for it! This chapter will help you figure out what kind of dog would be good for you. Notice we did not say a perfect dog or an ideal dog or the dog of your dreams. For there are no perfect dogs, just as there are no perfect people, and the idea of a dream dog encourages the risky notion that if you just make the right choice, the dog will do the rest. If you acquire a dog with that thought in mind, disappointment is likely to result. And when people become disappointed in their dogs, too often it's the dog who suffers.

So Many Dogs!

Where to begin? There are so many kinds of dogs, so many sizes and shapes and personalities. It's true that in many ways, a dog is a dog is a dog. But it's also true that no two are alike. Which are the most important characteristics to look for? Which are least important?

And what about you? Don't forget the other side of the equation. What kind of an owner will you be? Firm and consistent, or moody and permissive? Are you looking for a hiking partner, or a couch-potato companion? What kind of dog are you best suited to own? Believe it or not, the dog you want and the dog that wants you may *not* be the same! Since your dog-to-be can't undertake a search for his good owner, it's up to you to do the choosing with both parties' best interests in mind.

Later in this chapter we'll look at many factors that you should think about in choosing the kind of dog who is likely to fulfill most of your expectations, and whose needs you can meet in exchange. But first we should look at what all dogs need. Because whether large or small, purebred or mixed-breed, male or female, all dogs require some basic things that they can no longer provide for themselves. To honor our covenant with dogs, it is up to us to make sure they get these essentials for a high-quality dog-life. If you're honestly unable or unwilling to do so, for the life of your canine companion, you're not yet in a position to offer a good home to a dog.

What All Dogs Need to Live in Human Families

We are used to categorizing human needs as physical, mental, emotional, and social. (In Western society, we're just beginning to add spiritual to the list.) Dogs, too, have a variety of needs. A human being may be able to survive in solitary confinement, on nothing but bread and water, but he or she certainly can't thrive there. Likewise, a dog may survive on the end of a chain with occasional scraps thrown over the fence and mud puddles to drink from; but the dog can't do well in that situation. To prosper, and, at the same time, to make the best possible partner for a human being, a dog's physical, behavioral, and social needs must be met. Fortunately, once you know what's wanted, it's not so hard to do. (See "Why I Love Sundays," page 34, for one dog's version of the good life.)

Physical Needs

Physical needs are pretty straightforward. They are those things that nourish and protect the body, and include the following:

FOOD AND WATER The subject of feeding your dog is so important that an entire chapter (chapter 8) is devoted to it. At this point, we only want to emphasize that people need to provide dogs with food specially formulated for dogs, and water. It's a mistake to think that a dog can flourish on odds and ends, even if the dog next door seems to. It's an even worse mistake to think a dog can feed herself as her ancestors did.

SHELTER FROM THE ELEMENTS The dog breeds found in the United States today were developed in many different parts of the world, so they vary widely in what kind of climate they are adapted for. In general, dogs need us to shelter them from extremes of heat and cold, from direct sun, high humidity, drenching rain, wind, snow, and ice.

VETERINARY CARE Advances in veterinary medicine over the past fifty years have made it possible to prevent, diagnose, and cure many diseases that used to be fatal to dogs, to correct defects, repair damage from accidents and injuries, control parasites, and extend the length and quality of their lives. To deny these benefits to your dog would be just as unwise and inappropriate as it would be to deny them to yourself or your children.

PHYSICAL EXERCISE Dogs are not sharks in the sense that they need to keep moving or die, but all dogs (like all people) benefit from regular activities that keep bones and muscles strong and flexible, cleanse the body of wastes and toxins, burn excess energy, and release natural calming chemicals into the bloodstream. However, it is not enough to give a dog two fenced acres to run in by himself; many dogs (like many people) will not initiate physical activity; it is up to us to exercise — and supervise — them.

GENERAL CARE Most if not all modern dogs need us to help them with their personal hygiene. This includes regular grooming, which ranges from very minimal to very extensive (and expensive) depending on coat type, bathing as needed, cleaning ears and teeth, and controlling fleas and ticks. Dogs that don't exercise enough on rough ground need their nails clipped, as well.

PROTECTION FROM LOSS OR INJURY The modern world, urban, suburban, and rural, is filled with peril for an unattended dog. Lassie notwithstanding, dogs are not homing pigeons; they are not born with street smarts or traffic savvy; they consume poison as readily as pot roast; they take candy from strangers; and they don't necessarily know enough to pick on someone their own size. Dogs need us to protect their very lives, but our "weapons" are simplicity itself: collars and leashes, ID tags, and fences.

Behavioral Needs

A dog needs to be allowed to be a dog, to live as a dog, to do the things dogs do. We've grouped a dog's behavioral needs in three categories:

SOCIAL ORDER Dogs evolved as pack animals. All members had greater and lesser amounts of status. Status could and did change as dominant young males and females challenged established leaders, but at any given time, there was a hierarchy, a "pecking order." Dogs are still governed by pack law. This legacy means that they need two things from humans in order to feel secure: They need to be part of a group, and the group has to have order. When you bring a dog home, your family becomes his "pack" or perhaps more accurately, his "team" — whether it's just the two of you, or whether you have a spouse, children, older relatives, other dogs, and other pets. From his perspective, the team needs a captain (if no one volunteers, he probably will) — presumably, it will be you. As team captain, it's your job to make sure that your new dog knows what position he plays in various family games, and what the rules are.

ATTENTION Dogs are creatures of habit and need something to do to organize their time. Fortunately for us, they're wonderfully flexible about what it is. What they're less flexible about is our participation. More than anything, they want to be with their people. Then the simplest little rituals, where they know what to expect and then it happens, give a tremendous boost to their well-being.

PERMISSION TO BE A DOG There are a number of things that dogs do, normally and naturally, just because they're dogs. Among other activities, they chew, bark, dig, sniff, chase things that move, scratch and lick themselves, and investigate new scents and people. Unfortunately, many of these activities, so deeply gratifying to dogs, are unacceptable to their owners or other humans. As owners, we need to find ways to allow our dogs to be dogs, while at the same time setting limits we can live with and respecting others' rights.

Social Needs

If dogs were still wolves and lived in packs, not a single one would fail to find his or her niche in wolf society, even if it meant leaving home to start a new pack. Within a human family, a dog needs to find a niche in a society that's foreign to him. If he can't, his prospects of getting a second chance with another family are poor. Here are some things that will help a dog fit in:

CONSISTENCY Closely related to the dog's need for social order is her need for fair, consistent rules and expectations. The reason that our

The wolf's pack has been replaced by the modern dog's human family. (Kevin and Jamey Bower and Bandit)

dogs need consistent treatment from us is because dogs and people have no common language. Imagine how difficult it would be to communicate with a complete stranger if neither of you could understand a single word the other was saying. Even so, as fellow humans, you could share smiles, shrug your shoulders, shake your heads, gesture with your hands. You and your dog would be at a greater disadvantage than that. She would have to learn what your gestures and words meant if she was to have any hope of knowing what you expected of her. How much harder her job would be if you were inconsistent.

SOCIALIZATION To fit into our lives and lifestyles, dogs need what we might call social skills. For their own sake as well as ours, they need to be accepting of and trustworthy with at least the people who move in and out of our family orbit, any other animals who share our homes, and the veterinarian and other professionals they will come in contact with. Most puppies are born with outgoing, friendly natures, but without proper treatment, training, and the right kinds of experiences, they can grow up fearful, aloof, nervous, destructive, domineering, uncooperative, and unpredictable. It is up to us to provide and to continue to provide our dogs with the social experiences they will need always to fit comfortably into our lives.

ADAPTATION   Adaptation is to environment what socialization is to people. Whether you live in a teeming city with wailing sirens or down the road from a sheep ranch, your dog needs to be comfortable with the sights and sounds, the smells and textures and sensations of your lifestyle. If she can't go along and fit in, she'll be left behind. She needs you to expose her patiently and purposefully to what she needs to know.

CONTROL   Finally, dogs need to be under our control whenever lack of control might get them into trouble. If allowed to follow their instincts, unspayed females and unneutered males, in particular, may roam, mark territory with urine, fight with other dogs, kill cats and other small animals, become overly protective of their territory and family members, and run with other dogs in predatory packs. What unspayed females and unneutered males definitely will do is bring more unwanted puppies into the world. Measured against the kinds of trouble dogs can get into, keeping them under control is astonishingly simple and cost-effective. Spaying and neutering are the lion's share of control. Supervision, together with care and attention to encourage self-control, supplies the rest.

Special Dogs, Special Needs

"Special" dogs are for special people (you know who you are). If you feel strongly called to make an additional commitment in time, resources, patience, oversight, or caring — perhaps all of the above — consider acquiring a dog that is special in one of the following ways. Of course, you already know the rewards are special, too.

Dogs Who Are Very Large

Expect such dogs (more than one hundred pounds) to need somewhat more living space, to cost more to feed, and to have a shorter life span than small

I know today is what they call Sunday because of the church bells. My person will be getting up soon, even though it's Sunday, because he thinks I have the right to a regular schedule.

I love Sundays because we always go for breakfast at our friend Natalie's. My person wishes Natalie wouldn't "spoil me" with treats, but he doesn't want to hurt Natalie's feelings. So he gives me half-rations of my dog food at dinnertime; that way I don't overeat.

I'm trying to wait patiently until it's time to go, but I'm too excited. I sit by the door awhile, even though it's not time yet, and once or twice, a whine escapes. My person is in the other room putting on his shoes, but he hears me. He tells me to be quiet. Something about his voice makes me feel calmer, and that helps me wait a little longer.

At last it's time to go. As usual, I'm wearing my no-pull harness. Going to Natalie's is the only time I wear the harness, but if I don't, I pull so hard against my collar that I gag and gasp all the way up the street. Even though I wear the harness, I still have to wear my collar, because my ID, license, and rabies tags are on it. I feel a little overdressed, but my person always says, "Better safe than sorry." He makes one last trip into the kitchen to get some plastic bags for our trip, and we're off!

In the elevator are several of our neighbors, and they all make a fuss over me. Usually I go over to each one for a pat and a wiggle, but I'm not in the mood. My person apologizes for me: "Sparky's got his mind on other things," he says. "I knew when I got him that he'd be tenacious, and he sure is." I guess I'm rude, but I can't help it.

Out on the street I scoot quickly over the curb and take care of my business in the usual place. My person scoops it up with the bag and we cross the street to the trash barrel. Now we're really on our way!

I know the route by heart. We pass right by my veterinarian's office. When I go there, Dr. Ackerman's assistant always gives me a biscuit. She tells everyone in the waiting room that I'm the only dog who comes bounding *in* the door and gets dragged *out*. That's because my person took me in to meet everybody (and get a biscuit) before I had to get my first injections. Even after my neutering operation, I still like to go there. "First impressions are lasting impressions with knuckleheads like Sparky," my person says.

The next landmark is the playground where we go on weekday mornings to play with my ball. That's another real fun thing to do. A lot of my dog friends are there. We only spend about fifteen minutes, but by the time I've leaped into the air and caught that ball about fifty times, I'm pretty well pooped. I try not to fall asleep on the couch before my person leaves for work, but sometimes I do. To tell the truth, sometimes I'm just waking up again when he comes home!

I can't talk anymore now. Natalie's building is right ahead. These last few minutes are the worst. I hope I don't start whining. I hope the elevator comes right away. I hope I get a scrambled egg today. I hope I get some leftover fish. I hope . . . *Nnnnhhh-nnnnhhh-nnnnhhh.* . . .

dogs. Very large or giant dogs are best handled by a physically fit owner with good upper-body strength and maximum tolerance for giant-size cleanup chores. Other factors to consider are that extra-large dogs need large cars or vans to be transported in, probably will have trouble with stairs as they get older, and may be unwelcome when you travel or visit friends. Very large dogs are more prone to structural defects, particularly in their hips.

Dogs Who Are Very Small

Tiny or "toy" dogs (less than ten pounds) are somewhat fragile because of their small size. They can be seriously injured by falling or jumping off tables or out of a person's arms. They are not suited to homes with small or boisterous children; they are less able to withstand cold, wet weather than other dogs; and they need to be carefully supervised while interacting with larger dogs and other animals. Don't be fooled into thinking that a small dog will be easier to handle and manage than a larger dog. Most toys are in perpetual motion, and unless accustomed to having all moving parts handled from earliest puppyhood, are determined to resist virtually anything you might attempt to do to their mouths, eyes, ears, and feet. Tiny dogs also are prone to structural defects, particularly in the knees, and often have problems with their teeth.

Dogs Who Are Very Active

Dogs with extremely high energy levels (notably purebred or mixed terriers, setters and pointers, and working collies) need a lot of vigorous, regular exercise. They do best with people who are active, outdoor types and live where there are safe places for their dogs to run, hike, or swim. Owners need to be fairly tolerant of some overactivity indoors and low key about household furnishings.

Expect large dogs to need somewhat more living space, cost more to feed, and have a shorter life span than small dogs. (Laura Wasson and Sunny)

Puppies

The time commitment to raise and train, feed, clean up after, supervise, and safeguard your chewables from puppies under six months is huge. You must be long on patience and willing to accept several months of puppy mistakes, mishaps, and messes. Expect to pass at least one full season living with baby gates blocking doorways and stairwells, electric cords and woodwork "painted" with hot sauce, a spring clip on your garbage pail lid, and all wastebaskets sitting atop tables and counters.

Dogs Who Are Older

In contrast to the havoc a puppy can wreak on a household, a dog more than seven years old may make the most tranquil adjustment of any dog you might choose. However, you may have to meet an older dog more than halfway in retraining her to new routines, and you may need to give her more time really to warm up to you. You should also be aware that veterinary problems (and expenses) are likely to come sooner rather than later, and that your time together will be relatively short.

Dogs with Special Needs

Some very special people are willing to offer a home to a dog with some kind of disability. The dog might be partially or completely blind or deaf, have a missing limb, epilepsy, diabetes, allergies, or another chronic condition that requires regular or lifelong treatment. A different kind of special need is found in the dog who has been mistreated or abandoned and is particularly fearful or clingy. There may be restrictions on what you and your special dog can do together, and you may find few friends who want the responsibility of caring for him in your absence. Depending on the type and extent of disability, you may face higher veterinary bills from the outset. All dogs with special needs require maximum patience and understanding, and an iron-clad commitment to their ongoing care.

Dogs, Wolves, Wolf Hybrids

Although all breeds of dogs are descended from the wolf, you must not lose sight of the fact that dogs are not wolves, wolves are not dogs, and wolf hybrids are not a happy combination of the two. What all dogs have in common is domestication. And what sets dogs apart from wolves, no matter how similar they may appear, is also domestication.

With human intervention, dogs and wolves can and do interbreed, resulting in what is called a wolf hybrid. By the late 1980s, wolf hybrids had become enormously popular, because many people believed that these animals could neatly bridge the wild and domestic worlds, possessing the best characteristics of both parents. Not so. Genetics just doesn't work that way. For example, a very tall man and a very short woman do not have children of average height; they have either very tall or very short children, or some of each. Wolf hybrids, rather than being wolves who act like dogs, tend to be misfits who cannot function well in either a wild or a domestic environment. More aggressive than wolves, more timid than dogs, difficult or impossible to train or trust, what wolf hybrids mostly are is unpredictable — which, ironically, is just the opposite of the trait humans valued in those captive wolf pups some fourteen thousand years ago. So in your search for your good dog, you've one less kind of canine to consider. The field is still vast and wide open.

Wanted: One Good Dog

You would have a much easier time choosing a dog if dogs didn't come in such mind-boggling variety. Fortunately, Americans are used to making choices. No people at any place or time in history have been blessed (some say cursed) with so much diversity in goods, services, fashion, music, career tracks, belief systems, lifestyles, cultures, and worldviews. Not surprisingly, we've even got a variety of approaches to choosing a dog!

What most approaches you could try have in common is that they encourage you to take a personal inventory, to think about your physical space, the makeup of your family, your interests and lifestyle, and how much time you're prepared to spend caring for a dog. We will do that, too, but we will also be thinking about the other part of this partnership, the dog. We'll be keeping in mind the different needs of different kinds of dogs, as well as the needs of all dogs, outlined above.

Taking a personal inventory is basically a matter of asking yourself the right questions, and being frank and thorough in your answers. (Your Inventory Answer Sheet is found on page 50.) The questions are drawn from what dog owners repeatedly give as reasons for surrendering dogs to shelters. That means it's critically important to address these issues *before* you choose a dog. There are no right or wrong answers, only what's true for you. The point of taking this inventory is to gather information about two things: yourself as an owner, and what kind of dog you're suited for. After you've completed your worksheet, continue reading to see what your answers could mean to your dog.

Part A: Yourself as a Dog Owner

All of the questions in this part call for a *yes* answer. However, *no* answers to some questions don't necessarily mean that you should not get a dog. They mean that some action on your part is called for, and/or that there are some restrictions on the kind of dog that would be a good choice for you.

Are You Allowed to Have a Dog?
The time to make sure that your landlord allows dogs is before, not after, you bring one home. (Get permission in writing — ideally it should be part of your lease — since a verbal agreement can be broken if tenant/landowner relations become strained.) If you're not certain whether or not your landlord or town has any restrictions on how many, what sizes, or what breeds of dogs may live there, find out. You can keep two hearts from being broken.

Can You Afford a Dog at This Time?
The only way you can answer this question responsibly is to get out paper and pencil, plug in some real numbers, and extend them forward over fifteen years, over ten years, and over five years. If you currently or recently have owned a dog, you have access to approximate figures for your area. If

this will be your first dog, you have to find out the cost of food, supplies, spaying/neutering, training, licensing, regular veterinary care, then budget for a few extraordinary expenses (chapter 5 addresses in detail the subject of finances). Unless money is truly "not an issue," this one exercise can help you focus in on the best age dog to think about, or even the best size.

Have You Considered the Neighbors — Present and Future?

Unless you have no close neighbors and no chance of getting any, you need to give them more than a passing thought as you consider getting a dog. Not only should your dog not disturb your neighbors, but you should also consider the effect that your neighbors (and their children, dogs, cats, other pets, or livestock) are likely to have on your dog. If you live in an apartment building, remember how frequently neighbors can change and make sure your dog will give new tenants no legitimate reason to object to having him live next door.

Are You, or Another Adult, Prepared to Be the Dog's "Owner"?

No matter how many people are in your family, it's important that one person, an adult, take responsibility for the dog. This is the person who will be captain of the team where the dog is concerned. Certainly all family members can share the dog, play with the dog, and love the dog. What the responsible adult is really responsible for is making sure the dog is secure about his status within the family's social structure. This is almost automatic if the responsible person is the one who primarily feeds and trains the dog.

Do You Know How to Care for a Dog?

Many dog books rank dog breeds by how hard they are to train, and some even caution that certain breeds are not suited for first-time owners. This is true enough. It is also true that all dogs require a certain amount of know-how. How to feed, groom, and handle your dog, as well as when to take her to the veterinarian, is easily learned. But no dog, and certainly no puppy, is going to arrive at your home with the ability to figure out on her own what's expected of her. Yet teaching your dog how to fit into your family is not a matter of common sense. To teach her, you first have to understand how she learns. Most people find this fascinating and fun, but it does take some time and effort. If you don't already know how to train a dog, make sure you feel committed to finding out.

It's important that no one in the household be negative, uneasy, or uncertain about adding a dog to the family. (Geoffrey and Holly Bouton and a potential adoptee)

Do All Family Members Agree about Getting a Dog?

It's important that no one be negative, uneasy, or uncertain about adding a dog to your household. Find out ahead of time if any family member (or prospective family member) is allergic to dogs by spending time with different types; don't depend on assurances that this or that type of dog is hypoallergenic; it is not dog hair but dog dander that people are allergic to, and all dogs have dander. Happily, there are products that can help make dogs less allergenic to sensitive people.

Is Your Family Situation a Stable One?

Acquiring a dog really does need in many ways to be equated with adopting a child. Dogs are entitled to permanent homes. This is easier to ensure if your family is established. Young singles may easily fall in love with someone who doesn't like dogs. Unhappy unions are not likely to become happy ones by adding a dog. Young professionals who are just starting careers may need to relocate across the country or the world. Childless young couples should consider a dog and future children as equally important aspects of family planning.

Are Your Children Six Years Old or Older?

Having young children imposes some restrictions on the kind of dog that is suitable for your family to own. Notably excluded, in general, are very young puppies, very small dogs of any age, and adult dogs not used to being around children. In addition, the responsible adult should always be present to supervise any dog and children under six. Another adult such as a baby-sitter is not an acceptable substitute.

Will the Dog Be the Only Pet in Your Home?

The presence of other pets may restrict the kind of dog for which your home would be suitable. No incoming adult dog should be expected to be indifferent to small animals, including cats, rabbits, ferrets, hamsters, and birds. A resident adult dog needs to be introduced to a prospective new dog to assess compatibility. Incoming puppies are at risk of being injured by cats and other established pets, and all interactions must be supervised at first.

Can Your Schedule Accommodate the Needs of a Dog?

Different kinds and ages of dogs vary in terms of how often they need to be fed and allowed to eliminate, as well as how much care, exercise, and training they need. However, all dogs need some amount of care, and they need it on a reasonably reliable schedule. If no one is home for eight hours at a time, you'll want to make provision for an adult dog to have the opportunity to eliminate. Puppies need to relieve themselves every few hours. If you work long hours, reliable neighbors and professional dog walkers are two options, as are dog doors leading to fenced yards. Very small breeds may be trained to eliminate indoors on newspaper.

Can Your Lifestyle Accommodate the Needs of a Dog?

A dog should complement and enhance your lifestyle, but there are some ways of living that are incompatible with a dog's basic need to be a fully integrated member of the family. If your family is constantly "on the go," meaning that everyone is away from home as much as or more than they're there, or if you travel frequently for pleasure or business, you probably can't provide a suitable home for a dog at this time.

Are You Free of Any Physical Limitations or Health Problems That Would Interfere with Your Ability to Own a Dog?

Caring for almost any kind of dog is pretty physical. Tiny dogs weigh next to nothing, but there's a tremendous amount of bending down involved. Even medium-size dogs are remarkably strong and fast, and large and giant dogs, no matter how calm, cannot be physically controlled by a frail person. Every dog owner needs to be able to participate in training classes with the dog. Finally, as a responsible owner, you will want to have a contingency plan in place from the outset in the event that you become temporarily or permanently unable to care for your dog.

Part B: A Good Dog for You

The questions in Part B will help you to focus in on the kind of dog that is most likely to fit easily, well, and permanently into your home. Keep the discussion from Part A in mind as you answer Part B.

What Size Dog Should You Get?

As you may know, dogs range in size from several pounds to almost two hundred, and from between seven or eight inches in height to well over three feet. For comparison purposes, we classify them as very small or toy (under 15 pounds), small (15–30 pounds), medium (30–60 pounds), large (60–100 pounds), and extra-large or giant (over 100 pounds). If your plan is to bring your dog to the office every day, a good choice might be a toy dog. If you're a hiking enthusiast who's looking for a trail buddy, you'll probably want a larger, sturdier type. For most people, a small or medium-size dog is most practical. It's neither fragile nor too powerful to handle, is big enough to play and romp with, and is small enough to transport easily. All other things being equal, a medium-size dog with a "regular" shape is less likely than extreme types to have structural defects.

What Age?

As already noted, puppies under six months are labor- and time-intensive. Puppies over six months and young dogs under about eighteen months are far sturdier than young puppies, and their basic personality is more apparent. These adolescent dogs are full of energy and enthusiasm, but can pay attention long enough to learn new things quickly. Best of all, they still have most of their lives ahead of them. If you don't like surprises, a dog over two years may be your best bet. Dogs live an average of about twelve years, with very small dogs living longer and very large ones being shorter lived.

What about Health?

It may seem obvious that you will want your dog to be healthy (as noted, some people willingly accept the challenge of a dog with special health needs). Still, it's important to remember that a dog is a living thing, not an appliance under warranty to "work" for a given length of time. Some genetic pitfalls were discussed in chapter 2, and of course you should try to avoid these when you choose a dog. You'll also want to do your best to make sure the dog you select is in good health (see Checklist for Health, page 47). Beyond that, a reasonable attitude toward your dog's health should be the same

A dog should suit
your lifestyle.

as it is toward that of your friends, family, and spouse: "in sickness and in health, till death you do part."

What Kind of Temperament Will "Fit" Your Household?

A dog's temperament is partially inherited, partially shaped by his interactions with his mother and littermates, and very much affected by early experiences, including treatment by people. Temperament in dogs ranges from very timid to extremely bold, from placid to excitable, from submissive to aggressive, from very people-oriented to quite aloof and independent. And while most dogs do have a basic temperament, it's common for dogs to display different behaviors in different situations and with different people

For most people, a small- or medium-size dog is most practical. (Lalita Ragland and Essence)

and animals. Temperament is an important factor in training a dog; people-oriented dogs with medium levels of other characteristics are generally easiest to teach. You should also think about the emotional climate within your family and look for a temperament that seems compatible. Shelter adoption counselors, a veterinarian, experienced dog trainers, and some breeders can help you assess the temperament of a dog you're considering.

Do You Need a Dog Who's "Good with Children"?

This subject was raised in Part A, and if you have children under six, you may need to note some restrictions with regard to the size and age of your dog, as well as her temperament. Most dogs who are properly socialized as puppies to older, responsible children will grow up to be trustworthy with children.

Will the Dog Have to Be Left Home Alone?

Some dogs have a great deal more difficulty than others being calm when they are left at home alone. This is mostly due to early experiences and never having been taught how to behave when alone. It's hard to imagine any dog not needing this skill, though, and you should either choose a dog that has already demonstrated it or resolve to teach it to a puppy. (For help overcoming what is called separation anxiety, see chapter 19.)

What Activity Level Can You Accommodate?

What you need to know about activity level is that it doesn't just apply when you're in the mood to jog five miles or throw a ball three hundred times. A dog's activity level tends to be more constant than that, even allowing for the fact that most dogs slow down as they get older. Another way to think about your dog's activity level and how it will mesh with your own is to consider his activity level not so much in terms of what he does, but how quickly and passionately he does it.

How Much Training Are You up To?

Your dog needs to be under your control, which means that you have to train her. (See chapter 14 for a complete discussion of obedience training.) In addition to housetraining, she needs to be trained to walk on a leash, not to bite, and to come when called. A dog who will sit, lie down, not jump up, and stop barking, on command, is much easier to live with than one who raises an eyebrow at such suggestions. As already noted, some dogs are easier to train than others because they are more people-oriented, more eager to please, and less easily distracted by sights, sounds, and smells. Nevertheless, training any dog requires patience, practice, and consistency. If you find yourself falling in love with an independent, inattentive, easily distracted dog, make sure you love a good challenge and are totally committed to working long and hard at her training.

Do You Have a Particular Breed in Mind?

If you're absolutely certain that a beagle or a boxer or a (fill in the blank) is the dog for you, your search may be simpler. But unless you've already owned and enjoyed at least two of that breed, you might want to ask yourself why you feel as sure as you do. (A minimum of two is important, because if you've only owned one, you may be confusing the breed with the individual dog!) If the dog's overall appearance, size, coloring, and coat type are of primary importance, you're on pretty safe ground in choosing by breed. But if you expect a particular temperament in your beagle, boxer, or whatever, remember that inheritance is only one of the factors that determine temperament. If you're a cautious consumer who feels more confidence in the quality and predictability of a "name brand" dog who's backed by "papers," your faith may be misplaced. Registration papers are actually an identification and record-keeping tool, not a warranty of quality, temperament, or health (see Papers and Pedigrees: What Do They Mean?, page 49).

Do "Looks" Matter to You?

Beauty, as they say, is in the eye of the beholder. Another thing they say is that handsome is as handsome does. Certainly, it makes sense to like the way your dog looks. Something you should know about looks in dogs, however, is that they often affect function or convenience in ways that may not be obvious to you. For instance, wrinkled skin, bowed legs, a pushed-in face, or a long, flowing coat may strike a strongly responsive chord within you. But wrinkles can trap moisture and odors, bowed legs limit running and jumping, pushed-in faces cause problems in breathing, and long, flowing coats become filthy, matted, and smelly without daily care. The further a dog's looks vary from what nature intended — a small wolf or coyote type — the more upkeep and/or functional problems you should expect.

How Much Shedding Can You Live With?

One way or another, dog hair has to be reckoned with. There are a few coat types that are not shed (curly coats, as in poodles, long, flowing types that are similar to human hair, and some wiry types associated with terriers). However, the kinds of coats that aren't shed require continual care to keep the dog clean and to prevent the skin, eyes, ears, and genitals from becoming irritated with matter that becomes trapped in the hair. The vast majority of dogs do shed, although the thicker and bushier the coat, the more you can expect on your furniture, floors, and clothes. On the bright side, dog hair can be spun and made into warm, "loyal" garments.

Is Digging an Issue?

All dogs like to dig — except terriers, who *love* to dig. Given the right kind of earth, most dogs will gladly dig in it. If you have a yard or garden where your dog will spend a lot of unsupervised time, she is likely to discover the pleasures of hole-digging. If you don't mind, then digging isn't an issue. If you do mind, you probably shouldn't choose a terrier or terrier mix, and you will need to come up with a way to resolve this conflict of views on digging (see chapter 20 for solutions to many common behavior problems). The simplest and fairest solution might be to set aside one area (away from the fence to discourage tunneling) as a digging pit for your dog.

How Much Barking?

Virtually all dogs bark. Some breeds do tend to bark a lot more or a lot less than others, but that doesn't mean that any individual dog necessarily reads the manual. There are three things to keep in mind as you think about barking. One is that barking is communication; dogs bark for a reason (from their point of view). Two is that a relentlessly barking dog is almost bound to be objectionable to your neighbors, if not to you (most nuisance barking occurs when dogs are left alone). Three is that dogs can be trained not to bark (see chapter 20).

Can the Dog Have a Strong Predatory Instinct?

Since all dogs are believed to be descended from the wolf, and the wolf is a predator, it stands to reason that there is a predation instinct present to some extent in all dogs. Most dogs that have been bred to hunt (terriers and hounds, in particular) still have a strong instinct. So, unless a terrier or hound is raised with cats, birds, or small furred animals, for example, these breeds are not good choices if you have such animals in or around your home and would like to keep them there. However, once *any* dog has hunted, it is not easy to train him not to. This should definitely be a consideration if you choose an adult dog of any breed.

Reputable sources will not knowingly offer sick dogs or puppies for sale or adoption. On the other hand, most situations where large groups of dogs are offered to the public are stressful to the dogs, and a basically healthy animal may come down with a minor infection or other temporary condition. Other problems may be more serious and/or difficult to cure. The following checklist will help you detect possible problems.

- *Does the dog appear healthy?* Investigate further such signs as shaking or tilting the head, pawing at eyes or ears, and repeatedly scratching or licking a particular body part. If the dog is a puppy, is he active, playful, and interested in his surroundings? A very quiet, still puppy may be ill or in pain. A thin puppy with a potbelly very likely is infested with worms.
- *Does the dog move naturally?* Limping or favoring a limb signals pain. Also look for hesitation to move or jump and an unnatural gait, such as swinging the hips from side to side or giving a little hop every few paces.
- *Are there signs of infection?* These include thick, colored, or crusty discharge from the eyes or nose; sneezing or coughing; and red, hot, inflamed ears. Dark, crumbling debris inside the ear probably means ear mites.
- *Are the skin and coat clear and clean?* Check for flakes and scales, sores and rashes, bare patches, offensive odor, very dry and dull or very oily hair. Examine the skin in the groin area for fleas.
- *Are the teeth and gums white and pink, respectively?* Signs that point to the need for veterinary attention are excessive buildup of brown deposits on the teeth, bad odor, and gums that are red along the tooth line.

CHECKLIST FOR HEALTH

Where Do You Stand on Aggression?

Like barking, aggressive behavior is communication for dogs; there is always a reason (from the dog's point of view). Certain working and herding breeds and mixes may be more likely than other dogs to become protective of people and territory, but aggressiveness can and does occur in all breeds and in mixed-breeds. Aggression is much easier to prevent, through early socialization, sterilization, and training, than it is to correct later on (see chapter 21). No dog should ever be trained to be aggressive, and no dog should be trained as a "guard" or "attack" dog. There are many dogs who are friendly to people but aggressive toward other dogs, particularly, but not only, if they have not been spayed or neutered. Dog-to-dog aggression tends to be most common between dogs of the same sex, more prevalent among terriers and working breeds such as Doberman pinschers, rottweilers, Akitas, and Great Danes, and less likely among hounds and sporting dogs such as retrievers, setters, and spaniels. Nevertheless, any dog can be aggressive toward other dogs. There is no good reason to want your dog to be aggressive, as it certainly puts all kinds of restrictions on your freedom of movement, as well as your dog's. Early and ongoing socialization with other dogs, as well as spaying and neutering, can prevent a lot of dog-to-dog aggression, but it's really not within our control to make any two dogs like each other.

A dog with "papers" is a dog with a kind of canine birth certificate that attests to the fact that he or she is purebred. He's eligible to be, as it's called, "registered." And he's eligible to be registered for one reason only: because both of his parents were registered, and all four grandparents were registered, and all eight great-grandparents were registered, and so on. The record of the dog's ancestry, his family tree, is his pedigree.

And what does that do for you? If you own a registered, purebred dog, what does it really mean?

It means you have a piece of paper that tells you your dog's name (presumably you know this already), his date of birth (useful if you do parties), his parents' names (do you really care?), and his breed.

The fact that your dog is a purebred beagle, boxer, or whatever is what his "papers" certify. But again: Does being purebred matter? What can you expect from a purebred dog?

You can expect your purebred beagle, for example, to look more or less like other beagles (same general size and shape, same colors and texture of coat, same kind of tail, same shape ears, probably the same distinctive vocalizing).

You should not expect a purebred dog to have a particular kind of temperament or character, such as sociable, easygoing, independent, eager to please, courageous, or protective, or to have particular aptitudes, such as the instinct to keep a group of cloven-footed animals clumped together, to freeze in the presence of feathers, to retrieve dead things from icy water, or to hurtle headlong down a dark hole in pursuit of unidentified small creatures. Your dog may have typical character and aptitude for his breed, but he may not.

What you absolutely cannot expect in your registered purebred dog is good health or freedom from genetic defects (all dogs, including mixed-breeds, are heir to some genetic defects, but some pure breeds are at much higher risk than others). At no point in the backward reach of record-keeping that supports purebred registration in this country has a single animal been required to pass any kind of screening exam, even if one existed, for health or soundness. Certainly, some individual breeders have their own high standards, but purebred registries in the United States do not require dogs to be tested for either physical or temperamental health. Your own purebred dog may never be sick a day in his life. Or, he may never be anything but.

The bottom line on "papers," and on pure breeding itself, is that when it comes to all the qualities of companionship, they are irrelevant.

INVENTORY ANSWER SHEET

Part **A**

Yourself as a Dog Owner

Question	Yes or No	Actions You Might Take
Are you allowed to have a dog?		
Can you afford a dog at this time?		
Have you considered the neighbors?		
Are you prepared to be the dog's "owner"?		
Do you know how to care for a dog?		
Do all family members agree about getting a dog?		
Is your family situation stable?		
Are your children six years old or older?		

Will the dog be the only pet in your home?		
Can your schedule accommodate the needs of a dog?		
Can your lifestyle accommodate the needs of a dog?		
Are you free of any physical limitations or health problems that would interfere with your ability to own a dog?		

Part B

A Good Dog for You

Question	Answer and Comments
What size dog should you get?	
What age?	
What about health?	

What kind of
temperament will
"fit" your household?

Do you need a dog
that's "good with
children"?

Will the dog have to
be left home alone?

What activity level
can you accommodate?

How much training
are you up to?

Do you have a
particular breed in mind?

Do "looks" matter to you?

How much shedding
can you live with?

Is digging an issue?

How much barking?

Can the dog have a strong
predatory instinct?

Where do you stand
on aggression?

Summary

With any luck, you're ending this chapter with certainty that you're ready to
get a dog, and a great deal more clarity about the kind of dog you want. In
the next chapter, we'll examine the different sources of dogs and puppies,
and explain how experienced trainers and counselors can help you evaluate
individual dogs and make that very important choice.

4

Finding Your Dog

The homework's been done. You've narrowed down the field to the type of dog — in general terms — that matches up well with your lifestyle and expectations. At last it's time to start looking at live animals. But where do you look?

Sources of dogs, and there are basically six, are not all created equal. It's important to understand the differences among the various sources of dogs as well as among different individual sellers within the various sources, if you are to make the best possible choice — for your sake and for your dog's.

Sources of Dogs

Pet Shops

Pet shops supply mostly purebred puppies from roughly two to six months of age, but increasing numbers of popular mixed-breed puppies as well, such as the "cockapoo" (cocker spaniel/poodle cross) and "Pekapoo" (Pekingese/poodle cross). Salespeople in pet shops may have little in-depth knowledge about dogs. Their primary objective is to sell, not to find the best home for the puppy in the window. As businesspeople, pet shop managers may want you to be a satisfied customer, but they really are not equipped to assure that you are. For one thing, most pet shop "stock" is supplied by puppy mills, large commercial breeding facilities where minimal care or no care at all is given to the health or well-being of either the parents or the puppies. Second, in order to be in the store at eight weeks of age — when they are most irresistible — pet shop puppies are removed from their mothers and subjected to the trauma of shipping at an age that is too young for the puppy's emotional or physical health. Third, in the pet shop environment, puppies do not receive the individual attention, social interactions, preliminary housetraining, or other kinds of experiences that would help them adapt easily to their future homes.

Because of the middlemen involved, and because of the high rent of premium mall space and other desirable locations, pet shop puppies generally are more expensive than puppies from other sources. Thirteen states (see Appendix I) have passed so-called lemon laws that require pet shops to refund the purchase price of or replace any puppy found to be ill within a few weeks, and seven of the thirteen allow between six months' and a year's worth of protection for puppies found to have congenital or hereditary defects. The most enlightened laws, passed in eight of the thirteen states, allow the consumer to keep the dog and be reimbursed for medical expenses up to the purchase price of the animal. Lemon laws without this provision may offer some financial protection to the consumer (you), but do nothing to comfort the heartbroken family (yours) that has already fallen in love with the unsound, unstable, or chronically ill puppy.

Backyard or Casual Breeders

These breeders include our friends, relatives, and neighbors and account for most of the puppies advertised in local newspapers, veterinarians' offices, feed stores, and on community bulletin boards, telephone poles, or mailboxes. These breeders of both purebreds and mixed-breeds usually know very little about canine health and genetics and are primarily motivated to find homes for their puppies, not to make sure that you and the puppy are a good match. Puppies may or may not have received socialization and early training. Puppies from this source are priced to sell (some are "free to a good home"), but unless you have a written contract with the seller, you have no recourse in the event that problems develop.

Hobby/Show ("Professional") Breeders

These breeders offer purebred puppies of different ages as well as adolescent and adult dogs. Most hobby breeders are very knowledgeable about their breed and their line, although some may be blind to undesirable traits in their animals. An exception would be breeders of extreme types of dogs such as very large, very protective, or very tiny and fragile. These breeders are likely to be well aware of the fact that their dogs are not for everyone and would easily recognize and probably refuse to sell to an individual or home they deem to be unsuitable. Hobby breeders in general are very careful about screening potential buyers of their puppies and offer follow-up support on diet, training, and living with their dogs. It's important to note, however, that there are all kinds of hobby breeders: some good, some average, some poor and unethical across the board.

Responsible hobby breeders almost always sell puppies on contracts that offer some protection to both parties, and many will take back (even insist on having returned) a puppy who doesn't work out at any time, for any reason. Mother dogs usually will have received good health care, and puppies from this source often have had substantial early socialization and training.

Hobby breeders invariably have two kinds of puppies for sale and charge very different amounts for each. The first is the puppy with "show" potential, meaning that even at an early age, the puppy appears to be a particularly good specimen of his breed. The breeder will very likely want this puppy to be shown to a championship title and eventually used at stud; the breeder's contract will specify this. The second kind of puppy a breeder has for sale, and there are many more of these, is the so-called pet-quality puppy. From the breeder's point of view, this puppy, even if completely healthy in mind and body, nevertheless possesses some "flaws" that mean her show prospects are nil. Usually these flaws are cosmetic in nature, such as too much white in a black coat, or ears that are too large or two small. The flaws certainly do not make the puppy any less able to be a wonderful pet for someone, but the truly responsible breeder's contract will stipulate that the puppy shall not be bred, and in fact be spayed or neutered.

While the price of a puppy with show potential can be very high, pet-quality puppies from a hobby breeder may actually cost less than you will pay at a pet shop, depending on factors such as popularity of the breed, litter size, and the number of hobby breeders available locally. Pet puppies from a hobby breeder invariably will cost more than you would pay to a backyard breeder or at a local shelter.

Animal Shelters

Animal shelters offer dogs and puppies of all sizes, shapes, ages, and personalities, both mixed-breeds and purebreds. The dogs who are available for adoption at animal shelters have found their way there for a wide variety of reasons. Responsible animal shelters carefully evaluate the dogs who come to them and place for adoption only those that they feel will make a good pet for the right home. To help assure that a good "match" is made, many shelters provide adoption counseling services and/or offer follow-up assistance in the form of group training classes and counseling to solve problems. Shelter dogs are not sold, but a reasonable adoption fee is set to help defray expenses for food, vaccinations, deworming, and spay/neuter surgery. As is true of other sources of dogs, there are all kinds of animal shelters too: some good, some average, some poor. Don't leave your common sense at the door.

Rescue Leagues

Rescue leagues are in essence private, single-breed networks of hobby breeders who offer foster homes to dogs and occasionally puppies of that breed until they are ready for adoption. Purebreds find their way to rescue leagues in a number of ways. Some are found dogs, some are "rescued" from failed breeding operations or from boarding kennels and veterinarians where they were left and never reclaimed. Probably most rescue dogs are obtained through the cooperation of knowledgeable hobby breeders and the staff at local animal shelters, who agree that these dogs may need more intensive and specialized attention than the shelter can provide and where it is presumed they are less likely to find new homes.

Dogs adopted from rescue leagues usually have been screened for health and temperament and rehabilitated if necessary, then kept in foster care until permanent homes can be found. Rescue dogs are not sold, but adopters usually are required to reimburse the league for veterinary and other costs that have been incurred. Follow-up assistance to deal with any problems usually is provided, and adopters are required to return their dogs to the league if they cannot be kept for any reason.

Found Dogs

Found dogs are complete unknowns. They can be young or old, mixed-breeds or purebreds, sound or unsound, and there are as many reasons why they are at large as there are at-large dogs. Whether they find you or you find them, there's often a sense of destiny about the meeting that overrides practical considerations regarding suitability, timing, convenience, and any preconceived ideas about what kind of dog you're looking for — or even if you're looking for a dog at all! Giving a home to a found dog is very much a matter of "making the best of it," and many of these acquisitions don't work out well for dog or owner, though large numbers certainly do. Because taking in a stray dog is usually an impulsive if noble act, it cannot be recommended as a way to find a companion for the long run.

We noted above that all sources of dogs are not created equal. Nor are they all equally good choices from a humane viewpoint. As you set out to find your very own dog, you might want to keep this thought in mind: Where you go for your dog can either *en*courage or *dis*courage the continuing overproduction of dogs in this country. Puppy mills, backyard breeders, and professional breeders alike, although for different reasons, will continue to produce puppies as long as they can sell or even give them away. On the other hand, adopting a dog from a shelter or rescue league, or giving a good home to the dog you find wandering by the side of the road (or at least taking it to the nearest shelter) cannot possibly encourage anyone to continue to breed more dogs while there still are so many "extras." Your first priority, of course, should be to find the best possible dog for you. You can do that *and* give a home to a dog that badly needs one by adopting your dog from your local humane society or animal shelter. Virtually every prospective dog owner is likely to find the best possible dog for him at his local shelter — if not on his first visit, then on a subsequent one. If you never do another thing for dogs, by adopting yours at an animal shelter you'll have done your share to repair the canine covenant.

Making the Match

In chapter 3 you learned how important it is that you figure out what kind of dog will suit you. But the question remains: How will you know when you've found her? The answer is that, probably, *you* won't. You'll need the help of someone who knows how to evaluate dogs in terms of their basic temperament and behavior and who is strongly motivated to find a loving, safe, and permanent home for every dog in his or her care. The person most likely to fill this double bill is the adoption counselor at your local animal shelter. On the other hand, if you're absolutely certain that you want a particular purebred dog, you may do well not only at an animal shelter, but also at a rescue league or a hobby breeder's kennel, where knowledgeable people will help you choose among the individual animals they have available. Both groups are likely to go to some length to make sure you will be able to provide a good home for one of their dogs, asking many "personal" questions about your prior dog-owning experiences as well as about where and how you live. Bear in mind, however, that many purebred adult and young dogs are available at animal shelters, too. As a matter of fact, all across the country at any given time, some 25 percent of the shelter population of dogs consists of purebreds.

Puppy mills are large-scale commercial dog-breeding establishments where dogs are kept in inhumane conditions. (HSUS/Baker photo)

Adoption Counseling

Adoption counseling is a service that more and more shelters have begun to provide to improve their adoption success rate. The last thing that a responsible shelter wants is for the new home to not work out and for the dog to go through the trauma of being relinquished a second time. For the most part the days are gone when an adoptive family would simply show up at the shelter door, pick out a dog, put down a few dollars, and leave. Today's adopter should expect and, if you think about it, welcome the opportunity to fill out an application and have an extensive private conversation with a counselor. Adoption counseling consists of three separate parts: determining whether the prospective dog owner is likely to provide the loving, safe, and permanent home every dog is entitled to; selecting a dog who will most likely match up well with the adopter's lifestyle and expectations; and providing information at the time of adoption as well as follow-up counseling and training. The goal of adoption counseling is to empower the new owner to be an educated and responsible one.

The Prospective Dog Owner

If you do decide to adopt your dog from an animal shelter, what will be required of you? This will vary from shelter to shelter, but usually includes two components:

THE APPLICATION   The application or written questionnaire will establish who you are, where you live (many shelters will adopt out only to town or county residents and to those with landlord approval), and whether you meet the basic requirements of responsible dog ownership.

Shelters will want to be sure that you have enough time to care for, train, exercise, and interact with the dog, adequate living quarters for the kind of dog you hope to adopt, and enough money to provide quality food, supplies, veterinary care, professional grooming, if necessary, and incidentals. Shelters also want to be sure that you have the right reason for wanting a dog in the first place. That reason will always be companionship. If your dog turns out to be a good watchdog, or keeps raccoons and rabbits away from your garden, or ultimately saves your entire family from fire, that's all gravy. But it's not why you initially get a dog. (To grasp easily the right reason for wanting a dog, think about any eight-year-old you've ever known, perhaps even yourself, who was dying for a dog. Children may not make the most responsible caretakers of dogs, but they do seem to know intuitively that dogs are for loving.) On the adoption application, you may be asked to provide references to substantiate what you say, particularly if you've owned a dog or dogs in the past.

THE INTERVIEW In the interview, the adoption counselor is trying to determine if you possess the "Three C's" of the qualified adopter: Commitment, Compassion, and Capability to care for a dog humanely. Among the adoption interview questions recommended by The Humane Society of the United States are the following:

- What brings you to our shelter for a dog?
- Is there any particular reason you prefer a dog/puppy?
- What kinds of dogs do you find hard to deal with?
- What kinds of behavior do you feel unable to accept?
- What would make you likely to turn down a particular animal?
- What do you see as normal puppyhood problems?
- What will you expect of the dog you adopt?
- What do you think the dog will expect of you?
- What leisure activities does your family enjoy together?
- What kinds of activities do you see yourself doing with an adopted dog?
- Will the whole family share in the care of the dog?
- Tell me about a typical day in your household.
- Tell me about some of your past (or present) pets.
- Did your family have dogs when you were a child? Tell me about those experiences. Is there anything you would do differently from what your parents did in raising a dog?
- Describe your neighborhood for me in terms of the dogs living there. Are there lots of dogs and cats already? Are there nuisance problems? Do you and your neighbors get along?

Thousands of lifelong partnerships begin every day at animal shelters across the country.

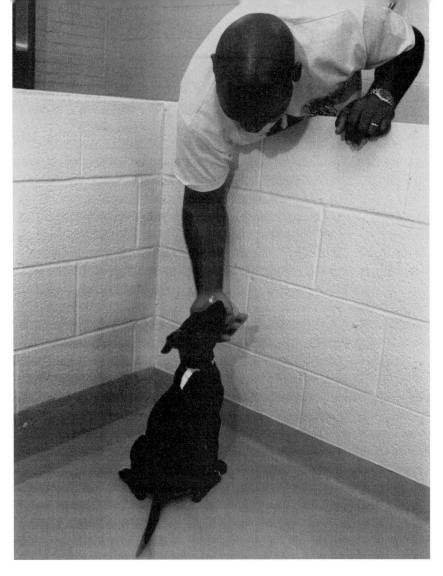

- How do you feel about pet sterilization? Do you have any concerns or questions?
- How do you feel about signing a legal contract saying you will have your dog licensed and vaccinated, sterilized, and trained — in effect, saying that you will be a responsible dog owner?

Some potential adopters feel insulted by these questions. It seems they're being given the third degree. If you think you'd feel that way too, it might help to understand why shelters put people through this process. First, they have the dog's best interests at heart, and experience has shown that asking the right questions is a good way to help a prospective owner make a good choice — or decide not to choose at all. Interview questions are also intended to make sure the prospective owner meets with no surprises when she brings her new dog home, i.e., that she has a pretty realistic idea of the cost, time, and commitment that will be involved.

Also, don't forget that there are never enough good homes for the multitudes of dogs needing one. This means that any counselor sitting across from you will truly want to be able to approve your application. The only thing she will want more is to do right by the dog. Her questions, therefore, are intended to help both the shelter *and* the adopter (you) avoid mistakes; this is why it is in your best interest not only to answer her questions fully but to provide any additional information you think is important.

After all this, is it possible that you will *not* be approved to adopt the dog you have selected? Yes, it is possible. This is a good time to rethink what kind of dog you're looking for, and why. Discuss with the counselor what concerns she has. If they make sense to you, you may very well be able to choose a different dog, one whom she will heartily approve. On the other hand, it is possible that you will not be approved to adopt any dog at that time. Should that happen, the adoption counselor will tell you why. Even though you may feel bitterly disappointed, try to be grateful you went to a shelter where someone was able to be more objective than you might have been yourself about your abilities to care for your dog.

The Right Dog

Enough negative thinking! Let's assume that you've sailed happily through a prescreening interview and are ready to select a dog from among those on the premises, or that you've already walked through the kennels and have selected what you think is your dream dog. At this point, one of four things can happen. The counselor may agree with what you've decided about a good kind of dog for you *and* with your actual selection; she may agree with your decision but not with your actual selection; she may agree with your decision but not have a dog of that kind to show you at the moment; or she may disagree with some aspect of your basic decision about what kind of dog you should get. Let's consider each scenario in turn:

AGREES WITH DECISION/AGREES WITH CHOICE Imagine you're an at-home mom with three children between the ages of five and eleven. You decide you'd like a mellow, midsize mixed-breed dog, at least one year old, with an easy-care coat. You and your husband wander slowly through the shelter kennels with your children, referring often to the notebook in your hand. The criteria you've decided upon are listed down the left side of a page. Particular dogs who are "in the running" are listed on the right side. When you've seen every dog, you reverse your steps and reconsider the dogs you've listed in the notebook. Finally you find yourselves rooted in front of one kennel, looking down into the bright eyes of a largish tan dog with four white feet. The dog, whose name is Bob, is two and a half and bigger than you'd visualized. On the other hand, he seems calm and steady, attentive without being hyper. The dog's coat is short and coarse — the kind that looks like a quick brushing once a week will do it. You go back out to the office to tell the adoption counselor which dog you're interested in, and she warmly agrees that Bob would seem a really good fit for your family.

AGREES WITH DECISION/DISAGREES WITH CHOICE Unlike some people, you see your choice as easy. All you want is a big friendly couch-potato dog and you don't care what gender, what color, or even what age as long as he or she is not a puppy. You live in the country, work at home, and are looking for a dog who just likes to hang out, a live-and-let-live type who's good steady company. The counselor goes with you into the kennel area and points out a kind of funny-looking dog that she says is part basset hound and part something else, maybe retriever. But in the same kennel you spot what looks like an Irish setter and ask, "How about him?" The counselor shakes her head. She says the setter is not nearly as laid-back as he appears at the moment, mostly because his natural exuberance is depressed by being in the shelter with a lot of strange, loud dogs. The counselor goes on to say that setters generally have a high activity level and need lots of vigorous exercise. This particular dog, she adds, was brought to the shelter because the young working couple who owned him had found him "too much to handle." You look again at the red setter and now can almost sense the energy locked inside the dog's slender body. It no longer is so easy to see this dog lying upside down on your well-worn leather sofa by the stove, his head lolling over the side. Your glance swings back to the basset mix. He really *is* a nice lazy-looking dog. . . .

AGREES WITH DECISION/DOES NOT HAVE A DOG SUITABLE FOR YOU AT THE MOMENT You've always known that when you got a dog, she (or he) would be a purebred beagle. The first dog you remember from your childhood was a black-and-white beagle named Betsy, whom your neighbors had gotten as a puppy from the city shelter. In no time at all, Betsy seemed to belong equally to all the children in town. Years later, one of your college housemates had a male beagle named Uncle Joe, and just like Betsy — as well as the comic strip beagle named Snoopy — Joe seemed to accept all the residents of the house as his alternate owners. Probably beagles aren't the world's brightest dogs, but you don't see yourself teaching tricks to a dog in any case. As you tell all this to the counselor, she looks a little dubious. "You do understand that all dogs are unique?" she asks. "That not all beagles will have the same 'democratic' temperament?" You do know this, you tell her, but it's the democratic kind of beagle that you want. The counselor says that they do get beagles from time to time and that she will call you if one comes in whom she thinks is the type you'd like. It's a deal. You've known for a long time that what's worth having is worth waiting for.

DISAGREES WITH SOME ASPECT OF DECISION Your old dog died seven years ago. Since then you've retired from the school system and have been diagnosed with a heart condition. You've been thinking more and more about getting a new dog and your doctor wants you to stay active, so it seems like a good time. At the shelter you fall in love with an adorable nine-week-old Akita-mix puppy. You really like the idea of having something to cuddle and mother again. But when you tell the counselor your choice, he warmly agrees that puppies are just about irresistible, then quietly asks you to remember how much energy puppies have and how much mess and upset they leave in their wake during those first six months. He points out that even adult dogs are like children in that they need and depend on us for everything. On the other hand, he says, adults come with the distinct advantage of having their permanent teeth (no overwhelming need to chew, chew, chew), full control of their bowels and bladders, and a far less intense interest in testing, tasting, exploring, unraveling, unearthing, devouring whole, and generally being into every last thing they encounter. The counselor asks if you'd ever thought about adopting a small older dog, one who could snuggle in your arms and offer affection and companionship, but without so much caffeine. A few hours later, you realize you've done a 180. You've spent time with three adult dogs and are growing more and more comfortable with the thought that your new dog is going to be Joli, a small, outgoing, four-year-old poodle — whose curl-covered face just happens to give him the look of a perennial puppy.

When a Shelter Does Not Offer Counseling

Unfortunately, not all shelters have the funds to provide adoption counseling at this time, although the trend is definitely in that direction. If coun-

TRUE OR FALSE

	TRUE	FALSE
1. Shelter dogs are "problem" dogs — that's why their owners gave them away.	——	——
2. Shelter dogs are all older mixed-breeds. Don't go to a shelter looking for a puppy or a purebred.	——	——
3. When you adopt a shelter dog, you have no way of knowing anything about its history.	——	——
4. In choosing a shelter dog, stay away from the shy and quiet ones and also from the hyper ones.	——	——
5. You should never bring home a shelter dog if you have other dogs at home. The shelter dog is bound to have some diseases or parasites from being in the shelter.	——	——
6. Shelter dogs primarily have been picked up as strays. After being on the streets, they rarely can become a good pet.	——	——
7. Shelter dogs are in desperate need of new homes. By adopting one, you're probably saving a life.	——	——

seling is not offered in your area, ask the shelter manager whom you can call or write to urge that this service be provided in the future. Then plan to enlist the help of someone who can go with you to the shelter on your next visit to help you choose your dog wisely. What kind of person? Use these tips as a guideline:

- Select a person who has in-depth knowledge of dogs and dog behavior, and is familiar with many breeds and mixed-breeds. Professional trainers, obedience instructors, and behavioral consultants are good examples. Maybe a staff member from your veterinary hospital would be willing to go along.
- Select a person who can be reasonably objective and disinterested. For all their knowledge and experience, people who have a long and exclusive association with one breed or type of dog may have difficulty being objective. This includes hobby breeders, some dog trainers, and some obedience competitors.

- Meet ahead of time with the person to make sure he or she understands what you are looking for or can help you focus your thinking. Be clear about what you expect.
- Plan to spend as much time as it takes; it is not necessary, or even desirable, to make up your mind in one visit. Recognize that the dog for you may very well *not* be in residence the first or even second time you stop by, and that there's too much at stake to be in a hurry. As long as your expectations are reasonable, your dog will come along. While you're waiting, there are many advance preparations you can make. See chapter 5 for details.

At the end of the day, a dog is a dog, whether he wandered onto your back porch in a snowstorm or melted your heart gazing at you through the window of the pet shop in the mall. As we said at the beginning of this chapter, all sources of dogs are not created equal, and we hope we've persuaded you to stop by your local humane shelter when you're ready to get your dog. However, once you've decided upon a particular dog, no matter the source, the playing field is leveled and the clock reset to zero. All dogs have the same birthright to a safe, loving, lifetime home.

THE TRUTH ABOUT SHELTER DOGS: A QUIZ

ANSWERS

1. *False.* There are many reasons why dogs are surrendered to shelters. Although owners sometimes cite various kinds of problems as the reasons why they are surrendering their dogs, closer scrutiny usually reveals that the owner had unrealistic expectations about dogs or did not choose the kind of dog that would fit into his or her lifestyle.

2. *False.* Approximately 25 percent of shelter dogs are purebreds, and most shelters have puppies most of the time, particularly during the spring months.

3. *False.* Often a dog is surrendered by his owner, who provides a lot of information about him. However, even if a dog does not come with a history, most shelters give all animals a thorough health examination as well as carefully observe dogs for behavioral characteristics; this information is available for the benefit of adopters.

4. *Not necessarily true.* Many dogs are "not themselves" in the shelter environment, particularly in the adoption kennels, which are often noisy and crowded. It's very useful to be able to spend some time with the dog in a quiet place away from the hubbub, and many shelters now provide such a space. Shelter staff observations of dogs can often shed additional light on their true temperament, whether they appear overly quiet or overly boisterous.

5. *False and true.* Most shelters evaluate dogs for health and arrange for vaccinations, parasite control, and treatment of preexisting conditions. Still, it would be unwise to bring home a shelter dog — or any dog — if you have a young puppy at home or a dog who has not yet been fully immunized. Additionally, you should plan to keep your resident dogs and your new dog — from whatever source — separated for about two weeks, the incubation period for most contagious diseases of dogs.

6. *False.* Perhaps 50 percent of a shelter's population of dogs are lost or abandoned and have been picked up by animal control; the other 50 percent are surrendered by their owners. Even so, there is no reason why a dog who has been out on his own for a while cannot make a wonderful companion. There is no direct correlation between being on the street and bonding with people, nor on the other hand with being "free" and wanting to run loose forever. These are certainly among the factors that adoption counselors evaluate before placing a dog with a family.

7. *True.* The pet overpopulation problem in this country is such that perfectly good dogs who would make wonderful pets unfortunately will be euthanized in order to make room for new dogs coming in who also deserve their chance to find a loving home.

Getting Ready

5

You're almost there! Red ink marks the date on the calendar when you get to bring home your brand-new puppy or dog. Whether or not it's your first, this is a time of happy anticipation. It should also be a time of busy preparation.

What's to prepare? you ask. Well, would you bring a human baby home without at least a box of diapers and a crib? A new dog, particularly a new puppy, requires almost as much planning. After all, a human baby cannot move around during the first few months while you're figuring out what you're doing. To help make sure your dog's entrance into your life is as smooth as possible, here are some ways you can prepare your home, your car, and especially yourself, for the new arrival.

The Trip Home

You might think the first order of business is stocking up on dog food, but unless the Dog Stork drops your new dog down the chimney, you'll have to pick him up somewhere and bring him home. Accidents happen! Maybe the drive is longer than a puppy's bladder can handle, and you have to make a bathroom stop. This is precisely the time when a frisky puppy or disoriented adult dog may dash off — over the nearest hilltop or into oncoming traffic.

To be safe, your new dog should wear a collar and leash and an ID tag from the very beginning. Also, resist the temptation to place him on your lap or on the seat beside you where you can cuddle and reassure him. There will be plenty of time to cuddle once you've gotten him home. The best and safest places for your new dog to ride in the car are inside a dog crate or behind a barrier made for this purpose. (Later on, once you've accustomed him to it gradually, you may choose to use a secure seat harness for your dog.) If one of these is your ultimate goal for him, it makes every kind of sense to place him there from the very beginning. This doesn't mean that you shouldn't interact with your dog on the trip home. By all means, talk pleasantly to him as you drive. Tell him how happy you are to have found him and what a great life you're going to have together. He won't understand a single word, but your matter-of-fact voice from the front seat will reassure without rewarding him for being frightened.

Following are the primary things you'll need for that all-important first trip together. Look for these at your local pet-supply store. Also, some shelters have a small supply of pet-related goods for sale that will help you get your new dog safely home, including a temporary ID tag and an application for a permanent one.

COLLAR An excellent first collar is the nylon buckle collar. It is light-weight, strong, inexpensive, and comes in a variety of plain and designer patterns and colors. Find the correct size by measuring around your dog's neck, then adding two inches. For puppies and immature dogs, you will need to replace the collar once or twice during the first year. An adjustable nylon collar that will "grow" with a puppy is economical, but if your dog is very tiny, an adjustable collar may be too bulky and heavy. For the tiniest puppies, you may find that a nylon cat collar offers the best fit. Collars made of cotton are also available, but may not be as strong or durable as nylon. For humane reasons, metal choke or pinch collars should be used for training purposes only, not for wearing day-to-day.

LEAD For your dog's first lead, also called a leash, choose nylon or cotton webbing of about the same width as his collar, equipped with a swivel and safety snap, which is less likely to pop open when you don't want it to. Most leads come in four- or six-foot lengths, with the shorter length more appropriate for smaller dogs and puppies. Leads much longer than six feet, including retractable leads, give you less control of your dog and therefore are not appropriate walking leads in most situations. (In some cities, owners can be ticketed for walking their dog on a lead longer than six feet.) Very short "traffic" leads of only a foot or so in length prevent a dog from lowering his head to the ground and walking in a way that's normal and natural for dogs; for that reason, traffic leads are not comfortable or appropriate for your new companion.

ID TAG   Many a dog has been tragically lost while her owner was intending to get a proper identification tag. Avoid this heartbreak by ordering a tag as soon as you get your dog, or even better, in advance, if you're taking the time we recommend to look for the right dog for your household. If you haven't settled on a name, just use Dog Doe; after all, the critical information on the tag is *your* name and telephone numbers (daytime and evening). If there isn't time, you can make or purchase a temporary tag while you wait for an engraved one to arrive in the mail. (Note: At the time of adoption, many shelters provide temporary tags on which you can write your name and telephone numbers.) When you take your dog to a veterinarian for his first exam — which you should do within the first day or two — ask about tattooing or microchip implantation if the shelter hasn't already educated you about them. These are the two methods of permanent identification currently available, which you may wish to consider as additional insurance in case your dog ever becomes lost or stolen. Tattooing is usually done inside the thigh. It is not painful, but the noise and vibration of the tattoo needle may unnerve some dogs. Microchipping involves injecting a chip the size of a grain of rice under the skin between the shoulder blades. A code that yields your name and address is imbedded in the chip and can be read by a scanning device. "Chipping" is quick and almost painless. The cost of these procedures runs between $15 and $35 or more, depending on who performs them and where. A shelter may charge as little as $8 to implant a microchip. An additional $25 to $35 is necessary to register a tattoo or microchip with one of the national registry organizations.

CRATE   A sturdy crate that confines your dog is the safest way for her to travel. Not only will she not be roaming around the car, creating a dangerous distraction for the driver, but she will be protected from sliding off the seat or into the windshield if you need to stop suddenly. In case of a serious automobile accident, a dog who has been confined within a crate is not as likely to suddenly find herself standing on the highway as one seated in the front seat. Nor will police or emergency medical personnel be as likely to hesitate to enter your vehicle to rescue her or even you. Tragically, there have been instances where an unconfined dog, instinctively attempting to "protect" her unconscious owner in the wake of an accident, has delayed police and EMTs from assisting the dog's owner for fear of their safety.

Dog crates or "kennels" come in two basic types: the mostly solid plastic types approved by airlines for shipping dogs, and the mostly open wire crates.

For use in your car, the wire crate is the better choice. It allows air to circulate more readily and allows your dog to take in all the sights. Crates are also recommended for teaching your dog not to eliminate in the house (see Housetraining later in this chapter); you certainly may use the same crate for both purposes, but if you intend to take your dog on frequent car trips, you'll probably find it more convenient to have two. Dog crates can cost anywhere from about thirty to several hundred dollars, depending on the size and construction, so plan to purchase one that your dog will not outgrow. To do this, estimate how large she will be when fully grown (of course there's no guessing involved when you adopt an adult dog!), then select a crate that will allow her to stand with her head up, turn around, stretch, and sleep comfortably on her side with her legs fully extended. Bigger than that is not better.

VEHICLE BARRIER A truly marvelous invention is the adjustable barrier for station wagons, utility vehicles, vans, and minivans. The metal bar barrier is easy to install and remove, yet forms a secure seethrough wall that separates the passenger compartment from the back of the vehicle where the dog rides. Vehicle barriers protect your dog as well as your upholstery, and in automobile accidents may keep your dog inside your car and still allow rescue personnel to offer aid to human victims. An associated travel item is the window vent barrier, a wire mesh device of similar construction that allows you to roll down a window for ventilation without allowing your dog to jump out of the car or a stranger to stick his arm in! The vent barrier also prevents your dog from sticking her head out of the window while your car is in motion — a primary cause of eye injury because of airborne dirt and cinders.

CAR HARNESS The car harness is an adjustable, nonbinding restraint that is designed to be hooked up to the seat belts in your automobile. Like young children restrained by seat belts, dogs will not have as much freedom to move around as they'd like, but they will be protected from injury in the case of sudden stops, and they will not be able to interfere with the driver. For dogs under about ten pounds, there is also a car seat that can be used with the harness. The car seat simply elevates the small dog so she can see out of the window, which of course she very much wants to do. Please note that car seats without harnesses are unsafe, as a sudden stop can send the small dog flying. Also, keep in mind that some dogs do not adjust easily to these kinds of restraints. You might want to borrow one from a friend or construct something that simulates a harness or car seat before you invest good money in a device to which your own particular dog says, "No thanks, Mom."

Housetraining

Methods of housetraining are discussed in detail in chapter 12. However, since housetraining should begin the first moment of your dog's first day in his new home, you might want to take the time now to think through just how you will handle this critically important training program.

- Decide whether you want to train your dog to eliminate on newspapers inside the house (paper-training), to wait until you take him outdoors, or a combination of both. Figure on four to eight outings a day at first, and discuss with family members who will firmly commit to which shifts. Put this schedule in writing and put it up wherever you post other important notices and reminders.
- Purchase a dog crate that you will use to teach your dog to "hold it" during housetraining and possibly designate as his permanent bed as well (see Basic Care, below). Other housetraining materials that you should have on hand are large quantities of a cleanser or disinfectant suitable for tile and linoleum. An enzymatic pet odor/stain remover, which you can purchase in most pet-supply stores, will be a godsend for the inevitable accidents on rugs, carpeting, wood, and other porous surfaces.
- A major component of any housetraining program is being able to confine your dog to a smallish area where he can be monitored at all times. You don't want to wait until your dog is squatting on your Persian carpet to think about when and where he will be confined during the housetraining program. Once you've selected the area (the kitchen or pantry, with washable floor and close proximity to the center of family life, is ideal), purchase or construct baby gates or another kind of barrier that you can use to confine the dog to the room or a section of it. If your yard is not fully fenced and escape-proof, now is the time to see to that. Don't forget to inspect the locks and/or gates. A simple latch is no match for a dog determined to find out how much greener the grass is on the other side of the fence.

Basic Care

Another area where advance planning can pay big dividends is in setting up and stocking some special places for the dog to use. The closest analogy in human terms would be the nursery and layette.

- Select a place where your dog will sleep and eat. During the housetraining period, especially for puppies, these will be close by one another. The critical considerations are that your dog not be isolated from you any more than necessary, that he be restricted at first to a small area that can be easily cleaned, and that the entire area lend itself to thorough puppy-proofing. (Note that even an adult dog who appears to be thoroughly housetrained may be overwhelmed at first by too much freedom in your home, especially if he spent any length of time closely confined in a shelter environment. Such a dog may feel more secure and adjust more quickly to his new living quarters if you keep him confined to a small area for the first week or so.) Kitchens usually are the ideal place. Their only drawback is that they invariably are full of dangerous cleaning products, under-the-sink poisons, and other hazards. Safeguard your dog by figuring out ahead of time how to keep all cupboard doors securely fastened (child-proofing fasteners work for dogs as well), the contents of the garbage pail or cat's litter box inaccessible, and the dog himself away from the stove, where boiling liquids or spattering grease may land on him.
- Obtain a suitable bed. The dog crate discussed above can do triple duty. It can be your dog's safe haven while traveling, the device that assures he will be easily housetrained, and a permanent place of his own for sleeping or for retreating to when he wants to be alone. Be advised that no matter what you may think ahead of time, if you don't obtain a bed for your new dog and fully expect him to use it, there's every likelihood that his bed will turn out to be your bed. This is not helpful for housetraining. In addition, it's not a good idea to allow this in the beginning unless you intend to allow it forever. Dogs have a hard enough time learning all the "rules" that go along with living in a human pack without having what's okay change from day to day.
- Get two bowls, one for food and one for water. Bowls should be nonchewable, impossible to tip over, resistant to being pushed all over the room, and easy to clean. Beware of hand-painted ceramics or dishes not expressly intended for food, as paints may contain lead or other toxic substances. You can never go wrong with stainless steel or heat-resistant glass.
- Decide on what to feed your dog (see chapter 8). If possible, always start out with the food the dog or puppy is currently eating. Get in a week's supply and gradually mix the old food together with the diet you'd prefer to feed. "No abrupt changes" is always good advice, but particularly during housetraining.
- Get together a few safe toys to introduce one at a time. Avoid toys with small parts that can be swallowed, toys that may splinter, or toys that con-

tain ingredients you wouldn't want to put in your human child's mouth. If your dog is a puppy or a dog under nine or ten months, have on hand some nylon or heavy rubber chew toys for use during teething.

- Purchase whatever grooming tools and supplies you will need to care for your dog's coat, eyes and ears, nails, and teeth. The basics include a brush and comb (the exact type will depend on the kind of hair your dog has or will have as he grows older), cotton balls dipped in warm water for removing any discharge from the corners of the eyes, cotton balls and canine ear-cleaning solution for removing dirt and/or wax from the ears, a toothbrush and toothpaste made especially for dogs for daily teeth cleaning, and a nail clipper made for dogs. (Nails, by the way, should be clipped every week, not because they need shortening that often, but because dogs usually dislike the procedure so much that they should be kept well habituated to it.) To bathe your dog — and only if he's truly dirty — requires a shampoo made for dogs as well as a spray attachment for your sink or bathtub, depending on his size. Dogs with long coats that keep growing like human hair and dogs with very thick coats that develop mats probably will need to be groomed by a professional every month or so. Tips on grooming and bathing your new dog are given in chapter 13.

- Designate an area where all your dog's "stuff" will be kept. You want to be able to find things when you or other family members need them. Also, the very act of setting aside a shelf in the pantry or a drawer in the kitchen will help to impress upon you that this new dog is here to stay and that he has legitimate needs and requirements that are distinctly his own.

- Prepare to begin assembling first-aid and emergency kits for your dog. In later chapters we will talk in depth about the items that should be in each, but for now, note this as something to attend to as soon as possible. Unfortunately, neither accidents and injuries nor natural or manmade disasters wait until we are ready for them. If you want to start collecting kit materials immediately, see chapters 10 and 11 for details.

- Buy a small notebook or binder where you will faithfully record all of your dog's vital statistics and veterinary data (the purposes and use of this notebook are discussed fully in Your Dog's Veterinary Records Book in chapter 9). Also jot down important numbers, such as the veterinarian's office, the emergency clinic, your shelter's customer service desk, or perhaps the number of the breed rescue committee or the professional breeder who sold you your dog. Writing down these numbers will

A dog will make herself
comfortable on your bed.
(Kathy Milani's Bailey)

remind you that you undoubtedly *will* need some help with your new dog from time to time. It will also reassure you that you can find that help quickly when the need arises.

Safety Precautions

Chapter 7 goes into detail about the various hazards to dogs and how to guard against them. For now, if you just attend to the following, you will be a giant step ahead of the game:

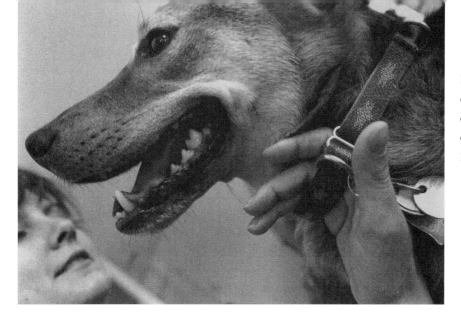

Make sure you can insert two or three fingers between your dog's neck and his collar to ensure a correct fit. (Tamara Hamilton and Cika Kola)

- Carefully examine any areas where your dog will spend time and "proof" them for common hazards (poisonous plants, flowers, trees, and shrubs; toxic chemicals in the house, garage, and laundry room; pesticides, electric cords, broken glass and litter, wood chips and shavings, pressure-treated building materials such as deck and playground wood, workshop debris, and unsafe chewables of all kinds, including human medicines). A different but important kind of hazard to your dog is any object in his space that is valuable to you and that he might inadvertently break or damage, thus causing you to be upset with him. Do both of you a favor by removing or protecting such items before an accident happens.
- Do not get into the habit of turning your dog outside into the yard by himself. He needs you to spend time with him in the yard — leashed at first as you walk the perimeter of your property, gently pulling back if he goes toward property lines. In addition, make sure your yard provides protection from the elements as well as a securely locking gate. Be absolutely certain that the yard is injury-proof and escape-proof, remembering that a motivated dog is a marvel at jumping and digging. Check to make sure that no chemicals (fertilizer, weed killer, pesticides, rodent poison, snail bait) have been applied to any yard areas that your new dog will have access to. In flea and tick season, treat the yard a few weeks before the dog is due to arrive.

Two can share a flying disk, a safe toy when used under supervision. (Gorman Bechard's Kilgore and Casey)

Professional Care

The time to carefully search out the professionals who will help you care for your new dog is now, before you need them.

VETERINARIAN Locate a veterinarian or veterinary clinic you feel comfortable with. (See chapter 6 for a checklist of things to look for.) Don't assume that this will necessarily be the most conveniently located practice.

EMERGENCY CLINIC Few veterinarians have round-the-clock coverage, which means that when their clinic is closed, clients are referred to emergency-care facilities. Before you need to, find out where your veterinarian refers emergencies. Take a drive there to make sure you can find it in an emergency, when your head may be swimming with worry.

TRAINING CLASS Puppy kindergarten as well as classes for older puppies and dogs is highly recommended to get you and your dog on the same page, as they say, in terms of building good communication and a relationship that works for both of you. Check out more than one training program (first see chapter 14, Training) and find out when the next class begins. Early registration may well be necessary. Note: At some shelters, training classes may even be included in the adoption fee.

SUBSTITUTE CARE If you are like most dog owners, the day will come when you will need to find someone else to care for your dog for an evening, a half-day, a weekend, or a week. Options may include a professional dog walker, a reputable professional pet-sitter or boarding kennel, or even a friend or relative who is willing and able to step in and help. Your goal here should be to leave your dog with someone who will

care for him as conscientiously and humanely as you would. Time spent interviewing and selecting substitute caregivers is time invested in your dog's well-being and your own peace of mind.

Education

If you are a first-time dog owner, or even if you're not, there probably are quite a few subjects relative to owning a dog that you know you're a little fuzzy about. New interests may spark as you step into your role and discover that the more you put into owning your new dog, the more you both get out of it.

- Find out about dog licensing in your area by checking with your veterinarian, or your local humane society or animal care and control agency, and obtain an application. Be sure you know which vaccinations, if any, are required before a license can be issued. Many states require proof of rabies vaccination in order to purchase a license.
- Make a point of becoming acquainted with staff at your local humane society, no matter where you acquired your dog. The humane society is an excellent source of information on all aspects of dog ownership. It will be aware of local laws regarding dogs, including licensing requirements, leash laws, and penalties for noncompliance, whether and where there are local dog parks or runs where owners can exercise their dogs off-lead, and if there are any local ordinances restricting dog ownership. For example, you may find that there are some restrictions on ownership of

certain breeds, such as pit bulls and wolf hybrids. Restrictions may include muzzling the dog in public, restraining the dog on your property behind specific kinds of barriers, and carrying a certain amount of liability insurance in the event your dog bites someone. Other kinds of restrictions on dog ownership, usually instituted by property/homeowners' associations and landlords, may affect the size and number of dogs you may own. If there are such restrictions where you live, you certainly need to know about them *before* you select a particular dog, not after.

- Browse through the pet section of your local library or bookstore to become aware of the broad range of books written about dogs. A comprehensive illustrated veterinary guide, for instance, will answer many basic questions although it will never substitute for the services of your own veterinarian.

- Sample a few magazines about dogs and think about subscribing to one that looks as if it will keep you up-to-date on current issues relative to dogs' health and well-being as well as provide news about legal and public policy issues regarding dog ownership.

- Get to know about any organizations in your area or nationally that advocate for dogs and are most likely to have current information on local issues and regulations. (See chapter 17, Activism.)

Practical Matters

- Make up a realistic budget for caring for your dog (see Your Canine Bank Account, below). New and experienced dog owners alike often are astonished to discover how much it can cost to take good care of a dog. Veterinary diagnostics and care are improving all the time, but the cost for quality service is increasing just as rapidly. And veterinary care is only one, albeit the biggest, item in a realistic canine budget plan.

- Budget for time as well as money. Dogs do take time — a lot when they're very young, often a lot again when they're old, and a goodly amount on a daily basis for all the years in between. In the beginning weeks and months, figure that you will be spending at least two hours a day on puppy stuff — handling and grooming, housetraining, teaching basic manners and socializing, preparing food, cleaning up puddles, getting your questions answered, and of course, cooing and cuddling. An adult dog will spare you some of the bending and stooping and mopping up that a young puppy requires, but even adult dogs need at least one hour of quality time with you every day (it's quality for you too!). Even

Setting up a bank account for your dog (and why not put it in a real bank where it can earn interest?) will remind you on a regular basis that quality dog care *will* cost money. It will also give you peace of mind in knowing that you are reasonably prepared for the unexpected as well as for the routine costs of owning a dog. Here are the major categories you might want to budget for:

VETERINARY CARE This is the biggie. Dogs typically have high start-up costs when they receive their initial series of vaccinations as well as surgery to be spayed or neutered; moderate but ongoing maintenance costs through the major part of their lives, including annual or semiannual checkups, booster shots, heartworm preventive, blood tests to screen for hidden problems, fecal exams to detect parasites, and dental care; and then high old-age costs as they become prey to the same geriatric changes in heart, kidneys, joints, and other body systems that we are. Accidents and acute or chronic illnesses are impossible to predict, but they happen. You might want to add a budget line for "unexpected veterinary expenses," and contribute to it regularly and generously. It would not be a bad idea to have several hundred dollars or more in this account if you can manage it (if you never have to use it, and one would hope you won't, it will still be sitting there, drawing interest). This amount may seem high, but a single X ray can cost $100, as can an ultrasound exam in the case of soft-tissue disease or damage. Routine annual boosters, including a checkup, can run roughly $60, a stool exam for parasites an additional $15, and a year's supply of heartworm medicine almost $100.

For help estimating the broad range of veterinary costs, have a frank conversation with a few veterinarians in your area. If you explain that you are asking in order to be able to budget for quality care for the lifetime of your pet, most veterinarians will be more than happy to work with you on plugging in some realistic numbers. If you already know that you are going to get a particular breed of dog, the veterinarian may be able to be even more realistic in his estimates, as some breeds are plagued with particular veterinary conditions with well-known associated costs.

IDENTIFICATION This includes at the very least one ID tag or several, depending on whether or not you move from time to time. Tattooing or implanting a dog with a microchip costs more, particularly when you add in the cost of the lifetime or annual registration fees — without which the tattoo or chip is useless. Some veterinarians and shelters implant microchips and can tell you the cost; pet-supply stores or local newspapers may carry advertisements of people who do tattooing.

BASIC SUPPLIES These include items you will purchase only once, such as a dog crate or possibly two, a dog bed if you don't use the crate for that purpose, baby gates, outdoor fencing, a doghouse or temporary shelter while the dog is outside, food and water bowls, and grooming tools. Supplies you will have to replace weekly, seasonally, or from time to time include dog food and supplements, collar and lead, medical and disaster supplies, grooming supplies as opposed to tools, toys, chews, and foul-weather wear.

EDUCATIONAL MATERIALS The major educational expense you should budget for is one or two series of puppy socialization or basic obedience training classes (figure about $50 to $75 a series from local obedience clubs, and less or maybe no charge at all from your local shelter. Private group classes can cost several times that much). Other educational expenses could include such things as an annual subscription to an interesting and informative dog magazine; a video on training or emergency care; a seminar that addresses a subject of special interest, such as how dogs learn or the differences between dogs and wolves; and a comprehensive book on dogs as well as one or two small books that treat single subjects such as housetraining or teaching your dog tricks. These latter items are more in the category of "extras," but if you are interested, you should know that they can add up to a substantial sum of money over the life of your dog. Alternatively, informational pamphlets on health, training, and behavior can often be had for no charge at your humane society or veterinarian's office.

FEES These include your annual (in most places) dog license and also regular or periodic fees for such services as grooming, boarding, in-house sitting, or dog walking. A fee that could buy you considerable peace of mind would be a legal fee to have your attorney add a codicil to your will. This supplement would allow the executor of your estate to disperse funds immediately to a designated person who has agreed to care for your dog if you no longer can do so.

HEALTH INSURANCE Pet health insurance, intended to cover a large part of the expense of illnesses and accidents (rather than routine screening exams, vaccinations, and the like) is not particularly well known in the United States but does exist. Annual premiums vary depending on the age of your dog and when you take out the insurance, but the payout can be well worth it in the event that your dog is in an accident or develops a serious or chronic illness. (Preexisting conditions usually are not covered.) Ask your veterinarian for details and/or an application.

FINAL REMAINS Many first-time owners are surprised to discover that it can cost hundreds of dollars when their dog dies. Even if the dog dies at home of natural causes and you do not have to pay for euthanasia, you probably will still have to pay for disposal of his remains in whatever way is locally mandated. Private cremation, which returns your dog's ashes to you, or burial in a nearby pet cemetery obviously will cost more. Be aware that most municipalities prohibit "backyard burials." Again, your veterinarian or local animal care and control agency can give you some ballpark figures.

though puppy chores eventually will be replaced with adult maintenance routines, the time requirement will not change much. Always hold off getting a new dog until you have a block of time when you can stay at home and devote yourself to helping him settle in. A long weekend is the minimum; a few weeks would be better. If you were home all day and every day, from the dog's point of view, that would be ideal.

- Grim as it sounds, right at the beginning is the best time to address the "what if?" issues. What if something happens to you — who will care for your dog? Begin talking with one or two friends or family members about caring for your dog in case of your death or other emergency. Make sure to talk about the practical issues; a kind-hearted friend may have no idea at all of how much time and money may be involved. Once you've reached an agreement that both of you are comfortable with, have it put in writing and appended to your will. Inform your veterinarian and another person — a friend or family member — of your wishes so there's no question as to who will care for your dog in an emergency. This will allow your friend, in the event you become incapacitated, to gain immediate access to your dog and to any monies you may have earmarked for his care.

You can make daily grooming enjoyable for your dog if you establish an attitude of cooperation. (Tamara Hamilton and Cika Kola)

Health and Safety

The Right Veterinarian

6

Your dog's second-best friend is his veterinarian, and the veterinarian's office should be the second stop on his journey into your world. From an initial wellness exam shortly after your puppy or adult dog joins your family, through the initial series of vaccinations and then regular checkups and annual boosters, through the teenage, the middle, and, all too soon, the senior years, there will never be anyone besides you who is as committed to your dog as his very own veterinarian — assuming that you find the right veterinarian, that is.

The right veterinarian for your dog is a skilled professional, combining both the science and the art of healing. At the same time, the veterinarian is a wise counselor, offering both firm advice and a compassionate ear. The veterinarian's "people skills" are as important as her skill with animals, because there is a third traveler on this journey, and that is you.

How do you find the right veterinarian for your dog? You shop around. You may already have gone through a similar process to find doctors, dentists, and other health-care providers for yourself. Probably you asked your friends and relatives for suggestions, maybe you got recommendations from coworkers, sometimes you started with the Yellow Pages, and sometimes you had to try out a few before you found the one who really felt right for you. If you've been through this drill, then you already know that finding just the right doctor for your dog may take some looking. Sure it would be nice if the veterinarian down the street turned out to be this special person, and probably you will want to look there first. On the other hand, this relationship is too important to base solely on convenience or to leave to chance. Ideally, your dog will have and need only one veterinarian in his lifetime (unless of course you relocate, as so many of us do). With a little effort on your part, you can improve the odds that the first one is the right one.

Plan to start your search ahead of time — before you even get your dog, if you can. Call or drop in at several clinics that you are considering (see Sources of Veterinarians, page 97). Explain that you plan to add a new dog to your family soon and are looking for a veterinary hospital to help you care for your dog from day one. Then ask when it would be convenient for you to stop by for a few minutes to meet the staff, tour the facility, and learn about the hospital's policies and philosophy. In fact, you might ask if the veterinarian would be willing to advise you about the kind of dog you are considering (make sure to offer to pay for whatever time the doctor is able to make available).

Before you visit the hospital, spend some time preparing a checklist to make sure that you don't overlook significant factors. The checklist given below suggests a number of categories for you to think about. Ignore subject areas that don't seem relevant to you, and jot down any others that come to mind. Chances are, you won't be able to learn everything in your brief visit, so concentrate on the subjects that feel most important. Note: Many of your questions can be answered by your own observations, especially if there are other clients and dogs present at the time of your visit. Be considerate of the veterinarian's time and ask only those questions that cannot be answered in any other way.

Veterinary Checklist

Convenience
- location (Is the hospital reasonably convenient for you to get to, or at least not so inconvenient that you may put off taking your dog in on a regular basis?)
- parking
- hours
- appointment or walk-in basis (Both have advantages: the former helps eliminate long waits; the latter allows you more flexibility if your schedule is unpredictable.)

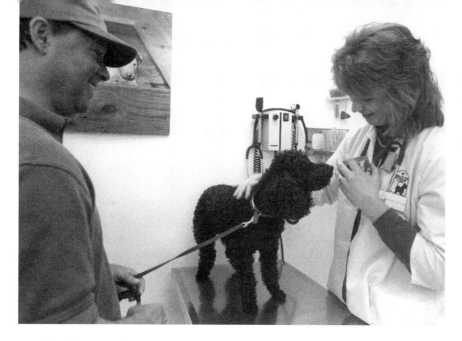

The right veterinarian listens to your concerns. (Lucy Olcott, D.V.M., Paul Scholl, and Toby)

- after-hours and emergency coverage (Does the veterinarian offer emergency and after-hours care? If not, does she have an arrangement with an independent emergency-care clinic in your area?)
- ancillary services (These are not essential veterinary services but if you need any of them, it might be nice to be able to obtain them at the same place your dog receives his veterinary care.)

    —— tattooing   —— microchip implantation

    —— boarding   —— grooming   —— nail clipping

- payment policies (Usually payment is expected at the time of treatment and can be made in cash, by credit card, or by personal check after you become an established client. Some veterinarians will allow you to pay in installments for large bills if you discuss this with them ahead of time. Others offer senior-citizen or multipet discounts.)
- policy regarding pet insurance (Can the hospital provide you with pet insurance applications? Will it accept copayment? Will it assist you in filing a claim?)

Hospital Facility

- cleanliness and brightness of waiting room, exam rooms, surgery, hospital kennels
- spaciousness (enough space in the waiting room, for instance, so that animals can be kept apart from one another)
- presence/absence of odors
- acceptable noise levels

- pet-health and pet-care literature or videotapes in the hospital waiting room
- privacy (Does the hospital offer time and space for dog owners to spend last moments with a terminally ill dog and/or deliberate over difficult decisions regarding treatment options?)
- AAHA member (Membership in the American Animal Hospital Association signifies that a veterinary hospital has met AAHA's standards in the areas of the facility, equipment, and quality care, although there certainly are many fine veterinary hospitals which for one reason or another have not chosen to pursue AAHA certification. To find out if a particular hospital is a member or to locate an AAHA-accredited hospital in your area, contact AAHA (see Choosing a Veterinary Hospital, Appendix II).

Diagnostic Capability

As a matter of convenience, it's nice if your veterinarian is able to perform in-house many of the tests your dog may need rather than having to send you to specialists for testing before a firm diagnosis can be reached. Increasing numbers of veterinary hospitals are beginning to expand their diagnostic capability beyond the standard X rays by acquiring additional pieces of diagnostic equipment and the expertise to use them. On the other hand, it is unrealistic to expect a private animal hospital to be able to afford CAT scanners and other highly specialized and very expensive kinds of equipment that can be found at veterinary schools and large referral hospitals. If two or three of the following are available at a clinic you are considering, it will make caring for your dog less complicated in the event that she becomes ill and the cause is unclear.

- X rays
- ultrasound
- EKG
- endoscopy

Office Systems

Veterinary hospitals vary widely in the kinds of records they keep and printed materials they provide. Computerized offices in particular are able to generate a great deal of useful information.

- new-client information packet (This could well answer many of your questions.)

- reminder cards (when your dog is due for vaccinations, heartworm medication, dental examination, etc.)
- complete treatment records (A veterinarian's own notes and findings must be kept for the life of the dog and a specified number of years beyond; a copy of your dog's records should be made available to you should you ever need or want them, possibly for a small copying fee although often free of charge.)
- printed certificates of vaccination and/or sterilization (Proof of rabies vaccination is required for travel or when you need to board your dog; proof of sterilization may be requested by local dog-licensing agencies.)
- itemized receipts (including medications given at time of treatment as well as prescribed for follow-up care; these receipts are particularly useful in the event you move or for some other reason change veterinarians and need to inform your dog's new doctor of tests, procedures, and medications your dog has had in the past)
- printed bulletins and fact sheets (Printed information and instructions relevant to any condition your dog is being treated for as well as such things as seasonal reminders of cold- or hot-weather hazards are appreciated by many dog owners and convey the veterinary hospital's ongoing interest in your dog's good health.)

Cost

Most veterinarians charge prices that are competitive for the area where they are located. However, dog owners on limited or fixed incomes may want to comparison-shop for one or more of the following basic procedures as a way of assessing whether a particular hospital tends to be above or below average for your area.

- office visit and examination
- set of vaccinations (distemper/hepatitis/leptospirosis/parainfluenza/parvovirus, and rabies)
- stool test for worms
- blood test for heartworm disease
- spay (nonpregnant)
- neuter

Note: If you obtained your dog from a shelter, the shelter may be able to refer you to one or more area veterinarians who have agreed to provide low-cost spay or neuter surgery for adopted dogs, and who then may become your dog's regular veterinarian. Alternatively, the shelter clinic may as a matter of policy sterilize and vaccinate all dogs at the time of adoption and continue to provide low-cost annual vaccinations. However, to help make sure this assistance will continue to be available to those who truly need it, your best course of action would be to refrain from seeking subsidized care if you are able to pay the going rates. Remember, too, that you will never establish the kind of relationship you want with a veterinarian, nor will she get to know your dog as well as she otherwise might, if you only take your dog to her when the price is right.

Professional Staff

Obviously the heart and soul of an animal hospital is the veterinary and other technical staff. It's not too difficult to keep looking if the veterinarian you speak with leaves you cold. On the other hand, the veterinarian with the great sense of humor who hugs your dog and chats happily for an hour may not turn out to be as open-minded as you'd like, or as willing to seek help from others when he doesn't have the answer. To avoid being overly influenced by personal vibes — which shouldn't be ignored either — force yourself to gather some data about the professional staff in the hospitals you are considering.

- number of veterinarians in the practice (Although a single veterinarian working alone may provide exceptional care for your dog, two or three heads often are better than one if in fact the veterinarians confer with one another on cases. On the other hand, some dog owners prefer to work with only one veterinarian. Ask to learn a particular hospital's policy.)
- number of technicians or other semiprofessional staff members in the practice (The technical staff is every bit as involved in the hands-on care of your dog as is the veterinarian. Technicians assist with diagnostic work as well as with treatments and assist during surgery. Often they are the "nurses" who feed and clean and administer TLC to your dog if she ever has to stay in the hospital. The presence of one or more veterinary technicians, who are state certified, may well mean that the veterinarian(s) themselves have more time to devote to understanding and managing your dog's case.)
- credentials (Look for diplomas and certificates to be displayed on the walls inside examination rooms.)
  —— current license to practice veterinary medicine in your state
  —— completed continuing education courses in areas of interest

———— membership in the American Veterinary Medical Association (AVMA) and in state and local veterinary medical associations. (Note: Association memberships certainly are criteria to use as part of your evaluation of a practice, but they alone do not mean that a veterinarian is exemplary in every way, any more than *not* being a member necessarily reflects poorly on a practitioner.)

- age of veterinarians in the practice (In a very general sense, an older practitioner usually will have the wisdom of his years and the great number of cases he has seen, while a younger veterinarian may bring familiarity with the most modern technologies and a mind more eager to embrace new ideas and methods. In any specific situation, however, this needs further investigation. Sometimes a recent graduate is more conservative than a veterinarian who has been in practice for thirty years! All other things being equal, though, it's nice to have both on your team.)

- languages spoken (If English is not your native language, it may mean a lot to you to find a veterinarian who can converse with you in your language. If not the veterinarian, find out if a technician or other staff member can serve as translator. You would not want to find yourself wondering whether or not your concerns were understood or if you completely understood the doctor's directions.)

- support staff (You may have as much or more contact with support staff as you do with the veterinary and technical staff. Note whether you find the support staff to be most or all of the following:
  ———— knowledgeable
  ———— concerned
  ———— compassionate
  ———— professional
  ———— able to communicate clearly
  ———— efficient in handling appointments and keeping records)

- type of practice (No longer does every veterinary hospital approach treatment in much the same way as every other. Chances are you will be attracted to the same kind of veterinary practice as you've selected for your own medical care. Don't hesitate to ask the veterinarian what kind of practice he provides.)

  - general traditional (An all-purpose small-animal veterinary practice offers a full range of medical, surgical, dental, and nutritional care for dogs and cats and possibly for birds, small mammals, and "exotics" as well; a traditional practice seeks to eliminate or at least reduce the signs and symptoms of illness, such as fever, pain, vomiting, diarrhea, respiratory distress, coughing, loss of appetite, bleeding, discharge, swelling, and itching, using drugs, diet, and surgery as needed.)

- specialized (In a practice limited to one specialty, such as cardiology or orthopedics, the practitioner should be board certified in that specialty, which means that he or she has had an additional two to four years of study and experience in the specialty area and has passed a rigorous examination; patients usually are referred to a specialty practice by a general-practice veterinarian.)
- alternative (Such a practice consists of one or more methods of inducing the body to heal itself, in which treatment protocols may have been carefully described, documented, and studied yet have not been and may be unable to be scientifically proven to cause the results that are claimed; see AVMA-recognized alternative modalities, below, for brief descriptions of the alternative modalities approved by the AVMA; other modalities exist and may become approved in the future.)

- policy regarding referrals to area specialists (The right veterinarian should not hesitate to refer a client to a specialist in the event that her dog's condition could be better managed by someone with advanced training in a particular discipline. Depending on population density and per capita incomes, the numbers and kinds of specialists may vary from area to area. Many veterinary specialists are located at veterinary colleges and large referral hospitals. Try to find out which kinds of specialists the veterinarian you are considering has worked with.)
  - —— cardiologists
  - —— neurologists
  - —— oncologists
  - —— orthopedists
  - —— ophthalmologists
  - —— behaviorists
  - —— alternative practitioners
- communication skills (The right veterinarian will be able to elicit vital information from you as well as clearly explain treatment options and possible outcomes, and instruct you in home care. She will also show genuine interest in your observations and intuitions about your dog, as no one knows your dog better than you do.)
- handling of your pet (The veterinarian and other staff members should display knowledge, skill, patience, and a humane approach in handling

your dog. If your dog was so unruly or so fearful/aggressive that the staff was restricted in their ability to examine and treat her, you should expect the right veterinarian to offer you a referral to a qualified trainer or behavioral counselor.)

- accessibility by telephone (Many veterinarians have specified phone hours when you may call to discuss your dog's condition if she is under treatment. Those that do not should return calls reasonably promptly or at specified times.)

Ethics

From a humane point of view, some aspects of veterinary practice cannot be recommended. Find out whether veterinarians you are considering perform the following procedures and perhaps others that you personally find unacceptable.

- cosmetic surgery such as cropping ears and docking tails
- dog breeding (artificial insemination of client dogs or assistance in natural breeding)
- convenience euthanasia (performing euthanasia at the owner's request on a dog who is not terminally ill or suffering, for "reasons" that appear trivial)

Community Outreach

Many veterinary hospitals are active in their communities, supporting local legislation to improve conditions for animals and participating in educational events of various kinds. It does not seem unreasonable to expect your veterinarian to take part in one or more community programs.

- collaboration with area shelters on low-cost spaying/neutering
- public positions on animal-welfare issues (leash laws, anti-dogfighting, humane law enforcement, and dedicated dog parks)
- public education initiatives (workshops on such subjects as first aid, heartworm protection, spaying/neutering, parasite control)

Alternative Veterinary Care

A relatively new and rapidly expanding kind of veterinary practice, alternative or "complementary" veterinary medicine includes a number of very different modalities, each of which requires substantial additional study before a veterinarian should expect to use it effectively and safely. In some alternative modalities formal educational programs have already been established and certification procedures are in place. (Note that alternative veterinary care for your dog should be sought only from a licensed veterinarian or from a licensed or certified "people" practitioner to whom your regular veterinarian has referred you and with whom he or she is collaborating in the care of your dog.)

The American Veterinary Medical Association has recently published guidelines that specify for the first time which alternative modalities are to be considered a legitimate part of standard veterinary practice, to be employed only by licensed veterinarians following the completion of advanced study and certification programs.

- veterinary acupuncture, and acutherapy (the use of special needles, magnets, low-level lasers, and other devices to stimulate specific "acupoints" on the body, believed to be associated with the functioning of particular organs and physical structures)
- veterinary chiropractic (manipulation and "adjustment" of the spine and skeletal structures in order to relieve pressure on nerves, thus relieving pain and improving function of the muscles and organs served by those nerves)
- veterinary physical therapy (the use of such noninvasive techniques as stretching, heat and cold applications, ultrasound, hydrotherapy, and specific exercises to rehabilitate animals following injury)
- massage therapy (the use of the hands to rub or knead soft tissues for the purpose of increasing circulation and relaxing muscles)
- veterinary homeopathy (a medical system in which conditions in animals are treated by administering infinitesimal doses of substances that have been shown to produce symptoms in healthy animals similar to those being observed in the animal being treated; prescribing specific "remedies" according to the individual animal's symptoms is believed to aid the body's own efforts to rid itself of disease and return to health)
- veterinary botanical medicine (the use of plants and plant derivatives as medicines, sometimes to be taken internally and sometimes to be applied to the skin)
- nutraceutical medicine (using familiar nutrients such as vitamins, minerals, enzymes, and amino acids in amounts that cause them to act as therapeutic agents in the body)
- holistic veterinary medicine (the practice of combining alternative and conventional modalities together, both to diagnose and treat disease)

Sources of Veterinarians

Yellow Pages

The veterinary section in the Yellow Pages (check both Animal Hospital and Veterinarian listings) probably is the best way to begin your search for the right veterinarian. You'll be able to gauge how many options you have close to home and how many more within, say, a 15–20-minute drive. Not all the listed veterinarians will have large display ads, but a number will. (Incidentally, the size of an advertisement cannot be considered a sure sign of anything except the fact that that particular veterinarian believes in the power of advertising.) In large cities where there may be stiff competition among a dozen or more veterinary hospitals, the ads can give you an idea of what the veterinarians themselves think is noteworthy about their practices. In fact, you may be able to make some progress on your checklist just by reading the ads. For instance, an ad may state that a particular hospital is an AAHA member, that twenty-four-hour nursing and emergency care is available, that both appointments and walk-ins are accommodated, and that endoscopy and ultrasound are done in-house.

Personal Referrals

Probably the most common source of personal referrals are friends and relatives who live in the same or neighboring communities. Take advantage of your close relationship to ask blunt questions about why they would recommend their veterinarian to you. Just make sure your questions go after real information, not just about their feelings. If you live in the city, it's a simple enough matter to approach people walking dogs in your neighborhood and ask them if they can recommend a veterinarian. Undoubtedly you'll find that most will use the hospital that is closest to where they live. There may actually be more to learn from someone who doesn't, and she will probably be more than happy to tell you why she doesn't like Dr. Closest.

Professional Referrals

Pet professionals such as dog breeders, dog trainers, and groomers in the normal course of their businesses will come to hear from their clients a great many comments about all the veterinarians in the area that they serve. Over time, even without personal knowledge of individual veterinarians, the trainer or groomer may begin to form positive, negative, or neutral impressions of them. It may very well be that these opinions are well founded, i.e., that if two dozen people commented that Dr. Frost is cold and lacking in compassion, this probably is true. What you should keep in mind about this source of referral, however, is that it may hide a conflict of interest. For example, a dog trainer who profits from the referrals sent to him by a veterinarian may reciprocate by mentioning that veterinarian's name every time someone casually asks.

Veterinary Medical Associations

The AVMA as well as local veterinary medical associations will be happy to help you locate a licensed veterinarian, or a veterinary specialist, in your area. In sparsely populated regions, this alone can be worth the cost of the telephone call. Note that the associations do not "rate" the veterinarians on their files but will verify their membership status. You might also want to put in a call to your state board of veterinary medicine to inquire about any

THE GOOD VETERINARY CLIENT

You and your veterinarian are partners in caring for your dog. He supplies the knowledge and skill, you supply the cooperation and the commitment to carry out his recommendations. Here are some ways you can help make both jobs easier:

- Make an initial appointment as soon as you acquire the dog, even if the dog seems perfectly well and has already been vaccinated — a first stress-free visit can set the tone for all future visits.
- See your veterinarian regularly, not just when your dog is sick.
- Socialize and train your dog; keep your dog clean and groomed and at a healthy weight (though primarily for the dog's benefit, these practices will also enable your veterinarian to more easily examine, handle, and treat your dog when necessary).
- Learn how to observe your dog for signs that something isn't right.
- Do not play veterinarian — bring your dog to the veterinarian at the first sign of a problem (see chapter 9).
- Don't expect your veterinarian to be expert in all fields — occasionally he may need to refer you to a specialist for diagnosis or treatment of certain conditions.
- Do expect your veterinarian to be able to help with nonmedical problems, too; your veterinarian most likely has expertise in dealing with behavior problems and is also your best source for referrals to qualified dog trainers and animal behaviorists.

complaints received about a particular veterinarian. Some *will* tell the caller if the veterinarian has been successfully sued for malpractice.

If you never gave much thought to finding a veterinarian, you may be daunted by what could be starting to feel like a Very Big Deal. Don't be. Whether or not you "got into" searching for your dog, by now we trust you realize how important it is to find the right dog for you. Finding the right veterinarian is just as important — particularly if you already had your dog when you bought this book.

7

Ounces of Prevention

All of our grandmothers were right: An ounce of prevention *is* worth a pound of cure. Here are many ounces of prevention. Implement as many as you can for tons of benefits.

Spaying or Neutering

Spaying or neutering your dog is one of the most effective ways to prevent a number of physical and behavioral problems in male and female dogs. (It goes without saying that it prevents more hapless puppies from being brought into a world with too few homes.)

- cancer of reproductive organs (uterus, mammary glands, testicles)
- pregnancy-associated health risks to the female dog (death during labor or delivery, toxemia of pregnancy, infection of the uterus, infection of the mammary glands)
- sex-linked behaviors in the male (roaming, urine-marking, fighting with competing males, howling if unable to get to females in season, inattentiveness and regression in training)

- "heat"-related problems with the female (bleeding on furniture and carpets for several weeks twice a year, attracting all the male dogs in the neighborhood to your doorstep, causing you to redouble your efforts to keep your dog from escaping)

Veterinary Wellness Checkups

Don't wait until your dog is sick to visit the veterinarian, by which time minor conditions may have had a chance to become major ones. After your new puppy or dog's initial checkup, and two or three follow-up visits to complete her first vaccination series, ask your veterinarian how often you should plan to return. An annual visit to bring the dog's vaccinations up to date is the absolute *minimum* you should contemplate. One other visit during the year would allow the veterinarian to monitor her growth, weight, and overall condition, examine and possibly clean her teeth, check her stool for parasites, discuss any training or behavior problems, and get to know better how she looks and acts when she is well. The annual or biannual visit is also an opportunity for the veterinarian to tell you about new procedures and products.

Grooming/Handling Checkups

These exams are performed by you, every week for the first few months and thereafter as often as your dog's coat requires care. (This can range from every other day for dogs with long, soft, or bushy coats to perhaps twice-monthly sessions for dogs with very short coats.) Setting up a schedule for grooming and handling will help you (and your dog) get into a routine for "personal care" that you should plan to follow for the life of your dog. In addition, these sessions will allow you to become so familiar with all parts of your dog's body that you'll be likely to notice any lumps or bumps, swelling, painful spots, itchy spots, flaking skin, hair loss, or other changes that should be brought to your veterinarian's attention. Another important benefit is that you'll be sure to spot fleas and ticks when there are just a few. Maybe the greatest benefit of all, though, is that touching your dog during regular and unhurried grooming sessions will increase the feeling of connectedness between you and your dog, making these sessions favorite "together times." A grooming session should include:

BRUSHING AND COMBING With your dog lying or standing on a table that is waist-high on you, first brush the entire body, back, sides, legs, tail, stomach, and so on in order to open up the coat, stimulate the skin, and remove dirt, dander, and dead hair. Follow through with a comb, making sure you are able to comb the hair right down to the skin (as you do your own). Be careful not to pull against any mats or tangles; tease them apart with your fingers, then gently pull the comb through a few hairs at a time.

EAR CLEANING Check the ears for dirt and waxy buildup, dark debris, or offensive odor (if any are found, or if the ears are painful, you will need to have your veterinarian clean the ears and perhaps treat the dog for ear mites or an infection). Use a cotton ball moistened with a little baby oil to clean the inside of the ear flaps. Carefully clean inside the canals too, inserting your finger no deeper than you can see.

TEETH CLEANING Wrap a piece of gauze or rough cloth around your finger and rub it across your dog's teeth, particularly the outside edges next to the cheeks. Or, try using a doggy toothbrush and one of the flavored toothpastes made for dogs (available from your veterinarian) — many dogs really like it! For best results, brush your dog's teeth every day or at least every other day. If you're unsure of how to proceed, ask your veterinarian to demonstrate proper technique.

BATHING Dogs should be bathed only when they are truly dirty, although giving your dog a few baths during the first month or so and very occasionally thereafter is a good idea because it will familiarize her with the procedure. Brushing and combing usually remove enough dead hair and debris so that a bath isn't necessary, whereas too-frequent bathing can dry out the skin and cause it to itch, possibly setting up an itch-scratch-irritate-itch-scratch cycle that can take on a life of its own.

Bathe small dogs in the kitchen sink and large ones in the tub or outdoors in the yard in nice weather. Attach a hose to the faucet and wet the dog down with warm water. Then apply a baby shampoo or shampoo designed for dogs and work it through the coat. Rinse thoroughly, then towel dry, taking care not to retangle any long hair. For soft-coated breeds, you may want to use a detangler, which is like hair conditioner made for dogs. Allow the dog to air-dry in a draft-free room, or dry carefully with a hand-held dryer while brushing gently. (You may have to introduce the dryer in stages until your dog gets used to the sound and the feel of the warm air.)

NAIL CLIPPING While the nails are soft from the bath, clip off the tips of any that are long enough to touch the floor when the dog is standing. If you haven't bathed the dog, clip the nails anyway. Use a nail clipper intended for dogs (available at pet-supply stores), hold the paw gently but firmly, and remove only the portion that curves downward. Talk encouragingly to your dog as you work, praising him often for bravely enduring this procedure.

If you cut back too deeply into the nail, i.e., in the portion that is horizontal, you may nick the vein in the nail, causing pain and bleeding (if your dog has white nails, the vein will be visible and you can avoid it easily; unfortunately, the veins cannot be seen in black nails). If they've been nicked even once, most dogs will resist nail clipping forever after. If you're uncertain, ask your veterinarian to demonstrate for you before you attempt cutting nails on your own.

Disease Prevention

There seems to be more evidence every day that we humans can help prevent disease and disability by exercising, eating well, and managing the stress in our lives. The same is true for our dogs, but in their case, we're the ones who are in control of their diet, their exercise, and their lifestyle. At this point, just start thinking about the fact that your focus on prevention can have a big impact on your dog's health and welfare — and on your pocketbook and peace of mind. Detailed suggestions regarding diet, health, and exercise will be found in chapters 8, 9, and 15.

Safety Precautions and Ways of Avoiding "Trouble"

Dogs are not famous for staying away from things that can hurt them or for avoiding behavior that can get them into trouble with others. Even though it's their behavior, preventing the behavior is our responsibility. It's up to us to look around, figure out where the hazards are, and take appropriate actions.

In the Home, Workshop, and Garage
- things that can poison (cleansers, soaps, ammonia, detergents and bleaches, insect sprays and pesticides, perfumes, colognes, and aftershave, vitamins and medications, office and crafts supplies, chocolate, poinsettia, mistletoe, dumbcane, cactus, and philodendron, pressure-treated lumber, paints and solvents, gasoline, fuel oil, and, above all, antifreeze)

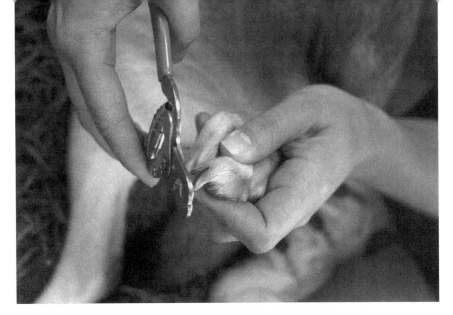

Grasping the foot firmly but gently to prevent your dog from flinching, clip only the portion of the nail that curls downward, taking care not to nick the vein (visible in white nails only)

- things that can burn (tub water, boiling liquids, open flames, cigarettes, plugged-in appliances)
- things that can electrocute (chewed-through lamp cord, appliance and Christmas tree light cords)
- things that can strangle, choke, or obstruct (choke collars, slip nooses, small balls, string, sanitary tampons, sponges, poultry bones, pantyhose)
- things that can topple, crush, or allow falls (precariously situated appliances, especially on tabletops where food is placed, high-piled boxes, top-heavy open filing cabinets, unstacked lumber or construction debris, ramps and open staircases)
- things that can get a dog in trouble with neighbors, delivery people, other family members, or even with you (barking, howling, and whining, chewing and scratching, urinating and defecating indoors and on others' property, jumping up on/mounting, growling, snapping, and biting)

Outdoors
- things that can poison (spilled or leaked antifreeze, fertilizers, weed killers, grass that's just been treated with pesticides, snail and slug bait, rat and mouse poison, certain toads, acorns, apple seeds, wild mushrooms, yew shrub berries, oleander, azalea, honeysuckle, rhubarb)
- things that can wound (broken glass, metal can lids, nails and spikes, barbed wire)
- things that can allow escape or theft (unlatched gates or doors, electronic shock-collar fencing, shallow-dug fencing, too-low fencing, too-large collars, worn leashes, leashes in the hands of small children)

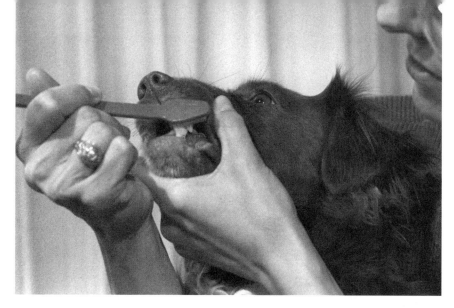

You should brush your dog's teeth three to four times a week. Gently stabilize your dog's jaw as you brush his teeth. (Leslie Sinclair, D.V.M., and Brownie)

- things that can burn, parch, chill, or freeze (road salts, shadeless yards in summertime, overturned water bowls, unheated and noninsulated doghouses, exposure to wet, wind, and subfreezing temperatures)
- things that can attack (other dogs, coyotes, bees, wasps, fire ants, black widow spiders, venomous snakes, scorpions)
- things that can be attacked (cats, birds, rabbits, children, mail carriers and other delivery or service personnel)

In the Car or Truck
- things that risk health or death (being left inside for even a few minutes in hot weather, being left too long in subfreezing weather, being unrestrained in the event of a sudden stop or collision, being left in a running car within a closed space, ingesting spilled windshield detergent or antifreeze, being transported in the open bed of a pickup truck)
- things that could get a dog in trouble (destroying car interior while left alone, urinating or defecating out of anxiety, biting the hands of children reaching in through the window)
- things that permit escape or theft (open windows, unlocked doors, being unrestrained in the event of a car crash, being visible, vulnerable, and unattended)

Legal Precautions

Depending on where you live, there are doubtless some and perhaps many ordinances that affect your dog and you as a dog owner. Not being aware of

these laws unfortunately does not mean that they don't apply to you. In order to prevent your dog from running afoul of a legal requirement, check with your veterinarian and health department about those that involve health, with your animal control officer or local humane society for those that involve the public, and with your insurance agent for those that involve liability. For one-stop shopping, visit your local public library or the law library in your county courthouse, and look up "Dogs" or "Animals" in your municipal code. Many local governments, usually through the animal control agency, produce booklets that explain pet-related laws. In most municipalities, the most common ordinances include the following:

- dog licensing (Usually good for one year, the dog license is a community's way of keeping track of its canine population; your dog's license tag, if always worn on his collar, is also a way that authorities can reunite him with you should he become lost.)

- rabies vaccination (Every state in the union now requires that dogs be vaccinated against rabies; each time your veterinarian vaccinates your dog, she will give you a tag that you should firmly affix to his collar; in many areas, rabies-vaccination and dog-licensing requirements are linked, meaning that a dog cannot be licensed unless he is first vaccinated for rabies.)
- leash laws (Many cities and towns now have leash laws, which require that all dogs be on a leash while within the town limits and/or in all areas not otherwise designated; violators may be subject to a fine, and unleashed dogs may be picked up and impounded.)
- pooper-scooper laws (These laws require dog owners to pick up their dog's feces immediately if deposited anywhere but on their own property; violators may be required to pay a fine.)
- nuisance laws (Communities differ in the specific behaviors that are deemed to be a nuisance; the most common are barking, howling, or whining.)
- "dangerous" or "vicious" dog laws (Usually local but in some cases state laws, these laws generally impose secure confinement measures while on the owner's property and muzzling in public of dogs who have without provocation threatened or caused injury to a person or in some cases a domestic animal; another frequent tenet of a dangerous dog law is that the owner must carry a specified amount of liability insurance in order to compensate victims for damage the dog may cause.)
- breed-specific laws (These are similar to dangerous dog laws but unfairly discriminatory — and when contested in court, sometimes overthrown — in that they impose restrictions on dogs solely on the basis of their breed or breed type; overwhelmingly, breed-specific laws target pit bulls, although several terrier breeds, Rottweilers, Doberman pinschers, chow chows, and others have also been named in some proposals.)

Dog-Limiting Policies to Be Aware Of

Condominium boards and landlords of rental properties may legally limit by number or size, restrict in terms of access, or completely forbid dogs on their properties; public properties and spaces, wilderness areas, and private businesses may deny access to all but assistance dogs; airlines may limit the number of dogs in the cabin on any flight and must deny cabin access to any dog too large to fit under a seat)

Lost-Dog Prevention

Owners of lost dogs describe a unique kind of distress, clearly due to the belief that they are responsible. In fact, most loss *is* preventable; even theft can be made far less likely.

Practical Tips to Avoid Loss or Theft

- Make sure yards are escape-proof; periodically examine fencing and latches.
- Do not use electronic shock-collar fencing containment systems; they are not foolproof.
- Do not chain or tie your dog outdoors; chains can break, ropes can fray or be cut.
- Supervise your dog while she's in the yard; don't give this responsibility to small children.
- Train your dog not to dash through open doors.
- Obtain help for a dog with separation anxiety; in the meantime, make sure your dog is confined away from windows.
- Walk and exercise your dog on-leash, even in areas such as national parks where they may be allowed off-leash; periodically check leashes, collars, and harnesses for wear.
- Keep an especially firm grip on your dog's leash during parades, fireworks, in unfamiliar settings, and at all times if your dog is high-strung; slide the handle over your wrist rather than hold it only with your fingers.
- Allow your dog off-leash only in designated and secure areas such as municipal dog parks.
- Make sure your dog's collar fits properly; dogs can easily slip out of a collar that is too large.
- Never tie your dog outside a store or shop.
- Never leave your dog unattended in your car or truck.
- Never leave your dog with anyone you do not know and trust.
- Never board your dog at a kennel you have not carefully investigated and inspected.

Permanent Identification Brings Peace of Mind

- Make sure your dog is always wearing his collar and ID tag; the tag should include your name, address, and home and work telephone numbers.
- Attach your dog's license and rabies tag to his collar as well; these also allow your dog to be traced to you.

- When traveling, make sure your dog is wearing your vacation or temporary address as well as your permanent one.
- For added protection, have your dog tattooed or microchipped (and don't forget to register the tattoo or chip number) as well as tagged; unfortunately, collars and tags can be lost or removed.

A Lost-Dog Kit Can Make the Difference

At home or when traveling, have at the ready a lost-dog kit that contains the following:

- a recent photograph of your dog
- blank paper and waterproof ink for making up an ad
- tacks, hammer, and nails and waterproof tape for hanging flyers in different locations
- telephone numbers of local animal shelters and national tattoo and microchip registries
- an earmarked sum of money to cover the expenses of searching for your dog (copying costs, telephone calls, postage and envelopes to mail flyers to selected mailing lists, reward, or donation)

Emergency and Disaster Preparedness

When an emergency or natural disaster occurs, it's already too late to start thinking about how to provide for your dog. But by being prepared, panic can be avoided and chances for "weathering the storm" can be greatly improved. Detailed suggestions for preparing for emergencies and disasters can be found in chapters 10 and 11, respectively.

Despite the well-documented benefits of sterilizing both male and female dogs, there are always some owners who decide not to have the surgery performed because of a variety of mistaken beliefs. Do *you* know the facts? Take the test below and find out.

TRUE OR FALSE

		TRUE	FALSE
1.	As long as females are sterilized, males don't need to be.	——	——
2.	Females should have at least one litter or they will be high-strung and nervous.	——	——
3.	Males will not attain full size and strength if they are neutered.	——	——
4.	Sterilized dogs are not protective of their families and do not make good watchdogs.	——	——
5.	Sterilized dogs may become less active and put on weight.	——	——
6.	Sterilizing solves behavior problems.	——	——
7.	Sterilizing can be done at any age.	——	——
8.	Sterilized dogs make better pets.	——	——

ANSWERS

1. *False.* Owners of male and female dogs share the responsibility for not contributing to the pet overpopulation problem. In addition to preventing them from siring litters, there are sound physical and behavioral reasons for neutering males.

2. *False.* There is no connection between temperament and motherhood. Furthermore, a nervous mother is likely to pass the trait on to some or all of her puppies.

3. *False.* The only physical difference seen between neutered males and intact males in one study designed specifically to study such differences was in the size of the penis. Overall physical size and weight were the same for both groups, even in dogs who had been neutered as young as seven weeks, and neutered males of some large breeds of dogs were actually taller and longer than intact males of the same breeds at the same age.

4. *False.* The instinct to bark at strangers or to protect family members is not linked to gender or to whether or not a dog is sterilized, although females in heat and roaming males are less protective of their homes than sterilized dogs. In addition, a female with a litter of puppies is likely to be protective of

them, which could actually make her temporarily less devoted and in some cases even aggressive toward her human family members.

5. *True.* Some sterilized dogs may require a managed diet and exercise regimen to maintain the same weight after sterilization. So do some unsterilized dogs as they become older. So yes, it's true that some dogs will gain weight after being sterilized, but they should still be sterilized for all the reasons given previously. If there *is* a weight gain, consult with your veterinarian to determine the best diet and exercise regimen. Possible options include feeding smaller portions, feeding a diet designed for less active dogs, substituting low-calorie snacks such as raw vegetables for some of the dog's daily biscuit ration, and taking longer, more frequent walks and increasing active play.

6. *True and False.* Sterilization may ameliorate or eliminate in at least some dogs those behavior "problems" that are directly influenced by the presence of sex hormones in the blood (urine-marking, mounting, howling, roaming, aggression). Sterilization cannot be expected to affect other undesirable behaviors or temperamental defects.

7. *True.* Sterilizing can be done as young as eight weeks of age, with no increased surgical or postoperative risks reported. Females who are sterilized before their first heat cycle are at much lower risk for mammary tumors than are females who are sterilized after even one or two cycles. Both male and female dogs remain fertile throughout their lives; therefore, older animals should still be sterilized in order to prevent uterine infection in females, to ameliorate some undesirable behaviors in males, and to prevent more puppies from being born. Although there is a somewhat increased risk from anesthesia for dogs over the age of seven years, this can be overcome by careful presurgical evaluation and careful monitoring of the patient before, during, and after surgery. The benefits to even the older dog usually outweigh the risks.

8. *True.* Even if there were no health, hygiene, cleanliness, behavioral, or ethical factors to consider, dogs — males and females — who are not subject to the stress, discomfort, and distraction of the female's heat cycle are more dependable, attentive, and devoted companions.

8

Food and Feeding

It really is true that we are what we eat — whether "we" are humans or dogs. More is learned every day about the benefits of optimum nutrition, not only in maintaining health but in helping to cure disease. Granted, we've all known some dogs who've lived to a healthy old age on nothing but table scraps. But how much healthier, and how much longer, might they have lived on a more complete and balanced diet? Then again, scraps from a table where lean meat, whole grains, and fresh vegetables are served — rather than hot dogs, French fries, and sugary desserts — could actually though accidentally provide a pretty good diet for a dog.

Dog Food vs. People Food

Historically, dogs have been fed differently and apart from their human families. In earliest times, wild dogs were allowed to scavenge around human camps, supplementing what they could hunt for themselves with whatever humans had cast out as garbage or offal. In later times, dogs were more likely to be "fed," although their diets for the most part consisted of what humans found unfit or unpalatable. Today, with dogs mostly considered members of the family, they have their very own aisle in the supermarket, stacked with an impressive array of foods, snacks, biscuits, and treats. In pet-supply stores, both popular and little-known brands of foods as well as different kinds of nutritional supplements and an even greater selection of snacks and treats can be found. The tremendous variety and ready availability of specially prepared dog foods doesn't mean that no one feeds table scraps or homemade meals anymore. Most of us, however, are very happy to feed our dogs a commercial diet. We already have enough to do. In addition, it's comforting to know that someone else has come up with a formula for complete and balanced nutrition for our dogs.

Complete and Balanced

If you're a dedicated label-reader, as anyone who takes nutrition seriously almost has to be, there is a lot of useful information to be had on dog food cans and packages (see Reading the Label, page 117). But if you're the type who just wants to know that the food is "good" for your dog, there are three things to look for on the label. The first is the phrase "complete and balanced." It means that the food contains everything that dogs are known to need in their diets (except water) and in the correct proportions.

The second phrase to look for, which usually appears in conjunction with the first, is the "ages and stages" designation. No longer is one dog food required to nourish dogs through all life stages. Today's dog foods are formulated as complete and balanced nutrition either for "growth and reproduction" or "adult maintenance." Levels of certain nutrients are higher in the former than the latter, so you should be careful to select a food that is appropriate for your dog's life stage. As a rule of thumb, puppy food should generally be fed until about one year of age and then gradually replaced with an adult formula. In addition, some manufacturers also provide "lite" foods for overweight/couch-potato canines, senior diets for older dogs, and high-performance foods for working dogs with exceptionally high energy requirements.

The third thing to look for on a dog food can or package is the acronym "AAFCO" (pronounced *af'-ko*), which stands for the Association of American Feed Control Officials, a kind of watchdog agency for pet and other animal foods in this country. If the label states that AAFCO guidelines or procedures were followed and substantiate that the food provides complete and balanced nutrition, you can go ahead and feed the product with confidence that your dog will be getting the right proportions of protein, fat, fiber, vitamins, and minerals in his diet. Even so, you still have a lot of choices to make.

What Kind of Food?

The dog food industry is a multibillion-dollar enterprise in the United States. Small wonder that there are many kinds of diets, all competing for your dog food dollars.

Commercial Diets

There are three primary classes of commercial diets to choose among: generic, name-brand, and premium. In general, the quality of diet increases from generic to premium brands, although there are company and product exceptions to this rule.

GENERIC DOG FOODS Many large supermarket chains offer "generic" or "store brand" dog foods for considerably less money than the name brands that may appear on the same shelf. Generic dog foods are considered to be of lower quality than their popular counterparts, and are unlikely to provide optimal nutrition. For added assurance, look on the labels for a reference to either feeding trials or nutrient profiles that adhere to AAFCO guidelines. It goes without saying that a food that does *not* claim to be complete and balanced almost certainly is not!

BRAND-NAME DOG FOODS These are the canine equivalent of the Stouffer's and Swanson's dinners that you can buy for yourself at the supermarket, and the supermarket is exactly where you can find the dog foods as well. Recognizable "name brands" for dogs include Purina, Alpo, Cycle (formerly Gaines), and Ken'l Ration. These brands have been around long enough to have earned a high degree of consumer confidence and are generally of good quality.

PREMIUM FOODS The manufacturers of these diets have gone to extra trouble and expense in preparing their foods, and they cost more as a result. Popular premium diets include Iams and Science Diet. Additionally, Purina and some of the other manufacturers of name brands have begun to add premium foods to their product lines for those owners who are willing to spend more for higher quality. Premium foods are mostly found in pet-supply and specialty stores.

(A word about quality. When we talk about "quality" in a diet, we are talking primarily about the quality of the ingredients. For instance, the protein source in a generic chicken diet food may be the legs and beaks of processed chickens; in a name-brand food it may be chicken organs such as the gizzard or intestines; and in a premium food, it may be chicken meat, much as we would eat ourselves. The same differences exist in turkey diets, beef diets, etc., and the price of the diet varies with the quality of the ingredients.)

Specialty Diets

As the term suggests, specialty foods are formulated for special purposes or for a specialized segment of the market. Some specialty foods include:

NATURAL DOG FOODS These are foods to which no chemically altered ingredients have been added. In general, that means no dyes, no colorings, no artificial flavors, and no artificial preservatives. Manufacturers of natural dog foods include Wysong, Abady, Pet Guard, Solid Gold, Nature's Recipe, and Natural Life. In addition, some of the giant pet food companies are beginning to add a more "natural" pet food to their product lines for those pet owners who are concerned about chemical preservatives and other additives. Natural dog foods are sold primarily in pet-supply stores and health-food stores; they cost more than brand-name foods and generally are in the same range as premium diets.

ORGANIC DOG FOODS Made with ingredients that were grown (grains and vegetables) or raised (meat, poultry, and fish) without chemicals such as insecticides, fertilizers, hormones, and antibiotics, organic diets are either fresh or are carefully processed to maintain freshness as well as naturally preserved; they are largely local or regional products that may be found in some health-food stores or in special holistic pet-supply stores.

VEGETARIAN DOG FOODS Dog owners who are vegetarians often feel more comfortable feeding their pets a vegetarian diet as well. Prepared vegetarian diets for pets are available in some health-food and holistic pet care stores. Because some nutrients are believed to be available in highest quality only from animal-based protein sources, you probably should discuss with your veterinarian the label of any vegetarian food you are considering. You want to make sure it meets your dog's specific nutritional needs.

Prescription Diets

COMMERCIAL PRESCRIPTION DIETS Formulated to treat a number of veterinary conditions, the best known of these are the Hill's diets that are prescribed by and are available only through veterinarians. Prescription diets exist to help manage conditions such as heart, kidney, and liver disease, as well as to assist dogs with allergies, fat intolerance, and other conditions.

HOMEMADE THERAPEUTIC DIETS Some holistic veterinarians advocate feeding dogs a diet consisting of raw, fresh, whole foods, as a lifelong way of feeding and/or as part of an overall therapeutic regimen for dogs with various chronic conditions. These diets are very labor-intensive. They require fresh, preferably organic foods, usually available at local farmers markets or health-food stores, which are then prepared at home according to recipes that are written specifically for dogs.

What Texture Dog Food?

Dog foods come in three "textures": canned, semimoist, and dry. Each has its pros and cons.

Canned Food

PROS most palatable; very convenient (compare opening a can with starting from scratch with fresh, wet ingredients); most appealing to owners (canned foods look most like what people think dogs like)

CONS most expensive; uneaten portions spoil if left out at room temperature; most likely to lead to overeating if fed free-choice; "messiest" food for dogs with beards and long ear fringes

Semimoist Food

PROS lightweight and portable; very convenient; no preparation or cleanup required; will not spoil at room temperature; no mess for dogs with long hair

CONS contains many additives and preservatives, including sugars, in order to retain moisture yet not spoil; moderately expensive

Dry Food

PROS least expensive; will not spoil at room temperature; allows free-choice feeding; helps promote healthy teeth and gums; no mess for dogs with long hair

CONS least palatable unless fed from an early age

Which texture food you feed is largely a personal choice — not so much your dog's but yours, as he is likely to eat readily whatever you accustom him

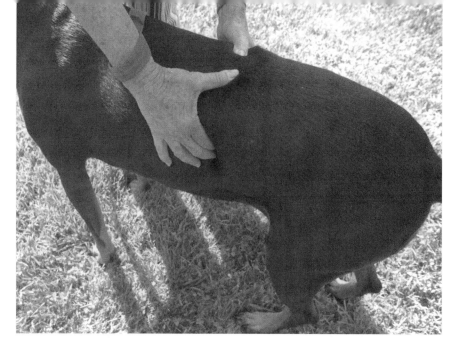

You should be able to feel your dog's ribs individually under her coat only by exerting gentle pressure if she is at her ideal weight.

to eating. Mixing dry and canned foods together is a good way to obtain the benefits of both, and some packages include suggestions for how much of each to use. Semimoist food, even if complete and balanced, is less recommended because of its additives. However, if you feed it just often enough so that it remains familiar to your dog's system, its handy, resealable, and, for many dogs, single-portion packaged, requiring no preparation, mess, or cleanup, which probably makes it the most convenient food to use when you're away from home or traveling.

Reading the Label

Fortunately for us, pet food manufacturers are required to put certain kinds of information on their labels. Just as important, they are not permitted to make claims that they cannot substantiate. In reading the label on a food you are considering, look for the following:

- identification of the product as complete and balanced nutrition, based on AAFCO guidelines, either for *growth and reproduction* or for *adult maintenance* (It would be just as much a mistake to feed your adult dog a puppy food that is too rich — too much protein, too much fat — as it would be to feed a puppy a food that is not rich enough in nutrients.)
- identification of the product as a snack or treat (These foods are not complete and balanced and cannot make up your dog's total diet without sup-

plementation. Feeding treats can lead to deficiencies of certain nutrients.)

- the order of ingredients (By law, the label must list ingredients in descending order by weight. Make sure that the protein source — meat, meat meal, or meat by-products — is near the top of the list, not near the bottom.)
- the quality of ingredients (As discussed above, this can take some decoding. In general, though, if a food is labeled as a chicken formula, look for *chicken,* meaning chicken meat, rather than *chicken by-products,* which could include indigestible parts of the chicken such as claws and feathers. Look for other ingredients that you recognize by name, such as rice or corn or soy. Note: Dogs with allergies may be troubled by foods with wheat, corn, or soy. Consult with your veterinarian regarding what food to feed.)
- guaranteed analysis (All dog food labels must state what percentage of the food is made up of protein, fat, fiber, and moisture. The "guaranteed analysis" data on the label lists the percentages as either a minimum amount [not less than] or a maximum [not more than]. To make use of these percentages, though, you must know how much of each nutrient your dog requires. As this varies with age, activity level, and other factors, ask your veterinarian what nutrient levels she recommends for your dog, then compare them to the numbers given on a dog food you are considering.
- manufacturer's address (All dog foods are required to have the manufacturer's address on the label. Use this to ask any questions that you have about the food. Use it also to register any complaints. For instance, if you find a food that your dog likes and does well on, but wish that the protein source was fresh chicken instead of chicken meal, which is cooked twice — once to make the chicken into powder, and again to process the meal into the food, thus losing more of the protein to heat — write a polite letter to the manufacturer expressing your opinion. It can't hurt, and you'll feel better for bothering.)

Testing the Diet

Reading dog food labels, asking questions, talking the matter over with your veterinarian, all are important steps in the process of choosing what food to feed your puppy or dog. In the end, though, the best test of any food is how well your dog does on it. Ask these questions:

Look at your dog from above to see if she has a definite hourglass figure with a definite waist. (Kathy Bauch's Kashiri and Ricky)

- Does he like it? The food your dog loves best may not necessarily be the best for him. On the other hand, you should be able to find one that he likes *and* that likes him.
- Is the food easily and well digested by your dog? Gas, bloating, loud gurgling noises after eating, loose, unformed stools, stools with undigested material in them, and very large stools are all signs that your dog is not digesting the food particularly well. Look for firm, well-formed, consistent stools that can be picked up easily and leave only a moist mark on the ground.
- How does your dog look? A shiny coat, clean skin (no flakes and scales), and clear eyes (no discharge) are good signs that your dog's diet agrees with her.

Supplements: Yes or No?

The "balanced" half of "complete and balanced" means that all nutrients are in the right proportion to one another. One of the things that manufacturers do in preparing their products is add all the essential vitamins and minerals (as well as other nutrients) that may be lacking in the ingredients they begin with or that are destroyed during the heating process. This means that if you supplement the dog food with vitamins and minerals, you may well be exceeding the recommended daily amounts of certain nutrients, which can be just as harmful as undersupplying them. You can also easily unbalance the food by adding more of a nutrient that needs to be in a particular relationship with another one. Therefore, supplements are only recommended when a deficiency exists — such as when the food you are feeding is not complete and balanced, or when your dog has a medical condition that requires additional amounts of certain nutrients. In other words, do not supplement your dog's diet unless recommended and supervised by your veterinarian.

Feeding Tips

First-time and even experienced dog owners can make some basic mealtime mistakes. Here are some feeding tips as well as some things to avoid.

- Feed puppies under three months four times a day, puppies between three and six months three times, and dogs over six months twice a day. Though many adult dogs seem to do well enough on one meal a day, there seems little doubt that two meals a day would be easier on the digestion, would help dogs maintain a consistent energy level, would avoid behavior problems associated with hunger and irritability, and would add interest to both ends of the day for your dog. Tiny breeds of dogs should definitely not be fed less than twice a day.
- Use the feeding instructions on the dog food package or can as a starting point in determining how much food to offer your dog each day. Don't be so rigid about the guidelines that you forget to observe your dog. If the dog leaves food behind or picks at it slowly, chances are you're feeding too much. If he gulps it down and continues to lick at the bowl after it's empty, you may be feeding too little. Most important, check your dog's weight (see Loving to Death, below) every few months so that you can correct any problems while they're small ones.
- Avoid any food that upsets your dog's digestion (spicy, very rich, fried, hard-to-digest foods, foods that cause gas, distress, very loose or very dry stools); avoid sugary sweets, fried foods, foods in chunks large enough to choke on, as well as poultry, fish, or pork bones; avoid foods that make your dog hyperactive or very thirsty or seem to leave him hungry again in a short time.
- Avoid chocolate completely — it contains theobromine, a substance that is poisonous to dogs.
- Feed your dog in an out-of-the-way but not isolated place, and at roughly the same times every day. At first you (or the dog's primary caretaker or leader) should feed the dog, but eventually all family members should

take turns feeding. All things being equal, it's a good idea to feed the dog after the family eats, and to ask her to sit quietly while the food is prepared and placed on the floor.

- Provide fresh water at all times.
- Prevent a finicky eater by offering a variety of foods or at least a variety of flavors of the same brand. Alternate canned and dry portions or mix the two together.
- Introduce new foods gradually, replacing perhaps a quarter of the regular food with that amount of the new product; then a half; then three-quarters; and finally dropping the old diet altogether.
- Use mealtime as a way to monitor your dog's health and overall well-being. Is there a change in appetite (eating more or less for more than a few days could signal some kind of health problem that your veterinarian should check out)? Does the dog seem hungry but hesitate to pick up food (which could mean pain in the mouth)? Does the dog's behavior toward food change? Does he become more protective (which could suggest some shift in the household dominance hierarchy that you should look at)? Does she begin to hoard or carry off food to another area (which could also be a dominance display, could mean you're overfeeding her — or could just be a quirk!)?
- Use treats sparingly and for a purpose, such as to train or to refresh training, or to help strangers make friends with your dog. Provide only wholesome treats (dog biscuits are fine, and there are several good brands to choose among) and ones that are low in calories (pieces of raw vegetables, bits of cheese or meat, or a few pieces of semimoist product kept for just this purpose). Whatever the treat, it should be something your dog finds particularly tasty, and all treats must be counted as part of your dog's daily food ration.

Roughly 25 percent of American dogs are considered to be obese or likely to become obese. Problems associated with obesity include skeletal stress, cardiopulmonary disease, diabetes, inflammation of the pancreas, greater susceptibility to heat stress, and if surgery is ever necessary, increased risk of anesthetic and surgical complications. The primary causes of obesity are overeating and lack of exercise. If you're not sure if your dog is on her way to obesity, or what to do about it, consider the following:

DO A HANDS-ON FAT CHECK Look at your dog from above to see if she has an "hourglass" figure with a definite waist behind her rib cage. See if there are fatty deposits over the base of the tail or hips. From the side, look to see if your dog has an abdominal tuck-up between the rib cage and the hind legs. Finally, stand over the dog and place your thumbs on her spine and curl your fingers lightly over her ribs. You should be able to locate and count each rib as you run your fingers over the rib cage.

KNOW THE CAUSES OF OBESITY Overfeeding, free-feeding, overtreating, too little exercise, spaying/neutering (without adjustment of caloric intake/output), medical conditions, and prescribed drugs may lead to weight gain. Discuss the situation with your veterinarian in order to decide which one(s) may apply in your dog's case. Then try one or more of the following techniques to correct them.

- Substitute "lite" items for more fattening ones, such as more fresh veggies and lo cal snacks.
- Give a half or a third of a dog biscuit instead of a whole one (your dog will never know).
- Guard against too rapid weight loss (this is as bad for dogs as it is for people); plan to have your medium-size dog lose no more than one-quarter pound a week until he reaches his ideal weight, then increase food gradually as long as he maintains the ideal weight (very small and very large dogs should lose proportionally — ask your veterinarian for guidance).
- Add an extra fifteen minutes of moderate exercise two or three times a day (increase gradually and only after your veterinarian gives the green light).
- Use behavior-modification techniques to eliminate begging (see chapter 18, Dog Behaviors/People Problems).
- Discuss your dog's weight and your plans to help her reduce with all family members; make sure none of them unknowingly sabotages your efforts.

- Weigh your dog regularly, especially when attempting to reduce her weight; most veterinarians would be amenable to having you stop by periodically for a weigh-in and to have the weight recorded in her medical record.
- Take a long, honest look at your own behavior around food and your dog; try to discover and eliminate any unconscious reasons you may have for indulging your dog, such as trying to make amends for leaving her home alone all day or trying to bribe her good behavior with a steady stream of goodies.
- Discuss with your veterinarian the possibility of switching to a high-fiber, low-calorie prescription diet.

9

Eye on Health

Just like their owners, dogs are heir to various illnesses — most minor, some major, all upsetting. While it may be inevitable that your dog will get sick from time to time, it's also true that a small amount of planning and routine good care can do a lot to catch problems while they're small, return your dog to health as quickly as possible, and generally minimize the distress of having your best friend under the weather.

Is Your Dog Sick?

No matter how keen your rapport with your dog, you cannot count on him to come and tell you when he's not feeling well. It's up to you to keep a watchful eye on his state of health. Here are some ways to do this:

- Have regular checkups by a veterinarian and periodic screening exams as recommended; ask your veterinarian how often she feels your dog should be seen and whether she will be sending reminder postcards (if not, enter your own reminders on the same calendar that you use for yourself and other family members).

- Maintain a veterinary records book for your dog in which you write down your dog's normal vital statistics (pulse, respiration rate, temperature, weight) and all veterinary "events" that occur (see Your Dog's Veterinary Records Book, page 139).
- Know your dog's normal appearance and behavior (color of gums, odor of ears, look and feel of coat, eating, drinking, and elimination habits, tolerance of light, noise, and handling, and overall activity and interest levels).
- Pay attention to and write down any changes — in behavior, appearance, or habits.
- Know the general warning signs of illness (changes in vital signs or behavior that last longer than a day, growths or lumps on or under the skin, bleeding, coughing, persistent scratching, change in gait or lameness, shivering or staggering, unwillingness to get up, move, or jump, hair loss, scaling, oily or oozing skin, loss of appetite, vomiting and/or diarrhea, and discharges from any body orifice).
- Whether you call your veterinarian first or just take the dog in to be examined, be prepared to provide as much specific information as possible (changes or symptoms you have observed, when they began, how often they occur, and any recent changes that may have been made in the dog's food, care, activity, or environment); if the symptoms you see are intestinal (vomiting or diarrhea), bring in a fresh stool sample.

What Could Be Wrong?

The number and kinds of conditions and diseases that afflict dogs are as extensive as those that afflict humans. Some can be prevented and/or cured, some cannot. Whether your dog turns out to be a little sick or a lot, your early observation that something is wrong and your prompt response are probably the most important factors in the outcome as well as in the financial and emotional cost. Here are the most common classes of canine illnesses, together with symptoms that you might expect to see — and that you should never ignore.

Internal and External Parasites
Parasites are living things, primarily insects ("bugs"), worms, and microscopic organisms called protozoa, which attach themselves to a "host" animal — in this case your dog — in order to survive. Some parasites do no

harm, some are nuisances, and some cause serious disease, even death. It is difficult or impossible to prevent your dog from ever playing host to parasites, particularly if she spends much time out of doors, and it is equally difficult to eliminate every single worm or bug that lands on your dog. A more realistic goal is to be ever-vigilant about the signs and symptoms of parasites and to initiate treatment before a full-blown infestation occurs. Fortunately, parasites are relatively easy to control with medication, especially if caught early, and in some cases there are effective preventive medications that you can give your dog on a regular basis or seasonally. Whenever you suspect parasites, take your dog to your veterinarian. He can identify the particular type of parasite that is infecting your dog and prescribe the most effective and safest medication. Also note that some internal and external parasites can infect people as well as animals, so your whole family has a stake in practicing very vigorous parasite control.

Here are the most common kinds of parasites that infect dogs, together with the signs and symptoms that should alert you to the possibility that your dog has picked something up:

INTESTINAL WORMS These include roundworms, hookworms, whipworms, and tapeworms. A puppy or dog can harbor one type or several types at the same time. The intestinal worms differ from one another in certain ways, but what they have in common is that they feed on ingested food in the intestines (hookworms also suck blood) and rob your puppy or dog of nutrition. Symptoms of intestinal worms include a voracious appetite yet an emaciated appearance, dry, dull coat, and diarrhea that may be bloody, watery, foul-smelling, or coated with mucus, depending on the type of worm.

Roundworms often are first noticed in the puppy's or dog's vomit or feces, and tapeworms, which resemble grains of rice, are noticed either in feces or in the hair around the anus. Whipworms and hookworms, however, are microscopic and cannot be seen by the owner.

Most puppies are born with some roundworms (which is why you should take a stool sample along on your puppy's first visit to the veterinarian). Generally, though, dogs contract worms either by walking or playing in soil that has been contaminated by the feces of infected dogs or, in the case of tapeworms, by eating infected fleas or infected mice and other rodents. If your dog spends time in grass or soil where strange dogs or other animals have access, having your dog's stool checked periodically will allow your veterinarian to detect the presence of worms before any symptoms develop.

HEARTWORMS Heartworms live in the chambers of the heart and the blood vessels of the lungs. If untreated, they can cause severe disability and death. Symptoms include a persistent cough, especially upon exertion, weight loss, and general fatigue. Dogs contract heartworm disease through the bite of infected mosquitoes. Heartworm disease is difficult and risky to treat, so prevention (through a monthly tablet your veterinarian will prescribe) is definitely the way to go.

Before you begin giving the tablets, however, your dog will need to have what's called a heartworm test, to make sure he isn't already infected. Assuming the test is negative, you can begin to give him the tablets, one a month, usually from April or May through October, when mosquitoes are in the environment. In areas of the country where mosquitoes live year-around, you may give your dog the medicine every month, but most veterinarians administer the heartworm test annually as a standard of care.

PROTOZOA Through poor sanitation, infected soil, and contact with the feces of infected animals, dogs may contract a number of different kinds of protozoa, microscopic organisms that mostly live in the intestines. Protozoa may cause diarrhea mixed with blood and/or mucus, dehydration, and anemia, though dogs with some protozoa seem to be unaffected until their systems are challenged by infestation with other parasites or by contracting another illness. Your veterinarian will probably want to rule out a protozoan infection if your puppy or dog has persistent diarrhea but no evidence of worms or other disease.

FLEAS, TICKS, AND MITES Fleas and ticks are external parasites that live on your dog, biting the skin to suck blood, causing itching, allergic skin conditions, and sometimes transmitting serious diseases as well. Fleas and ticks are small but are clearly visible on your dog if you look in the groin area (for fleas), where there usually is little hair, or around the head and on the ears (for ticks). Fleas and ticks are picked up out of doors, from others dogs, or from infested areas indoors or out. Mites, on the other hand, are too small to be seen by the naked eye. Different types live in the skin, in the hair follicles, or in the ear canal, causing irritation, discomfort, intense itching, crusty skin, or patches of hair loss, depending on the mite. Mites are either transmitted to puppies from their mother, or are spread by close contact with infected dogs. If your puppy or dog is scratching persistently or pawing at her ears, or if you discover fleas or ticks when you are performing your weekly grooming check, make an appointment with your veterinarian so that your dog can be put on the appropriate medication to control the problem.

Digestive Upsets

The symptoms of digestive upsets in dogs are pretty much the same as they are in people: vomiting, gas, bloating, flatulence, and diarrhea. If your dog could rub her stomach and groan, the picture would be complete. It is a rare dog who doesn't have occasional bouts of "indigestion," simply because dogs have very poor judgment about what they eat. Uncomplicated cases of digestive upset, caused by eating too much, eating the wrong thing, even eating something unfamiliar, usually resolve within twenty-four hours just by "resting the stomach" (withholding food and giving only minute amounts of water), much as they do in humans.

Just as in people, however, vomiting and diarrhea can be symptoms of dozens of other conditions, including intestinal parasites, mentioned above, food allergy, poisoning, a contagious disease (see page 129), kidney, liver, or other serious diseases, including certain cancers. Therefore, vomiting and/or diarrhea that lasts longer than twenty-four hours, or that is very frequent (more than, say, three or four times), that is mixed with blood or mucus, or that is accompanied by other symptoms such as fever, pain, trembling, or agitation should be looked into right away by your veterinarian. Because young puppies easily become dehydrated, take your puppy to the veterinarian if there is more than one occurrence of diarrhea or vomiting.

Your careful observations of vomiting or diarrhea (when it started, whether anything in particular seemed to precede it, what the dog vomited or what the stool looked like, how often it has happened, how the dog has been acting otherwise, and what things you have tried to resolve the problem) will help your veterinarian narrow down the great number of possibilities that exist whenever these symptoms are present.

Allergies

Allergies seem to be on the increase, in dogs and cats as well as in humans. Theories to explain this abound. Some point to all the pollutants in our air, water, and food supply. Others suspect that weakened/impaired immune systems are the root of the problem, which only raises more questions as to why immune systems should be so fragile. In purebred dogs especially, genetics is often suspected as a contributing factor. Regardless of the reason, allergic responses in dogs are far from rare events. Your dog may be allergic to some component in his dog food, to saliva from the flea that bit him, to the dye in the carpet he sleeps on, to pollen in the air, or to a medication prescribed by your veterinarian. Different symptoms may be seen. Most common are red, runny, and itchy eyes, red, itchy skin with a rash or eruptions, particularly on the back near the base of the tail, hives, hair loss, inflamed ears or toes, and digestive upsets (gas, gurgling, perhaps diarrhea). Allergies can be relatively minor annoyances, they can make your dog's life miserable, or they can be life-threatening. An allergic response to part of the dog's own body is called autoimmune disease; these diseases are chronic and serious. One potentially lethal allergic response, to an insect bite or sting, for example, is called anaphylactic shock; symptoms of this are itching and swelling at the sting site, hives that spread, vomiting or diarrhea, and increasing difficulty breathing. (This is a true emergency and is discussed in chapter 10.) Any symptoms of allergy should send you and your dog to the veterinarian promptly. Skin that is scratched at incessantly can easily become damaged, setting up a fertile environment for a bacterial infection in addition to the allergic rash.

Accidents and Injuries

If there's anything positive that can be said about an accident or traumatic injury, it's that it is usually pretty hard not to notice one has occurred. The telltale signs of pain, limping, immobility, obviously broken bones or dislocations, lacerations, bleeding wounds, torn ears, injured eyes, and so on should precipitate a visit to your veterinarian, with or without first aid being applied before the dog is moved. Injuries that may be more difficult to detect immediately are those of internal organs following a fall or to the brain following a blow to the head. Certainly if you know your dog fell from a height or was hit by a car, you should immediately take the dog to the veterinarian for a thorough checkup even if she seems completely normal. In cases where you are unaware that an accident has taken place, it may well be your ongoing care in observing your dog and taking seriously any changes in function or behavior that will get your dog to her doctor sooner rather than later.

Contagious Diseases

A puppy or dog whose vaccinations are kept up-to-date is very unlikely to come down with one of the major contagious diseases of dogs, since effective vaccinations currently exist for such diseases — unless, of course, a "new" disease comes along, as parvovirus did in 1978 (see the following table). Unvaccinated dogs may contract from infected dogs, or in the case of rabies, from any infected mammal, one or more of the following infectious diseases. Early symptoms are listed for each, and should prompt you to see your veterinarian immediately while the chances of recovery are best (though not guaranteed).

Disease	Early Symptoms
distemper	watery discharge from the eyes and nose, loss of appetite, depression, chills and fever
hepatitis	fever, loss of appetite, vomiting, abdominal pain, and an inflamed liver; another strain of the virus causes a respiratory disease, with runny nose, sneezing, coughing, wheezing, and labored breathing
leptospirosis	high fever, abdominal pain, liver enlargement, vomiting, loss of appetite, nosebleeds, and blood in the stool
canine parainfluenza	sneezing, runny nose and eyes, coughing, and fever
canine parvovirus	explosive watery and bloody diarrhea, persistent vomiting, high fever, and acute abdominal pain
rabies	sudden behavioral changes, paralysis of the jaw, lack of coordination, and seizures

These contagious diseases range from very debilitating to frequently fatal to fatal in all cases. They are what you risk if you do not have your puppy properly vaccinated beginning at the age of about eight weeks. There is a "five-in-one" shot (designated as DHLPP) that includes distemper, hepatitis, leptospirosis, parainfluenza, and parvovirus. A rabies vaccination may be given at the same time, but as a separate injection. Some owners — and some veterinarians — prefer not to vaccinate for all six diseases at once, because in some cases this can present too large a challenge to the immune system. Better results may be had by separating the vaccinations by a month or so. This is something you should discuss with your veterinarian.

Serious Illnesses

Serious illnesses in dogs are mostly the same as serious illnesses in people: heart disease, pneumonia and other diseases of the lung, anemias and other blood diseases, degenerative joint diseases, diseases of the liver, kidney, stomach, pancreas, bladder, bowel, reproductive and other organs, and many different kinds of cancers. Some serious illnesses are completely curable; others can be managed with medication, diet, surgery, and other therapies, resulting in a good quality of life; and some diseases are currently incurable and come with a poor prognosis. Symptoms obviously vary depending on the illness. What this means is that your best offense in protecting your dog against serious illness is a good defense: regular visits to your veterinarian, spaying or neutering as a means to prevent diseases of the reproductive organs, screening examinations as recommended, especially as your dog gets older, and your own careful observation and prompt investigation of anything out of the ordinary.

Genetic Diseases

Diseases or defects that regularly occur more frequently among related animals than within the general population are considered to be wholly or partially genetic, or inherited. There are many hundreds of known genetic defects in the dog (which is still not as many as there are in people!). Genetic disease is most often talked about in relation to purebred dogs, although mixed-breeds suffer from many kinds of inherited diseases as well. Genetic defects can affect virtually any part of the body; they can cause few practical problems for the dog or they can cause endless suffering, disability, and death. For example, genes control the number and placement of teeth in the jaw, and some breeds frequently have two, three, or more missing teeth. This is hardly a serious problem, although it is a genetic defect. On the other end of the spectrum is von Willebrand's disease, a bleeding disorder caused by a defect in the dog's clotting system. A dog with von Willebrand's disease could literally bleed to death by having his nails cut too short.

You cannot protect your dog from genetic disease if he is already born, and unless you intend to return him for a refund or replacement, there is no urgent reason to initiate a myriad of tests to try to find out whether or not he has inherited one or more defects. (In chapter 4 we talked about the so-called lemon laws that offer consumers some compensation for pet store puppies found to be suffering from congenital or inherited defects.) On the other hand, it certainly is in your own and your dog's best interests to educate yourself as fully as possible about any genetic defects known to exist in the breed you have chosen (ideally, you will do this before you decide on a particular purebred). Your veterinarian will probably be aware of at least the more common genetic diseases that are prevalent in your type of dog and will have these possibilities in the back of his mind if your dog should develop symptoms of one of those diseases. From your independent study of these problems, you can greatly assist your veterinarian by calling to her attention facts that she may have overlooked.

Visits to Your Veterinarian

If your dog is sick, make the most of your visit to the veterinarian by being prepared and by having some kind of checklist to help you remember to get all your questions answered. Here are some suggestions:

- Write down ahead of time any observations you want to share about your dog's health and behavior, and any questions that you want to ask.
- Review your notes from the last visit so you can follow up on anything that needs attention.
- Take along a pad to record your veterinarian's comments and instructions.
- Ask for demonstrations of any unfamiliar procedures you are asked to perform at home.
- If you believe you cannot perform a certain procedure, say so — there may be an alternative.
- Ask if there are any side effects of treatments that are given or medications prescribed, and find out what you should do if you see them.

Nursing Procedures

At some point in time, your veterinarian may ask you to follow up her treatment at the hospital with certain kinds of home care. You may also be asked to monitor your dog's vital signs so that you can report her progress to the veterinarian by telephone. Rather than wait until your dog is sick, think about practicing some common "nursing procedures" on your dog ahead of time, when both of you are calm. Touching your dog in this way from your earliest days together, just as in grooming her regularly, is a profound bonding experience. It will engender the level of mutual trust that will be needed for you to perform these procedures when your dog is ill. As always, ask your veterinarian to demonstrate procedures first.

Taking Your Dog's Temperature

1. If your dog will stay on command, you can do this alone; if he or she is likely to wander off, ask a friend to restrain her gently at the head.
2. Use a rectal or digital thermometer intended for children; if using a mercury thermometer, be sure to shake it down.
3. Lubricate the tip of the thermometer with a water-based lubricant or petroleum jelly.
4. With your dog either standing or lying down, hold the tail up with one hand and steadily but gently insert the thermometer into the rectum with the other. Insert the thermometer to where the mercury (silver line) is visible on a mercury thermometer or to a point just past the tip on a digital thermometer. If the thermometer seems to meet up with a fecal mass, withdraw it slightly and angle it around the mass until it can be inserted to the depth recommended.
5. Maintain a loose grip on both your dog and the thermometer; leave the thermometer inserted for three minutes (mercury) or until it beeps (digital).
6. Remove and read (digital); look for where the silver line stops on a mercury thermometer and read the numbers at that point.

Taking Your Dog's Pulse

Ask your dog to lie down, then roll her over on her right side. Then choose one of two sites to take her pulse.

OVER THE HEART

1. Gently bend the left front leg at the elbow and bring the elbow back to where it touches the chest.
2. Place your hand or a stethoscope (you can purchase one at any drugstore) over this area to feel or hear and count heartbeats. Count heartbeats while you look at the second hand of a watch. If your dog is lying comfortably, count for sixty seconds; if she is not, count for six seconds and multiply that number by 10 to get the number of heartbeats per minute.

IN THE GROIN

1. With your dog on her side, lift the upper back leg away from the lower back leg.
2. Place your two fingers as high up as possible on the inside of either leg, just where the leg meets the body wall. Use a light touch or you will not be able to feel the pulse.
3. Feel for the pulse in the middle of the leg (midway between the front and back), where you can feel a recess. Count the number of beats while looking at the second hand of a watch.

(Note: You may find it easier to do this with your dog standing. Have him stand facing away from you, and reach your hand around the front of his rear leg and place your fingertips along the inside of the leg.)

Giving Liquid Medication

1. Use a baby dosing syringe or eyedropper with measurements marked on it. Fill the applicator with medicine to the correct mark.
2. If you have an assistant, ask her to hold your dog's head loosely to steady it and tilt the muzzle upward slightly so the liquid can roll to the back of the mouth. If you're alone, you may be able to rest your dog's chin on your knee to accomplish the same thing.
3. Pick one side of your dog's face and place your finger into the space between her lower teeth and cheek. Pull the cheek outward slightly, and use your other hand to dispense the medication slowly into the space, taking care not to dispense it faster than she can swallow.
4. If the medicine has an unpleasant taste, your dog may try to spit it out. In that case, wrap your hand around her muzzle and hold it gently shut while tilting her head back and blowing softly on her nose to encourage swallowing.

Giving Pills

1. Before you begin, wave a delectable tidbit such as a bit of cheese in front of your dog's nose. The scent should start his saliva flowing, which will make it easier for the pill to slide down his throat.
2. If you are right-handed, sit with your dog on your left. Place your left hand over your dog's muzzle, midway between his eyes and his nose, and tilt his head back to about a forty-five-degree angle. This should cause his mouth to open, even if only slightly.

3. Press gently but firmly inward against his upper lips. If you roll his upper lips over his teeth, he will be less likely to bear down on your fingers.
4. Grasp the pill between your thumb and forefinger. Placing your middle finger on or just behind the lower front teeth, gently pull the dog's lower jaw down and place the pill as far back as you can, in the center of the base of the tongue. If your dog is calm, insert your fingers into his mouth and give the pill a little push over the back of his tongue.
5. Close your dog's mouth and hold it closed, stroking his throat until he swallows. If he licks his nose when you release his muzzle, you can be pretty certain he's swallowed the pill.

Cleaning a Wound

1. Cleanse wounds strictly according to the schedule given by your veterinarian (usually twice or three times a day), and use the cleansing solution she recommends, with cotton-tipped swabs, sterile gauze pads, or a bulb syringe, depending on the size of the wound to be cleansed.
2. Carefully remove the soiled bandage, if there is one, after noting how it was applied so that you can duplicate the technique. Gather enough clean toweling or other material to absorb whatever liquid runs off the area.
3. If possible, have an assistant at hand to hold your dog's head steady in case she is startled by the cleansing solution as it comes in contact with the tissue.
4. If the wound is large, use a syringe to flush the wound until all debris is removed and/or the solution runs clear. Alternatively, apply the cleansing solution to large gauze pads and gently wipe the wound clean. For small wounds, use a smaller syringe to flush the area or a saturated swab gently to wipe it clean.
5. Cover the wound with a clean sterile bandage (only if directed to do so or if your dog will not stop licking at the wound), and tape it loosely in place with adhesive tape.
6. Continue cleansing the wound until debris no longer accumulates in it, or as directed by your veterinarian.

Administering Medicine into the Ear

1. Before applying ear medication, lift the ear flap and use a cotton-tipped swab to gently remove any traces of old medication and debris, being careful to keep the swab vertical and parallel to the side of the dog's head. Be careful not to insert the swab any farther than you can see (you may

To administer liquid medication, fill a baby-dosing syringe or eyedropper with the medicine, place your finger into the space between your dog's lower teeth and cheek, then pull the cheek outward slightly, using the other hand to dispense the liquid slowly into the space created. Take care not to administer more liquid than the dog can swallow.

accidentally pack debris against the eardrum), and try to twirl the swab and lift out the debris rather than compact it.

2. Stand or kneel by your dog, on the same side as the ear you will be medicating.

3. Lift the ear flap (if there is one) straight up above the dog's head and insert the nozzle of the tube into the ear canal. Squeeze out three or four drops.

4. Rub and massage the base of the ear to work the medicine well into the canal (if you're doing it right, you should hear a squishing sound).

Administering Medicine into the Eye

1. Position yourself slightly above and behind your dog.

2. To steady the hand you will use to administer the medication, rest the side of it that is opposite your thumb on the bone above your dog's upper eyelid.

3. With the palm of your other hand under the dog's chin to support his head, tilt the head backward slightly.

4. With the thumb of this same hand, pull down the dog's lower eyelid.

5. Place drops or ointment directly on the eye. Avoid touching the eye with the tip of the dispenser. If you find it difficult to drop ointment into your dog's eye, dispense the required amount onto the tip of your (clean) index finger, and touch the ointment to your dog's eye as if you are inserting a contact lens.

Gently pull the dog's lower jaw down and place the pill as far back as you can on the center of the tongue. Close your dog's mouth and hold it closed gently, stroking his throat until he swallows.

Force-Feeding

1. Blend canned dog food with enough water to make a loose paste.
2. Fill a syringe with the food paste.
3. Using the same method as for administering liquid medication, place a quantity of the food into the pouch between the dog's teeth and cheek.
4. Administer only as much food as recommended by your veterinarian, and administer it slowly enough for the dog to swallow.

With a calm and cooperative dog, you can medicate the ear by lifting the ear flap with one hand and compressing the bulb of the dropper with the other, squeezing out three or four drops of medicine.

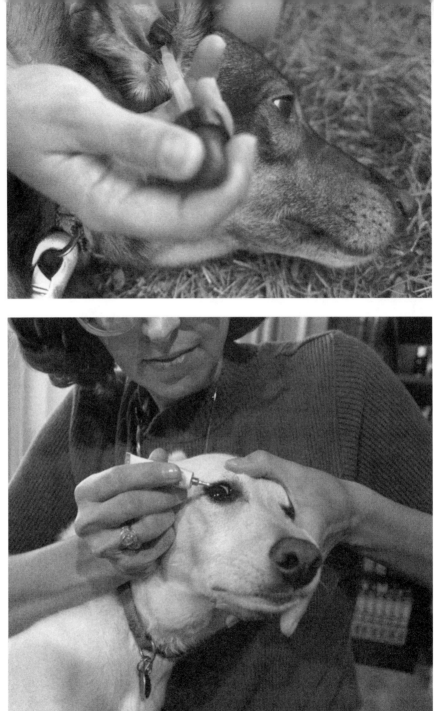

To administer medicine into the eye, rest the hand you are using to administer the medicine on the bone above your dog's upper eyelid and, with the palm of your other hand under his chin for support, tilt his head slightly backward. With the thumb of this same hand, pull down the dog's eyelid, then place the drops or ointment directly on the eye. (Leslie Sinclair, D.V.M., and Bailey)

The purpose of a veterinary records book is to keep all of your dog's health information in one place so that you can more fully participate in his care. Veterinary records books are available in some pet specialty stores, but you can also make your own book using an ordinary three-ring binder with tabs to divide the book into convenient sections. Here are suggestions for what you might include and how you might organize the material. Feel free to compress, add to, or modify these suggestions in any ways that make sense to you.

Section One: OWNER AND DOG ID

- your name, address, telephone numbers; your pet health insurance policy number (if you have such a policy)
- your dog's name, sex, birth date or approximate age when acquired, breed, color/markings, height/weight (with room to update as your dog grows), your dog's license number, her tattoo or microchip numbers, registry names and telephone numbers
- your dog's "vital statistics": resting pulse, resting respiration rate, and normal temperature, set alongside the average vital signs for dogs in general (pulse 120–160 beats per minute for puppies, 100–160 beats per minute for dogs under 30 pounds, and 60–100 beats per minute for all others; respiration 10 to 30 breaths and up to 200 pants per minute; temperature between 99.5 and 102.5 degrees Fahrenheit, by rectum)
- your veterinarian's name, address, and telephone numbers (leave space to add additional veterinarians in the future, including referral veterinarians); emergency clinic address and telephone number, National Animal Poison Control Center hotline numbers
- other professional caregivers with addresses and telephone numbers, such as your boarding kennel, groomer, pet sitter, pet ambulance or other transport service
- up-to-date Alternate Caregiver instruction sheets, including names, addresses, and telephone numbers along with feeding amounts and times, exercise rituals and places, and medication schedule, if any (it's a good idea to keep these sheets up-to-date at all times in case of an emergency)

Section Two: VACCINATION RECORD

Eventually you will need several pages for this information, as vaccinations should be updated every year.

- date and expiration date (Note: In some states, three-year rabies vaccines [boosters] are recognized after the initial one-year series. However, if you go one day beyond the expiration date, you must start the series over again.)
- your dog's age
- type of vaccination
- tag number (rabies only)

Section Three: INCIDENTS

Record in this section all health-related events, whether or not they lead to a visit to the veterinarian. For each incident, record:

- date
- nature of incident
- any actions taken (including periodic checks of the dog's temperature, pulse, and respiration rates)
- outcome or resolution

Section Four: VETERINARY EXAMINATIONS

Veterinary examinations may be for routine annual checkups and vaccinations, or they may arise out of incidents such as those you might record in Section Three. For each exam include:

- date of examination
- purpose
- findings
- recommendations or treatment

Section Five: DIAGNOSTIC TESTS

- date of test
- type of test (stool test, urinalysis, heartworm test, skin scraping, complete blood count, X ray, ultrasound, electrocardiogram, other)

- test results (leave a few lines to record the test results as reported back to you by your veterinarian)
- recommendations or treatment

Section Six: MEDICATION SCHEDULES

Whenever your veterinarian prescribes medication for your dog, create a daily log so that you will be sure to give all medicines at the prescribed times and until they are gone unless otherwise instructed. The following table is one way to set up your log. After listing all medications across the top of the page, all you have to do each day is write in the time that you give each to your dog.

| Drug | Antibiotic (7 days) | | Eyedrops (10 days) | | |
	Morning	*Evening*	*Morning*	*Afternoon*	*Night*
8/9	8:00	8:00	7:00	3:00	11:00
8/10					
8/11					

Section Seven: SURGERY

- date of surgery
- purpose
- outcome
- date discharged
- postoperative home care

TIPS FOR USING YOUR DOG'S VETERINARY RECORDS BOOK

- Keep your book in a place so handy that you'll be sure to remember to use it regularly.
- If the book is too large to take with you to the veterinarian's office on each visit, use a small pad instead and transpose your notes later.
- Punch holes in such documents as itemized receipts from your veterinarian, vaccination, spay/neuter and health certificates, and copies of laboratory tests and add them to the appropriate sections in the book.
- Make sure other family members are familiar with the records book and can make and access relevant entries in your absence.
- Mark your calendar with a reminder of the next round of tests, vaccinations, medication(s) to be given, so that these dates don't slip by unnoticed.

10

Emergency!

What could be more harrowing than a life-or-death emergency involving your dog, when immediate skillful calm action is needed — and there's no one there but you? In chapter 7 we discussed prevention at length, but it bears repeating here that many emergencies can be avoided altogether if we establish and maintain really good habits in the way we care for our dogs. For example, if we simply never ever allow our dog off-leash outside an escape-proof enclosure, we are effectively preventing him from being hit by a car. If we take the same precautions with our dogs around water and/or frozen ponds that we do when young children are involved, including making them wear life vests while in a boat (such gear *is* available for dogs!), chances are excellent that we will never have to try to cope with a drowning emergency. Indoors, puppy-proofing our homes is as important as child-proofing them, and it's essentially the same process: Anything that is labeled or deemed hazardous to children should be considered hazardous to our dogs!

Probably nothing could ever completely prepare you for a life-or-death emergency involving your dog. Still, there are some things you can do ahead of time to improve the chances that you'll be able to keep a cool head and be effective if your dog's life ever depends upon it.

General Precautions

- Discuss potential emergencies with your veterinarian, particularly any that your dog may be more likely to encounter (for example, if you take your dog along on vacation to rattlesnake country, you might ask your veterinarian to review what you should do in the event of snakebite); ask her to demonstrate emergency procedures on your dog and to critique your efforts to perform the same maneuvers.
- Know the location and telephone number of your local emergency clinic and how to get there; make a practice run so you won't be slowed down by darkness, confusing signs, or one-way streets.
- Have a first-aid kit always at the ready (see Your Dog's First-Aid Kit, page 159) — preferably one for your home and one for your car.
- Take a course in first aid and CPR for humans; encourage your veterinarian to sponsor a pet first-aid seminar for interested clients of her practice.
- Post emergency numbers by the telephone or where you can find them easily (veterinarian, emergency clinic, car service, National Animal Poison Control Center).

Is It an Emergency?

In trying to determine whether or not a particular situation is an emergency, keep this thought in mind: An emergency is not determined by what happened; it is determined by how your dog is responding to what happened. For example, a fall — even a fall from a considerable distance — is not *necessarily* an emergency. If your dog loses consciousness from the fall, or appears paralyzed after the fall, that would be the emergency. Some spectacular falls, as we all know, result in only minor injuries. On the other hand, any dog who has sustained a high fall, even if he appears unfazed, should be examined by a veterinarian as soon as possible and carefully observed in the meantime. But that is a bit different from a frantic high-speed dash to the emergency clinic or from hysterically calling your veterinarian at home on New Year's Day.

By definition, then, an emergency is any situation where immediate action is needed to keep your dog from dying or suffering irreversible damage. According to this definition, there are only a handful of situations that *al-*

ways call for an emergency response. If your dog should ever exhibit one of the following, call the nearest veterinarian or emergency clinic, describe the symptoms as accurately as you can, and rush your dog to the hospital. (You may also need to begin emergency first aid on the way to the hospital. See Emergency First-Aid Procedures, page 151.)

- uncontrollable bleeding
- extremely labored breathing
- seizures
- sudden paralysis
- shock (severe weakness, inactivity, lack of normal responses to the environment, depression)
- unconsciousness
- continuous vomiting or diarrhea

Even though the list of emergency symptoms is short, there are many events that are likely to, or inevitably will, cause one or more of them to occur. Sometimes a serious but undiagnosed illness is the cause, although it would be unlikely that you would not have seen other signs first. Most often these symptoms accompany some kind of traumatic accident.

Following are some of the more common reasons why dogs are seen in emergency rooms every day, together with some things you might need to do if this happens to your dog. (Incidentally, note how many of these events really are preventable.)

Animal Encounters

Encounters with unfriendly animals can be life-threatening. For example, if your very small dog is grabbed and shaken by a larger dog, internal injuries can occur even if the skin isn't broken and nothing looks wrong. Puncture wounds may easily become infected unless they are properly drained and antibiotics are administered. (Signs of an infected puncture wound are abscess — a pus-filled, painful swelling at the wound site — fever, loss of appetite, and lethargy.) Even if there are no puncture wounds, there may be underlying muscle, soft tissue, and bone damage.

Other animal encounters that should be considered potential emergencies include: bee stings; bites of any kind, including by insects you're not familiar with, and certainly by such animals as bats, scorpions, and snakes (see Snakebite and Stings and Bites, later in this section); cat scratches to the eye; porcupine quills anywhere; skunk spray to the eyes. If your dog is bitten by a wild animal that you or she kills, wrap the animal up (without touching it directly) and take it with you to the veterinarian so it can be sent to a laboratory and examined for rabies.

External Bleeding

Bleeding is usually caused by cuts from broken glass and other sharp objects, lacerations from falling and being dragged, as in a fall or accident, or by accidents where limbs are broken and protrude through the skin. If your dog is bleeding from an injury, you may need to stem the loss of blood. Bleeding from a cut should stop within five minutes or so. If it does not, or if bleeding is profuse, apply a pressure bandage. In very rare circumstances, an artery or a vein may be cut; this kind of bleeding is difficult to stop and may require a tourniquet (see Emergency First-Aid Procedures, page 151). To make a pressure bandage, place a gauze pad or folded square of clean, absorbent material directly over the wound and apply firm pressure with your hand. Even if the bleeding stops, proceed to the veterinarian, as the wound may need sutures in order to heal properly.

Internal Bleeding

Bleeding of the internal organs, evidenced by blood in the urine, or by blood flowing from the nose, mouth, or other orifices, typically follows trauma. Internal bleeding may not be visible, but is frequently indicated by difficult breathing, abdominal pain, or shock (see Shock, page 149). If none of the other emergency signs are present, cover the dog loosely for warmth and seek immediate help.

Broken Bones

Dogs suffer broken bones when they jump, fall, or are dropped from heights as well as in car accidents and other kinds of trauma. Suspect broken bones after an accident when the dog is in obvious pain and will not bear weight on one of his legs.

Broken (fractured) bones can be excruciating, and your dog may try to bite you out of pain and fear. Getting bitten will certainly make you less effective in an emergency, so before you do anything else, take the precaution of placing a muzzle on your dog (see Emergency First-Aid Procedures, page 151). If you can immobilize your dog in a box or carrier or by strapping her down on a flat, rigid surface (equivalent to a human stretcher), do so and go immediately to the nearest veterinary hospital. Do *not* attempt to realign the bone. If you cannot immobilize your dog, make a temporary splint for the broken limb by wrapping it loosely, in the position you find it, in some kind of firm casing, such as a thickly rolled newspaper, then taping it. The splint

If you cannot immobilize your dog, make a temporary splint for the broken limb in some kind of firm casting. (Courtesy of the American Red Cross)

must include the joints above and below the fracture. If the broken bone is protruding through the skin, wash the area with water or saline (one teaspoon of salt to a quart of warm water), put a sterile gauze pad or piece of clean cloth over the area, and tape it loosely in place.

A broken spine is a true emergency. Your dog may not appear to be in pain, but may show partial or complete paralysis. Moving a dog in this condition is risky, possibly causing further damage to the spinal cord and nerves. Try to prevent the dog from moving on his own. Restrain him at the head, chest, and hips in such a way that his back and neck do not bend or twist (unless he is very small, you will need assistance to do this) and carefully slide a board or other rigid structure under his body for transport to the hospital.

Choking

Dogs, like people, can choke to death if an object becomes lodged in the throat (unlike people, dogs more often choke on a ball or other toy than they do on a chunk of food). Signs of choking are frantic pawing at the mouth, possibly coughing and gagging. If the obstruction is complete and the object is not promptly removed, unconsciousness and death will follow. If there are two people available, you should head for the emergency clinic immediately. While one drives, the other should try to remove the object, as there is very little time to lose. If you are by yourself, you probably should concentrate on trying to dislodge the object. If your dog appears to have died (no breath and no pulse), call a friend to rush you to the nearest emergency clinic but immediately begin CPR yourself (see Emergency First-Aid Procedures both for dislodging objects from the throat [page 157] and for CPR [page 156]). Do not stop CPR just because you see no response; your efforts may at least keep the blood circulating to the brain.

Dislocations

Dislocations, usually of the elbow or hip, are primarily caused by trauma, although there are also genetic defects that cause various joints, especially knees, to be less stable in affected breeds. In cases of trauma, bones may be dislocated rather than broken. Signs of dislocation are pain and (in the elbow) a limb that may turn in or out at an odd angle, or (in the hip) a leg that appears shorter or longer than the other. Dislocations need prompt veterinary attention. After twenty-four hours, dislocations may require surgery to repair. If a board or rigid structure is available, immobilize your dog on the board using tape or strips of torn cloth to prevent her from moving. If you cannot immobilize your dog and the dislocation is of the elbow, splint the joint in the position it is in using rolled newspaper or another material that will not bend. Do not attempt to reposition the bone yourself.

Drowning

Most dogs are good swimmers, but they can get in trouble by leaping into bodies of water that they can't get out of, such as swimming pools or even, if the dog is very small, bathtubs. If your dog appears to have drowned, the first thing to do is to lift his hips high above his head to allow the water to run out. Should that be enough to revive him, thank your lucky stars, but take him to the veterinarian anyway, as antibiotics may be needed to prevent pneumonia. If you can detect neither breath nor pulse, contact a friend to rush you to the veterinarian while you perform CPR on your dog. Do not cease your efforts, even if you see no response.

Heatstroke

Heatstroke primarily occurs when a dog is left in a car in hot weather. But it can happen in other situations, such as when you take your dog for a walk on a very hot day. Unlike humans, dogs cannot perspire; the only way they can cool themselves is by panting. This mechanism cannot keep up with the rapidly rising temperatures inside a car (or other enclosure, including a yard with no shade). If your dog suffers from any kind of airway problem, either because of her structure (short muzzle) or some illness (collapsing trachea or respiratory problem), she is even more susceptible to heatstroke. Heatstroke is easy to recognize by the dog's frantic panting, terrible anxiety, red tongue, and thick saliva.

A dog suffering from heatstroke must be cooled immediately. If you have a thermometer handy, take her temperature. A reading over 106 degrees Fahrenheit is extremely critical, but any reading above normal, (99.5–102.5 degrees), together with other symptoms, warrants an emergency response.

Depending on where you are, begin by hosing or spraying her with cool water for a minute or two, or by taking her into an air-conditioned room. Place water-soaked towels or cold packs on the head, neck, feet, chest and abdomen. Turn on a fan and point it in her direction. After a few minutes, retake the dog's temperature. Even if she appears to recover, she should be taken immediately to a veterinarian for evaluation.

Poisoning

Dogs do not use good judgment when it comes to eating things they shouldn't. They can be poisoned by licking up antifreeze, eating poison that was set out for snails, slugs, mice, or roaches, eating a poisonous plant, or even grass that has been treated with a chemical — the list is almost endless. Symptoms of poisoning include vomiting and/or diarrhea, seizures, trembling, staggering, drowsiness, depression, drooling, or foaming at the mouth.

If you suspect your dog has eaten poison, call your veterinarian or emergency veterinary clinic and follow instructions while rushing the dog to the hospital. If you know exactly what the poison was, how much your dog ate, and how long ago he ate it, the clinic will be better able to advise you. How far away you are from professional help will likely determine whether or not you are asked to begin first aid at home. An alternative is to call the National Animal Poison Control Center at (800) 548-2423 (there is a fee for the call and you must use a major credit card) or (900) 680-0000 (charges will appear on your telephone bill). Even if you do, you should still have your dog examined by a veterinarian as soon as possible.

Few poisons have specific antidotes, so the first step in emergency treatment usually is to induce vomiting. *Do not induce vomiting, however, unless instructed to do so, as this can sometimes cause even more harm.* Agents that will induce vomiting are hydrogen peroxide 3 percent solution, about a teaspoonful for every ten pounds of body weight, every fifteen to twenty minutes, repeated twice; or table salt, one-half to one teaspoonful placed far back in the mouth.

Remember: A poisonous substance on your dog's coat will very likely soon be a poison in his stomach. If you cannot simply cut away the hair containing the substance, you must remove the poison completely with mild soap and water. Do not use pet shampoos unless you are certain they contain no insecticides, as that would only add to the problem. Oily substances such as gasoline, household oil, or motor oil should first be soaked well with mineral or vegetable oil, then removed with soap and water.

Shock

Shock occurs when some event disturbs the normal circulation of blood and oxygen to the tissues and organs. Trauma that results in heavy blood loss is the most common cause, but shock can also be caused by heatstroke, poisoning, drowning, electric shock, and other accidents. Shock is a life-threatening situation.

Suspect shock following an accident if your dog appears depressed and unusually quiet. The mucous membranes of the mouth — i.e., gums and inner lips — which normally are pink (except for some breeds that normally have black mucous membranes), will appear pale. The pulse will be weak. The most important sign that deep shock is present is a slow capillary refill time. To check this, press firmly against your dog's gums for a second or two, then release. The depression left by your finger will appear white. The time it takes to return to normal color is the time it takes for capillaries (tiny blood vessels beneath the skin) to refill with blood. Anything over a second or two is abnormal; hold the dog with his head slightly lower than his heart, cover him with a thermal blanket or other light covering to preserve body heat, and rush him to a veterinarian. (Note: Earlier stages of shock when the body is trying to compensate for decreased blood flow may present an almost opposite picture, with pulses that appear normal or even stronger than usual and mucous membranes that appear redder than usual and have normal capillary refill times.)

Snakebite

A bite by a venomous snake is a life-threatening event to your dog. If you're not sure whether or not a snake is venomous, assume that it is and treat the bite as a veterinary emergency.

Signs of snakebite may include some or all of the following: rapid and extensive swelling and redness at the site of the bite and surrounding areas, two round puncture wounds perhaps in conjunction with horseshoe-shaped teeth marks (nonvenomous snakes and some venomous snakes, such as the coral snake, don't have fangs, so the puncture wounds will be absent although teeth marks may be seen), excruciating pain, excitability, panting and drooling, diarrhea, vomiting, weakness, seizures, and collapse. Though all venomous snakebites are critically serious, bites on the head, lips, neck, and body are the most deadly in the shortest length of time. Several bites obviously are worse than a single one.

If your dog has been bitten by a venomous snake, the first thing you must do is restrain her. The pain from snakebite may be so intense that your dog tries to run away, which spreads the venom through the bloodstream even faster. Immobilize your dog as quickly as you can, and try to keep her lying flat.

Your dog's survival may very well depend on how quickly you can get her to a veterinarian or emergency clinic. If possible, call ahead to say you are on your way and describe the snake in as much detail as you can so that the veterinarian on duty can be prepared. Then rush your dog to the hospital, preferably with a friend doing the driving. En route, put on gloves and wash the wound with water and mild soap. Do not cut open the wound or attempt to suck out the poison. If you've had to kill the snake to protect yourself or your dog, bring the body along for the veterinarian to identify positively. Treatment will consist of specific antivenin to neutralize the venom, intravenous fluids, and treatment for shock.

Stings and Bites

Some dogs have allergic responses to the stings of bees and the bites of spiders, fire ants, and other insects. To limit the amount of poison that enters your dog's bloodstream, remove the sting by brushing against it several times with the back of a knife or the edge of a credit card (do not use your fingers or tweezers to remove the sting, as you will squeeze more poison into the wound).

A mild allergic response to a bite or sting would be redness, swelling, hives, and itching and pain at the bite site that may last for days. If the dog is allowed to scratch at the bite, infection can follow. To prevent this from happening, apply a topical cortisone cream (to control itching) and an antibiotic ointment (to fight infection). These are available as over-the-counter medications for people, or you can obtain such supplies from your veterinarian. If your dog's response is somewhat stronger, you might also administer an over-the-counter antihistamine containing diphenhydramine, such as Benadryl. (Note: Use Benadryl that contains diphenhydramine *only*. Sometimes other chemicals are included that could be dangerous to dogs.) This is something you should have discussed in advance with your veterinarian. Dosages are 10 mg. for dogs less than 30 pounds, 25 mg. for dogs 30–50 pounds, and 50 mg. for dogs heavier than 50 pounds.

An extreme allergic reaction to stings and bites, called anaphylactic shock, is also possible. This system-wide response can lead to rapid swelling

To make a muzzle, make a single loop in a necktie, stocking, or strip of gauze or nylon leash and slip the loop over your dog's nose. Tighten the loop, allowing enough room for your dog to breathe or pant slightly. Crisscross the two ends under his chin and bring them behind the ears and crisscross them again. Tie the loose ends in a bow behind the ears.

of the breathing passages and a drop in blood pressure, resulting in respiratory failure and death in a matter of minutes. The only effective treatment for anaphylaxis is adrenaline (epinephrine). Owners of dogs who have already had at least one allergic reaction to a bee sting should ask their veterinarian for a prescription for a bee-sting kit for their dog, in the case of an emergency. The kit will contain a premeasured amount of epinephrine, correct for your dog; make sure you understand exactly how to use the kit.

Emergency First-Aid Procedures

How to Make a Muzzle

There are a variety of muzzles on the market, in sizes to fit all dogs. If you do not have a muzzle in an emergency situation, use the following steps to make one on the spot. *Never muzzle your dog if he is unconscious, vomiting, or having difficulty breathing.*

1. Start with a piece of material at least 18 inches long. Gauze works best, but a nylon leash, stocking, necktie, or any piece of cloth can be used.
2. Make a single loop in the material that is large enough to drop over your dog's nose *and* allow you to keep your hands away from his mouth. (Remember: You're muzzling your dog to prevent him from biting you in fear and pain.)
3. For maximum safety, you should position yourself above and behind your dog and slip the loop over his nose while talking to him calmly so he'll know where you are.

4. Tighten the loop down on top of the nose, but not so tight that your dog can't breathe or pant with a *slightly* open mouth.

5. Bring an end of the material down each side of your dog's muzzle, criss-cross the two ends under his chin, bring them back behind the ears and crisscross them again. If your dog is a short-nosed type, now bring one end of the material down the nose from the forehead, pass it under the loop over the nose, bring it back up the nose, and tie it to the other end around the neck. For dogs with normal length muzzles, you can skip this step and just tie the loose ends of the material in a bow behind the ears.

How to Stop Bleeding

Profuse bleeding can lead to death in a relatively short time, so you must take steps to stop or at least slow down the loss of blood. Unfortunately, techniques to stop bleeding can cause permanent damage if performed improperly or inappropriately. Use them in the order given below, which presents the safest method first (direct pressure technique) and the most risky (the tourniquet) last. Only if the technique you are using has failed within a minute to stop or slow profuse bleeding should you move on to the next.

DIRECT PRESSURE TECHNIQUE

1. If possible, raise the bleeding body part above the level of the heart (do not do this if the wound is on a limb that appears to be broken).

2. Take a folded piece of gauze or other clean cloth and place it directly over the wound. Apply steady pressure with your hand on top of the cloth. If the cloth soaks through with blood, apply a second cloth over the first so that you don't disturb any clot that may be forming. Continue to apply direct pressure on your way to the nearest veterinarian.

3. Very rarely, an artery or vein may be cut. However, if blood is spurting from the wound in a rhythmic fashion, an artery may have been cut. In addition to direct pressure over the wound, hold the area just *above* the wound with your hand to close off the blood vessel to the area. If blood is flowing heavily but is not spurting and is steady rather than rhythmic, the bleeding vessel is likely a vein; hold the area just *below* the wound to shut off the blood vessel.

4. If holding above or below the wound fails to stop bleeding within about ten or fifteen seconds, apply a pressure bandage of gauze or clean cloth, secured in place with tape, an Ace bandage, shredded T-shirt, or strips of towel. Wrap the bandage snugly but not tightly. If the wound

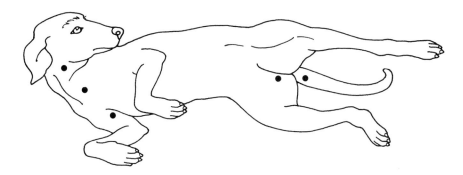

Apply firm, even pressure to the pressure point that corresponds to where your dog is bleeding. (Courtesy of the American Red Cross)

is on a limb, check repeatedly for swelling or chilling of the toes; these indicate that your bandage is too tight and you will need to loosen it a little.

5. If you still have not significantly stopped the bleeding, you will need to try the following:

PRESSURE POINT TECHNIQUE

Apply firm, even pressure to the pressure point (area from which blood vessels travel) that corresponds to where your dog is bleeding. Release pressure slightly, for a few seconds, every ten minutes.

- *Front limbs* Place three fingers up and into the armpit on the side with the bleeding limb.
- *Back limbs* Place three fingers to the area of the inner thigh where the leg meets the body wall, on the side with the bleeding limb.
- *Head* Place three fingers at the base of the lower jaw (the angle just below the ear) on the same side and below where the bleeding is occurring.
- *Neck* Place three fingers in the soft groove next to the windpipe (which feels round and hard) on the side of the neck where the bleeding is occurring, just below the wound. Be sure not to apply pressure to the windpipe itself.

Tourniquet

It is rarely if ever necessary to use a tourniquet to stop bleeding. The use of a tourniquet may damage nerves and blood supply to the injured area. Use this technique only as a last resort for severe uncontrollable bleeding and seek veterinary care immediately. Use only on limbs or the tail — *never* on the neck.

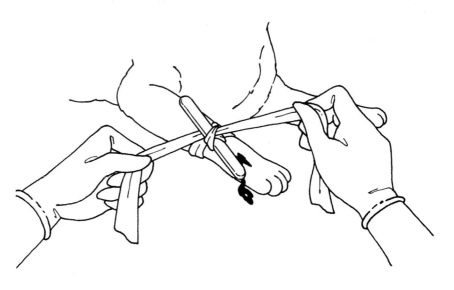

1. Wrap a wide (about 2 inches) strip of gauze, cloth, a necktie, belt, or similar object twice around the limb above the area that is bleeding. Do not make a knot.
2. Tighten the gauze or cloth by wrapping each end around a rigid object such as a stick. Turn the stick slowly and just enough to stop blood flow.
3. Write down the exact time you applied the tourniquet.
4. Every ten minutes, loosen the tie for about ten seconds. This will help prevent permanent damage and possible loss of the limb due to the interruption in the blood supply.

Remember: Most wounds will have some bleeding. A clean, moderate-pressure bandage is almost always appropriate. Holding off veins or arteries or the use of a tourniquet is rarely, if ever, necessary.

How to Perform Artificial Respiration

Artificial respiration, also called *rescue breathing* or *mouth-to-nose resuscitation,* is an attempt to breathe for a dog who is unconscious and has stopped breathing for whatever reason. (If you have reason to suspect there is an object stuck in the dog's throat, either because you noticed him struggling and gasping to breathe, or because he is prone to chewing on rawhide or balls, you should first try to remove the obstruction. See How to Dislodge an Object Caught in the Throat, page 157.)

To have the best chance of success, artificial respiration should begin immediately. Before you begin, however, it is important to make sure that your dog is not breathing on his own. Check for respiration by holding a tissue or cotton ball just in front of his nostrils. If the tissue moves, your dog is still breathing. If breathing is loud or gasping or very labored, there is every likelihood that it will soon stop. Call a friend to drive you to the nearest veterinary hospital and prepare to begin artificial respiration and perhaps heart massage as well (see CPR, below).

1. Lay your dog on his right side on a flat, hard surface.
2. Open the mouth, extend the neck, and pull the tongue forward, then remove any foreign material or vomit from the mouth. On medium- and large-size dogs, close the mouth again and create a seal by gently holding it shut with your hand. On dogs smaller than about 30 pounds, your mouth will seal their mouth and nose.
3. Position your head so you can see your dog's chest, then blow into his nose four or five times in quick succession. Do not blow with tremendous force; as long as you can see the chest expand, you are blowing hard enough.
4. Release and watch the chest fall.
5. Repeat either until the dog breathes on his own or until you can turn him over to your veterinarian.

How to Perform CPR

Cardiopulmonary resuscitation (CPR) is performed on a dog who has stopped breathing *and* has no pulse, who for all intents and purposes has died. Do not assume that there is no pulse just because the dog is not breathing. (Review Taking Your Dog's Pulse, page 133.) It is dangerous and unnecessary to attempt CPR on a dog who is conscious. To check for consciousness, use your thumbnail to pinch the skin between the toes on a rear foot. If the dog is conscious and responds to you, then his heart is beating.

If there is neither breath nor pulse, call a friend to drive you to the nearest veterinary hospital, notify the veterinarian that you are on your way, and proceed with CPR in the car. If there are two people to work on the dog, you can work together at the same time. If you must work alone, you will have to alternate between performing artificial respiration and massaging the heart. Perform CPR with your dog lying on her right side, on a firm, flat surface if possible. Choose the method that corresponds to the size of your dog.

LESS THAN 30 POUNDS

1. Kneel next to your dog, with her chest facing you.
2. Place the palm of one of your hands over her ribs at the point where the elbow touches the chest. Place your other hand opposite the first, underneath her chest.

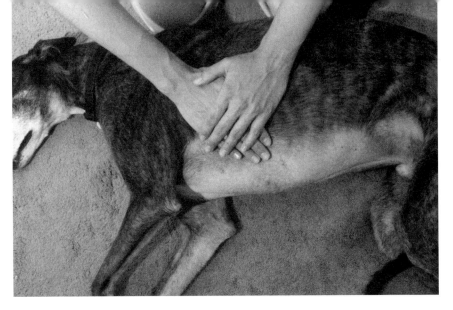

To administer CPR to a dog weighing between 30 and 90 pounds, stand or kneel with your dog's back to you; extend your arms and cup your hands over each other; then compress the chest at the point were the left elbow lies when pulled back to the chest. CPR should not be administered on a conscious dog.

3. Compress the chest 1/2 to 1 inch, at the rate of one compression a second (count out the seconds by saying 1–one thousand, 2–one thousand, 3–one thousand, etc.).
4. If you are working alone, do five compressions for each breath, then check for a pulse.
5. If there are two of you, do three compressions for each breath, then check for a pulse.
6. Continue CPR until your dog has a strong heartbeat and pulse.

30 TO 90 POUNDS

1. Stand or kneel with your dog's back to you.
2. Extend your arms and cup your hands over each other.
3. Compress the chest at the point where the left elbow lies when pulled back to the chest.
4. Compress so the chest moves about 1 to 3 inches with each compression.
5. If working alone, do five compressions for each breath, then check for a pulse.
6. If there are two of you, compress the chest at a rate of two or three compressions for each breath, then check for a pulse.
7. Continue with CPR until your dog has a strong heartbeat and pulse.

OVER 90 POUNDS

1. Use the same basic technique as for a dog between 30 and 90 pounds.
2. If working alone, do ten compressions for each breath, then check for a pulse.

3. If there are two of you, compress the chest at a rate of six compressions for each breath, then check for a pulse.
4. Continue CPR until your dog has a strong heartbeat and pulse.

(Note: It is highly recommended that you receive instruction in CPR for your pets, just as for people. Sources of instruction include your veterinarian, your local shelter, and your Red Cross chapter. Books and even videos on this subject are no substitute for a hands-on course.)

How to Dislodge an Object Caught in the Throat

The technique for dislodging an object from a dog's throat is similar to the Heimlich maneuver for people. It may be performed with a dog who is still conscious (take care not to get bitten!) or one who has lost consciousness.

1. Open your dog's mouth and look into the back of her throat. If you can see the object, carefully sweep from side to side with your finger to try to remove it. Be careful not to push it farther into the throat.
2. If your dog is unconscious, pull the tongue forward to remove any object that may be present.
3. If your dog is small enough for you to lift and suspend, hold her by the hips with her head hanging down. If she is too large for you to suspend, hold her hind legs in the air (like a wheelbarrow) so her head hangs down. If the object does not come out by doing this, do the following:

- Have your dog either stand or lie down.
- Place your arms around her waist with your hands under her stomach.
- Close your hands together to make a fist and place the fist just behind the last rib.
- Compress the abdomen by pushing up with your fist five times in rapid succession.
- If your dog is not breathing, breathe five breaths into her mouth. (See How to Perform Artificial Respiration, above.)
- If even a small amount of air can get past the obstruction, your abdominal compressions will be more effective.
- If this does not work, strike your dog sharply between the shoulder blades with the flat side of your hand, then repeat the abdominal compressions.

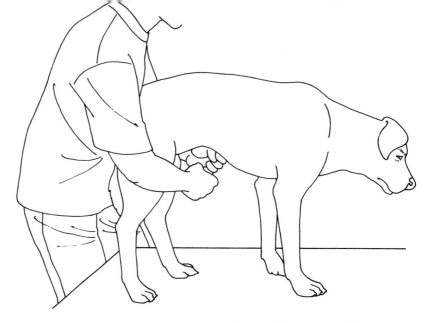

To dislodge an object caught in a dog's throat, use a procedure similar to the Heimlich maneuver performed on humans. (Courtesy of the American Red Cross)

- Carefully sweep your dog's mouth with your finger to see if you can now dislodge the object, if it has not come out on its own.
- Once the object is dislodged, stop the thrusts. If your dog has neither breath nor pulse, initiate CPR. In either case proceed at once to the nearest veterinary hospital.

There is peace of mind in knowing where to lay your hands on items you may need in an emergency. Make a point of examining the contents of your first-aid kit every three months to make sure tubes haven't burst, liquids haven't spilled or evaporated, expiration dates haven't been passed, batteries haven't died, and rubber items haven't degraded. Consider making up two identical kits, one for the home and one for the car.

- adhesive tape, hypoallergenic
- antibacterial ointment
- antihistamine (liquid diphenhydramine)
- bee-sting kit (prescribed by your veterinarian)
- cardboard strips or pieces of wood (to make splints)
- cotton balls, cotton swabs, rolled cotton
- medicine to control diarrhea (bismuth subsalicylate, kaolin-pectate, or something prescribed by your veterinarian)
- eyedropper or dosing syringe
- eyewash (sterile saline) and sterile eye lubricant
- flashlight
- gauze pads and gauze rolls of several sizes
- hydrogen peroxide (3 percent solution)
- latex gloves
- lubricant (water-based and sterile)
- muzzle or material to make a muzzle
- rubbing alcohol (isopropyl)
- scissors
- single-edge razor blade and suction device (or snakebite kit in some geographic areas, prescribed by your veterinarian)
- sterile pads, nonstick (for dressings)
- thermal blanket
- thermometer (pediatric rectal, or digital)
- tourniquet material
- towels and clean cloths
- tweezers

11

Before Disaster Strikes

Each year seems to bring its own crop of natural disasters. For days we huddle in front of our television sets, feeling concern and compassion for the latest victims of tornado, flood, drought, wildfire, hurricane, or blizzard. Each year also brings its share of man-made disasters: fires, both accidental and intentional, hazardous-material spills, including oil, and industrial or municipal accidents that can result in loss of power, water, cooking and heating fuel, telephones, and other essential services. Such disasters not only take human and animal lives and destroy property, but often require people to be evacuated from their homes.

Often, when people are evacuated and taken to municipal or Red Cross shelters, they are shocked to learn that their pets cannot accompany them (with the exception of service animals, who assist people with disabilities). Dogs and other animals left behind in situations that are considered unsafe for humans face an uncertain fate. For starters, any situation that is unsafe for humans is equally unsafe for animals; animals left behind can get injured, sick, lost, or killed. Second, residents who expect to return to their homes within a few hours may find themselves prohibited from returning for days, weeks, and even longer. If you've never had occasion to think about this before, think of it now: What would happen to your dog (and other pets) if some kind of disaster happened where you live and you were required to leave your home for safety's sake?

Many disasters are unanticipated and/or unpredictable. Some give a few days' or hours' warning. Whatever the situation, the best defense against disaster is a strong offense. That means only one thing: being prepared, having a "What-if?" plan.

Disaster Plan One: Widespread Disasters

This plan most obviously applies to major natural disasters such as earthquakes, floods, seasonal wildfires, and hurricanes, which typically involve an entire community. That doesn't mean, however, that it's relevant only to people who live over a fault line, along the Atlantic seaboard, or on the banks of a major river. A key element of widespread disaster is that many of the normal sources of help, including your own veterinary and emergency clinic, your cousin Mae across town where you and your dog are always welcome, the boarding kennel that your dog thinks of as summer camp, the pet supermart three miles away, even the pharmacy where you've done business for years, are probably affected in exactly the same way you are. This may not be true; there are plenty of examples of devastation on one side of the street and blue skies on the other. In fact, your veterinarian and Cousin Mae may be just waiting for you to call — but don't count on it. None of you may even have a working telephone!

To afford reasonable peace of mind, your disaster plan should include the following elements:

A Safe Place to Take Your Pets
The foremost concern in planning for disaster is to safeguard your family members, which of course includes your dog and other animals. This means that if you have to leave your home, they go, too. Don't let anyone assure you that you'll be home again by a certain time; in a disaster situation, no one can know that for sure. Temporary housing includes:

- friends and relatives outside your area who will take in you and your animals
- hotels/motels outside your area that take pets (Research this subject now, before you need the information. Directories of hotel/motel chains

and individual innkeepers who welcome pets can be found in bookstores, in pet specialty stores, and through mail-order catalogs.)

- boarding kennels or veterinarians outside your area who board companion animals (An option that would separate you from your pets is obviously less desirable than one that would not, but this may be something you have to consider. If so, and in fact even if you don't expect ever to need them, check out facilities ahead of time with particular attention to how likely they would be to remain unaffected by natural disasters. For example, a boarding kennel situated in a low-lying area along the coast, along an estuary, or even alongside an inland riverbank would not be a good bet during high rains, floods, or storms at sea.)
- local animal shelters (Local humane societies and shelters are usually inundated with animals during disasters — if in fact they are able to continue operations themselves. Consequently, they should be considered only as a last resort. Do investigate ahead of time, though, to see if local shelters operate a foster program involving a network of private, volunteer foster homes during times of crisis, and find out whether contingency plans can be made in advance.)

A Portable Pet Disaster-Supplies Kit

For maximum peace of mind, your disaster kit should include the following:

- your pets' first-aid kits (first-aid kits for dogs were discussed in chapter 10)
- medical records, medications, spay/neuter certificate, current vaccination certificates, especially for rabies (If you are maintaining a veterinary records book for your dog, recommended in chapter 9, just bring along the book.)
- leashes, harnesses, and/or carriers to transport your dog and other pets safely and prevent escape (Be aware that hotels and motels may require that pets be crated when unattended in guest rooms.)
- current photos of your pets (These may come in handy if one of your animals becomes separated from you and you need to reclaim him, or if he should become lost and you need to make up lost-pet flyers.)
- a few days' supply of your pets' regular food and water (this is not a good time for digestive upsets caused by sudden changes) as well as a can opener and feeding bowls
- feeding information and other particulars about your pets' personalities and care, together with the name and number of your regular veterinarian

- bedding and toys, if easily transportable (Even a small item that smells like home may comfort your pet in a strange new environment.)

A Checklist to Follow as Disaster Approaches

A short checklist taped someplace where you can't miss it, perhaps on the outside of your first-aid kit, will help assure that you don't forget last-minute details.

- Confirm temporary housing arrangements for yourself and your animals. (Note: Do this at the first official watch or warning. You don't want to delay and risk finding that you've lost telephone service. In the event that local telephone service is interrupted, you may still be able to get through on a cell phone, although in certain kinds of disasters, even the cells may be down.)
- Double-check that your animals' ID tags are current and are securely attached to their collars. If not, make up or purchase in a pet-supply store a temporary ID tag for each of your animals. If you are making your own, cut out small pieces of heavy paper. Write on each the name, address and telephone number of where you will be staying temporarily, reinforce and waterproof the tags with transparent tape, punch a hole in them, and attach them to your pets' collars with a piece of string.
- Gather your disaster supplies together. Either put them in your car or collect them in one place so that nothing will be left behind when/if it comes time to evacuate.
- Keep your animals indoors at all times for their protection and safety, as well as to allow a quick and orderly exit if you have to leave abruptly. Make sure that leashes and carriers are at the ready.

Note: You may not be home when the evacuation order comes. Find out if a trusted neighbor would be willing to take your pets and meet you at a prearranged location. This person should be comfortable with your pets, know where your animals are likely to be, know where your pet disaster-supplies kit is kept, and have a key to your home. If you use a pet-sitting service, they may be available to help, but discuss the possibility well in advance.

Disaster Plan Two: Localized Disasters

A localized disaster is unlikely to affect a whole town or community, so many of your normal avenues of help should be available to you. For example, a fire or explosion in your high-rise apartment building may cause a complete loss of services and/or the evacuation of all tenants. However, once you get to the street with your pets, you should be able to make your way to or be picked up by nearby friends or relatives who have agreed in advance to shelter you in just such an emergency.

On the other hand, local disasters are less likely than major natural disasters to give any advance warning. Therefore, it is even more important in these cases that you have a "What-if?" plan in place and that you review it on a regular basis. One good time for annual review would be the date each year when your pets are re-vaccinated; as you add up-to-date vaccination certificates to your veterinary records book, take an extra few minutes to think about your disaster plans and update any aspects that need it. For instance, if you've changed any diets over the past year, now would be a good time to replace the old food with the new in your disaster kit.

To be reasonably prepared for localized disasters, make the following arrangements:

- Discuss with two or more friends, neighbors, or relatives in the area whether they would be willing and able to take in you and your dog on short notice if it ever became necessary. Reconfirm this arrangement from time to time.
- Make it a point to visit these friends with your pets every so often. It will be less upsetting for everyone, especially for your animals, if their temporary home is somewhere they've been before. If there are other pets living at the home, it's important to know ahead of time that all the animals will at least tolerate each other.
- Have on hand several blank temporary ID tags with the names, addresses, and telephone numbers of the friends who have agreed to take you into their homes. As you're evacuating your residence, attach an appropriate tag to each of your pets' collar next to their permanent ID tags.
- Have on hand the following supplies:
  - a sturdy leash, harness, or carrier to transport your animals safely and prevent escape (Keep these items where you can get at them quickly, not in the back of a closet.)

- your pets' first-aid kits, as discussed in chapter 10
- any medications your pets are currently taking, along with the medication schedule you are following, in writing
- a few days' supply of your pets' regular food and water (this is not a good time for digestive upsets caused by sudden changes)
- feeding information and other particulars about your animals' personalities and care, along with the number of your regular veterinarian (You may need to leave your pets with your friends for a day at a time while you run errands, go to work, or attend to the business of getting back into your home.)
- current photos of your pets (These may come in handy if one of them gets away from you or your friends in an unfamiliar environment and runs off.)
- bedding and toys, if easily transportable (When you're not there with them, small items from home may comfort your pets in a strange new environment.)

Disaster Plan Three: Personal Disaster

Potentially the greatest disaster that can befall your pets is losing their human caretaker(s). Obviously the disaster would be greatest if the entire family were lost. If only you, the primary caretaker, were lost, and you were married or had a significant other, or had grown responsible children at home, presumably these family members would continue to care for the family pets in the ways all of you had agreed to at the outset.

If you live alone, or do not feel that other family members are able to manage the ongoing care of your pets, the situation is quite different. Even if you've taken the step of finding someone who will care for them in the event of your death and have had your estate attorney spell this out in writing in your will, there's more to be done. It could take weeks or months before the provisions of your will are executed — what happens to your companions in the meantime?

Suppose a freak accident took your life on your way home from work one day. What would happen to your pets that very night? Would they be fed and walked and given their medication? If you live alone, who would be contacted, and when? Would that person even know what pets you have, much less what provisions you may have made for their ongoing care?

Here are some steps you can take to make sure there is an orderly transition of care for your beloved companions:

If you are ever separated from your dog during a disaster, your relief at your reunion will be enormous.

- Make arrangements ahead of time with at least two trusted persons who live nearby, know your animals, and have access to your home. Ideally, at least one should be at home during the day. Make whatever financial arrangements are necessary so that funds will be immediately available for your pets' feeding and veterinary care.
- Verify that both temporary caregivers know the location of your veterinary records book, and know that in it they will find current feeding, exercise, and medication instructions for each of your animals.
- Give neighbors or your building superintendent, in writing, the names and telephone numbers of the persons you have given permission to enter your home and care for your animals. Also, give your temporary caregivers a written letter of introduction to your superintendent or to whomever it may concern so that they will not be denied access to your home or apartment.
- Inform both temporary caretakers of the other's identity, address, and telephone number so they can coordinate with one another if necessary.
- Ask these persons to try to let you know whenever they plan to be away for more than a day or two in order to avoid the possibility that both will be unavailable at the same time.
- Make sure you always carry wallet instructions to health, law-enforcement, or other professionals to promptly contact one of your foster caregivers in the event that you are in an accident and immediately hospitalized or killed outright.
- Make sure both of your foster caregivers have copies of whatever provisions have been made in your will regarding the permanent care of your

animals in the event of your death. And make sure that the executor of your will is aware of the arrangements you have made for the temporary care of your companion animals.

- Delicate as the situation may seem, you should make sure that your alternate caregivers are "on record." To underscore the serious nature of the commitment you are asking them to undertake, write out a simple agreement that they and you will sign and date. In the agreement, spell out the temporary responsibilities and rights that you are transferring to them, in the best interests of your pets.

TRAINING FOR DISASTERS

During a disaster, your dog's world (and yours!) can easily turn upside down. His or her survival could depend on being able to keep his cool in chaotic and unfamiliar circumstances. The following tips will help your dog cope more easily should disaster strike (and every ordinary day as well):

- Regularly expose your puppy or dog to crowds, noisy scenes with sirens and flashing lights — whatever hustle and bustle can be found in your environment.
- Accustom your dog to riding in all kinds of vehicles.
- Accustom your dog to climbing open stairs and walking across a variety of uneven and unusual surfaces.
- Train your dog to be leashed by, handled by, and to go with other persons, with or without you present.
- Periodically vary your dog's diet so that he will not refuse to eat in the event that his regular food is unavailable.
- Continuously expose your dog to being in close proximity to strange dogs and other domestic animals.
- Regularly refresh your dog's training to be confined in a crate as well as to wear a muzzle.

You and your dog should be able to negotiate calmly a maze of distractions on a busy downtown street. (Frank Loftus and Sunshine)

Care and Training

Housetraining 12

Housetraining is Job One for you and your dog. Note we did not say house-*breaking,* as the process has been called until quite recently and as it still is called in some quarters. The term *housebreaking,* and the harsh methods that accompanied it, such as rubbing a dog's nose in his "mistakes," or hitting him with a rolled-up newspaper, implies that dogs must be broken of the bad behavior of relieving themselves indoors if they are to live as our household companions. In happy contrast, today we speak of house*training,* much as we speak of toilet training for children. The term reflects not only an entirely different way of teaching, but an entirely different perspective on our relationship to our dogs.

In chapter 5 we introduced the subject of housetraining. You were encouraged to think about which method of training you wanted to use, to purchase a dog crate, and to plan where you would confine your dog during the housetraining process. Ideally, housetraining begins the moment you walk in the door with your new puppy or dog. But if it's already too late for that, don't despair. Just start now. The job will still get done, though it may be a little harder and take a little longer.

The best way to approach housetraining is to recognize at the outset that a few weeks of intensive effort now will pay off handsomely in many years of living with a dog who can be trusted not to soil the house. For your dog's part, even though she has no say in the matter, the cost/benefit ratio is the same. Being confined and restricted for a few weeks is a small price to pay for years and years of freedom: freedom to accompany you from room to room and on all your travels, as well as freedom from being left behind, from being confined to a small area, and from being endlessly scolded and confused about why her people are unhappy with her.

Training Methods

Training your dog where she should eliminate (or training her to do anything else for that matter) is a two-step process. First you have to show her — in a way that she can understand — what you want her to do. Then, whenever she does it that way, you have to reward her. This will help impress upon her that good things happen when she performs or behaves in a certain way.

Housetraining methods build on the dog's basic instinct to eliminate away from her "den" or sleeping/eating area. Therefore, what you need to do is confine your untrained puppy or dog to a cozy den or crate at all times when you cannot actively observe her; this will prevent her from making innocent mistakes all over your house, especially on rugs and carpets, where any lingering odor will draw her back again and again. At the same time, however, you must provide your dog with ample opportunities to relieve herself in an area of your choosing, whether indoors or out, as well as for supervised exploration, exercise, and play with all members of the family. After many repetitions of using her designated area, with enthusiastic praise for doing so, she will learn what is expected of her. Then and only then can you extend the amount of time that she can spend outside her crate, although still within a limited space that can be easily cleaned. When housetraining is complete, your dog will have free run of your entire home (providing you don't wish to restrict her from certain areas for other reasons), whether anyone is there or not.

There are two methods of training your dog where she should eliminate: paper-training and housetraining. Either way, at the end of the training period your dog should clearly understand where she can "go" and where she can't. The training period can vary from a few weeks to a few months, depending on the age of your dog, her health, whether or not she's already been allowed to develop bad habits, and how consistent you and other family members are in your training efforts. Note that a dog who regularly eliminates outdoors simply because you let her out into the yard a dozen or more times a day, or "on demand," is not necessarily housetrained in the sense of clearly knowing where she can and cannot go. This could become clear should you suddenly find yourself living on the fourth floor of an apartment building in town, with no backyard just a step off the kitchen.

To help you decide which training method to use, consider the pros and cons of each:

Paper-Training

(Paper-training means training your dog to eliminate indoors on newspapers or other material that has been placed in a designated spot.)

PROS

- Paper-training provides a fast, easy, and *permanent* method for very small dogs who live in apartment buildings and who will always eliminate indoors.
- It's a practical but *temporary* approach for young puppies who are not yet fully immunized and therefore should not go where other dogs go and/or who are still too young (under about twelve weeks) to have complete sphincter control and cannot make it to the street or yard.
- Owners who work long hours and can't be home at the same time every day find paper-training very helpful.
- Some senior owners or owners with infirmities may not be able to walk a dog three or four times a day and cannot safely walk outdoors in rain, snow, ice, extreme cold or heat/humidity. (Let's hope these owners have selected small dogs.)

CONS

- Paper-training is not practical as a permanent method for any but small dogs (approximately twenty pounds or less).
- It can be difficult for male dogs who lift their legs to urinate. (Male dogs who were neutered at an early age may not lift their legs; paper-training would therefore be appropriate for them.)
- Dogs who are paper-trained learn *where* to eliminate but not necessarily *when* (i.e., to "hold it").
- Some level of mess and/or odor in the house is unavoidable; paper-training is not recommended in homes with small children.
- Paper-training results in loss of space in kitchen, bath, or other room with washable floor-covering.
- Dogs who have been paper-trained may refuse to eliminate outdoors on the occasions when this is desirable or necessary (i.e., spending a day

Since successful housetraining builds on the dog's basic instinct to eliminate away from his "den," you'll need to confine him to a cozy den (in this case, his crate) at all times when you cannot actively observe him during housetraining. (Leslie Sinclair's Moses)

outdoors with the family, when traveling, going to veterinarian or dog groomer).

Housetraining

(Housetraining means training a dog to "hold it" until taken outdoors to eliminate.)

PROS

- There is no mess/odor in the home.
- You do not need to set aside an area of the home for the dog's toilet.
- Housetraining teaches the dog *where* to eliminate and also *when*.
- A predictable housetraining schedule (including feeding schedule) establishes consistency, which is reassuring to the dog, but also impresses on the owner how well her dog responds to consistent routines.
- A dog who is housetrained can accompany her owner anywhere that dogs are welcome.

CONS

- The owner is strictly bound by the dog's housetraining schedule, especially during the first month.
- The owner and dog are at the mercy of the elements.
- Housetraining can be slower and more difficult, especially in the case of older dogs, of dogs who have been inconsistently trained, or if the family lives in an apartment building.
- Dogs who have been thoroughly housetrained will usually suffer considerable discomfort before they will relieve themselves indoors in an emergency or in the rare situation when you might want them to.

Advance Preparations

- Plan to be home for several days or, even better, a week or more when you first bring home your dog.
- Have your dog examined thoroughly by your veterinarian and have her stool checked for parasites. Dogs with intestinal or urinary tract infections, or with diarrhea for any reason, will be difficult to housetrain.
- If you haven't already purchased a dog crate, do so now (see chapter 5 for advice on the purchase and multiple uses of crates). Accustom your dog to her crate by feeding her inside it before beginning her formal housetraining. (Note: Never scold your dog while she is inside her crate or use the crate to punish her. The crate is to be her "den," her very own place of rest and refuge, so all her associations with it should be pleasant ones.)
- Make sure your dog is accustomed to being on a leash before you take her outdoors.
- Feed your dog a consistent amount of food and at the same times each day. Use only high-quality food and clean water. Not only is this important to good health, but a premium diet with high-quality ingredients also is more completely digested by your dog. This, in turn, helps train your dog's system toward regular, consistent bowel movements.

The Training Schedule

During housetraining, your dog's entire day should be divided into time/activity slots and taped up on the refrigerator for easy reference by all family members. After housetraining, it certainly won't hurt to maintain the same basic schedule for feeding and taking your dog outdoors. (You'll never go wrong by bringing a fairly high degree of routine and predictability to your dog's daily life.)

Your dog's daily schedule should consist of several repeating cycles of these four basic activities: going outdoors or to her papers (about ten minutes each); playing and exploring within a limited area, such as the kitchen (about twenty minutes each); eating and drinking (about thirty minutes at a time; take up food and water after thirty minutes); and being confined in her crate or other small area that she will not want to soil (three or four hours at a stretch). Note that your dog's and especially your puppy's natural rhythm is to relieve herself after sleeping, after playing, after eating and/or drinking, and after being confined for a length of time.

Also note that if you work all day, there will be a period of more than eight hours when your dog is confined. Clearly this is not the ideal situation, and you are encouraged to try to find a trustworthy neighbor or professional pet-sitter who will come in and add an additional cycle to the middle part of the day.

How to Paper-Train Your Dog

Materials
- a dog crate or small confined area that will represent the dog's den, ideally located in the kitchen or other room where the floor can easily be cleaned but which is also near the center of family life
- baby-gate or other barrier to keep your dog in the kitchen during the times she is allowed to play and explore
- standard-size newspapers, stacked about eight sheets high, always in the same location (you may substitute an uncovered litter box and litter if you prefer)
- enzymatic odor remover, available in pet-supply stores

Schedule
- Make up a schedule for your dog according to her age (remember that puppies under three months should eat four times a day, puppies between three and six months three times, and dogs over six months twice a day; be sure to schedule time to eliminate after each meal as well as after waking, playing, and being confined).
- Discuss the schedule with all family members; if several people are going to share in housetraining duties, clearly assign all time slots so that the schedule is rigorously maintained.

Steps
- Begin by following the schedule you've set up, but don't hesitate to add or subtract minutes from different activities if it becomes obvious that your individual dog needs more or less time for certain ones.
- Ignore your schedule whenever you see signs that your dog is ready to eliminate; typical signs include circling, sniffing the floor, and appearing to be restlessly looking for something.
- The first few times you take your dog to her papers, gently hold her there until she uses them; do not distract her by petting or talking.
- Praise her warmly as she is "performing." (Note: Offer only a word or

two of mild praise if paper-training is being used temporarily; you do not want to really congratulate your dog now for something you will not want her to do in a few weeks.)

- Remove soiled papers right away and put down clean ones, but leave one used paper on top to remind your dog of what she's supposed to do here.
- After your dog is promptly using the papers, start calling her to walk to them rather than placing her on them; it's important that she begin to move toward them on her own.
- Whenever you catch your dog making a mistake, i.e., *in the act* of urinating or defecating anywhere except on the papers, startle her by firmly saying "No" (no need to yell) and immediately take her to the papers; if she finishes there, praise her warmly (again, praise her sparingly if paper-training is only a temporary approach).
- Dogs instinctively return to the same areas again and again to eliminate, and their extraordinary sense of smell will easily lead them to "the spots"; therefore you should thoroughly clean and deodorize any areas where mistakes were made to avoid inadvertently allowing your dog to be drawn back to them.
- As your dog makes fewer and fewer mistakes and finally no mistakes for a week, you can begin to extend her playtime until confinement inside her crate or small area is no longer needed; if she relapses, go back a step and maintain for another week the last schedule that allowed her to be successful, then gradually increase her playtime again.
- Only when your dog has made no mistakes in the kitchen for a week should you begin to allow her into other rooms of the house; even then, observe her closely at first so you can correct any mistakes that she may make.

How to Housetrain Your Dog

Materials
- a dog crate or small confined area that will represent the dog's den, ideally located in the kitchen or other room where the floor can easily be cleaned but which is also near the center of family life
- baby-gate or other barrier to keep your dog in the kitchen during the times she is allowed to play and explore
- enzymatic odor remover, available in pet-supply stores

Schedule
See How to Paper-Train Your Dog, above.

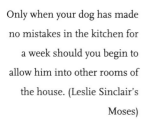

Only when your dog has made no mistakes in the kitchen for a week should you begin to allow him into other rooms of the house. (Leslie Sinclair's Moses)

Steps

- Begin by following the schedule you've set up, but don't hesitate to add or subtract minutes from different activities if it becomes obvious that your individual dog needs more or less time for certain ones.
- Ignore your schedule whenever you see signs that your dog is ready to eliminate; typical signs include circling, sniffing the floor, and appearing to be restlessly looking for something.
- When you take your dog outdoors, always take her to the place you've already decided shall be the bathroom area, and keep walking her back and forth on-leash until she eliminates; if your dog is a male, direct him to

appropriate vertical structures — which do not include flowers, bushes and shrubs, mailboxes, or anyone's personal property, including automobile tires.

- Be prepared with a particular word or phrase (for example, "It's time!" or "Let's do it!"), which you will utter as you see the first signs that she's about to perform. Praise enthusiastically; in time, this phrase will become an effective command to your dog and she will actually eliminate when requested to do so. (Obviously, you should not make this request unless you are pretty sure that she has a need to do so at the time!)
- Do not distract your dog by petting or talking, but praise her warmly as she begins to perform.
- Pick up your dog's feces and dispose of them in a proper receptacle.
- During housetraining, you must teach your dog that the first order of business when she gets outdoors is to eliminate. You can do this by always taking her directly to her bathroom area, gently distracting her from other activities, and firmly saying "No" (no need to yell) every time she begins to wander off. Then bring her back to the spot, and as you do so, remind her why she's there by repeating "It's time!" When she does finally begin to perform, praise her with great enthusiasm. After that, she can get to sniff and explore, meet other dogs and people, and generally enjoy the great outdoors.
- Whenever you catch your dog making a mistake, i.e., *in the act* of urinating or defecating indoors, startle her by firmly saying "No" and immediately take her to her outdoor area; if she finishes there, praise her warmly.
- Thoroughly clean and deodorize any indoor areas where mistakes were made to avoid inadvertently allowing your dog to be drawn back to them.
- As your dog makes fewer and fewer mistakes and finally no mistakes for a week, you can begin to extend her playtime until confinement inside her crate or small area is no longer needed; if she relapses, go back a step and maintain for another week the last schedule that allowed her to be successful, then gradually increase her playtime again.
- Only when your dog has made no mistakes in her enclosed area for a week should you begin to allow her into other rooms of the house; even then, observe her closely at first so you can correct any mistakes that she may make.

To make a success at housetraining, take your dog(s) outside on a schedule and supervise elimination habits. (Frank Loftus, Bailey, and Brownie)

Success?

How do you know when your dog has been thoroughly housetrained? Here are some good indicators:

- She has had no mistakes for at least a month while having free run of the house.
- You find yourself completely confident when you are away from home that she will either use her papers or will wait until you get home to take her out. (Note: Even a thoroughly housetrained dog may make mistakes under very stressful circumstances. Examples include the presence of

new animals or even new people in the home; the absence of accustomed persons or animals; injury or illness; a change in diet; a sudden change in the familiar environment, i.e., a large and noisy party or a substantial home construction or restoration project. Try not to overreact to one or two mistakes during such circumstances.)

- If friends invite you and your dog to visit for a few days, you are reasonably confident that the dog's training will be maintained away from home as well.
- Don't hesitate to set your own standards for how good is good enough, but remember that if something should happen to you, a thoroughly housetrained dog stands a better chance of finding another loving home.

HOUSETRAINING TIPS

- Be consistent. It's best to have one person handle housetraining, but all family members and any substitute dog walkers should try to follow your method and schedule.
- Learn your dog's natural schedule (all are different) and always be guided by it rather than your own arbitrary schedule.
- Even after housetraining is complete and you are taking your dog for nice long walks around the neighborhood, make it a point to have her continue to eliminate as soon as she gets outdoors. This will come in very handy when the weather is freezing or when you are in a rush to get somewhere.
- Take steps to avoid becoming irritated and impatient. For example, roll up rugs during housetraining, remove any objects that can be damaged, and always leave plenty of time for each trip outdoors.
- Prevent accidents from happening as much as possible (by maintaining consistent feeding routines with a quality diet, avoiding rawhide, table scraps, fatty or salty foods during the training period, and by adhering to your schedule). Be scrupulous about deodorizing mistakes so your dog won't be tempted to return to the same spot again and again. Also, make sure that your actions, e.g., coming home very late or feeding unfamiliar foods that may cause diarrhea, don't force your dog to make mistakes (very occasional mistakes should do no permanent harm).
- Once your dog knows what's expected, and the possibility of illness has been ruled out, don't hesitate to correct with your voice; physical punishment is never appropriate, doesn't work, and will harm your relationship with your dog. Remember to correct *only* if you catch the dog in the act of making a mistake.
- Unless you don't mind walking your dog "on demand," be on guard against the Mom-I-have-to-go-out! con. This is when your dog begins to ask to go out at times when you're pretty sure she doesn't really need to. If your suspicion is correct, ignore subsequent requests but at the same time make extra sure that you are feeding and taking her out at the usual times and frequencies. She should soon settle back into the schedule you established during housetraining.
- If you adopt a dog who is claimed to be thoroughly housetrained, be prepared to allow the dog one or possibly two mistakes before deciding that remedial action is needed. If it seems that remedial action is needed, follow the approach outlined in How to Housetrain Your Dog, above.
- Reward yourself appropriately for keeping calm and being patient with your dog. You deserve it!

Socialization and Handling

As you gaze into the warm eyes of your new puppy or dog, it's easy to think that this really is another human being after all. Enjoy the feeling of kinship, but remind yourself of the truth: Your dog is a dog. Certainly he's willing and able to become a full-fledged member of your family. Nevertheless, he's still a different species and will need help in adjusting to Life With You. Two tools that you can use to give him that help are socialization and handling.

Socialization

One of the key reasons that dogs have been our best friends for thousands of years is that dogs, like children, are remarkably flexible in adapting to the families, communities, and lifestyles in which they find themselves. This is particularly true when dogs are puppies, or if they were exposed to many different kinds of experiences when they were young. Luckily for us, dogs have evolved with both the capacity to fit into a human family and the desire to do so. But capacity and desire are not enough to assure that a particular dog fits smoothly into a particular family or into any family. What improves the odds is a special kind of training called socialization.

What Is Socialization?

To socialize is to prepare for companionship with others, to adapt in such ways as to fit the needs of a particular society. Mostly the term is used in reference to children. For instance, the properly socialized child is the one who learns at a very early age how to communicate, play, share, and cooperate with others, as well as how to resolve conflicts peaceably. The child needs to acquire these social qualities and abilities — called *skills* — in order to get along well with members of her family and with peers and adults in school, in the community, and ultimately in the larger society. Happily, social skills are *not* built by drill, practice, and hard work; they develop quite naturally as long as the child has the right kinds of early experiences with people.

Socialization in dogs is a similar process. The dog inherits from his parents the capacity and desire to bond tightly and permanently with his human family. But the specific qualities and abilities — *skills* — that he'll need to do so, including such things as being able to turn a deaf ear to the vacuum cleaner, a blind eye to the scampering kitten, and a tolerant attitude toward the letter carrier, are not passed down. It is up to us to help our dogs acquire these skills.

What Skills Will Your Dog Need?

Pretend for a moment that the dog who comes to live at your house was raised away from human beings during the first year of his life. It would be easy enough to understand that he would be completely unfamiliar with any sights, sounds, sensations, and interactions that had not occurred in his dogs-only environment. How much these unfamiliar sensations and experiences might faze him, whether he would respond by trembling or by growling, and how quickly or well he might eventually adapt to them would largely depend on the temperament this particular dog had been born with.

Chances are good of course that your dog was *not* raised in a dogs-only environment. He was, however, raised in a specific environment and had specific experiences there that may or may not be similar to those he will encounter as a member of your family. You can help your puppy or even your adult dog to fit smoothly into your life by *socializing* him, that is, by gently and systematically introducing him (see How Dogs Are Socialized, below) to as many as possible of the things that he may reasonably be expected to see, hear, and tolerate as a member of your family. Note that your home, your neighborhood, and your personal lifestyle will each present a fresh set of social challenges (other beings) and environmental challenges (sights, sounds, and other sensations) for your dog. The following lists include many of the things most modern dogs need to be able to handle calmly. As you read through them, jot down any others that are likely to confront the dog who comes to live with you.

In Your Home

SIGHTS other dogs, cats, birds, small mammals such as gerbils and hamsters; children; people of many sizes and proportions, dressed in flowing fabrics, uniforms, work boots, high heels, flapping raincoats, and acting in a variety of ways such as running, jumping, making sudden and/or strange motions; empty rooms, cluttered rooms, small dark spaces, cavernous rooms with flickering lights and shadows

SOUNDS banging pots and pans; laughing, crying, and screaming children; the stereo, vacuum, telephone, doorbell, teakettle, kitchen timer, dishwasher, clothes washer; alarm clock, smoke alarms, security alarms

OTHER SENSATIONS polished hardwood floors, carpets, tiles, steps, and open stairs

THINGS TO TOLERATE all family members and other household pets; delivery persons as well as visiting friends and strangers; confinement in a crate; handling all over the body (see Handling, page 190), including being petted or massaged; being groomed and bathed; being examined by the veterinarian; having nails clipped; wearing a collar and leash, coat and/or raincoat; being left alone for lengths of time; being required to sleep in a designated place

In Your Neighborhood

CITY SIGHTS AND SOUNDS honking horns, sirens, airplanes, fire trucks, firecrackers, backfiring automobiles, loudspeakers, heavy construction equipment, underground trains, air brakes; flapping flags and awnings, metal signs clanging in the wind; crowds of people of many sizes, shapes, types, and ages; people jogging, bicycling, rollerblading, jumping rope, playing games in the street; inebriated, staggering, and disoriented people who may be behaving in bizarre ways

SUBURBAN AND RURAL SIGHTS AND SOUNDS noises of domestic and wild animals; delivery persons and vehicles; thunderstorms; sirens; trains; gunfire during hunting season; other animals such as squirrels, rabbits, cats, birds, and snakes.

OTHER SENSATIONS elevators, escalators, revolving doors; street grates, cobblestones, rock salt, debris and litter; mown lawns, wild grasses and cut fields; gravel, shale, and cinders; running water, deep snow and ice, mud and marshland, loose and hard-packed sand

THINGS TO TOLERATE crowded streets; being approached by strange dogs, cats, other animals, and people; noisy children's toys and neighborhood games; pouring rain, sleet, and snow, high wailing winds; elderly and infirm people and equipment such as walkers, canes, wheelchairs

Within Your Lifestyle

Lifestyles vary tremendously. A young couple with a strong interest in athletics and the outdoor life might spend their leisure time running, cycling, swimming, hiking, and camping. A family-oriented family with roots and relatives in the area may be engaged in large noisy meals with many people, birthday parties, backyard barbecues, and lawn games involving all the cousins as well as droves of visiting children from the neighborhood. A trio of roommates in a large city may do a lot of social entertaining, with late nights, loud music, heated discussion, and a constantly changing cast of characters. A fast-track household may consist of two young professionals who work long, irregular hours, a child in preschool, a new baby, his nanny, a housekeeper, and a dog walker; a key characteristic of this family's lifestyle is that no two days are ever quite the same. Obviously, the family dogs in these scenarios will need different kinds of social skills to participate fully and happily in family life.

What are the key characteristics of *your* lifestyle? Orderly and predictable? Chaotic and fast-paced? Do you "stay put" or do you travel a lot? Do you often bring people home? Do you never? How often does your dog come in contact with other dogs? Cats? Children? Is he home alone a lot? Is he ever?

As you think about your lifestyle, jot down the kinds of sights, sounds, and experiences your dog will encounter on a regular basis. At the end of this chapter you will find a "Socialization Agenda," which will help you plan ways to make sure your dog acquires the particular social and environmental skills he'll need as a member of your family.

How Dogs Are Socialized

Dogs are socialized in two ways: naturally and normally within their litters during the first few months of life, and/or deliberately, by their breeders and subsequent owners. A puppy's first few months are as important to his future development as are a child's first few years to his. The lucky puppies of the world have parents who are healthy both physically and mentally, and soon after birth find themselves in homes where they are wanted and where they are raised with love and attention to their need for both stimulation and security. These puppies make the easiest adjustment to their new homes because they've already had many chances to encounter new things and have developed self-confidence as well as trust in people. Less lucky puppies don't get as good a start in life. Some simply are not well socialized in those important first few months, others may actually be neglected or mistreated in ways that cause them to be fearful, which makes them more difficult to train and slower to adjust to change. For instance, these puppies or adult dogs may come to their new homes with no prior experience of young children, loud noises, other dogs, walking on a leash, or riding in the car.

As mentioned above, socialization is not hard work — for you or for your dog. It is a simple process of figuring out what your dog needs to get used to in the environment, then introducing him to those things in a way that will help him accept them calmly rather than try to run away from them or attack them. In many cases, being exposed once or twice to something unfamiliar is all it takes. In others, it may take many repetitions and much patience on your part.

To gain a little perspective on this process, think back to when you were a child. Remember how easy it was for you to master some new things, maybe riding a bike or doing long division — even if your best friend took twice as long? Remember some things that were impossibly hard or scary to you, maybe going into the attic or climbing a tree, although everyone else found them fun? Didn't you finally get the hang of some of the hard things? Aren't some of them scary to this day? As you socialize your dog, keep reminding yourself that he is the child you once were. Have patience if he's having a tough time. Let him have some monsters under his bed, too.

Steps for Socializing Your Dog

Suppose, for example, that you acquire a dog who has really never been around children. You realize that sooner or later your dog will encounter children — on the street, in the park, at the veterinarian's. Rather than wait until that happens and hope for the best, why not take steps now to help your dog get used to children before he's suddenly confronted with a half-dozen who all want to hug him at once?

The following technique may be modified as necessary to socialize your dog to any new sight, sound, sensation, person, and experience. The key ingredients are to start out slowly; observe your dog and let *him* show *you* when he's ready for the next step; praise your dog for any and all progress; and gradually make the process more challenging (by making the sound louder, the people noisier, the car ride longer).

Sample Socialization Process for Dogs Who Lack Experience with Children

1. Introduce your dog to children slowly, one at a time, a little at a time, and observe him closely for signs that he is comfortable. For instance, if your dog has never been around a young child, stage the introduction in a neutral place (away from your home and other areas that your dog may feel are "his") so that territoriality and possessiveness will not complicate the picture. Select your child carefully; to begin, you want a calm child who will play quietly at a distance and not attempt to run up to your dog.

2. Keep your dog on a loose leash and allow him to investigate the child at his own pace. Don't force a face-to-face meeting. If it takes three, four, or more trials before your dog relaxes in the child's presence, that's fine. (You'll know he's relaxed when he looks away from the child, investigates other objects in the area, sits or lies down.) When your dog is comfortable with the child at twenty to thirty feet, try moving in a little closer.

3. Praise your dog for being calm, for being curious, for stepping closer, for sitting or lying down near the child, and so on. Praise warmly but don't overdo it and excite your dog. Do not attempt to correct your dog for not showing a positive response, as this will only add to his uneasiness.

4. Handle and direct your dog as little as possible; he will grow more confident if he walks toward, sniffs, and eventually lies down near the child on his own.

5. Continue to observe your dog. If he seems comfortable at twenty feet but not at ten, back off a little and give it more time.

6. When your dog seems reasonably comfortable, invite the child to give your dog a small tidbit by slowly tossing (not hurling!) it toward your dog. Eventually your dog may be willing to approach the child for the treat. (Do not encourage hand-feeding if your dog has any tendency to grab.)

7. Once your dog has "mastered" this child, it's time to introduce him to children of other ages and activity levels and in various locations. Proceed slowly in each case. If all continues to go well, present him with two children at once, then three or more.

8. The final step should be bringing a child into your home. Even if there's been no difficulty at any step along the way, use care in "staging" this event. Once again, select a child you can be sure will not attempt to grab at the dog or try to corner him or take things away from him.

Vigilant adults should monitor all interactions between small children and dogs, even the family dogs, no matter how friendly and reliable they may be. (Laura, Kevin, and Jamey Bower with Bandit and Barnabe)

9. Once your dog has shown he can handle himself around children, make sure you bring him into contact with them at regular intervals in order to make sure the positive response isn't lost.

Additional Facts about Socialization

IT BEGINS WITH MOM Ideally, puppies are socialized by their mothers, littermates, and possibly unrelated dogs to get along with other dogs. Breeders or owners of the mother dog then carry the process forward, gently introducing puppies to many sensory experiences during the first few months of life.

SELECTION IS IMPORTANT Part of the new owner's task in choosing a puppy or dog is to select one that appears curious, trusting, and confident. This is a good sign that the dog has had positive social experiences in the past.

START ON DAY ONE Whatever age your dog is when you acquire him, begin on the first day slowly to show him the ropes in his new home. Enrolling a puppy or adolescent dog in a puppy class for the purpose of building social skills with new dogs is recommended. This also offers a good opportunity to observe any areas that may need special attention as the puppy gets a little older.

YOUR DOG'S NEVER TOO OLD An older puppy or an adult dog who has had limited experience in the world, as long as he has a basically sound temperament and has not been mistreated, can adapt quite easily to a whole new cast of characters and circumstances in his new home. Tune in to your own dog to see how much growth he may be capable of. Even shy and fearful adult dogs can gain in self-confidence, although this will likely require great patience and perseverance on your part. In such cases, don't expect your dog ever to become boldly self-confident. At the same time, don't be surprised if a miracle occurs (dogs are good at that).

KEEP ON SOCIALIZING   The socialization process need never end. Just as people enjoy learning new things all their lives, dogs also enjoy new experiences. A steady and ongoing effort to expose your dog to new sights, sounds, terrain, people, and activities will keep his flexibility quotient at the highest possible level.

Handling

We humans can be forgiven for making the assumption that all dogs — or any dog — can be easily and safely handled. The majority that we have known or casually encountered probably could be. Newborn puppies are easily handled, even by strangers. It is not true, however, that dogs who receive little handling when they are young will nevertheless grow up to be tolerant of handling, particularly of their mouths, feet, tails, and sometimes other areas that may vary from individual to individual. What this means is that if we need our dog to accept having all parts of his body manipulated — and we really *do* need that — then it is up to us to see that he does. Fortunately, all we need do is accustom him to this kind of handling from an early age. If you have acquired an adult dog unaccustomed to this kind of handling, however, don't despair. Through repeated lessons, administered with patience, even an adult dog unaccustomed to handling can be taught to accept it.

What Is Handling?

Just as the name implies, handling is literally to touch, hold, or manipulate with the hands. Handling falls into two classes: *affectionate handling,* as in patting or stroking, and *handling for a specific purpose,* such as to examine, transport, treat, groom, or train. Most dogs appear to enjoy it when their owners gently rub their ears or scratch their bellies. Still, the dog who readily accepts and even solicits being patted on the chest may strenuously resist other kinds of handling. The only sure-fire way to make sure your dog will submit to specific kinds of handling is to introduce him to them when he is young (ideally), in small stages over time, kindly but firmly, with encouragement and praise. Refresh this training on a regular basis. Dogs go through different stages of development as they mature, whereby something they seemed to like yesterday is frightening by tomorrow. These stages

Teaching your dog to be handled — including being lifted and transported — makes him much easier to live with. (Leslie Sinclair, D.V.M., and Moses)

take place rapidly and dramatically during a puppy's first few months but continue to occur to some extent all through a dog's life.

What Kind of Handling?

In order to hold his own in our modern world, the average dog will need to master the following kinds of "hands-on" experiences — certainly when the hands are his owner's, but also when they are the hands of a friendly stranger:

- patting/stroking — for the pleasure of both dog and owner; as an aid in training
- handling of the eyes, ears, mouth — to examine, clean, or medicate
- handling of the whole body — to examine, massage, or treat; to lift, transport, restrain
- working with the coat — to examine and treat the skin or to groom
- bathing and drying — for general hygiene or in treatment of skin or other diseases
- handling of the feet and nails — to examine, treat, cleanse, and trim

Accustoming your dog to being handled in these ways brings obvious benefits to both of you as well as to caregivers and other persons who come in contact with your dog. In addition, teaching your dog to be handled will make him that much easier to live with, train, and enjoy.

SOCIALIZATION AGENDA

This chart will help you plan learning experiences for your dog. To use it, think about both ordinary and unusual events of a typical year in *your* life. Assume that your dog (of course!) will participate with you in these events. Then think about what new skills the dog may need — i.e., anything that he doesn't already know — in order to do so. Finally, jot down how you will make sure he acquires the skills. We are presenting one common scenario as an example, but of course you should complete a chart that is based on your own lifestyle.

SAMPLE TABLE

Family Event	Skills My Dog Will Need in Order to Participate	Ways to Help My Dog Develop Skills
Summer — annual family vacation at campground in mountains	Comfort with long car rides	Gradually accustom dog to riding in car
	Ability to rest quietly in crate in car	Carefully train dog to spend time in crate
	Ability to remain reasonably calm during frequent thunderstorms in mountains	Begin immediately to expose dog to loud rumbling noises in the outdoors and also to recordings of thunderstorms at gradually increasing volume; plan for pleasurable activities to take place at the same time
	Acceptance of and sociability with other dogs and children in close proximity to family cabin	Bring dog into close social contact with as many other dogs, children, and adults as possible; encourage them to play with and around your dog

Training 14

Training — or what is often called obedience training — is one of the best things that could ever happen to you and your dog. An obedience-trained dog has learned her manners — not just to sit, or lie down, or come to you (after all, she could do those things without being taught) — but to do them when asked, or "on command." There is little likelihood that an obedience-trained dog will lose her home because of unruly, uncooperative behavior.

Through the training process, a dog learns two (at least) other things: that in certain circumstances she is expected to behave in a certain way; and that there are some things she isn't supposed to do at all. Well-trained dogs, like well-mannered children, are a joy to live with. Not only are they happy to be under your control and do what you ask, but they also have developed self-control, meaning that in novel situations, they will actually turn to you for approval — any parent's dream come true.

Training benefits you and your entire family as well. Together, you all learn how dogs learn. You learn what kind of leaders you must be in order to earn the respect and obedience you need from your dog if you're all to live happily ever after. Without exception, obedience training should be part of the early experience of every dog, dog owner, and family.

What Is Obedience Training?

Obedience training is an educational program for dogs and their owners. Typically, a professional obedience trainer or instructor teaches owners how their dogs' minds work and what they must do in order to make their wishes clear to their dogs. For their part, dogs learn that when they do certain things, good things happen, and that when they do other things, not-so-good things happen. Ultimately, what obedience training does is give owners the tools they need to control their dogs' behavior in almost any situation just by eliciting a prompt response to simple commands such as "Sit," "Stay," and "Come" — not for the purpose of showing the dog who's boss, or to impress the neighbors, but to keep the dog safe, quiet, and unobtrusive when walking down the street, at the veterinary hospital, in the homes of friends, when you have company, or every night at dinnertime. In other words, obedience training helps make sure your dog doesn't wear out her welcome in your home and heart.

As excellent an idea as obedience training is, take care in selecting a trainer. Some highly qualified trainers have acquired a great deal of knowledge over the years about how dogs learn and how best to teach them. They are truly interested in helping you find the best way to work with your individual dog — which can vary depending on factors such as your dog's age, personality, and temperament as well as on your dexterity, sense of timing, and ability to be alternately firm and enthusiastic with your dog. Humane obedience trainers seek to *induce* compliance on the dog's part by advocating positive ways of affecting the dog's behavior, such as food, attention, play, or praise; inhumane trainers *compel* compliance through harshly negative techniques such as yelling, choking, shaking, striking, or "stringing up" (lifting the dog's head by the collar until his front feet leave the floor), or by confinement and isolation.

Positive obedience training always deepens the bond between dog and owner and often prevents behavior problems from developing. (Note: Obedience training alone is not likely to resolve behavior problems that already exist, although it often is part of an overall strategy in problem resolution. See Part Five of this book, Problem Solving, for ways to resolve common behavior problems.) A positive training experience also helps the dog accept and depend on her owner, not herself, as pack leader, and she'll respond to commands happily, reliably, and without fear of what will happen if she doesn't. In contrast, dogs who are taught by harsh methods may learn to do what is expected of them, but they do so out of fear, not out of respect. The owner whose dog fears him will never know the deeply satisfying bond that develops out of mutual respect and trust.

It's also important to understand what obedience training *isn't*. It isn't a family sending off their dog to be trained by someone else while they wait at home for the new and improved companion to be returned to them. (Would you send your children off to be raised by someone else? If so, would you really expect to know and understand them and to have earned their respect when they returned?) Dog training is a two-way street. Both dog and owner need to participate actively in the process, become familiar with one another, and learn the rules of getting along together.

How Obedience Training Works

Obedience training relies on four elements to help a dog to perform a particular action in a particular way when she receives the command to do so: *consistency, timing, reward or correction,* and *repetition.* The basic sequence of events is as follows:

When the dog is first learning a command, the "Sit" command for example, the owner will guide her into a sitting position using the same motions each time (consistency) just as the word "Sit" is spoken (timing); then, just as the dog begins to lower herself to the ground (timing), she is warmly praised (reward) for doing as she was asked. This sequence is repeated in the same way many times (consistency and repetition) until the owner has no doubt that the dog knows what "Sit" means and the dog knows that her owner is pleased with her if she complies.

The other side of the reward coin is correction. If the dog knows what is expected but refuses to comply, the owner says "No!" (correction) together with (timing) a quick snap on the leash (additional correction). This will help the dog begin to associate the word "No" with a mildly unpleasant physical correction. The command "Sit" is then repeated (consistency, repetition), and if the dog once again begins to sit (timing), she is praised (reward). When you repeat these elements over and over — consistent command, proper timing, and prompt reward or correction, and especially when all members of the family do the same, the dog will learn what is wanted and what payoff she can expect. More important, she will recognize your leadership. And because she is a dog, a very social pack animal who thrives on routine and an unambiguous pecking order, she'll be motivated to please you in order to receive your praise (or occasional other goodies such as a treat, a quick game, or a friendly pat).

What about Punishment?

The idea of punishment has fallen into disfavor as a method of teaching either dogs or children, and some would argue that this has had unfortunate consequences. Whatever happened to "spare the rod and spoil the child"? some of our elders want to know. Likewise, some dog trainers who learned their profession in the military, where modern dog training has its roots, or from others who had learned it there, decry the "warm and fuzzy" approach to training dogs where trainers never "let the dog know who's boss."

In fact, punishment, in and of itself, is *not* a bad thing, so long as it is never harsh, abusive, or painful. Appropriately used, it's a teaching tool. Punishment is the opposite of reward. Just as you reward desirable behavior, you punish undesirable behavior. If you ask your dog to sit and she promptly sits, you tell her she's great and give her a pat. That's her reward, and it is intended to encourage her to continue to repeat her prompt sitting behavior. On the other hand, if your puppy starts circling around and sniffing the living room carpet, a sure sign he's about to eliminate there, and you startle him with a disapproving "No!" that's his punishment (these days we more often say "correction," but we're talking about the same basic concept), and this punishment is intended to discourage him from repeating his eliminating-in-the-house behavior. When rewards are paired with *appropriate* punishment, lessons may be learned more quickly and possibly more permanently.

The key word is "appropriate." In the training of dogs, punishment can be a verbal reprimand, withdrawal of attention, or something physical that might range from the toss of a can of pennies to startle the dog to a mild tug on the leash. What it *cannot* be is a violent tug on the leash or any other action that is uncomfortable, frightening, or painful for a dog.

What harsh or abusive methods of training dogs overlook, and why they are never appropriate, humane, or even particularly effective, is that like rewards, punishment is intended to teach, not to mete out some notion of human justice. If you were to toss your dog a treat every time you felt warm and affectionate toward her, regardless of what she was doing or not doing, you would quickly undermine the usefulness of the food reward as a teaching tool intended to encourage your dog to repeat specific desirable behavior. Likewise, using harsh punishment when you are feeling disappointment, anger, or impatience with your dog is not only inhumane but will quickly undermine the effectiveness of the verbal rebuke or the withdrawal of attention as a way of discouraging him from repeating behavior that you don't like. Just as important, both the dog and you will have lost the possibility of the deep bond that can only develop on a foundation of kindness and trust.

How Dogs Learn

Dogs are born knowing how to suckle, to cry when they're hungry or frightened, to snuggle against their mother and littermates to keep warm, and many other things. Things dogs are born knowing are called instincts. Dogs also learn many things from their mothers and littermates, and from other dogs, cats, and different animals they are raised with. Typically, they learn how roughly they can play with one another, whether and how they can get/keep more of the toys and treats, that some other dogs are fun to play with and some aren't, and that cats sometimes scratch. Through their early experiences in their first home and then in yours, dogs learn about many different sights and sounds, about the people they meet and how they look, smell, sound, and act. By trial and error and by doing things themselves, they learn that they can open a door or get you to open it and that if they stand by your side as you prepare dinner, some bits of food may occasionally fall to the floor. From the day they are born, in any and all circumstances, dogs are learning — whether or not anyone is consciously trying to teach them. So if we want our dogs to learn our household rules rather than just develop their own way of doing things, it's up to us to train them.

If fact, we do deliberately set out to teach our dogs certain things that they need or we want them to know. Housetraining is probably the first purposeful training a dog receives. Socialization and handling are other kinds of learning experiences that begin, or should begin, on the very first day. But unfortunately, not everyone thinks about the need for obedience training until the dog is a year old, fast and strong and almost completely unmanageable. The whole process is much, much easier if you begin when your dog is a puppy, but it's certainly not too late to start whenever you acquire your dog. Fortunately, most dogs are never too old to learn. But how do you get started?

Different Training Formats

Any individual or group of individuals who feel they know how to train dogs can offer obedience instruction to the public. There are no state or federal agencies that regulate this kind of training. As a result, obedience training is offered almost everywhere, if you know where to look. And because it is not regulated, there is tremendous variation in the qualifications of those who teach it, in the methods that they use, and in the formats for instruction. In most areas of the country, training is available in the following ways:

- group classes — offered by private trainers, humane societies and shelters, 4-H and obedience clubs, some municipal governments through adult education or continuing education programs at schools or community centers
- individual lessons — either in your home or at the trainer's school
- self-help training — at home with the help of a book (such as this one), audio tape, videotape, or CD-ROM.
- off-site training — where the dog is sent to the trainer's facility, either for the day or for the duration of training, and is then returned "trained" to the owner

Highly Recommended

GROUP CLASSES These are recommended for all dogs and owners. In a group situation, dogs learn to accept other dogs and attend to their owners in spite of distractions; dogs learn to accept handling by other owners as well as trainers; owners — who may feel awkward and inept at first — are supported in their efforts by others who are "in the same boat"; owners get to see a variety of dog types, personalities, and temperaments, and to understand that each dog has her own best way of learning.

Group classes usually are divided into Puppy Classes, for youngsters between eight and sixteen weeks of age, and Regular Classes, for dogs six months of age and older. In addition, some Puppy Classes may be further divided by the size of the puppies, so that tiny toy puppies weighing only a few pounds won't be overwhelmed by puppies who already weigh twenty pounds or more at ten or twelve weeks of age.

Recommended

INDIVIDUAL LESSONS These offer you one-on-one instruction and feedback as you train your dog under the eye of the instructor. However, since there are no other dogs or people present, it is impossible to achieve the same degree of confidence about how reliably your dog will respond when there are other dogs and people around to distract her. In private instruction you also miss the opportunity to learn by observing other dogs and trainers or to benefit from the camaraderie of others at those inevitable times when you doubt that either you or your dog will ever figure this out.

SELF-HELP TRAINING   This method is recommended in the unusual circumstance where no classes are available, or scheduling problems exist that will delay training for many months. Even after dogs have learned the basic commands, however, it is recommended that as soon as possible they be enrolled in a training class for the added benefits of being trained as part of a group of other dogs and owners.

Not Recommended

OFF-SITE TRAINING   A program in which the dog is sent to a trainer and returned when the work has been completed could never be recommended. The most important elements of obedience training are that the owner and the owner's family learn to be humane and effective leaders to the dog and the dog and the owner develop a bond that will form the basis for their entire relationship together. If the family does not participate actively in the training of the dog, these benefits are lost. It may even happen that the dog who responds perfectly for the off-site trainer responds very poorly if at all for the owner when the trainer is not present. And as a worst-case scenario, you cannot be certain how humane a trainer's methods are if you are not physically there to witness them.

Note: Behavioral counseling or behavioral modification is not obedience training, but is a special kind of training that may be necessary when problems arise that are beyond the knowledge or experience of the ordinary professional dog trainer. Behavioral counseling is supplied by some veterinarians who have an interest in companion animal behavior and by other professionals who have years of postgraduate study in animal behavior as well as extensive practical experience helping people resolve behavior problems in their dogs. Typically, veterinarians can provide counseling to owners of dogs with most basic behavior problems. Veterinarians will refer clients whose dogs have more complex problems to an applied or certified animal behaviorist or behavioral counselor, although sometimes the referral will be made by the professional obedience trainer who recognizes that the problem is more than simple lack of training. (See chapter 18 for help in distinguishing the problems of the untrained dog or the dog with a medical problem from those of dogs with true behavior problems.)

How to Choose an Obedience Training Program

Locating Programs

No matter what kind of obedience program (group, individual, etc.) you are contemplating, use these resources to start your search for a program for you and your dog:

- your own veterinarian for the names of area trainers she recommends
- your local humane society or shelter (some offer obedience classes of their own, often as part of the adoption package)
- friends and neighbors whose dogs appear well-mannered
- other pet professionals, such as groomers, dog walkers, kennel operators, who are in a position to know local trainers as well as to hear comments (for and against) from many dog owners
- the Yellow Pages (under Pet Training) for public, private, and shelter-run training programs
- the American Kennel Club for a list of affiliated obedience clubs in your area
- the National 4-H Council for clubs in your area that may offer obedience training for school-age children and their dogs.

Evaluating Programs

Once you have a few programs to consider, use these criteria to compare them to one another:

- credentials of trainer(s), including number of years in business; how they themselves were trained; what methods they advocate (how dogs are rewarded, how they are corrected, whether punishment is used and, if so, what kind); whether or not the trainers are members of any national training associations (Note: Membership in the National Association of Dog Obedience Instructors, NADOI, requires a peer approval process and includes assurance that trainers use humane methods; other membership associations may have different [or no] criteria — you must ask in order to determine how much weight to give to such memberships.)
- the trainer's willingness to let you observe training sessions in progress and to speak with dog owners currently in training (An ideal approach is to observe several dog/owner teams at the beginning of the series of classes, then return after five or six weeks to see how much progress has been made.)

- your own personal observations of the program in action, noting the kinds of equipment in use (plain buckle collars? choke training collars? prong or pinch collars? head halters rather than collars?); the way owners are expected to correct their dogs; the apparent attitudes of both dog and owner (are they having fun together?); the general cleanliness, efficiency, punctuality, and overall professionalism of the facility
- price (Expect a wide range of prices, with the lowest being shelter or obedience club group classes and the highest being private in-home lessons from a well-established trainer.)

Picking a Group Class

If you decide to enroll your dog and yourself in a group class (hurrah!), look for one that has the following features:

- classes for puppies beginning at the age of eight weeks, in which the whole family participates (Many future behavior problems can be prevented if puppies spend six or eight weeks in a setting where they play and interact with many other puppies, and are handled and socialized not only by their own family members but by other children, adults, and the class trainers as well.)
- classes for adult dogs (over six months usually) who are licensed and vaccinated (Classes may be divided into basic, beginners, intermediate, etc., depending on whether the dog and owner have had any prior training.)
- an exclusion policy that excludes dogs who appear ill at a given class session, or dogs who are aggressive to other dogs or to people (However, aggressive dogs should be excluded solely on their own behavior, not because they happen to be certain breeds, breed mixtures, or types of dogs.)
- trainer teaches owner to teach dog (Over a course of six to eight weeks, the dog is trained to one of two standards: [1] basic obedience, where the dog learns to perform a set of basic behaviors on command, usually including the "Come," the "Sit," the "Stay," the "Down," and the "Heel"; [2] "Canine Good Citizen," a program designed by the American Kennel Club to encourage owners to train their dogs to be well-behaved at home, in public, and in the company of other dogs. Dogs learn to remain calm and quiet around other dogs, to walk nicely on leash amid distractions, to allow themselves to be patted, groomed, and handled by strangers, to be left alone with a stranger, and to obey a few basic commands such as "Come," "Sit," "Down," and "Stay.")

- dog and owner "teams" learning at their own pace, although slow teams may receive extra attention in order to help them keep up
- humane collars and leashes required by trainer (no prong or electric collars; no choke collars at all, or at least none for puppies under one year or for dogs weighing less than forty pounds and/or with necks smaller than sixteen inches; even then, choke or "training" collars should be used humanely, i.e., tugged gently and immediately released, and only for the purpose of discouraging unwanted behavior, never for showing the dog who's boss or teaching him a lesson he'll never forget)
- no harsh treatment of dogs permitted by trainers or by owners (On the off-chance that you witness harsh or abusive treatment of a dog, either by the dog's owner or by the trainer, be very clear that this is not something you will tolerate. Your options are to object to the group director and/or the person involved, and if you do not receive assurance that the abusive behavior will stop, to leave the group. It could be very effective to write up and document your experience and send copies to your local humane society or animal care and control agency, which has responsibility to investigate complaints of animal cruelty. Beyond that, you may wish to file a complaint with the Better Business Bureau and/or the Department of Consumer Affairs. Finally, if this trainer was recommended to you by your veterinarian or someone else in a position to influence others, you certainly will want to let that person know what you discovered so that he or she may rethink whether to continue to endorse that individual or group.)
- referrals to certified animal behaviorists if dogs have a history of aggression or display aggression (or other complex behavior problems such as extreme fearfulness)
- limited class size, based on the number of trainers available and the size of the facility (Inexperienced dogs in particular and owners who have not yet learned how to control their dogs should not be crowded together.)
- practice by dog/owner teams (and family members) every day at home between class sessions, but with cautions against lengthy practice sessions or too many repetitions (Remember: Obedience should be fun!)
- ample rewards to dogs for all their progress — with praise, attention, patting, a favorite toy or game, or a tidbit of food

Setting Your Own Training Goals

Before signing up for any training program, take the time to ask yourself what you really hope to achieve with your dog.

In your mind's eye, how would your trained dog behave in the following everyday situations?

- The doorbell rings.
- You and your dog meet another dog and owner on the street.
- You want your dog to stop teasing the cat, to get off the furniture, to drop a morsel of food he just found on the street.
- Your dog is in the veterinarian's waiting room; on the examination table.
- Your welfare or property is threatened.

Do you think your goals are realistic and achievable for you and for your dog?

- Why or why not?
- If not, what adjustments can you make to assure that you start off with realistic and achievable goals?

Be assertive about what you want.

- Decide what your dog *really* needs to know as your companion (not what you may have seen some dog do on the Discovery channel).
- Choose the program that most closely offers the level of training that you feel is important for you, your dog, and your family situation.
- Make sure that other family members stay involved in the program and avoid mixing methods and/or goals, which will confuse your dog. (It is very important that the entire family participate actively in training the dog and make every effort to be sure that they are consistent in their use of commands, which kinds of behaviors are praiseworthy, and which warrant some kind of correction. Some dogs are able to work out on their own what they can get away with from the man of the house as opposed to the teenage son, but for most dogs this is confusing and leads to stress and sometimes behavior problems.)
- Set your very own standard of perfection for your dog's (and your!) performance — it may be quite different from other teams' and from the trainer's. Concentrate on trying to achieve what's meaningful for you, and remember that training should be fun for your dog.

A head halter provides maximum control, without choking, when walking dogs who may pull too hard on standard leashes. (Barbara DeMambro and Lady)

Until You Get to Class

If the puppy class you want to join is midsession and the next one doesn't start for four weeks, you don't have to lose the time altogether. Ask your veterinarian if she can put you in touch with another client or two who have young puppies, and organize your own informal play group. Even if the puppies just play together for twenty minutes at a time while all the adults and children sit in a circle around them, they will still be learning stuff that it's good for puppies to know.

Meanwhile, you can begin at home to teach your puppy or untrained dog the basics.

Equipment

- a small handful of your dog's dry diet, or bits of broken-up dog biscuits
- a well-fitted buckle collar made of nylon, and a nylon leash either six or seven feet long (A head halter, which allows you to lead the dog by his muzzle rather than by pulling against his neck, may also be used.)

Picking a Time to Train

Pick a time when your puppy isn't exhausted from a play session, hasn't just eaten, and doesn't need to eliminate. Keep the sessions very short — a minute or two for very young puppies and no more than five minutes for older dogs.

Your Voice

Develop three distinct training voices to help your dog distinguish your meaning.

- a command, e.g., "Sit" (Say this in a conversational tone, as if you were saying "I'm asking you to please *sit*.")
- praise, e.g., "Good girl" (Say this in a high-pitched and happy voice, as if you were saying "Hooray!")
- correction, e.g., "No" (Say this is a low-pitched, displeased tone. Pretend you're saying, "Just say *'No!'*" Never shout at or berate your dog verbally.)

Knowing When to Stop

No matter how long you've been training, if your puppy or dog begins to tire, or get bored or antsy, it's time to stop. Try to end each session on a positive note, when your dog has just succeeded at something and you've been able to praise him. Keep an eye on your own mental state during training sessions; if you find yourself getting frustrated, impatient, or inconsistent, it's *definitely* time to stop.

Note: Different trainers, books, and videotapes may advocate slightly different methods of teaching the following basic skills. There is no single right and only way to teach your dog. Rest assured, however, that the steps outlined below have worked successfully for millions of owners and dogs.

Teaching the "Sit"

1. Attach your dog's leash to her collar so that you have some control over your dog's movement.
2. With your dog standing, position yourself along one of her sides (if you are right-handed, it probably will be easier if she is on your left), hold a

bit of food high over her head, and move your hand slightly to the rear. Say "Sit." As she raises her head to follow your hand, her body may automatically lower into a sit. If so, praise her immediately ("Gooood girrrrl!") and give her the tidbit.

3. Repeat the command and action the same way several more times. She will quickly associate the word "Sit" with the action on her part that gets her the praise and the food.

4. If your dog doesn't sit, do not give her either tidbit or praise. Simply look and move slightly away from her and wait several minutes before trying again. Do not even think about correcting her for not sitting at this point. Corrections are appropriate only when your dog knows what to do but doesn't do it.

5. If your dog doesn't automatically sit when the morsel is above her head, try gently pulling up on the leash with your right hand while scooping your left hand behind her hind legs to collapse her legs into a sitting position as you say "Sit." Even the beginning of a squat is cause for praise. Try again, and be ready with your enthusiastic praise for all moves in the right direction. Correctly timed praise should come out of your mouth as your dog is *deciding* to sit. That way she'll more quickly connect what she's doing with the reward she gets from you. (Use as little physical manipulation of your dog as possible. They really learn a lot better and faster if they move their bodies into position by themselves.)

Teaching the "Stay"

1. Only begin teaching the "Stay" when your puppy is reliable with the "Sit."

2. Proceed in stages; do not move forward to the next stage until your puppy knows the one you're working on now.

3. Stand on your puppy's right side, with the leash attached to her collar. Ask her to sit. Praise her for sitting.

4. Immediately slide the palm of your left hand down and backward, to a point just in front of your dog's nose. Say "Stay" as you do so.

5. If your puppy stays for a second or two, praise her calmly and slowly, as in "Gooood girrrrl! Staaaaay!" (excited praise may cause her to jump up), then release her with a word like "Okay" and let her wander off.

6. If your puppy doesn't stay, give a gentle tug on the leash while saying "No." This should just startle her a little. As she hesitates, ask her to sit again, praise her, and again give the hand signal and verbal command, "Stay." If she stays at all, praise her immediately.

7. As the puppy begins to understand that "Stay" means to remain sitting, and eventually stays every time for five or ten seconds, you can begin with *your right foot* to walk a little bit away from her (the right foot, being farther away from your dog, is less likely to tempt her to move out when you do). Should she begin to get up, give a tug on the leash, say "No," replace her in the sitting position, praise her, and try the "Stay" again.

8. Gradually increase the distance that you walk away after giving the "Stay" command. If your dog stays well at four feet but gets up at eight, go back to four feet for a while before you try to increase the distance again. Eventually you should be able to walk between twenty and thirty feet away without difficulty, which is probably as far as you'd ever have a practical reason to leave your dog.

9. Don't repeat the "Stay" command more than two or three times in one training session. Increase the time the dog is asked to stay very gradually, to about one minute by the time she is six months old.

Teaching the "Down"

1. Begin with your dog in a sitting position with the leash attached to her collar.

2. Using a bit of food as a lure, hold the food between your dog's front legs, directly under her nose, and slowly lower your hand to the ground and then drag it along the ground away from her as you say "Down." Don't get too far in front of your dog's nose. In order to follow the food, she must automatically lower her body into a down position. You can reinforce the motion by pulling gently down on the leash at the same time that you lure the dog with the food.

3. Praise the dog for even beginning to go down. (Lying down puts a dog in a vulnerable position. It is not something most dogs do easily, so your praise should reflect the fact that your dog has done something very special in acknowledging your leadership in this way.)

4. If instead of going down, the dog gets up from the "Sit," give a tug on the leash, say "No," ask her to sit again, praise her, then once again attempt the "Down" sequence.

5. Once your dog goes down, squat next to her, looking away, and try to get her to relax in that position. Eventually you may wish to leave your dog on a "Down" for a half hour or more, while you're eating dinner for instance, so you really don't want to give her a "Down-Stay" command that you won't be in a physical position to correct if she breaks it. So for the "Down," it's best for her to begin to associate it with relaxing indefinitely

until you release her with an "Okay" or overriding command such as "Come."

Teaching the "Come"

1. Begin teaching the "Come" in locations where there are few or no distractions.

2. From just a few feet away from your puppy, crouch down on her level, open your arms, call her name, and then say "Come" in a very excited voice. Praise the puppy as soon as she begins to move toward you, continuing until she has reached you.

3. For a puppy who does not come readily to this encouragement, try getting her attention and then either running away while calling her to "Come," or backing away facing her. Praise her as soon as she moves toward you and continue as long as she is on her way. Look away and stop praising if the puppy stops and wanders off. You do not want to repeat the command if you hope to have your dog come on the first command (which can be important for safety's sake). Once your dog knows the "Come," you can begin to correct her gently for failing to come when called. Do this by saying "No" as you give the leash a tug. When you've gotten her attention, repeat the "Come" command with open arms and happy praise for any forward motion.

4. Once you've added some distractions to the training scene, you may need to use a bit of food to keep the puppy's focus on you. Do this every time while the puppy is learning the lesson; once she knows it, offer food only every once in a while.

Teaching to Heel

1. Heeling is taught with your dog on your left side. It does not matter how close or far away the dog stands from your left leg, or if her head is a few inches in front of your leg or a few inches behind. If she basically stays with you on your left side, that's sufficient for virtually any practical purpose. Only ask your dog to heel when there's a good reason for her to do so, such as when you're on a crowded street or need to move quickly to your destination.

2. To get your dog to heel along happily at your side, you have to be interesting. Say her name, pat your leg, and then say "Heel" to get her started. Make sure the leash stays slack and do everything you can to get and keep her attention. Praise her for keeping up with you, talk to her, give her the occasional bit of food, keep up a brisk pace, make frequent zigs and zags, and keep the lessons short (only a minute or two).

You can teach your dog to heel happily — in a group setting or at home — if you can make the exercise fun and interesting. (Peter Muldoon and Chester)

3. Once your dog knows what the command "Heel" means, you can begin to start her off with a short tug and the word "Heel" or "Let's go." Whenever she stops heeling, meaning that she stops to sniff the ground, or veers off in another direction, say "No," give the leash a tug, repeat the word "Heel," and praise her when she once again begins to walk with you.

4. Always release your dog from heeling with a particular word and/or gesture, such as "Okay" or "Free," together perhaps with a particular kind of pat that she'll come to associate with being released from the "Heel."

5. At the same time that you teach your dog to heel, which really means to keep her focus on you as you walk together, teach her that there's another kind of walking, perhaps on your own property or in a deserted section of the park, where she can stop and start and sniff pretty much as she pleases. This "lesson" is distinguished by not having any commands to start or stop, and no requirement that she be on your left side. Try to let your dog walk freely as often as possible. Since she is a dog, it will always be more fun for her to sniff and explore all the delicious aromas in the great outdoors than to walk with her head up and her focus on you.

Note: There are many additional commands that you can teach your dog to make life together more pleasant. Some examples are "Off," when you want her to get off the furniture; "Leave it," when you want her to drop something she's picked up or gone over to investigate; "Wait," if you don't want her to go through doors until you have; "Place," if you wish to direct her to a particular spot, such as her bed or crate; and "Jump," to encourage her up into the car or onto another surface. Everything you teach your dog is one more opportunity to reinforce the relationship between you as well as for both of you to gain the practical benefits of her new skill. While most obedience classes only teach the basics, some may offer additional training in advanced classes. Alternatively, once you know how your dog learns and how to teach her, you'll find yourself able to devise ways to train new commands yourself. Enjoy learning new, even zany things together. For instance, how about "Time for bed" or "Clean the floor!" (A good dog is faster at picking up wayward pieces of carrot or apple than the best vacuum cleaner ever made! Incidentally, you may very well impress the neighbors, too!)

"MY DREAM TRAINER"

By Your Dog

- keeps sessions short and fun
- doesn't care if I'm not perfect
- figures out what she's doing before trying it out on me
- doesn't expect me to understand English
- stops the lesson if she starts to "lose it"
- avoids training me when I'm tired, starved, stressed-out, or under the weather — or when she is
- warms me up with a little brisk walk before starting our lesson
- helps me to succeed (makes sure I can crawl before she asks me to walk)
- often calls me by my new name (Goooood Boy!)
- goes easy on my nerves (doesn't feel she has to scream)
- always ends our sessions on a high note (when I've finally gotten it right)
- tells me I'm the best dog ever

More and more "people doctors" are telling their groaning patients that they really must make physical exercise a regular part of their daily life, that human bodies were designed to walk and climb, hunt and gather, lift and haul — not to sit in front of a computer for half the day and in front of a television set for the other half. Veterinary doctors could be even more emphatic about their patients' need to use their bodies vigorously every day. Before they teamed up with man, wild dogs searched out, ran down, and killed their own food, in the process traveling many miles in all kinds of weather, feeding and raising their families as best they could, and patrolling and defending their territory from intruders. Once domesticated by man and selectively bred to assist their owners in various ways, dogs worked hard for a living: keeping pace all day with hunters on horseback to point, flush, and retrieve game from land and water; pulling heavy loads on snow, ice, and dry ground; herding farm animals over mountainous terrain and/or defending flocks from predators; going underground to rout and do battle with den-dwelling animals who otherwise took a heavy toll on farmers' crops and flocks.

By comparison, the vast majority of today's dogs are acquired as companions; they are not expected to do anything but bring joy and happiness into our lives. They do this fully and well. On the other hand, the need of dogs to be active and physical and at least have the illusion that they're working at something hasn't gone away. Today's dog is like a skilled laborer who's been promoted to supervisor; in many ways his lot has improved, but deep down he may sadly miss the hard physical work that left him tired but relaxed at the end of the day. The way to give this back to your dog is through regular physical exercise. Fortunately, most dogs don't need a second invitation to exercise, though their owners often do. If you're such an owner, just look deeply into those ever-ready eyes — and consider yourself invited!

What Exercise for Dogs Is — or Should Be

AN ENERGY-BURNING, WHOLE-BODY WORKOUT   Exercise is fifteen to thirty minutes a day of hard play that may include such activities as swimming, trotting, or running, chasing objects that bounce unpredictably or zig and zag, jumping over low obstacles or into the air to catch things, making lots of quick turns, and climbing hills or stairs. Exercise is *not* a leisurely walk with stops every fifteen feet, nor is it dashing out to catch a flying disk and then flopping on the ground to chew it for a while — though even these activities are *far* better than none (as they are for humans!). (See chapter 16 for many kinds of active games you can play with your dog.)

GRADUATED AND REGULAR   See your veterinarian to make sure your dog is in good health before you begin any exercise program. Even then, start out at a moderate pace and build up gradually to longer walks, steeper climbs, more retrieves over rugged ground, and so on. And once you've begun, plan to exercise on a regular basis. Three days of lazing about, then a four-hour hike is not the prudent way — for you or your dog.

AGE-APPROPRIATE   It's just common sense to consider your dog's age in planning an exercise program, and you may want to talk to your veterinarian about what she thinks would be appropriate. Don't, however, design a program that's based on age alone. The best program is one that your dog anticipates eagerly and enjoys from start to finish and that does not leave your dog stiff, sore, and exhausted afterward.

PRACTICAL   A practical exercise program is one that you will be able to participate in cheerfully on a regular basis without too much cost and inconvenience. An hour's drive to a park with a lake where your dog can swim sounds like a fine idea for the occasional weekend jaunt, but probably won't be something you can do on weekdays without beginning to feel overwhelmed.

ENJOYABLE   The best workout in the world isn't right for your dog if your dog doesn't enjoy the activity. For example, you may think that a half hour of steady retrieving is just the ticket for your Labrador, but your Lab may be one of the rare retrievers who could not care less about putting a stick in his mouth, much less bringing it back to you.

SAFE Your dog is not likely to have safety on his mind when he's streaking down a hill after a flying disk or thrashing wildly in the undergrowth looking for the ball you hit for him to retrieve. You're the one who has to think about fleas and ticks, broken glass, poisonous snakes, and all the other hazards that may await. Dogs who are exercised after dark should wear collars or vests with reflective strips to make them more visible to passing motorists.

LEGAL It's up to you to make sure that the activities you plan for your dog are legal, that the property you're on is public land, and that it may be used for the purpose for which you are using it.

CONSIDERATE OF OTHERS Even if you and your dog have a perfect right to take your place alongside all the other joggers who circle a lake in the park every morning, be considerate of others who may be frightened if your big black off-leash dog appears to be running right at them and their small child or tiny Chihuahua. It's all too easy for irate non–dog owners to band together and have dogs banned from recreational areas, based on their experiences with irresponsible pet owners and uncontrolled dogs. Put your dog on-leash or decide to go out an hour earlier to beat the crowd.

What Exercise for Dogs Isn't

SOMETHING A SINGLE DOG DOES SPONTANEOUSLY Happy as the average dog may be to join you on the path, trail, or beach, it's a rare dog who takes the initiative to exercise. (Many humans will readily recognize this phenomenon.)

SOMETHING TWO OR MORE DOGS NECESSARILY DO TOGETHER Two dogs who will play together for hours on end in your living room, once let out to romp in the yard may stand side by side at the back door, waiting to be let back in. Your participation is the missing ingredient. (Be honored!)

SOMETHING UNSUPERVISED Your dog's exercise should not be unsupervised any more than anything else he does outdoors (or indoors, for that matter, if he's still in the puppy stage).

SOMETHING THAT'S DONE ON THE END OF A CHAIN IN THE YARD Some dog owners are under the impression that their dogs, like their children, are hard at play as long as they're out in the sunshine and fresh air. Even if a dog had the room to run around freely on the end of a chain, chances are that his spirit would be so dejected from the social isolation or so frustrated at all the things that were just beyond his reach that the only "exercise" he'd get would be from barking out his loneliness, chewing his feet in boredom, or pacing back and forth in frustration.

SOMETHING THAT HAPPENS IN NICE WEATHER ONLY A regular program of exercise cannot wait for clear days and mild temperatures. In most regions of the country, it's possible for the truly dedicated to get outdoors for at least short periods of exercise all year round. It may mean, however, that you have to avoid the hot part of the day in summer or the worst of winter's chill before sunrise and after sunset. Also, foul-weather gear for dogs is becoming as popular as it is for human athletes.

SOMETHING THAT'S LIKELY TO HAPPEN WITHOUT PLANNING Finally, it's best to face up to the fact that regular exercise with your dog probably is not going to happen just because you've decided it should. Until this new way of life becomes habitual, you probably will have to plan for it, get it on the calendar, and forbid yourself from renegotiating your decision every morning when the alarm goes off.

Benefits of Exercise

More is being learned every day about the way our mental and emotional states affect the way our bodies function, and vice versa. The long-suspected interconnectedness of the mind, body, emotions, and spirit are beginning to be able to be measured, both in people and in dogs. The upshot is that there no longer is any doubt that exercise stands right alongside a wholesome diet, clean air and water, and a stress-reduced lifestyle as an important component of health and well-being in humans and dogs alike. Benefits to your dog of regular, vigorous exercise include the following:

Effects on Physical Fitness

MUSCLES AND BONES Muscles and bones, as well as tendons and ligaments, are strengthened by exercise, making it less likely for dogs to injure themselves by sudden bursts of activity. Dogs who may have a genetic predisposition to structural abnormalities such as disk problems and hip dysplasia may actually have fewer symptoms as a result of regular *moderate* exercise that strengthens the muscles and provides for more stability in

Exercise is defined as an energy-burning, whole-body workout. (Karen Blessing, Anne Westall, and Blake)

the joints. (If your dog suffers from any kind of degenerative joint disease, ask your veterinarian for help in designing an exercise program that will strengthen your dog's muscles without overstressing his joints.)

DIGESTION/ELIMINATION Digestive problems such as gas, bloating, flatulence, and constipation seem to be less common in dogs who are physically active.

HEART AND LUNGS The capacity of the heart and lungs in dogs who regularly run or swim is considerably greater than in those who don't. They are able to maintain a high level of exertion longer and with less effort than dogs who are infrequently exercised.

ENERGY, STRENGTH, ENDURANCE, BALANCE, COORDINATION, FLEXIBILITY These key features of the canine athlete are just as evident as they are in human athletes. And just as in human athletes, a sure sign of too much or too intense exercise is decreased energy, strength, coordination, and even enthusiasm for a favored activity.

APPETITE Dogs who exercise regularly are much less likely to be overweight. Hard exercise not only burns calories but seems to discourage overeating. Who knows — maybe dogs overeat out of depression and anxiety, just as many people do!

Effects on Behavior Problems

RESTLESSNESS A dog with excess energy to burn may be restless, distracted, and irritable. Sustained exercise such as trotting, running, or swimming releases chemicals called endorphins into the brain, causing a general feeling of well-being that is nature's antidote to anxiety.

BOREDOM   Active dogs are generally alert and energetic. By combining physical exercise with problem solving, as in throwing a retrieving dummy into a lake for your dog to find and carry back, you can enhance the effect of the swimming exercise alone.

STRESS   Many modern dogs live relatively stressful lives just because there is so much change, ambiguity, and variability in their daily lives. Setting aside a specific block of time for daily exercise adds welcome routine to that part of their day — which in turn reduces their feelings of stress.

Effects on the Dog/Owner Partnership

QUALITY TIME   Exercising with your dog is an excellent way to spend quality time together. The activity and interaction with your dog should be absorbing enough so that your mind empties itself of other concerns and allows you to give your dog your undivided attention. Your dog, of course, could ask for no more than to be outdoors, get to do something fun, and spend time with you.

SHARED ACTIVITY   There is something about a cooperative endeavor with your dog that cements the bond between the two of you. This is true of giving him a bath, teaching him to shake hands, investigating side by side the damage that last night's storm did to your flower bed, and certainly exercising together. Though he may not be able to chat with you about his workout after it's over, his unflagging enthusiasm to get started and keep going as well as his happy exhaustion once he's back home in the living room say clearer than words that he had a really good time.

KNOWLEDGE AND UNDERSTANDING   There is a lot to be learned about your dog in the process of planning a sensible exercise program to increase his overall level of fitness while having fun together. Not only will you be able to see changes in his muscle tone, weight, and endurance, but you should also see positive changes in his behavior, particularly if he had been exhibiting the boredom and restlessness of an inactive life.

LEADERSHIP ROLE   Exercising with your dog is an unobtrusive way of enhancing your leadership role. Your dog will soon enough learn that the game begins and ends when you say so, and by occasionally asking your dog to execute a command, for instance to lie down while you change into your running shoes, you will be reassuring him that you are on the job as captain of the team.

Making It Happen

If you've ever resolved to get in shape yourself, you know that the best of intentions don't always translate into sustained action. Don't make the mistake of thinking it will be an altogether different story because the beneficiary of this fitness regimen is your dog. It won't happen that way. To improve the chances of success, concentrate on the following:

SCHEDULING   Take a careful look at your day and pick a time slot when you will almost always be able to spend at least fifteen minutes exercising with your dog. If you use a daily calendar to keep track of appointments and the like, treat these exercise periods like any other important commitment and enter them, say, for a week in advance. Get in the habit of making up any sessions that you have to miss. To honor your dog's craving for routine, try to exercise at the same time every day.

PREPARING IN ADVANCE   Even though exercising your dog is intended to be fun, it is also a serious conditioning or reconditioning program for him and possibly for you as well. You will be more likely to take it seriously if you spend time and effort in advance preparations. For instance, you may want to purchase certain equipment that will allow you to exercise regardless of the weather, or you may decide you'd like to get a collapsible water bowl that you can slip inside your knapsack.

REWARDING YOURSELF   Given how difficult it is to stick with any new regimen long enough for it to become a habit, you should be doubly generous in rewarding yourself appropriately for your efforts in making this work. Figure out what kinds of reinforcement will make you more likely to stick with the program, then make sure you cash them all in.

Keeping It Effective

VARIETY   To give your dog the benefits of different kinds of exercise, vary your activities. For instance, jogging builds cardiovascular fitness but does little for flexibility. To increase flexibility, include some jumping and catching activities such as flying disk.

FLEXIBILITY   There will be days when your dog shouldn't run — for instance, if he has a cut on his foot pad. Have in your back pocket some substitute activities, such as teaching the dog to sit up with front paws in the air (this strengthens back muscles without wear and tear on a sore foot). The important thing is to try to do some kind of exercise every day.

REGULARITY   Human couch potatoes are told that exercising every other day is often enough for maximum benefits, and that more isn't necessarily better. But some people need the discipline of exercising every day. Otherwise, every other day soon becomes every third day until they're managing to hit the trail only once a week. For your dog's sake and his love of routine, every day is probably not too often (though of course you will monitor him closely to make sure you're not overdoing it).

MONITORING Don't rely on general impressions alone to keep track of "how you're doing." Weigh your dog every week or two to make sure he's not losing weight (unless that's part of the plan, in which case you should weigh him every week to make sure weight loss is not too rapid). Observe your dog carefully for any signs of pain or lameness such as reluctance to get up; check his foot pads every few days to make sure they're not torn or abraded (dogs who don't exercise regularly tend to have thin foot pads that are easily injured; it takes a little while before exercise toughens them up). Also check your dog's vital statistics on a regular basis and compare them to what you've already recorded as his normal pulse, respiration rate, and temperature (see Your Dog's Veterinary Records Book at the end of chapter 9).

VET CHECKS Take your notes with you when you visit your veterinarian to have her examine your dog a few months into his new regimen — or sooner if requested to do so.

Keeping It Safe

BY LOCALE Different locales present different dangers that you should keep in mind as you go out to exercise. A wilderness area where you and your dog can hike might be a hard place to find help if one of you is injured. A city park with wonderful jogging trails may host a criminal element after dark that you really don't want to encounter.

BY TERRAIN Very rough terrain can be extremely hard on muscles and joints that are weak from years of inactivity. Such areas might best be avoided until your dog's (and your?) overall condition has improved. By contrast, icy city streets can be unbelievably slippery — and very conducive to sprains and muscle pulls — for one or both of you.

BY SEASON When you first begin exercising with your dog, you may not realize how heat and humidity can affect you — and especially him, because he cannot cool himself by perspiring. It's important to carry a supply of water for drinking and spritzing, but probably it's even wiser to avoid strenuous exercise on days when the temperature/humidity index is high enough to warrant warnings from your local television station. At the other extreme, a dog without a bushy undercoat can easily become chilled by wet weather combined with wind. Such dogs should wear sweaters that cover their chests and stomachs and should be kept moving to generate more body heat. (Observe your own dog; if he is shivering, he is cold.)

BY TIME OF DAY   The time of day when you exercise relates to other safety concerns, including temperature extremes and the possibility of finding yourself in need of help when no one is around. On the other hand, exercising very early or late can avoid other hazards such as traffic and human congestion. You will have to weigh the pros and cons of exercising at different times of day for the specific area in which you live.

BY EQUIPMENT   Collars or vests with reflective tape are important gear for exercising with your dog after dark. It goes without saying that your dog's collar (with ID tags) and leash should be inspected regularly for wear. Cold- and wet-weather gear, including dog boots for jagged ice and city streets covered with rock salt, can all help keep exercise safe for you and your dog.

BY PRECAUTION/PREVENTION   Do as much as you possibly can to protect your dog from the scourge of fleas, ticks, flies, wild animals, and dogs running at large. At the very least, speak to your veterinarian about flea and tick prevention and make sure all your dog's vaccinations — particularly rabies — are up-to-date. And it goes without saying that your male or female dog has been sterilized and will not be driven to run off in search of a mate when allowed off-lead.

BY TRAINING   One of the most effective ways to keep your dog safe in the great outdoors is by training him to obey promptly some basic commands such as "Come," "Down," and "Stay." If you've taken him through an obedience training course, you already have a significant degree of control over him. But for outdoor exercise, you might want to learn how to keep him under control when he is off-lead as well.

Keeping It Responsible

CONTROLLING YOUR DOG   One of the most responsible things you can do in terms of protecting the rights and property of others, as well as the health and safety of your dog, is to make sure your dog is *under your control at all times*. This doesn't mean that he's on a three-foot leash at your side. It means that he will respond promptly to your commands even from a distance and while distractions are present.

MAINTAINING VACCINATIONS   As long as your dog has been vaccinated, he cannot get infections from other dogs. Neither can he spread infection to other dogs who may not yet be fully immunized or who for one reason or another were not successfully immunized. Even unvaccinated dogs don't deserve to catch a potentially fatal disease just because their owners failed to keep their vaccinations up-to-date. Keep track of the vaccination certificates you receive from your veterinarian and have your dog's rabies tag attached to his collar. In case there's ever a question of when or if your dog was vaccinated, it's good to have the proof right at hand.

RESPECTING OTHERS' RIGHTS Don't get so enthusiastic about your dog's new exercise regimen that you forget the rights of others, monopolizing a small pond of water, for example, when others might want to enjoy it. Remind yourself frequently that you and your dog can suffer if non–dog owning citizens band together to have restrictions imposed on where you can be with your dog.

CLEANING UP AFTER YOUR DOG Now that it's the law virtually everywhere, nothing will turn the public against your dog faster than observing that you have failed to clean up your dog's feces. *Always* be prepared with extra paper towels or plastic baggies. There's nothing like a nice brisk run to stimulate your dog to have an additional bowel movement that you didn't expect and aren't prepared for.

OBEYING ORDINANCES REGARDING WHEN AND WHERE They may not be posted as prominently as you might wish, but ignorance of the local "rules" about where and when your dog is allowed to be off-leash in a city park is no defense. Check with your local humane society or Parks and Recreation Department — not necessarily with other dog owners — to be sure. Being a responsible dog owner includes knowing what your legal responsibilities are and complying with them.

Keeping It Fun

For Your Dog

RESPECTING HER SPECIAL INTERESTS Your dog will have favorite things, just like you do, and others that she's not so crazy about. You need only observe your dog to find out how she feels about whatever it is you're introducing. Under no circumstances should exercise be an activity that she doesn't truly enjoy.

RESPECTING HIS PACE If your dog happily retrieves a stick but walks it back to you rather than races back with it, so be it. At least he's moving on the way out. If his pace in both directions is snail-like, let him retrieve a few sticks for fun, but keep looking for something he may be willing to do at a brisker pace. And remember: Even this is *far* better than nothing, just as it is for humans.

RESPECTING HIS QUIRKS So he ducks whenever the flying disk goes overhead, or he only wants to wade in the pond instead of swimming. So be that, too. Maybe he'll climb stairs all day long for the treat at the top. Just keep looking — you'll find the things he really likes.

KNOWING WHEN TO STOP A trim young dog may tire more quickly than a pudgy older one. The only rule is that when *your* dog lets you know — by her body language, slowing pace, halfhearted attitude — that she's had it for the day, it's time to stop. Actually, it's a little past time to stop. As you get to know your dog's limitations better, you'll be able to stop before she gets really tired. It's important for you to discover this as soon as possible, because many a dog has run herself right into the ground. The spirit may be willing long after the body is unable.

For You

AVOIDING POTENTIAL UPSETS You know what ticks you off. Wanting your terrier to be fearless in the field, even if he's not. Having a soaking-wet dog shake himself all over your car. Having your dog stop in mid-stride to eat green grass at the roadside. Find ways to avoid these irritants, for your dog's sake as well as for your own. Keep your terrier on the sidewalk where he's happiest. Cover your car's backseat with an old towel. There's always a way, and it's always worth looking for.

MAKING ENOUGH TIME Neither you nor your dog will profit much from exercise under duress. Not enough time, getting a late start, needing to rush — these are not conducive to having a good workout that leaves you feeling refreshed. Go back to that schedule and make it work for you.

STAYING IN THE MOMENT Despite all the wonderful things about it, exercising with your dog can seem like one more chore if you let it. The best way to avoid that feeling is to experience the moment, the movement of your body, the breath going in and out of your lungs, your arm reaching back and then pulling forward to throw the ball. Even better, keep your eye on your dog. Be in her moment with her. Watch her body tense as you wind up. Notice the intensity in her eyes. Know how much this means to her. That's nice work if you can get it.

BEING MINDFUL OF BENEFITS Finally, think every once in a while about all the well-known benefits of exercise — for you and your dog. You may even want to keep a log that charts his progress over time. If you feel "the goals" have been accomplished and there's nothing more to achieve, go back to the drawing board and think up ways to add variety to the regimen. Come up with new activities so that every day of the week has its own program. Invite a friend to bring his dog so the four of you can work out together. As a last resort, tell your veterinarian you're thinking of cutting back or laying off for a while, and that you're not sure your dog is really getting any benefit anymore. Her reaction should get you back on track in a hurry!

TEN STEPS TO FORMING A NEIGHBORHOOD DOG PARK

If there really isn't any convenient outdoor space in your community where dogs can exercise (and socialize) off-lead, it may be time to petition your local community board to create a dog park. Activists in towns and communities across the nation have been successful in getting space set aside for this purpose. (To talk with some, contact The HSUS for names and addresses. Find out what works and what doesn't — you can benefit from the experience of others.) If you are interested in working to make a dog park a reality where you live, here are ten steps that others have found helpful.

1. Find a half-dozen or so others who share your enthusiasm and commitment. Give yourselves a name (for example, the Woodside Dog Owners Association) and advertise an open meeting, inviting other interested parties to attend. Make it clear that the purpose of the meeting is to draw up a plan for petitioning your community government for a fenced outdoor space that will be used exclusively as a dog park.

2. Create a proposal that specifies that the purpose of the park is to permit dog owners to exercise their dogs off-lead. Using statistics on the numbers of dogs who live in the area, suggest how much space will be needed, and list the kinds of amenities that will be necessary, such as lights, water, good drainage, grass, fencing, shade trees, benches for owners, trash receptacles, and convenient parking. Include in your request that the town or city maintain the property, collect garbage, and mow the grass — as it does in other municipal parks. Come up with cost estimates. In this era of budget-tightening, the cost issue is one of the biggies.

3. Know how funds will be raised to pay for things the group will be responsible for, such as stationery, printing, and postage, a supply of pooper scoopers and plastic bags, advertising and publicity, telephone and fax, educational activities such as tattoo clinics, first-aid seminars, and a newsletter to share information and tips on various subjects of interest to dog owners.

4. Don't overlook local funding sources. Various pet-related businesses, such as feed and supply stores, training schools, and grooming shops, and even veterinarians, might be interested in helping to sponsor the dog park in exchange

for publicity. On the other hand, branches of local government, such as the Parks and Recreation Department, may charge user fees that responsible dog owners are willing to pay for the benefits that they — and their dogs — get from the park.

5. Stipulate what the dog park rules and policies will be (for example, no aggressive dogs, no puppies under four months, no unlicensed or unvaccinated dogs, no unattended dogs, no continuously barking dogs or dogs who are otherwise out of control, no female dogs in season).

6. List the potential *benefits* to the community, such as fewer dogs running off-leash, thereby decreasing the risk of children being bitten or coming in contact with dog feces on playgrounds and other unrestricted areas. Stress also increased levels of owner responsibility in such areas as scooping up after their dogs, keeping dogs on-leash when not in the dog park, having their dogs licensed, vaccinated, and trained, and even obtaining professional help for serious problems like aggression.

7. So that your proposal is balanced, discuss possible *risks,* such as dogfights, biting incidents, owners who refuse to abide by the dog park rules and policies, resistance by other citizen groups, including those who don't want to lose part of their park to a group of dogs. Indicate how these problems will be managed (exclusion from the park for rules violations, presentation of statistics showing the percentage of taxpayers in the community who own dogs and therefore have a legitimate claim to part of the park for their recreational use).

8. Take time to meet with and enlist the support of animal control officers, veterinarians, and other local groups that stand to benefit from the creation of a dog park, including non–dog owners.

9. Request a hearing with city government to discuss your proposal, pointing out that your group of tax-paying residents only wants its fair share of public land to be set aside for this purpose.

10. When local government hears your proposal, send two or three calm, knowledgeable, and articulate association members to represent the group. Keep your eye on the prize and be willing to negotiate and compromise.

Chasing a flying disk is great
exercise. (Andrew Roberts
and Suka)

Enjoying Your Dog

Everyday Fun and Games | 16

If you love dressing to the nines and dining at four-star restaurants but your husband would rather be glacier skiing in Alaska, then you know firsthand that "fun and games" is a matter of personal preference. If so, you'll be relieved to know that we're *not* going to dictate which activities you must share with your dog in order to have fun together. That's really up to you and your dog, along with the rest of the family. Nevertheless, there are some "rules of play" that may help you discover all the ways your dog is able (*ready* and *willing* go without saying!) to share your life.

What's Fun for Dogs in General?
- social activities (being with their families)
- using their senses of smell, feeling (teeth), taste, hearing, sight
- mimicking natural hunting behaviors such as digging, chasing, grasping, mouthing, chewing, shaking, tossing
- investigating and exploring out-of-doors
- meeting challenges they can master
- being rewarded (by your attention, praise, petting, play, treats)

What Does *Your* Dog Like to Do?

- First and foremost, he wants to be with you — look for ways to include him in as many family activities as possible.
- Observe your dog to figure out what he can and cannot do. (Does he have physical limitations, such as very short legs, that would make it hard for him to be your jogging partner or emotional limitations, such as unwillingness to let you out of his sight, that would make hide-and-seek stressful for him?)
- Observe your dog's natural play behaviors to see where his instincts lead him. (Is he always digging? Is his nose always on the ground following a scent, or is it more often up in the air, sniffing the breeze? Does he pick up objects in his mouth and bring them to you, all on his own?)
- Keep an open mind about what your dog might like to do. (Encourage and "teach" new activities, then observe his response before deciding which to pursue, which to drop.)

What's in It for You?

Involving your dog deeply in your life is more than the answer to her prayers and the right thing to do. It offers many benefits to you, too:

- having a happy dog
- knowing it's in your power to make your dog happy
- having a tired dog
- having a calm dog
- having your dog's company much of the time
- getting outdoors more than you otherwise might
- building a deeper bond with your dog than you may have thought possible

"MY FAVORITE THINGS"

"I like to help Miss go through the mail in the breakfast nook. Actually, I don't care so much about the mail. What I really like is that she keeps me company while I stretch out on the bench and take a nap." — Toby, mixed-breed, nine years old

"Who would even *want* to resist fresh black earth in the garden? So many delicious possibilities for flying feet to uncover!" — JR, Jack Russell terrier, eight months old

For an active dog with a strong drive to retrieve, a game of ball is the ultimate reward. (Deborah Salem's Bonnie)

- earning the admiration of others ("Gee, *my* dog doesn't do anything but eat and sleep!")
- knowing you've motivated others to start spending more time with their dogs

General Prerequisites
- a dog who's housetrained
- a dog who's not aggressive
- a dog who's been spayed or neutered
- a dog who's vaccinated, licensed, and wears ID tags
- a dog who's under control (will sit, come, and stay on command; will walk on-leash without pulling)
- a dog who's been exposed to other dogs, many kinds of people, young children, other animals, cars, bicycles, various terrain, and so on
- a dog who's received his veterinarian's approval to engage in vigorous physical activities
- an owner who is prepared to protect her dog from whatever hazards may exist (fleas, ticks, mosquitoes, foxtails, poisonous plants, and unfriendly animals in fields, woods, and parks; dangerous debris in unfamiliar outdoor areas; the possibility of drowning or breaking a limb during specific activities; frostbite, heatstroke, and other seasonal hazards)

Things to Do with Your Dog

There is no limit to the number and kinds of things you can do with your dog. For clarity, our suggestions are being divided into *planned fun and games* and *spontaneous activities*. Planned activities are those that you decide in advance to do with your dog, and spontaneous activities are things that you may set out to do alone, then decide on the spur of the moment to invite your dog to do with you. The lists below are by no means complete — you definitely will add to them over time. In adding new activities, use as criteria that your dog participate voluntarily; that he never be compelled to do anything that he either fears or has no interest in; that the activities be safe; and that they not impinge on the rights of others, including other animals and wildlife.

Planned Fun and Games

SPORTS   Some physical activities come naturally to dogs, and dogs and owners can do them together.

- catch the disk (There are now disks made especially for dogs, in different sizes, that are easier on their mouths and teeth than the original flying saucer designed for human use; look for them in pet-supply stores and mail-order catalogs.)
- catch (Make sure balls are made of nontoxic materials and are not so small that they can be swallowed.)
- retrieving (The best choices are items specifically made for dogs to retrieve; avoid sticks or other objects with rough edges or sharp points.)

"MY FAVORITE THINGS"

"Bob's my guy. He's a wildlife artist. We put his easel in the Bronco and drive way up into the hills to look for animals to paint." — Red, Irish setter mix, four years old

"I love everything where I live now. I get to stay indoors with my new family and even though there's no grass inside our house, there are lots of pluses. Probably my favorite thing is listening to the tap-tap-tap of my mom's keyboard while I hang out under the desk with her feet." — Duchess, rottweiler, one year old

- walking (Walks can range from a slow amble around the neighborhood, where the dog is permitted to sniff every new scent laid down since his last outing, to something more like a power walk, where a brisk pace is maintained and stopping and sniffing are discouraged — though there's nothing to prohibit the last leg of the trip from being an amble, which gives your dog a chance to cool down from the physical exercise and use his nose to find out who and what is new in the neighborhood.)
- jogging (Condition your dog as you would yourself, increasing time and distance a little at a time; proceed gradually to allow your dog's foot pads to toughen; on hot, sunny days, make sure paved surfaces are not so hot that you cannot hold your hand on them for five to ten seconds.)
- running (ditto)
- hiking (Hiking can be surprisingly rigorous; begin on beginners' trails, bring along a supply of water for you and your dog, and be sure to keep your dog either on-leash or on a special nonrestrictive harness with ID tags securely attached.)
- swimming (Ask your veterinarian about products to protect your dog's eyes and ears from prolonged exposure to water.)

TRICKS   (things that dogs might do on their own, but when done on command, allow you to reward them, and in so doing, subtly reinforce your role as leader)

Notes on teaching tricks:
- You should feel free to teach your dog a trick any way that works, as long as you keep it positive and fun.
- Look for logical ways to break tricks down into distinct parts that can be taught sequentially; practice one part until your dog knows it well, then add another part and practice the two together, and so on.
- The general principles of obedience training apply to teaching tricks: Guide or lure the dog into a correct response; give a name to what you are asking and always use the same one; praise warmly just as the dog decides to comply; and repeat the whole procedure as often as necessary yet as briefly as possible in order to avoid turning the process into a drill.
- A tidbit of food used as a lure works especially well in teaching tricks, and what difference does it really make if your dog will only "perform" for his treat?
- Tricks range from very simple to quite complex, with the dog often deciding which is which. Often the very best tricks are those that just seem to evolve naturally from a particular dog's personality and interests. To

Even a routine walk with your dog can be an adventure.

"My favorite thing in the whole world is going with my dad to Mo Greene's to get the bagels on Sunday morning. At Greene's I play gently for a few minutes with Henry, Mo's old dog. Then Mo goes behind the counter and gets me a bit of turkey or a wedge of cheese." — Eloise, mixed-breed, one year old

"When Dad works in the yard, I get to help. Well, I don't really help, but I do get to be with him all day. Sometimes I follow behind him so closely that if he stops suddenly, I bump into his legs." — Vidalia, golden retriever, eight years old

encourage him to repeat something that he habitually or occasionally does, such as running in and crouching as you wind up to throw his ball, give the action a name that you will consistently use when you want him to do this. Then, faithfully reward him every time he repeats "Crouch" on command, and the next thing you know you'll be amazing your friends with a lively demonstration of "Scruffy Playing Shortstop."

Here is a selection of tricks to get you started. Challenge yourself to come up with at least one original trick of your own.

- roll over
- shake hands
- catch! (a biscuit or dog treat, cut-up vegetable pieces, a ball or other toy)
- play dead
- fetch (This is half of a retrieve, since you don't first throw the object out for him, and objects are usually such things as the daily paper, your slippers, or other household objects, perhaps one of his toys.)
- carry (his toy to or from the park, a small parcel home from the corner drugstore, or various objects you need when the two of you garden together)
- jump (straight up from a sitting position, over an obstacle that you point at, into the back of your station wagon, etc.)
- pirouette (turns in circles with head and front paws in the air)
- dance (lets you hold his paws lightly while you carefully lead him back and forth à la ballroom style)
- kiss (on the cheek, for hygienic reasons, though the slurpier the better)

GAMES Part sport, part trick, these are activities that include a learning component and also allow the dog to be rewarded.

- find it (by name, such as "the red ball" or "the biscuit" or "Bill" — the objects to be found may include family members, other pets, specific toys, hidden treats)
- hide and seek (best played with two people, one to hide and the other to command the dog to "Stay," then to "Find her")
- tug of war (Tug of war is extremely stimulating to dogs, as they seem to slip easily into the role of Great Gray battling a rival wolf for the leg of an antelope. To prevent your friendly game of "tug" from degenerating into a serious contest of wills — and possibly aggression — keep a close eye on how your dog is responding. Before you begin, he should know the

command "Leave it," or "Drop it," which applies to anything he takes in his mouth. If he's reliable about letting go of whatever you ask him to — and is then immediately rewarded for doing so — proceed with tug-of-war slowly, interrupting the game periodically by asking him to "Leave it." Make it very clear to your dog that this game begins and ends when you say so.)

- roughhouse (The same cautions apply here because the same danger exists; the game closely simulates fighting behavior and unless your dog is periodically reminded that you are in charge, aggressive/competitive feelings could be aroused.)

Spontaneous Activities

These activities are drawn from your everyday lifestyle. You are not designing these with your dog in mind as much as you are including her, just as you might include your children. Our examples are intended to show the wide range of possibilities.

- getting the mail (either riding the elevator to the lobby of an apartment building, strolling down the drive to the mailbox, or hopping into the car for a drive to the town post office; whichever the case, your dog might like to "carry" one piece home)
- "helping" with deliveries (going to the door, greeting the delivery person, snuffling the bags and boxes)
- watching television (Some dogs can really get interested in nature programs, but almost all dogs are likely to enjoy being with you on the couch!)

"MY FAVORITE THINGS"

"Are you kidding? When I see that ball come down off the shelf, my heart nearly bursts! One morning I caught it twenty-seven times in a row without missing. And believe me, Joey doesn't try to make it easy!" — Zack, mixed-breed, five years old

"I work six days a week and have to admit I hope I never retire. Our family owns a small convenience store on the main street in town, and it's my job to make everyone feel welcome and safe. I have lots of special friends who give me a happy thump on the shoulder when they see me. The best part is I can keep an eye on my folks." — King, Lab/shepherd mix, four years old

- running errands: on foot or in the car (Dogs just seem to know when they're going somewhere for a reason, as opposed to taking a casual ride or a walk; cautions include never ever tying a dog outside a store, even for a minute, or ever, ever leaving a dog unattended inside a car parked in the sun.)
- raking leaves (This is pure fun for your dog, but somewhat less fun for you if you really want those piles to stay neatly formed.)
- gardening (Watch out for toxic gardening supplies such as slug and snail bait, fertilizers, and pesticides.)
- doing laundry (Put away all detergents and other substances that a dog may like sampling but will surely regret later.)
- cleaning the attic (Attics hold hazards as well as treasures, so this might make a better task for an older, more sedate dog than for the youngster who still cannot contain her enthusiasm to taste, touch, and swallow.)
- making dinner (A kitchen filled with family members *and* the good smells of cooking food is like a magnet to a dog, but beware liquids boiling on the stove as well as the temptation to offer "just a taste" of everything in your pantry.)
- taking out the garbage (As in the case of getting the mail, dogs just like to go along on routine outings.)
- picking up the children from soccer practice or the spouse at the train station (A ride in the car for any reason is popular with most dogs who learned about car travel at an early age, but when it results in a reunion with family members — it's even better.)
- visiting friends (Knowing that your dog is welcome in the homes of your friends is one of the truly proud moments in a dog owner's life; for your dog, home is where her family is.)

"Mmm, let's see. That's a tough one. I really like sleeping in the hall closet next to the hot air register. That's during the day. In the evening I like sleeping on my mom's lap while she watches the Discovery channel. She always wakes me when there's something I need to see, even though she knows I can't see much anymore. Then she strokes me until I fall back asleep. Probably that's my favorite thing." — Lilli, Yorkshire terrier, fourteen years old

"MY FAVORITE THINGS"

Activities Not Recommended

Some activities that many people enjoy with their dogs nevertheless involve inhumane practices and cannot be recommended. Common events that are not recommended include the following:

- competitive events such as greyhound races or sled races (Because competition, winning, and profit motive are what drive these events, training methods are often and perhaps inevitably inhumane.)
- activities that exploit other animals (sport hunting, coon hunts, pursuit of rabbits, squirrels, birds, barnyard animals)
- high-risk activities (riding in the bed of a pickup truck, on motorcycles or surfboards, jumping out of airplanes, snorkeling)
- activities that your dog is not suited for, physically or emotionally
- activities that your dog doesn't want to participate in (in general or on a given day)

Activism 17

In the last chapter we discussed how sharing everyday activities with your dog could deepen the bond between you. Now let's look at a whole different category of activities that can also deepen your bond with your dog while helping to make the world a more hospitable place not just for you and your dog, but for all dogs and their owners.

The Canine "Cause": Then and Now

In earlier chapters we talked at length about the pretty shabby way that the human race, through the years, has repaid the dog for his loyalty and devotion. At almost all times in our shared history, dogs have been treasured and pampered by some and reviled and mistreated by others. Centuries ago, the same tribe or village, or even the same person, would feed and care for certain dogs while driving off or killing, perhaps eating, others. Today's version of this phenomenon is that there are people who dote on a certain breed but have little concern for others, and other people who value purebred dogs highly yet mixed-breeds not at all (or vice versa).

You may or may not be aware of the fact that dogs in this country, where they are so popular and populous as to be found in roughly four out of every ten households, nevertheless hold a relatively low station in terms of public policy. In many European cities, dogs may accompany their owners on trains and buses, to restaurants and shops of all kinds, to hotels, parks, and public monuments. In this country, exclusion is more the rule than the exception for the ordinary house pet (federal law now mandates that service dogs assisting people with disabilities shall have access to all public facilities and conveyances). In the worse cases, towns, cities, and even some states have tried to pass legislation that would completely ban certain breeds, such as the "pit bull," considered by the uninformed to be dangerous by nature because of the actions of some very irresponsible pit bull owners. Communities have passed ordinances that limit the number of dogs a person may own, as well as the maximum weight and size that a resident dog may be. Many landlords and cooperative/condominium boards have strict "No Pets" or "No Dogs" clauses in their leases and contracts.

Pro-Dog/Anti-Dog Forces

In the most simplistic terms, an ongoing war is being waged between those who like dogs and those who don't like dogs. To be more precise, it isn't really the dogs they don't like, but the behavior of dogs with irresponsible owners, who believe it is their inalienable right to own and breed a dog, yet whose failure to train, control, and confine their pets has resulted in dogs who infringe on the rights of others and generally make a public nuisance of themselves. The responsible pro-dog forces are fighting for their right to enjoy their own dogs in more ways and places and to see all dogs receive more protection from those who would exclude, neglect, exploit, or abuse them. The anti-dog forces are fighting just as hard to limit and restrict dogs so that they won't be further inconvenienced by those who bark, who deposit waste on lawns, sidewalks, playgrounds, and in many public places, who roam at large, who chase and frighten their children and themselves, and who harass or even kill livestock and wildlife.

In recent years, there have been a number of widely publicized exposés of the horrors of mass commercial dog-breeding establishments, where dogs are kept in inhumane conditions (so-called puppy mills); pet-theft rings that steal household pets from their own yards and sell them to research institutions; and irresponsible purebred breeders who have severely compromised the physical, emotional, and genetic health of many popular kinds of purebred dogs. The extensive media coverage of these problems the pet overpopulation problem has begun to make a difference. Some municipalities have imposed different kinds of measures designed to discourage the breeding of dogs, while others are offering financial incentives, such as lower license fees, to owners who spay or neuter their dogs. A number of states have passed puppy "lemon laws" to help protect consumers and curb the abuses of puppy mills. Some states are also increasing the penalty for animal abuse from a misdemeanor to a felony. At the same time, public support for national and local animal protection organizations has experienced phenomenal growth.

Encouraging as these trends are, there still is urgent work to be done. People who just want dogs to go away need to be helped to understand that the real problem is not the dogs but the irresponsible actions of their owners. Irresponsible owners, in turn, may be unaware of the consequences of their attitudes and actions, and, in addition, lack the knowledge and skills necessary to train and maintain their dogs in such ways that they are a pleasure rather than a nuisance at home and in the neighborhood. Finally, what the nation's dogs need are for more of us who treasure them to step forward and become activists in their behalf. If you would like to join the struggle to improve conditions for dogs and dog owners in this country, you'll find that there is no shortage of ways to help. Here are some groups that you may want to become involved with:

Local Shelters and Humane Organizations

An easy and effective way to help the dogs (and other animals) in your own community is to become a member or contributor to your local animal shelter or humane society. Not only will you support the organization's valuable work, but usually you also will receive a copy of its newsletter and other materials that will keep you abreast of events that are taking place in the community relative to animals. Many shelter newsletters spell out for people who want to contribute in practical ways shelter "wish lists," which may include everything from towels and blankets to office equipment and used cars.

If you'd be willing to contribute some of your time, shelters and humane groups always need volunteers to assist in carrying out many aspects of their work. So short-staffed are many humane organizations that

Volunteer adoption counselors match dogs with potential adopters at animal shelters across the country.

important programs simply could not be offered at all without a committed corps of volunteers. Some of the tasks that volunteers may take on include exercising and feeding dogs, cleaning kennels, grooming dogs to increase their chances of being adopted, socializing and handling puppies, helping in the adoptions and lost-and-found departments, working in the shelter's veterinary clinic, helping to organize fund-raisers, and assisting with humane education projects. If you would like to become a shelter volunteer, you may be asked to donate, say, a half-day a week and to commit to serve as a volunteer for a minimum of six months. Shelters request this commitment because they in turn must spend one to several weeks training new volunteers, depending on the demands of the department in which they choose to work. No matter how unrelated your "real" job may seem, you may find that your local humane organization has need of someone with your skills and background to help out with special projects of many kinds.

Another way to support your local shelter is to participate in fund-raising events. One of the most popular of these is the dog walk or "walk-a-thon." The walk-a-thon (and other community events) is designed to increase public awareness of the shelter's work and at the same time raise money for one or more of the shelter's programs. To participate in a walk-a-thon with your dog, you may be asked to pay a registration fee and sign your dog up for a course of, say, one, three, or five miles, depending on what you think he can comfortably do. You'll be encouraged (though not required) to invite as many of your friends, neighbors, and coworkers as you can get to "pledge" some set amount of money for each lap or measured distance of the course

Ordinary dogs and their owners can be trained to bring meaningful stimulation and comfort to people in nursing homes, hospitals, schools, and correctional institutions. (Frank Siteman/Courtesy Hills Pet Nutrition photo)

that you and your dog walk on the designated day. It goes without saying that in order to participate safely in a walk-a-thon, your dog should be well conditioned to walking the distance you set for yourselves, as well as socialized to other dogs of all types and sizes, people, children, and large noisy crowds. Participating dogs must be leashed, licensed, and vaccinated; no females in season may take part. Usually all contestants receive a T-shirt or other memento commemorating the event and sometimes prizes or other recognition may be offered for the dog/owner team that brings in the highest dollar amount of pledges. Participating in a walk-a-thon is a wholesome experience to share with your dog while allowing you to literally stand shoulder to shoulder with a larger body of dog owners in support of a common cause.

The Humane Society of the United States

The Humane Society of the United States (HSUS) was founded in 1954 "to promote the humane treatment of animals and to foster respect, understanding, and compassion for all creatures." A nonprofit organization with a constituency of more than five million persons, The HSUS is devoted to making the world safe for all animals through legal, educational, legislative, and investigative means.

Membership in The HSUS is your first-class ticket to armchair activism! As an HSUS member at the $10 per year (or higher) level, you may elect, at no additional charge, to join the HSUS Action Alert Team. This will bring you four times a year a copy of Animal Activist Alert, a newsletter filled with articles and news about many of the most pressing issues facing all animals and special alerts about local legislative issues. The *Animal Activist Alert* stories first will cause you to want your voice for animals to be heard, then spell out exactly how to get your message to the right people. (Of course, the same letter-writing, petition-signing, and other strategies that you use to help shape public policy on the state and national levels will apply equally well to your own hometown! A letter to the editor of your local newspaper, advocating a stiffer fine and swifter enforcement of leash-law offenders, for example, may garner so much support that additional funds will be found to add one more agent to your local animal control agency.)

Although the mission of The HSUS extends to all creatures (wildlife — including marine mammals, farm animals, and research animals), it concentrates many of its resources on companion animal issues — including the welfare, well-being, safety, and protection of dogs. Whether cosponsoring National Dog Bite Prevention Week, educating law-enforcement personnel on illegal dogfighting, or investigating conditions in puppy mills, The HSUS strives to assist and enhance responsible ownership of dogs. This book is one example. The HSUS has it headquarters in Washington, D.C.

Delta Society

The Delta Society is a national membership organization with a mandate "to promote animals helping people improve their health, independence and quality of life." It sponsors a national Pet Partners Program, which prepares and certifies ordinary dogs and owners to go out into their communities to bring meaningful stimulation and comfort to adults and children in sites as varied as nursing homes, hospitals, schools, and correctional institutions. To become certified as a Pet Partner, your dog would basically need to be able to pass the equivalent of the Canine Good Citizen test discussed in chapter 14.

Delta's premier event of the year is an annual conference, which is staged around the country, presenting several days of seminars on many subjects of interest to ordinary dog owners as well as a full slate of lectures and workshops for social workers, physical therapists, and other health-care professionals interested in learning more about the many ways that dogs (and other animals) can hasten and enhance the healing of persons who are ill, as well as assist individuals with disabilities of many kinds. Large numbers of volunteers are needed each year in a different part of the country to help with the massive task of hosting the annual conference. The Delta Society relies heavily on the work of volunteers to carry out its missions at the local level. The organization is headquartered in Renton, Washington.

Local Dog Owners' Networks

Yet another way to be active in the "dog cause" is to join or help organize a local network of concerned dog owners to address whatever needs exist in your own community. Some possible activities include rescue, rehabilitation, and foster care of stray and abandoned dogs, dog walking/pet-sitting exchange among members, consumers co-op, where members may obtain substantial discounts on foods and supplies by ordering in quantity, forming play groups for puppies and dogs to socialize, and sponsoring community "dog fairs" to attract and educate the public about responsible dog ownership as well as offer tattoo clinics, first-aid seminars, advice on housetraining, and other popular programs. Dog owners' networks may also lobby community boards to win approval of a designated dog park (see Ten Steps to Forming a Neighborhood Dog Park, page 222), and join with other groups to help shape local and state legislation relative to the rights and responsibilities of dog owners.

Local Obedience or Breed Specialty Clubs

American Kennel Club–affiliated and other all-breed and mixed-breed obedience training clubs offer public training classes for owners of purebreds and mixed-breeds. Affiliation with a local club often will give you access to many kinds of educational dog-related events that may not be widely advertised, such as tattoo/microchip clinics, temperament tests, Canine Good Citizen tests, and periodic club-sponsored lectures on a variety of subjects. If your dog is a purebred, there may be a specialty club in your area that offers a chance to learn from others valuable information on training, caring for, and living with that breed. To find out if there is an obedience training or specialty club in your area, contact your local humane society or the American Kennel Club in New York City or check the Yellow Pages.

Breed Rescue Leagues

Back in chapters 3 and 4, you learned about the good work that these one-breed sheltering groups do in "rescuing" purebreds from bad or uncertain situations, evaluating and rehabilitating them where possible, then fostering them until good, permanent homes can be found. If your dog is a purebred and you feel a particular affinity for other members of that breed, you may want to become involved with some aspect of the work done by these volunteer groups. Contact your local humane society to find out if there is a rescue league for your favorite breed at work in the area.

Just as important as the work you do in connection with a dog-related organization is the example you set every day as a responsible dog owner in your community. Here are some subtle and not-so-subtle things you can do:

- Obey leash laws at all times. Extend retractable leashes only when your dog will not interfere with people or other dogs; remember that children can easily become entangled in a leash that's played out sixteen feet or more.
- Never remove your dog's ID, license, and rabies tags from her collar. Not only do these offer protection if she becomes lost, but they also signal that this dog who clinks when she walks is clearly a dog who is valued.
- Don't allow your male dog to urinate on shrubs, bushes, or flowers, automobile tires, benches, bagged trash, or other items that people handle.
- Always scoop up after your dog; carry extra plastic bags to offer without sarcasm to dog owners who aren't scooping.
- Never leave your dog unattended outside a shop. If you see an unattended dog, wait with or near him until the owner returns. Make no speeches but tell the owner you were concerned because so many dogs are stolen under similar circumstances.
- Ask your dog to "Sit" in crowded spaces such as elevators, where non–dog owners may feel uncomfortable about the close proximity of your dog. Many people feel less threatened by a sitting dog than a standing one and will be reassured to see that your dog is under your control.
- Make a habit of publicly saying "please" and "thank you" when you ask your dog to do something. Your respect for your dog may give onlookers a new way to think about dog/owner relationships.
- Keep your dog's coat clean and brushed. A well-kept dog is also one who is valued.
- Whenever someone asks if your dog is a boy or a girl, answer the question fully (but nonaggressively): "spayed female" or "neutered male."
- Be alert for opportunities to share your concern about good veterinary care. For example, while exercising at the neighborhood dog park, walking around the neighborhood, or sitting in your veterinarian's waiting room, initiate non-

judgmental conversations about such topics as heartworm prevention, flea and tick preparations, "better" dog foods, and weight control.

- Never lose sight of the fact that the irresponsible dog owner down the street offers the greatest challenge and opportunity for your positive role-modeling; it is his or her actions that can do the most damage to your rights and those of your dog and *all* dogs.

Head and shoulders down,
tail up, your dog will invite
another to play through a play
bow. (Kathy Milani's Bailey
and Brownie)

Problem Solving

Dog Behaviors/People Problems 18

The word "behavior" has appeared hundreds of times already in this book, but until now we've never stopped to explain what we actually mean by dog behavior. You may have gotten the idea that mostly, behavior means misbehavior. Happily, you would be mostly wrong!

The first thing to understand is that dog behavior, in and of itself, is neither good nor bad. It is simply the stuff that dogs naturally do — just because they are dogs. Humans have human behavior, ducks have duck behavior, and dogs have dog behavior. As luck (bad luck in this case) would have it, though, some of the dog's natural behaviors just don't fit very well into human homes and family life. Take elimination behavior, for example. As long as your dog is able to keep his toilet area a comfortable distance away from his sleeping and eating quarters, he's happily expressing normal dog behavior. Whether his toilet ends up in the backyard or behind the living room sofa is immaterial to him. Through training, your dog can learn that you much prefer that he use the backyard, and he'll do his best to please you. Deep down, however, he'll never understand what all the fuss is about. Which is why some elderly dogs, who have grown senile (just like some elderly humans), may horrify their owners by rediscovering that really excellent spot behind the sofa.

Behavior Problem, Medical Problem, or Lack of Training?

Probably you've already heard about "behavior problems" in dogs. That's a good thing. If something is defined as a problem, at least it may have a solution. Before the early 1980s, when the idea that dogs (just like people!) could be treated for behavior problems first began to gain wide acceptance, many normal dogs who were just doing what came naturally were banished to a chain in the backyard, driven into the countryside to live as "nature," it was hoped, had intended, or dropped off at the local animal shelter to "find a new home." Today, the situation is much more hopeful. A dog who's behaving in ways that most people would find unacceptable is no longer considered bad; he's a dog with a behavior problem.

Before we go any further, it's important to distinguish between a behavior problem, a medical problem, and the lack of training. If your dog has never been effectively taught where and when to eliminate, for example, he doesn't necessarily have a behavior problem. Nor does a dog with internal parasites or a bladder infection necessarily have a behavior problem. Only if your dog has been given a clean bill of health by your veterinarian, has been carefully housetrained by methods similar to those described in chapter 12, and *still* is lifting his leg inside your home should you begin to suspect that he might have what we now call a "behavior problem."

Defining Behavior Problems

To understand how dog behavior problems can affect a household, imagine that your whole family agrees that your dog's incessant barking is a real problem. You've tried everything you can think of: obedience lessons, a squirt bottle, firm and consistent reprimands whenever he barks, even treats when he stops. Nothing has worked, and gradually you all are coming to the same sad conclusion: the dog has to go. He may be the sweetest, most agreeable dog in the world. Unfortunately, in his family's opinion, he has a behavior problem. (Fortunately, we now have many additional techniques for resolving barking problems effectively and humanely.)

In essence, then, a behavior problem is anything that a particular dog is doing that is jeopardizing his relationship with his owner. Remember that behavior — in this case, barking — is neither bad nor good. It is just something that dogs do under certain circumstances because they are dogs. Behavior problems are as varied and specific and intolerable as the dog's owner — or the neighbors, the landlord, or local ordinances — say they are.

To the dog, the behavior is completely normal and appropriate under the circumstances. Of course, we already know that when people have a problem with a dog, the dog has a very serious problem indeed.

Many dogs with such a problem are those who have been relinquished to animal shelters across the nation. Ironically, many dogs are there because of their *owners'* behavior problems, not their own — for instance, owners who didn't realize how much a dog would cost, or can't find the time necessary for properly housetraining the dog. The dilemma for these dogs is that many prospective owners have been led to believe that all shelter dogs have behavior problems. After all, the argument goes, why else would they be looking for new homes?

Certainly some shelter dogs have behavior problems, as do some dogs from pet shops, professional breeders, and other sources. Reputable shelters attempt to uncover problems and will advise prospective owners that Ben, for instance, needs to live in a one-dog household, or that Sheba is best suited for older, quiet adults. Labeling shelter dogs as problem dogs is inaccurate and unfair, both to the dogs and to the humans who might otherwise adopt them.

Even if this inaccurate assumption about shelter dogs were not an inaccurate assumption, the outlook would still be positive. Most behavior problems in dogs can be resolved. What's needed is time, commitment, and know-how. You supply the first two ingredients, we'll supply the rest.

Stuff That Dogs Just Naturally Do

What follows is a partial list of common dog behaviors that have the potential to become problems for their people. Some of the behaviors are things that dogs are born with, others seem to be learned as puppies and young dogs interact with their mother, their littermates, and other dogs in their environment, and some are under the control of hormones and show up as puppies grow older. If you ask "why?" about any particular dog behavior, you'll find the answer is always rooted in the kind of life that dogs once lived before they were domesticated. Note that we are not including in our list the many endearing dog behaviors that owners rarely complain of, behaviors such as always being ready to accompany us on a walk, submitting stoically to our hugs and kisses, and wriggling their whole bodies with joy whenever we come into view. Nor are we including the many neutral behaviors that go along with being a particular kind of dog, behaviors such as retrieving objects and bringing them to us; herding other animals, including the small children in the family, trying to keep them altogether; using their remarkable noses to follow interesting scent trails; or digging furiously in dirt and rocks to unearth small animals that live there. Note, however, that even these behaviors can occasionally get a dog in trouble.

Most dogs, given the chance, will do all of the following things at one time or another, although how much, how often, and how passionately will vary from dog to dog, breed to breed, and environment to environment. This last factor, environment, is crucial, because it is often by making changes in the home environment, including how we're interacting with our dog, that we are able to begin to resolve our dog's behavior problems.

BARK   Dogs bark for the same reason that people talk — to communicate. Dogs have a repertory of barks — different sounds for different occasions. Dogs probably never bark for no reason at all, but owners may often be unaware of the reason.

GROWL   Another form of vocal communication, growling is usually a warning. Roughly translated into people language, it means "I wouldn't do that if I were you. . . ."

HOWL   Probably all dogs can howl, although many never will have an occasion to do so. It seems that relatively few situations bring out the howl in a dog: extreme loneliness when isolated from his family; a prolonged rising wail, such as that produced by some kinds of sirens or even musical instruments; or the howl of another dog — or even a person.

CHEW   Virtually all puppies chew while their teeth are coming in, but many dogs continue to chew even as adults, although usually only in particular situations, such as when they are anxious, restless, or bored.

MOUTH   Very young puppies use their mouths instinctively to grab anything that moves. They mouth one another and their mother in their earliest games and play-fights, and in the process learn how much force they may use before hurting their playmates and being rebuffed. When taken into a human family, puppies will mouth their new pack members in the same way.

SNAP   Dogs snap to let others know they object to what the other is doing and may bite if they don't stop. They may or may not be bluffing.

BITE   Dogs bite defensively, either out of fear or in defense of territory or property, and/or aggressively, usually just long and hard enough to get someone else to stop what he or she is doing or to enforce their own position.

DIG   Digging is usually a means to an end: to bury or uncover something valuable, such as a bone, or to escape from an area of confinement, such as a fenced yard. Surfaces such as loose soil seem to be almost

Your dog has an inborn need to chew, so it is up to you to provide acceptable objects for chewing. (Pat Ragan's Filbert)

Mouthing is all in good fun among friends. (Kathy Milani's Bailey and Brownie)

Your dog can send a mixed message of submission and aggression. (Kathy Milani's Bailey)

253

irresistible to some dogs, and often the dog will dig a hole and then lie down in it, possibly enlarging it a little every day.

PULL/PUSH AGAINST RESISTANCE Dogs have a reflex to resist being physically pushed or pulled in a way that might unbalance them. Push against your dog's side and he will lean into you; push him from behind or from above and he will resist. Many dogs appear to "learn" to strain against their leashes as a way of countering the owner's constant pressure to pull them in the opposite direction.

BOND WITH FAMILY MEMBERS As highly social creatures, dogs and especially puppies under sixteen weeks of age form strong emotional attachments to their owners as well as to household children, other dogs, cats, and often miscellaneous resident animals. For the rest of their lives, dogs will prefer to be in the company of their "families" and will suffer varying degrees of discomfort if separated from them.

ESCAPE (from crate, room, home, yard, or other area of confinement) Many dogs never lose the strong instinctive pull toward freedom. This leads to many different kinds of behavior — e.g., jumping, digging, barking, pacing, scratching, whining — all aimed at the objective of gaining that freedom. Most dogs are very happy captives as long as they are with their owners, but if left alone, some may strive continually to escape.

GREET RETURNING "PACK" MEMBERS FACE-TO-FACE Dogs never seem to outgrow the great relief and pleasure they feel when family members return after any kind of absence. Their preferred way of greeting their humans is to sniff and/or lick us in the face.

JUMP UP In order to reach our faces, dogs lift up their front paws and lean against us; very short and/or energetic types may jump up and down on their hind legs in repeated efforts to get closer.

SLEEP ON FURNITURE Dogs find security in close physical contact with pack members while they are sleeping and therefore vulnerable. Furniture where we habitually sit, lounge, and sleep holds our scent more strongly than other areas of the house and allows our dogs to feel as close to us as possible, particularly when they are home alone.

PROTECT FOOD, BED, TOYS, PEOPLE, AND OTHER ANIMALS Within their families, many dogs are naturally possessive of their personal stuff. These dogs may growl, snap, or bite if they feel their possessions are threatened. With outsiders, dogs may be possessive of their people and their people's stuff. Protective behavior is much more pronounced in some breeds and individual dogs than in others.

INTERACT SOCIALLY WITH OTHER DOGS All dogs who spend their

Dogs smooch, too.

first six to eight weeks with other dogs know the rules of dog society and speak the language of dogs. This means that under whatever circumstances strange dogs gather together, each will attempt to find his or her place in the social hierarchy of the group. Weaker dogs will show deference to stronger dogs by submissive behaviors and body language, and the strongest dogs will adopt dominant postures and behaviors. If dogs meet on the personal territory of one or more rather than in a neutral zone such as a park or training class, the "balance of power" may well shift in favor of the dogs who are on their home turf.

DRIBBLE URINE TO SHOW SUBMISSION TO OWNER OR OTHER DOGS As pack animals, dogs also strive to find their niche in the social hierarchy of their families. Part of fitting in is showing proper deference to others whom they perceive as more powerful. They do this primarily with body language, but some timid types may also lower their bodies and dribble urine as one way of showing submissiveness.

ROLL IN FILTH For reasons we don't fully understand, dogs like to roll in foul substances that they encounter outdoors, including decaying carcasses of fish and animals and the feces of cows, horses, deer, and other wildlife.

EAT FECES Many dogs, given the opportunity, will eat their own feces as well as those of other dogs, cats, birds, wildlife, and a variety of domestic animals.

BURY STUFF Bones and biscuits with bonemeal in them are probably the most common items that dogs try to bury, but they are not the

In the midst of a playful tussle, one dog will submit to another's superior size by lying motionless.

only ones. Dogs who do not have access to a yard may do their "burying" among the cushions on the sofa.

DEFEND TERRITORY/CHALLENGE STRANGERS Once a dog has decided what territory is his — and "territory," to dogs, is not restricted to their owners' legal property lines — he will bark, growl, rush at, chase, and possibly attack other dogs or people who trespass upon it.

MARK TERRITORY WITH URINE Male dogs in particular will "mark" as much territory adjacent to their own as they feel confident enough to defend against other dogs.

ROAM Many dogs who are not confined will leave their property and roam around the neighborhood before returning home. Roaming may look like aimless wandering to us, but is more likely quite purposeful. Male dogs follow the scent of females in season and patrol the four corners of their territory; any dog may pursue other animals or interesting scents of all kinds, or travel to sources of food or good company.

FIGHT OTHER DOGS Nature did not design the dog to live harmoniously with dogs who are not members of his own social group. Strange dogs may fight over serious dog issues such as territory or breeding rights, or they may just get into the habit of fighting with particular dogs in the neighborhood whom they've fought with in the past. Even within a family, however, frequent short squabbles may break out between two or more dogs over preferred sleeping places, food, favored objects, proximity to the owner, or whenever emotions run high, such as when the doorbell rings. Some breeds of dogs that were developed to be protective, such as German shepherds, Dobermans, and rottweilers, or to be feisty, such as terriers and bull-and-terrier breeds, are more inclined than others to be quarrelsome among themselves or with other dogs. Breeds that have traditionally lived in large packs, such as beagles, foxhounds, and greyhounds, are more inclined to be peaceable.

MOUNT Nonsterilized male dogs in particular but also some females as well as sterilized males and females may exhibit the attention-seeking or sexual behavior of mounting other animals, the legs of the owner or visitors to the home, and inanimate objects of various kinds.

SNIFF ANAL REGION OF STRANGE DOGS When two dogs meet one another for the first time, and frequently on subsequent get-togethers if any length of time has passed, they sniff each other's anal regions as a way of introduction and investigation. Apparently dogs can tell a lot about each other's sexual and social status from the scent glands located near the rectum.

SNIFF URINE/FECES LEFT BY OTHER DOGS Dogs who are out for a walk will investigate who has passed that way recently by stopping to sniff every surface where other dogs have left urine or feces, often leaving urine markers of their own.

SHAKE OBJECTS HELD IN THE MOUTH This behavior is left over from the days when dogs hunted and killed small animals for food. It is most pronounced in dogs such as terriers who were developed by humans to kill large numbers of rats or other creatures in rapid succession.

INVESTIGATE Dogs have a strong reflex to investigate novel sights, sounds, smells, and objects in their environment. They do this by careful listening, sniffing, following, pawing, gripping, licking, and mouthing objects, particularly those that move in compelling ways and/or make provocative noises.

PREY-CHASE; KILL Small animals, such as human children, cats, birds, rodents, barnyard and woodland creatures who dart and flee, particularly if they squeal, may stimulate predatory (chasing, seizing, biting, or shaking to death) behavior in virtually any dog or group of dogs.

Does Your Dog Have a Problem?

As we said before, your dog's behavior is neither good nor bad, neither a boon nor a problem until you or someone in authority feels that it is. The surest evidence of this is that the very same behavior, for instance pulling against resistance, may be fun when you're playing tug-of-war in the yard with your puppy, but a real pain when you're walking him on-leash. Likewise, behavior you may value in your own dog, such as loud and insistent barking at unannounced strangers, you may not appreciate at all in the dog next door. Your dog's outright aggression toward strangers may appear to be an asset if your home and family is threatened, yet turn out to be a serious liability should he attack a guest in your living room.

In chapter 1 we examined some of the pitfalls of having unrealistic expectations of our dogs. Being aware of what constitutes natural dog behavior can help us to avoid being unpleasantly surprised when we discover that our male dog wants to tear into every other male dog on the street, or that our terrier cross is a four-wheel-drive digging dynamo. (See Problems Waiting to Happen, page 263, for some all-too-common examples of mismatches between owner expectations and dog behaviors.) Being aware of natural dog behavior can be reassuring, too, because behavior, even though natural and appropriate from the dog's point of view, can be changed. Things you may have thought you were stuck with . . . maybe you're not!

It's up to you to decide whether or not you and your dog have a problem. If it's a biggie, you undoubtedly already know. But in general, if you find yourself fed up, frustrated, or generally disappointed in your dog, it's time to take stock of what she may be doing that you'd rather she didn't. In your mind, separate your dog, whom you cherish, from her behavior, which you don't. As always, identifying the problem is the first step toward doing something about it. And remember: Most dog behavior problems can be resolved to both the owner's and the dog's satisfaction. Unfortunately, there are a few that cannot. (Suggestions for resolving some of the more common problems are given in chapters 19–22.)

Problems Great and Small

Dog behavior problems come in different sizes. Minor problems are things your dog may do that irritate you enough so that he is frequently "in the doghouse." Probably your response to these behaviors has been inconsistent, depending on your own mood and other factors, and attempts to correct the behavior have been unsuccessful. Examples of minor behavior problems are begging and/or whining, jumping up, pulling on-lead, digging holes, raiding the garbage pail, getting up on furniture, and boisterous, unruly behavior. This list is incomplete; you may need to add to it whatever specific thing your dog is innocently doing that has you convinced that the world's most headstrong animal is living at your house.

In contrast, a major behavior problem is anything that you find just about impossible to live with. Typically, the behavior causes so much tension between you and your dog that the entire relationship is at stake. Complaints of family members, neighbors, or others may add to the problem. Out of frustration, you may have begun to isolate the dog from some or many family activities or to resort to confining him for protracted periods of time — both of which are bound to make the basic problem worse, not to mention ruining your day-to-day relationship with your dog. Examples of major behavior problems are barking/howling, house-soiling, destructive behavior, escape behavior, fearful behavior, fighting, and aggressive behavior.

The Wisdom of Prevention

Of course it makes sense to do what you can to prevent problems from developing in the first place. It's always much easier to prevent trouble than to fix it once it's well established.

Much of the advice that has been offered in this book is intended to prevent problems between you and your dog, or your dog and the general public. Choosing a dog to fit your lifestyle and starting on day one to socialize your new companion, visiting a veterinarian regularly, putting primary attention on handling, housetraining, and learning to control your dog, as well as including him or her in all aspects of family life, are among the best ways to help prevent behavior problems from developing. Suggestions for preventing specific problems are given in the following three chapters, where common problems are discussed in detail.

Even if you do everything "right," there are no guarantees. You still may end up with a behavior problem. An adult dog may suddenly become very fearful of thunder and firecrackers, when she previously was not. You may never know why, but still she is keeping the house awake at night with her endless panting and pacing and is defecating indoors at the height of a storm or noisy parade. A dog who has easily accepted a succession of cats in his home may nevertheless have it in for your latest feline. It's not clear whether or not this could have been prevented; what *is* clear is that now three of you have a problem.

When it comes to prevention, an enthusiastic but reasonable approach seems best. Do your best to make sure your dog feels calm and secure in your home, don't berate yourself if you make a few mistakes, and most important, don't despair if you find yourself with a problem.

The Art of Acceptance

Some problems miraculously diminish if owners are able simply to adjust their expectations. There are no perfect dogs, just as there are no perfect people. Ask yourself: Do we really have a problem here or am I being unrealistic in my expectations? For example, sometimes a first-time owner will find her dog's exuberant personality "too much." All that ruckus in the house, the wagging tail knocking everything off the coffee table, the ever-present dirty paw prints on the kitchen cabinets . . . whether she gives the dog away or lives unhappily with the situation, such an owner may discover too late how small these problems really were. If you find yourself feeling chronically disgruntled with certain aspects of your dog's behavior, stop for a moment and think about how fully your dog accepts you, whether or not you walk him as far and as often as he'd like, hurry him along instead of stopping to enjoy every enchanting bush, hydrant, and lamppost, and throw his ball until he loses interest. What imperfections might your dog find in you, if he were so inclined?

The Process of Change

As we set out on the process of changing our dog's behavior — what professionals call behavior modification — our goal is to alter what the dog habitually does in certain situations in such a way that she becomes, or becomes again, someone we can live with happily ever after. Behavior modification does not deprive a dog of her right to behave like a dog. It does not take all the fun out of her life. In truth, dogs with behavior problems are not what you might call happy canine campers. Often their "misbehavior" is caused by stress and insecurity; ironically, modifying their behavior in ways that suit us better invariably suits the dog better, too. And it should come as no surprise that, almost always, our behavior toward our dog needs to be modified as well.

If you've ever tried to change any kind of behavior, perhaps your own eating or exercise habits or anything that your teenage children do, you already have an idea of how difficult it can be. Cheer up! Dog behavior in many cases is much easier to modify. Why? Because the dog doesn't have to look inside himself for motivation. That's your job!

To modify your dog's behavior, you will need a thorough analysis of the problem and a carefully thought-out remedial program that takes into account the dog's temperament, age, and health as well as the nature of the problem. Some problems you will be able to resolve by yourself, with the collaboration of your veterinarian and the cooperation of all family members.

For other problems, you may need the help of an animal behaviorist — a professional who is trained and experienced in resolving behavior problems in dogs. Problems of long standing usually will take longer to resolve, so it makes sense to get started as soon as possible. In most cases, the following steps will be useful:

WRITE OUT A HISTORY OF THE PROBLEM What does your dog actually do? Describe the behavior as explicitly as you can. At this point try to forget any conclusions you may already have come to about why your dog is doing what he's doing — stick with a very precise description. For example, you might say, "Max lifts his leg in several places around the house and leaves a small amount of urine in each place." Saying "urinating indoors" would not give as much information, and saying "urine-marking" would be a conclusion. Next, note how long the behavior has been going on. What can you recall about the circumstances under which it began? Had there been any recent changes in the family or in the dog's routine? How did you respond to the behavior when it first occurred? What was the result? When does the behavior occur now? Who else or what else is present?

TRY TO IDENTIFY THE CAUSE OF THE PROBLEM Now, with the complete history before you, can you clearly see the cause of the problem? For instance, if your notes show that Max only barks in the yard when the rest of the family is in the house, you can feel pretty certain that being isolated from the family is the cause of his barking. Many problems are more complex, however, and the cause will not be obvious.

IF POSSIBLE, ELIMINATE THE CAUSE In some cases, once you've identified the cause of a problem, the solution is obvious. For example, if you are Max's owner, keep him company in the yard (for safety's sake, dogs should not be left unsupervised in any case). If that prospect is unappealing for some reason, perhaps you can substitute a nice walk or a romp in the park for Max's yard time. Remember that your dog is a highly social animal and more than likely just wants to be with you — no matter how much you think he should enjoy the yard.

SEEK HELP IF NECESSARY Problems always have a cause, although you may not be able to decode your dog's behavior sufficiently to understand what it is. If the information given in the next four chapters isn't sufficient for you to work from, you will need to seek professional help. Trying to resolve a problem when you don't know its cause is at best foolish and could actually make the problem worse.

Getting the Help You Need

Help for resolving behavior problems is available in many forms. Begin by talking with your veterinarian. First of all, there may be a medical explanation for your dog's behavior (pain, impaired hearing or vision, parasites, improper diet, hormonal imbalances, neurological disorders), and this should be investigated before other possible causes are considered. If no health problem is discovered, your veterinarian may then have concrete suggestions to offer to help you resolve the problem. Unlike even a few decades ago, veterinarians now know quite a bit about animal behavior problems and can be a valuable resource in that regard. If the problem is very complex, your veterinarian should be able to refer you to a professional animal behaviorist, a person who has been professionally trained in resolving behavior problems in companion animals. Alternatively, the obedience trainer you located in chapter 14 may be experienced, although probably not professionally trained, in behavior modification techniques.

If you do decide to contact an animal behaviorist, be prepared to use the same kind of care in choosing one to work with that you used in selecting your veterinarian. You want someone you feel comfortable with, someone who clearly recognizes that behavior problems involve the dog and the humans and can only be resolved in the home setting with the participation of family members. The qualities of compassion, clear communication, knowledge, and strict adherence to humane methods are probably more to be relied upon than are so-called credentials.

Finally, don't overlook self-help materials. Every single day there are more books and articles available, more videotapes, more seminars, and more workshops on all aspects of dog behavior and how to solve problems. Check at your local library or bookstore for titles.

In Column A of the table below, you'll find a list of common behaviors that dog owners complain about. Column B, in contrast, describes the behavior that many of us actually expect instead, though we may not realize it. This is how we think our dog should act. In Column C, you'll see what our dogs might say about our expectations, if only they could talk!

The purpose of this exercise is to uncover areas where you may be disappointed or angered by the way your dog behaves, while at the same time expecting your dog to behave in a way that does not come naturally to dogs. Appreciating that your dog has an innately different point of view and will need your help and understanding to modify his behavior is key to building a true partnership between you.

So-Called Behavior Problem	The Owner's Expectations	The Dog's Point of View
Owner calls dog to come. Dog does not move.	My dog should come to me when I call.	Mm . . . I don't see any good reason why over there is better than right here; think I'll stay put. . . .
Stranger comes to door. Dog barks and will not stop.	My dog should bark to let me know someone is at the door, but stop when I tell him to.	My job is to bark until the stranger goes away.
Scottish terrier growls and lunges at other dogs while being walked.	My old Scottie got along with other dogs. So should this one.	I'm not her old Scottie. I'm me. And I don't like other dogs.
Dog chews furniture, woodwork, anything and everything when left home alone.	My dog is never destructive while I'm at home. He should be just as well behaved when I'm at work.	Don't leave me! I'm frightened! I don't like to be by myself!

So-Called Behavior Problem	The Owner's Expectations	The Dog's Point of View
Dog tries to run away from visiting children, but is cornered. Dog snaps.	My dog should be gentle with children.	I've never seen people like this before! Get them away from me!
Dog greets other dogs and people by sniffing them.	My dog should not sniff other dogs and people. It's embarrassing.	Let's get acquainted. I'll sniff you, and you can sniff me.
Dog goes over to neighbor's yard when let outdoors and "waters" all his bushes.	My dog should stay on my property.	I'm in charge of this street down to the corner. I need to mark everything so other dogs will know it's mine.
Dog explores widely when walked off leash.	My dog should stay near me when we take a walk. I shouldn't need to use a leash.	So much to see, so much to smell. I think I'll just go see where this trail leads.
Male dog lifts leg on umbrella stand by front door, by back door, on draperies by window looking out on the street.	There is no reason for my dog to piddle inside the house. He should hold it in unless we're outside.	When we were outdoors just now, I smelled the urine of other male dogs on this street. I need to let them know that this house is mine!
Dog jumps up to greet owner whenever she returns after being away.	Pepper is so high-strung sometimes. He should keep his feet on the floor and just wag his tail.	You're back! I want to greet you properly. If only your face weren't so far away . . . maybe if I jump. . . .

Home Alone 19

What's the loneliest you've ever felt in your whole life? Was it those first few nights at summer camp when you were ten? Was it being packed off to spend a whole week with relatives you didn't even know — and they had no kids? Perhaps it was the time you got separated from your second-grade class on the field trip to Playland or when your parents drove you to college that first September . . . and left you there. Can you conjure up the acute feelings of distress that engulfed you — loss of appetite, preoccupation with yourself and disinterest in others, inability to concentrate, restlessness, irritability? Do you remember knowing that you would do anything, give absolutely anything just to be back again with the old familiar faces? Then you can begin to understand what it's like for dogs to be separated from their people for prolonged periods of time.

When an eight-week-old puppy is taken from his mother and littermates to go to his new home, he suffers the pangs of separation for the first time. The first night or two, when he wakes up and finds himself alone in an unfamiliar bed, he may cry out. But he very quickly transfers the attachment he feels for his dog family over to his new "mother" and family members. Most often, during the ensuing days, weeks, and months, the puppy learns to be separated from his people without undue suffering — but not always. Some

dogs, for a variety of reasons, don't learn how to cope with separation. For these dogs, every separation is filled with anguish. And in today's world, where almost everybody is out of the home at least part of the day, these dogs — and these families — can be in for mountains of misery.

Signs of Separation Anxiety

Dogs are social creatures and don't like being alone. Period. As our household companions, however, they have had to learn to tolerate periods of isolation, and, adaptable creatures that they are, most have done so. Some dogs manage just fine as long as they have some familiar people or other animals around for company. Other dogs, however, cannot be comforted in the absence of a particular person, or occasionally a particular animal. For these dogs, being in their own home with all their familiar things is not enough. These dogs are suffering with what is known as "separation anxiety." It means that the dog becomes truly tense and fearful whenever he is apart from the person for whom he feels the strongest attachment. If the truth were known, probably all dogs feel at least minor discomfort when left alone, although usually not enough to take action to try to relieve the tension. The dog who suffers from separation anxiety, however, does take action. It's hard to miss the telltale signs:

HOUSE-SOILING   Dogs who clearly have been housetrained may "forget" their training when they are left alone. Defecation in particular suggests that the dog is feeling physical symptoms of anxiety (think about how your intestines feel when you have stage fright).

DESTRUCTIVE BEHAVIOR   If a dog chews furniture, woodwork, and household objects, scratches at walls, doors, and other barriers, digs, and/or generally "trashes" the environment — but only when left alone — separation anxiety is probably the cause. From the dog's point of view, taking action temporarily helps to discharge the restless energy that builds when he is under stress. Destructive behavior when left alone is particularly common in dogs who have come from shelters or been picked up as strays. It's probably not a matter of the dog fearing she will be abandoned again, as dogs cannot think abstractly as far as we know, but simply a common way for a dog previously traumatized during separation from her owners to respond when once again she finds herself in that very stressful situation.

ATTEMPTS TO ESCAPE Many dogs with separation problems try to escape from their homes or yards, presumably because their stress level is already so high that the additional frustration of confinement becomes unbearable. Dogs who suffer severe separation anxiety may injure themselves trying to claw and bite their way out of a crate or other enclosure. Others have jumped through glass windows, scaled fences, and dug their way out under fences.

CONTINUOUS BARKING OR HOWLING Another method of relieving stressful feelings is to bark or howl. Both are forms of communication for the dog, and what he is communicating is his distress over being alone. The unending barking says, "Rover to anyone. Rover to anyone. Come in. Come in. Over." A dog who howls is more likely saying, "Isn't *anybody* there? I feel so-o-o awful all alone." Dogs who are anxious at being alone may bark and howl incessantly — literally from the moment their owners walk out the door until they walk in again. Often owners find out about just how persistent their dog's barking is when they are confronted by irate neighbors!

SELF-MUTILATION Licking and chewing herself, usually on the front feet and forelegs, and sometimes to the point of hair loss, bleeding, and infection, is another attempt by the dog to manage her anxiety. As the skin becomes irritated from the constant licking, the dog licks more, to try to soothe it; soon a vicious cycle is in place that may carry over to times when the owner is at home as well.

GENERALLY ANXIOUS OR CLINGY BEHAVIOR A dog with separation anxiety often telegraphs distress signals as his owner prepares to leave the home. He may follow the owner closely from room to room, putting his front feet up on her and climbing in her lap if she should sit down. He also may lose interest in food, play, and other activities that normally are engaging, or perhaps sit by the front door as if to make sure he isn't left behind.

It goes without saying that your dog should *never* be punished for being afraid, as this can only make her more afraid. Owners sometimes assume that their dog's misbehavior when left alone is caused by spitefulness, as if the dog is letting them know that she didn't like what they did. It's natural enough for owners to think this way, as this is exactly what a human being might do in similar circumstances. Dogs, however, do not behave in this way.

What Causes Dogs to Fear Being Left Alone?

RANDOM OCCURRENCES   An individual dog's basic temperament, i.e., the way he is "wired," undoubtedly plays a role in the development of separation anxiety. So, too, may random experiences that occur while a developing puppy is with her litter. For example, if a thunderstorm raged during a time when the mother dog was away from the whelping box, the puppy's overall sense of security could be permanently affected. Periods of long separation, either from her litter or from her adoptive family during her first few months, can make her wary of being alone. Probably the most common cause of separation problems in a dog, however, is simply that she never was taught by her owners that separation, while admittedly no fun, isn't the end of the world, either.

AN UNNATURAL LEARNING ENVIRONMENT   In the wild, wolf and wild dog puppies are left behind for gradually increasing lengths of time so that being left and being returned to are learned at the same time. While they are "home alone," the wild pups have their world to explore and one another to play with. Older pack members are on hand for backup caretaking. In contrast, the single puppy or young dog whom we bring into our home may have none of this. It is our job, if only we realize it in time, to give our puppy as close a facsimile of the wild puppy's experience as we can. In this way the puppy will learn not to fear separation.

OVER-INDULGENCE   While you probably can never love your puppy too much, you *can* love her in ways that make her overly dependent on you rather than self-confident and secure about the world and her place in it. Never leaving the puppy alone in the beginning only delays her learning how to be alone. Making a huge fuss when you do leave and again when you return adds unnecessary emotion to what should be a calm, matter-of-fact process. Being a constant source of physical coddling, treats, and entertainment sets up expectations in your puppy for ongoing supplies of these things at a time when she should be learning to amuse herself with her toys and the view outside the window and to interact socially with other family members and resident animals as well as with you.

Preventing Separation Difficulties

Separation difficulties can plague our dogs, ourselves, and the relationships between us. The causes of these difficulties suggest what we can do to help prevent them.

PROVIDE EARLY TRAINING   It's always easiest to get off on the right foot with a puppy, but even new adult dogs will benefit from early experiences at being alone in your home. After a day or so to settle in, deliberately stage a calm "departure," even if you only go a hundred feet away and return after a minute or so. When you come back, greet the dog casually and just go about your business. Gradually increase the time you stay away until it's a half-day or longer. Another idea is to vary your departure and return times so your dog doesn't get in the habit of expecting you at a precise time. Someday you are sure to be late, and that could stir up enough tension in the dog to make him vulnerable. Even when there's every sign that your dog can handle being alone, refresh his home-alone training every few months.

BUILD SELF-CONFIDENCE   Anything and everything that enhances your dog's overall level of confidence and security is insurance against separation problems later on. You already know that a physically healthy dog (or person) is better able to ward off infections and disease than one who isn't in tip-top condition. Maintaining good emotional health offers your dog similar protection against behavior problems brought on by stress. Activities that build confidence include anything that allows the dog to be rewarded for desirable performance. Obedience exercises, doing something (a simple trick will do) to earn a treat or a pat are good choices.

BE YOUR DOG'S DEPENDABLE LEADER   In the sheer joy of having a canine companion, it's easy to lose sight of the fact that your dog needs to feel part of a clear social hierarchy. In most situations, you should be the one to make the decisions and initiate play, exercise, eating, and so forth. Then if you both feel comfortable with him running to the door and barking when visitors arrive, by all means feel free to let him do so. Don't forget, though, the qualities of leadership that are required of you: fairness, firmness, clarity, consistency.

SHARE THE CARING   One way to avoid making your dog overly dependent on you is to have other family members and even guests, once the dog is trained, participate in routine care and handling. Many dogs will always turn to one person in the household as their primary leader, but all humans, including supervised children, should be able to feed, walk, groom, and handle the dog. Dogs who recognize all family members as leaders are unlikely to require the presence of one person in particular in order to feel secure.

KEEP COOL   To some extent our dogs mirror and mimic our own behavior. That means that if we want our dog to respond calmly to whatever each new day brings, we need to act that way ourselves. We can get that message across by avoiding as many emotional indoor "scenes" as possible. Just as parents teach their children that the running and jumping and shouting they do on the playground is not okay indoors, we need to teach our dogs that the yard is the place for roughhousing and chasing and barking, but that indoors the drill is calm and quiet. We can do this by keeping our indoor greetings and leave-takings low-key, by speaking to the dog in a friendly, matter-of-fact tone, and keeping praise and petting warm but brief. A dog who is accustomed to being calm in the house with her family is less likely to become noisy and destructive there when left alone.

How Are Problems Triggered?

A puppy or dog who feels a little tense and insecure may have a *potential* problem being home alone but never get into trouble — until suddenly he does. Then, once he's spent an afternoon in frantic activity to try to relieve his anxiety, probably followed by a stern scolding from you when you return and find an accident on the rug or your furniture unstuffed, the stage is set for repeat performances. The dog's bad experience and your disapproval have made him more insecure, and he'll quickly recognize the scene when he finds himself in it again. Without your help, a long-playing drama may be about to unfold. But what triggered that first bad act? A number of possibilities are listed below. The common ingredient in each is that the dog already was a little (or a lot) insecure, and being left alone was the last straw.

THE FIRST PROLONGED PERIOD OF SEPARATION   If the family takes its first vacation, for example, and the dog is either being cared for by a pet-sitter at home or boarded at a kennel, the experience may trigger difficulty being home alone even for lengths of time that the dog handled easily in the past.

A CHANGE IN THE FAMILY'S ROUTINE   Any change that causes the dog to be left alone substantially more than before, such as an adult going back to work or a child going away to school, can trigger difficulties.

A DEATH IN THE FAMILY   The loss of a significant person or animal may bring on problems that may or may not ease as the dog becomes accustomed to her loss.

THE MOVE TO A NEW HOME   Moving to a new home or the ongoing upset of renovation to a current home may disorient the dog enough for her to have a hard time being alone.

BEING NEW TO THE HOUSEHOLD   Recently acquired and adopted dogs may go through a period of time when they feel so insecure in unfamiliar surroundings that they may fall apart if faced with the additional challenge of being left at home by themselves.

AGING   Changes in the brain as a dog ages (similar to Alzheimer's disease in humans) and various chronic illnesses and/or aches and pains associated with old age may increase a dog's base level of anxiety and cause him to be less able to handle the additional stress of being home alone.

Resolving Separation Anxiety

If your dog becomes anxious when left alone, you actually have two problems to resolve. The *immediate problem* is to find a way to eliminate whatever undesirable behaviors your dog expresses as she tries to cope with her anxiety. In other words, when you're away from home, how can you stop your dog from defecating on the landing at the top of the cellar steps, or from making the entire apartment building echo with her nonstop howling? (Chapter 20 contains step-by-step suggestions for resolving common behavior problems.) The *underlying problem,* of course, is to eliminate the root cause of the misbehavior — the tension your dog feels when she is separated from you. Until the underlying problem is addressed, you are really only suppressing the symptoms. Imagine that you're a gardener faced with an outgrowth of unsightly weeds among your prized begonias. If you hack a weed off at ground level but leave the roots behind, it's only a matter of time before the weed is back — more firmly anchored than before.

IMMEDIATE PROBLEM: STOPPING BAD BEHAVIOR   Depending on what your dog is doing, stopping it could be comparatively straightforward or more involved. Whatever the behavior, be cautious in putting any kind of "quick fix" into effect (more about the quick fix in chapter 20). There are many ways available to get rapid results, and some of them are completely safe, appropriate, and humane. Others may be fine in some cases but not in every case.

As an example, imagine that your dog chews the woodwork when you leave her alone. You might be tempted simply to lock her inside her crate while you're away. While this would effectively control the destruction, unfortunately it would only increase your dog's level of stress and discomfort. It could also be a very dangerous thing to do. Close confinement of an already restless dog might well cause her to try to chew or dig her way to freedom (especially since she's already a chewer). Many dogs have turned their mouths and paws into bloody pulp trying to get out of their crates, sometimes doing irreversible damage to themselves. Of course, this does not mean that crating a dog is a bad thing. You already know that the crate is highly recommended for housetraining.

UNDERLYING PROBLEM: ELIMINATING TENSION Every dog who has separation anxiety is different from every other. Some suffer only mildly, others mightily. Probably genetics is the major factor in some cases and environment is the major factor in others. Nevertheless, the task at hand — finding ways to reduce the stress your dog feels when she is left alone — is the same in every case. Here are some basic steps to follow and some thoughts to keep in mind:

- Diagnose the problem. The first step is to make sure that you're dealing with a separation problem and not something else that may result in some of the same behaviors. Take time to write down a detailed history of the problem. Questions to answer include: What does the dog do? Is she home alone when she does it? Has she ever been home alone and not done this? Does she appear uneasy when I'm getting ready to leave? Have there been any recent changes in our household or her routine that might have made her feel anxious?
- Rule out any medical component. Make an appointment with your veterinarian to make sure that there's no medical reason for your dog's behavior. Your veterinarian may prescribe anti-anxiety medication for your dog while you work with her to resolve her behavior problem. Obviously, medication alone is not the answer, as it will do nothing to eliminate the cause of the problem. Also, medication must be very carefully administered and monitored. Overdosing with some medications can actually *cause* problems as well as relieve them. For instance, overmedication of some products can cause hyperactivity.
- Build your dog's self-confidence. Work on implementing now the basic techniques discussed above under Preventing Separation Difficulties. These include brushing up on basic obedience, turning down the emotional volume in your home, especially regarding departures and homecomings, and discouraging your dog from being overly dependent on you.

- Teach your dog how to be calm when she's alone. The key to eliminating the stress your dog feels when she is left alone is to teach her to be calm in that situation. After all, she can't be both tense and calm at the same time! Try this technique:

1. Begin by making sure your dog is relaxed. For example, sit together quietly for five minutes or so in whatever room in your home she seems to find most comfortable. Avoid handling, petting, or even talking to the dog — just sort of hang out together in a calm, quiet way.

2. When the dog is relaxed and unsuspecting, get up and leave without saying a word. Do whatever you normally do when you go out (pick up your handbag, your car keys, etc.). Go out the door, walk a few hundred feet away, wait a minute or two, and then return.

3. Upon returning, ignore the dog completely for a few minutes. Then greet her with one or two words and go about your business in a calm, unhurried way.

4. Assuming the first experience went smoothly, begin to very gradually extend the distance you walk away from the house as well as the length of time you stay away. Vary the times of day when you leave and when you return to prevent the dog from becoming expectant at particular times. Watch for signs that the dog is anticipating your departure or becoming anxious while you are away; if you see any, go back a stage for a while before increasing your time away again.

5. When the dog is able to remain calm for ten minutes or so, begin to casually leave behind some new and absorbing things for her to do while you're gone. A sterilized bone or hard rubber toy, both of which are hollow inside, can be stuffed with cheese, for example, or with some of the dog's dry food mixed together with peanut butter, and this can provide a delectable challenge that will keep her happily occupied for quite some time. Whatever edible filling you choose, make sure it's something that really appeals to your dog.

6. Continue to extend the length of time that you are away. Don't hesitate to slow down or repeat steps whenever the dog seems to become restless.

7. Even when your dog seems to have learned that being alone is nothing to fear, be wary of backsliding. Pay particular attention to situations that may have caused problems in the past, such as a family vacation without the dog or major changes in the family makeup. If it so happens that the dog doesn't have to be alone for an extended period of time (weeks or months), make a point of "staging" some occasions to leave her. This training should be refreshed regularly and forever.

A hollow rubber toy filled with treats provides hours of occupation for a dog home alone. (Gorman Bechard's Casey)

Note: If this method does not seem to work for you, probably it is time to seek professional help in resolving the problem. Ask your veterinarian for suggestions or a referral.

STRESS REDUCERS

As social animals, all dogs are happier when they are with their families than when they are alone. Even dogs who display no classic symptoms of separation anxiety may nevertheless suffer some degree of upset. Try one or more of the following to make the time alone less stressful for your dog:

- Exercise your dog vigorously beforehand so he will be ready to rest quietly while you're away.
- Make sure your dog is comfortable during your absence (has access to his favorite places, including windows to look out, a secure den if he uses one, and your bed unless that's always off-limits; has toys to play with; has something to chew; won't need to eliminate during the time you'll be gone; won't be too hot or cold).
- Try to anticipate events that might trigger other problems, such as noise phobias (pending thunderstorms or fireworks) and take appropriate actions, such as closing all the windows, leaving on the radio or television with the volume turned fairly high, and/or clearing out a space for your dog inside a sound-muffling space, such as a closet in the interior of your home (i.e., away from windows), and allowing him free access to it.

Solving Common Problems

A few decades ago, the *Ladies' Home Journal* launched a popular feature called "Can This Marriage Be Saved?" Each month an embattled husband and wife separately tell their sides of the "story." Then a psychologist discusses the issues she sees facing the couple, ending with suggestions for resolving their differences. Without her, it seemed unlikely that the estranged couple ever would have found their way home.

The format of the column is an important part of its message. It shows that every story had two sides. It shows how different are the perspectives of the husband and the wife. It shows how poorly they communicate. And it shows that with commitment and work, there almost always is a way to make things better. Inevitably, the parties have to learn to talk to one another and to listen. Both have to change some of their ways.

So must it be with problems between you and your dog. You have to recognize that there are two very different points of view. You have to acknowledge that communication is key. With the help of a book like this one, you may be able to solve your problems yourself. Gravely serious problems, or any problem that has you asking "Can this relationship be saved?" probably will require professional help. Both you and your dog will have to change your ways.

Common Problems

The first set of problems discussed below are relatively minor for most dog owners. Some days they're just annoying, but other days they make you blow your top. The second set are major problems — though you may not always recognize that at first. They have you wishing you'd never got a dog (and you're not kidding). You honestly don't know how things got so out of hand.

But *we* do. At least we have some pretty good ideas. We also have suggestions you can try to make these problems go away. We have advice about what *not* to do.

We've kept our suggestions fairly general. Every situation is different, and you will need to experiment to find out what works best for you and your dog. The most important thing is to relax with this process. As you'll see, too much emotion — on your side or your dog's — is usually a factor in most behavior problems.

Feel free to take your time as you work to change your own and your dog's behavior. For instance, if we list three things you can do to try to stop a chewing problem, it's okay if you just work on one. If the situation improves somewhat and you're satisfied with that, feel good about what you've accomplished. Down the road you may decide to try for more.

Whatever you do, don't give up. On the other hand, don't try to convince yourself that things really aren't so bad. It's not okay to go through each day feeling disappointed in your dog. If you follow the suggestions below but your dog's behavior doesn't change, then it's time to seek professional help. Ask your veterinarian first. If he can't help personally, ask him if he can recommend a professional animal behaviorist (see chapter 18) or well-respected local dog trainer — a person, usually self-taught, who has many years of experience working with and training dogs, even though he probably has no professional training in animal behavior.

Minor Problems

Begging
CAUSES Dogs beg because they want something, usually food, *and* they've learned that begging will get it for them at least some of the time. Begging can be fairly unobtrusive, as when the dog lies quietly at your feet and watches your fork move from your plate to your mouth and back

again. Begging more often is accompanied by persistent whining, drooling, and occasional yawning (no, your dog's not bored — he's yawning to relieve the frustration that he's feeling). Some dogs inch ever closer as they beg, pawing or scratching at your leg or arm if the tidbits are too slow in arriving. It's important to realize that the uncertain outcome of begging (compared to having his food dish placed on the floor) means that there probably always is some amount of tension in the begging dog.

RESOLVING THE PROBLEM   If you'd never given your dog food from your hand or plate in the first place, you very likely would not have this problem today. Therefore, one way to stop your dog from begging is never again to give him anything (i.e., reward him) when he does. Some dogs may get discouraged and give up in a week or so, others may go on begging in vain for months. If you decide to try this tactic, you must be absolutely certain that you *never* relent or absentmindedly hand over a morsel, and that no one else does either. If you do, it's back to square one. You'll make it easier on yourself to "learn" this new behavior if you make some change in your customary way of doing things. For instance, if you tend to give your dog tidbits when you're cooking in the kitchen, half-watching television, try leaving the TV off or switching to the radio instead. A small change like this will help keep you focused for the first few days or week until *not* tossing pieces of food toward the dog begins to become automatic.

Another approach would be to train your dog to do something else at the times when he would normally beg. (If you need to refresh your training skills, go back to chapter 14.) For example, you might train him to go to a particular place and stay there quietly while the family is eating (he can't be two places at once). Whatever you decide to train as an alternative to begging, make sure to praise and reward the dog *only* when he does it quietly. Having your dog sitting in the next room whining or barking would probably not seem like much of an improvement.

Some dog owners truly don't mind if their dog begs as long as he doesn't whine (they think of it as sharing meals together). If you're one of these owners, concentrate your efforts on training your dog to be calm and silent while he sits and waits for handouts at your feet. Do this by giving him tidbits only when he's quiet, never when he's not.

WHAT NOT TO DO   When you think about it from the dog's point of view, begging is being fed on demand, although not very reliably. Being catered to one moment and denied or disciplined the next, which is what most of us indulgent owners tend to do, sends your dog mixed messages about who's really in charge. Remember: Dogs like as much consistency in the household rules as possible.

Boisterous, Unruly Behavior

CAUSES   Unruly behavior includes some or all of the following: not listening, being "on" all the time or "into" everything, excessive activity level indoors, resisting handling, always seeming to want to go left when you want to go right. Dogs are unruly for two main reasons: because they've never been trained not to be, which includes virtually all young puppies, and because they've been allowed to think they are *numero uno* in the household. Occasionally a dog may be restless, inattentive, and generally "difficult" because of a medical condition; if your dog has not had a veterinary checkup recently, probably you should schedule one to have the possibility of a physiological problem ruled out as the cause of her unruliness.

RESOLVING THE PROBLEM   If your dog is still in the puppy or adolescent stage, roughly two to ten months, and has not yet been routinely handled and socialized as discussed in chapter 13, or taught basic commands as outlined in chapter 14, she is simply running amok like a preschooler with lots of energy and no clear sense of what's okay and what's not okay to do. Depending on her age, this puppy is also growing increasingly uneasy about the lack of a social structure that clearly shows her her "place." Begin immediately to calmly but firmly handle and train your dog. Learning to sit or lie down is important, but even more important is learning that good things happen (warm praise, play, petting, treats) when she listens to you. This all makes such simple sense to a dog that your puppy should begin to seem less out of control almost immediately.

Unruly behavior in an older dog is more likely to be evidence that she has the idea that she's in charge. The usual reason for this is that puppy unruliness went overlooked or untreated. On the other hand, some dogs were born with more dominant personalities and may need daily reminders that they do not call the shots. In either case, you must begin immediately to be the dog's firm but fair leader. Do this by making it common practice to lead, both literally and figuratively, even if you don't feel like it or in some instances don't particularly care if your dog sets the pace. For example, make it a point to be first to eat meals or walk through doorways. Decide when a play period shall begin by bringing out toys anytime *except* when your dog is indicating that she'd like you to. Decide when play shall end by quietly taking the toys away and putting them out of reach. Be prepared *always* to resist your dog's artful enticements to play with her when she says so. The message you want to send your dog is that you are the source of many good and fun things, and her job is simply to wait for you to trot them out. Most likely the unruly dog will be difficult to walk on-lead, due to constant pulling in a different direction from the one you've set. (For help with that particular problem, see Pulling On-Lead, page 288.)

Once your dog understands that you're in charge, you may lighten up in areas where you truly don't care if she gets her way. But if you see generally bossy behavior begin to show up again, you will know that probably you are going to have to be the full-time leader on a permanent basis.

WHAT NOT TO DO Avoid making the problem worse by acting in an "unruly" manner yourself. Getting excited, angry, loud, or impatient with a dog who is already a bit out of control is likely to stimulate her to be even more unruly. An unruly dog needs to learn self-control, which comes from knowing how she is expected to behave and from feeling more secure in her role in the home. Restraining the dog from misbehaving (by crating, harshly jerking the lead, or any such methods), while it might seem to work temporarily, will do nothing to teach her self-control or help her feel more secure.

Chewing

CAUSES Chewing can be divided into two primary categories: puppy chewing and adult chewing. They are very different "problems."

Virtually all puppies chew. Puppies will chew in front of you as well as in your absence. From birth, they have an instinct to grab at and hold anything that moves around them as they use their mouths to investigate their world. While puppies' adult teeth are coming through the gums, roughly between four and six months of age, puppies chew almost continually in an effort to relieve discomfort. When older puppies grab and chew, they are also practicing hunting behavior inherited from their wild ancestors. You may notice them not only chewing on objects they find around the house but often also shaking them and tearing them to bits.

Adult dogs who are long past the teething stage may chew when they are anxious or bored, such as when left home alone or put out in the yard with nothing interesting to do. Aside from chewing bones or rawhide toys you've given them, adult dogs mostly chew in your absence.

Some dogs chew as a result of some kind of medical problem such as gum disease, stomach upsets, or conditions that cause great hunger. Your first goal must be to determine *why* your dog is chewing and then try to remove the cause. If you look at what else is going on when he chews, you should see important clues.

Almost any chewing by an adult dog will be destructive. Still, there is a difference between the kind of occasional chewing that might happen in specific situations, such as being confined in the car or in a small window-less bathroom, and the sort of mass destruction that can take place virtually anywhere and anytime a dog is left alone.

RESOLVING THE PROBLEM   Puppy chewing: Puppies *will* chew and that is that. If you go into puppy ownership with the cheerful expectation of sustaining some damage to household furnishings and personal items, you will not be as likely to view the behavior as a big problem. All other things being equal, it will pass. In the meantime, pick up any objects you don't want chewed and remove them from the area where the puppy is confined. "Paint" items that can't be removed, such as wood-work and table legs, with a bitter substance that your puppy will want to avoid. Commercial products are made for this purpose and will not harm your furniture, or you can use a hot pepper sauce or something else with a strong, sharp taste such as mouthwash (obviously the sub-stance must be safe and nontoxic). At the same time, offer your puppy safe and allowable items to chew, such as rawhide chew toys, nylon bones, and hard rubber toys. Make sure that whatever you offer is dis-similar from ordinary household objects. A puppy will not understand the difference, for instance, between an old sneaker and your good pair of Italian pumps.

Adult chewing: For the occasional chewers mentioned above, begin by looking for ways to relieve whatever anxiety or boredom the dog may be feel-ing. For instance, if your dog chews only when left in the car, try to avoid leaving him alone in the car. If you confine your dog in his crate or in a small room while you're away, try a different location where there's more to see, do, and interact with, such as a room with a large window overlooking the street or a garden. Experiment with giving the dog something that's chal-lenging and interesting and permissible to chew, such as a sterilized bone stuffed with cheese or peanut butter.

On the other hand, if your dog tends to chew destructively whenever he is left alone, no matter the circumstances, he probably has what experts call separation anxiety (see chapter 19 for a full discussion of this problem). In this case, think of the chewing as the symptom (it could be house-soiling, barking, or other misbehaviors). Your task is to find out what is causing the anxiety and then come up with ways to help your dog feel calmer in general, which will extend to your absence as well.

WHAT NOT TO DO   The most important thing not to do is punish the puppy or dog for chewing, particularly after the fact. If you come home and find chewing damage and punish (scold or isolate) the dog, he will not connect your actions with chewing; he will connect your actions only with your homecoming. Thereafter, whenever you leave your dog alone, he is likely to begin to become anxious as he dreads your return. That anxiety might actually cause him to chew more, to chew himself, scratch the walls, house-soil, or misbehave in other ways in order to relieve his anxiety. Neither is it a good idea to make an emotional fuss when, for instance, you see the remains of a prized wood sculpture; even negative attention to chewing is attention, and that may act as encouragement to your dog.

Digging

CAUSES   Dogs like to dig. It's a fun thing to do under normal circumstances and relieves tension and boredom when they are left alone. Some kinds of dogs, most notably terriers, have a true passion for digging. Teaching a terrier or any dedicated digger *not* to dig is swimming against the tide.

Other dogs dig to escape, and it's easy to determine if that's what's motivating your dog: Her efforts will clearly be concentrated around barriers.

RESOLVING THE PROBLEM   If your dog is digging to relieve tension and/or boredom, your best approach to resolving the problem will be to alleviate the uncomfortable feelings that are causing it. Begin by asking yourself whether it is really necessary for your dog to be alone in the yard in the first place. Perhaps you or another family member could join him there and throw him a ball or flying disk to catch.

A dog who digs out of boredom needs something more interesting to do when put out in the yard. Experiment with different options such as chew toys that you bring out only when she's alone in the yard (toys that lie around all the time lose their appeal after a while) or a doggy puzzle to solve, such as opening up an object to find the prize within. A large heavy carton box to tear apart to get at a biscuit you've placed inside is one possibility. (You'll have to clean up the debris, but that's a lot easier than filling in a hole and replanting grass.)

If your dog appears to dig just for the love of it and does it whenever the opportunity presents itself, you may want to reach a compromise position by giving him a place of his own where he can dig to his heart's content while leaving the rest of the yard intact. First, fill in any holes the dog has already started and cover them with plastic so he can't get at them. Next, select a digging location that's most acceptable to you. Then help your dog to understand that it's okay to dig there by burying something irresistible and praising him for digging to unearth it. Thereafter praise him whenever he uses this spot and scold him if you catch him beginning to dig elsewhere. If you wish, dress up your dog's excavation site by erecting a decorative fence around it and planting attractive flowers or ground cover outside the fence.

If your dog digs in order to escape from the yard, see Escape Behavior, page 298.

WHAT NOT TO DO Digging that occurs when you're not around should never be punished by shaming or scolding. Needless to say, harsh physical punishment is *never* appropriate. (Believe it or not, until quite recently one of the more popular "cures" for digging was to fill the hole with water, then push the dog's head under and hold it there. It's hard to imagine that this inhumane and completely misguided notion could ever have done anything but make the problem worse *and* erode the relationship between the dog and owner.) Attempting to control digging by not allowing the dog access to the yard may resolve the problem in one sense but surely comes at a very high price. Tethering or tying the dog on a rope or chain to restrict his movement and therefore his digging to one area is a very bad idea, especially when there are things crossing his line of vision that he normally would want to investigate. Tying out creates a sense of isolation, boredom, and tremendous frustration, and can lead to any number of new behavior problems, including barking, self-mutilation, and, most critically, aggression. Tethering a dog also presents physical danger to the dog in that the tether may snag on nearby objects, reducing even further the area in which the dog can move, possibly preventing him from getting to shade or his water bowl. The worst-case scenario, far more common than you might believe, is when the dog is tethered too close to a fence, attempts to leap the fence to escape his isolation/boredom/frustration — and hangs himself in the process.

Eating Stools

CAUSES No one is quite sure why dogs eat feces (usually their own but sometimes those of other dogs and/or other animals). Some apparently lack certain nutrients in their diets and are attempting to supplement them through the stool. Other dogs seem to eat stools (the formal name for the activity is *coprophagia*) only when the stool contains available nutrition, such as when the food has passed through the system undigested. Many puppies appear to "investigate" their own stools by eating them, and for some this can become a habit. Aside from spreading certain parasites from dog to dog, eating stools isn't really harmful to dogs as long as they've been vaccinated. It is, however, unacceptable to most dog owners.

RESOLVING THE PROBLEM If you suspect your dog may have a dietary problem, have your veterinarian give the dog a checkup. Avoid causing digestive upsets by introducing new foods gradually until your dog is able to handle the new nutrition. Do not overfeed! Dogs who are overfed tend to have looser stools, even diarrhea, and loose stools are more likely to contain undigested material, which in turn encourages coprophagia. Look for a firm, well-formed stool as a sign that you are feeding your dog the right amount of food.

Get in the habit of picking up the stool as soon as possible to eliminate the opportunity for the dog to eat it. Also, ask your veterinarian or pet-supply retailer for suggestions of commercial products that can be safely added to the dog's food in order to make the stool taste bad to the dog and thereby discourage coprophagia.

Training your dog not to eat stools requires you to be there when she eliminates and to teach her to "forget" about the stool. Do this by being prepared with some way of happily distracting her as soon as she eliminates. Just as she turns toward the stool, interrupt her with an invitation to play, chase a ball, go for a ride in the car, or other favorite thing. As soon as she complies, praise her warmly, in effect, for forgetting about the stool. Continue this practice until she eliminates and then immediately turns away from the stool on her own. If the problem has persisted for a long time, plan on refreshing this training every so often to avoid a relapse.

WHAT NOT TO DO If you witness your dog eating stools, try not to overreact. If you do, you run the risk of causing your dog enough apprehension that she will no longer eliminate in your presence. Also, avoid letting your dog see you clean up her excrement. Some dogs really do imitate the actions of their owners!

Raiding/Eating Garbage

CAUSES If you understand that your dog considers garbage an alternate food source, and sometimes a more appealing one than the dog's usual ration, it's easy enough to see why dogs would be interested. They don't have to be anxious or bored to turn to the garbage pail for relief, although it certainly can serve that purpose as well. Your approach to resolving this problem will require you to try to determine why your dog is doing this by looking at the circumstances in which it occurs.

RESOLVING THE PROBLEM   It's safe to say that dogs who never attempt to raid the garbage when it's clearly accessible to them have never been accidentally rewarded by finding something delicious there. Nor do their owners ever absentmindedly retrieve a morsel from the pail to give to the dog. Many dogs do get rewarded, though, and the bad habit of raiding the garbage pail is formed.

The simplest and most obvious way to resolve this problem is to make the garbage pail inaccessible by putting it in a closet, cabinet, or securely closed container. Another way is to make the garbage pail an object to be avoided. Do this by "booby-trapping" the pail with something that rattles noisily when it is disturbed, such as by setting an aluminum can with some pennies inside on the garbage pail lid. When the dog pushes his nose under the lid and the can of pennies crashes to the floor, the dog will be startled and in the future will associate the unpleasant noise with the pail. One good startle is enough for some dogs; others may require several negative experiences before they give the garbage pail a wide berth. Another deterrent would be to treat objects in the pail with hot sauce or another safe but strongly distasteful product. Afterward a small daub of the same substance on the pail lid should be enough to keep the dog convinced that she should keep her distance.

Dogs who only get into the garbage when they're alone most likely are doing so out of boredom or to relieve the stress of being alone. A number of steps for resolving problems associated with separation anxiety were given in chapter 19 (see Preventing Separation Difficulties, page 269). They include exercising your dog vigorously just before you depart, giving her something to do while you're gone, and implementing as many strategies as you can to bring your dog's overall stress level down.

Getting Up on Furniture

CAUSES   More often than not, dogs are invited or even placed on the furniture the first time by their owners. After that, they return to our sofas, chairs, and beds for the security of our scent, especially when we're gone. Many owners have no problem with this, though they may cover the upholstered pieces in loose fabric or plastic for ease of cleaning. It's also likely that some dogs are drawn to the den-like quality of furniture that partially encloses them within its upholstered back and arms. Since many dogs do seem to have "favorite" chairs, their owners compromise by designating that piece "the dog's chair," while making all other items off-limits. At some point sleeping on particular pieces at particular times of the day also becomes a routine that the dog, a creature of habit, repeats over and over.

RESOLVING THE PROBLEM If you are one of those owners who do mind their dog getting up on the furniture, following are some steps you can take to eliminate that behavior. In essence, you will have to break the dog's old habit by forming a new one, *and* you will have to find another way to give your dog an equal sense of security in your absence.

The first step is to find out when your dog goes up on the furniture. If it's only for a half hour in the morning after you leave, you could try coming up with something interesting for her to do instead during those few minutes, such as a special chew toy to work on or a bone to dig the center out of. If she spends most of the day dozing on the sofa, you'll need a different approach. Discourage her by planting a "snappy" motion-sensitive device upon the sofa to startle her away with an unexpected noise as she climbs on. At the same time, provide an attractive alternative. Many people give their dogs a chair of their own in the living room and maybe it's time to try that tack. Encourage your dog to jump into the chair by baiting it with something she likes to eat and take every opportunity to praise her for doing so. (Covering the chair with a washable sheet or throw will help you feel better about having a "dog chair" in your living room.) If you can't bring yourself to go this route, how about a dog bed on the floor instead? You may want to make this attractive to her at first by putting in it an article of your worn clothing and/or an enticing toy or tidbit.

It's always a good idea to take steps to increase your dog's overall sense of security so that feeling physically connected to you won't seem so important. You can do this in the usual ways: making sure she knows you are in charge by asking her to do little things to earn praise and petting, exercising her well before you leave so that she will be more inclined to rest quietly in her own bed, and cutting back on the amount of physical attention you give so that she won't miss you so much when you leave.

If your dog gets up on the furniture when you're home as well, treat the problem as a bad habit to be broken. Teach her the "Off" command, and treat, praise, and pet her only when she is off the furniture, never on. Catch her in the act of jumping up as often as you can and distract her with something she likes. When you're sitting on the sofa and she attempts to join you, point her toward a different destination and reinforce her with praise or a tidbit for going there.

WHAT NOT TO DO It would be a mistake to scold your dog harshly or physically correct her for getting up on the furniture, especially if

she's been allowed to do so in the past, as this will only build confusion and tension inside her. Covering the furniture in a way that makes it difficult or impossible for her actually to get on it probably would be counterproductive, meaning that it will do nothing to lessen the dog's desire to be there and may actually increase it by adding an element of frustration that she might seek to allay by going to the place that smells most comfortingly of you.

Jumping Up

CAUSES　Dogs jump up on their owners and visitors in an attempt to greet them face-to-face.

RESOLVING THE PROBLEM　The best way to discourage jumping up is to give the dog something different to do at the times when he normally would jump. For example, teaching your dog to sit on command will give you a way to keep him from jumping without having to scold or correct him for the undesirable behavior.

WHAT NOT TO DO　Avoid shouting at, kneeing in the belly, stepping on his rear feet, or using your hands to force your dog's front paws down when he greets you. This will not only frustrate his desire to greet you (or others) but will add unwanted emotion to the greeting and make the dog more unruly, not less.

Mounting

CAUSES　Dogs who have not been neutered are most likely to mount people's legs, upholstered furniture, throw pillows, and other inanimate

Keep your reunion low-key: if you bend down closer to your dog's level and speak to her calmly, she is less likely to jump up. (Deborah Salem and Bonnie)

objects, as well as attempt to mount same-gender dogs, the family cat, or almost anything else. Most mounting is seen in unneutered male dogs, but some females and sterilized animals mount people and inappropriate objects as well. Mounting is considered to be attention-seeking as well as sexual behavior.

RESOLVING THE PROBLEM Have your dog examined by your veterinarian for any urinary-tract or genital problems that could be contributing to this behavior. If your dog has not been sterilized, make an appointment to have this done. Sterilization is good insurance against mounting behavior but may not be effective once the dog is older and has formed a habit. Many veterinarians are now performing sterilization as early as two months. In the meantime, do nothing to encourage the behavior, including reacting strongly when your dog is engaging in it. Since mounting for many dogs begins with jumping up on their owners or on visitors, teaching the dog to sit whenever he begins to jump (see Jumping Up, above) will correct mounting behavior as well.

If mounting is only an occasional problem, you may be able to resolve it by turning quickly and walking away just as your dog begins to lift his forepaws. Or, you may discourage occasional mounting by tossing a ball or other favorite toy to distract the dog.

WHAT NOT TO DO   Avoid harsh scolding or rough handling of your dog. Also, removing the dog from the room during the times when mounting occurs, such as after dinner when everyone is gathered in the family room, or when company comes, does not address the problem and may well cause other problems to arise due to the frustration of isolation.

Pulling On-Lead

CAUSES   Dogs initially pull forward against their leads because they have an instinct to counter resistance. When they feel the lead pulling backward on them, which happens quite naturally as owners try to get the dog to slow down or change direction, the dog responds by pulling forward. A tug-of-war through the lead begins and can easily and quickly become ingrained. Unfortunately, the owner's response almost always is to pull backward even harder, making the problem worse, and at the same time to allow himself to be pulled along, teaching the dog that this is the way to success.

RESOLVING THE PROBLEM   Pulling on-lead will stop only when the lead does not pull back. One way to teach your dog that her lead will not pull back is to simply stop dead in your tracks as soon as you feel your dog reach the end of the lead and start to pull. Say nothing to the dog; in fact, don't even look at her if she turns around to look at you quizzically, which she probably will do fairly quickly. Just stand silently, concentrating on not pulling backward on the lead, and wait to feel the lead go slack. When it does, say, "Let's go" or whatever phrase you use to signal your dog to step forward. Chances are that within a step or two your dog will again take up the slack in the lead and begin pulling. Repeat the process. And repeat it again and again until the dog is carefully keeping slack in the lead on her own. At this point she will have learned that she cannot go where she wants to go if the lead is taut. The best part of this method is that your dog will not associate the correction with you at all.

Another way to train your dog not to pull is to start all over again to teach her how to walk on-lead. Use a six-foot lead, put your dog on whichever side you prefer, and use your usual expression to get her started forward. Every time she begins to get ahead of you, make an abrupt right-angle turn and walk right into her, cheerfully encouraging her again to walk forward. This action will achieve the same result, which is to prevent the lead from becoming taut, which would cause the dog to resist it. At the same time, the dog will begin to pace herself by your leg in order to avoid being walked into. Through repetition, your dog will learn that the way to walk comfortably with you is at your side. A third way to "solve" the problem of a dog who pulls on-lead is to use a no-pull harness on the dog (see Quick Fixes, page 306). In this case, the behavior will change even though the dog will not really have learned anything. Without the harness, the dog undoubtedly will revert to pulling.

WHAT NOT TO DO   The one thing that will undermine this method is inconsistency. Once you begin training your dog not to pull, you need to make sure that you never move forward when she is pulling. Anytime this happens, you will be back to square one and will have to start over. The longer the problem has existed, the longer it may take until your dog has learned a new way to walk. When you are ready to quit for the day, call the dog in to you before turning back.

Whining

CAUSES   Whining is a particular sound that a dog makes when he wants something quite badly and someone is present who can get it for him if only she will. A whining dog is excited and frustrated in about equal parts. Whining often accompanies begging. Puppies whine when they are first separated from their mothers and littermates, and some adult dogs whine when separated from their owners or other family members, but usually only when someone is there to hear them. Whining seems to be a "voice" that dogs use to ask for assistance, not just to complain to the darkness.

RESOLVING THE PROBLEM   You can always stop a dog from occasional whining by giving him whatever he is whining for, but you will only have succeeded in teaching the dog that whining is profitable. If you don't want him to learn this, it is best not to reward whining in the first place. A better way is to teach the dog that he will be successful in getting what he wants only if he is quiet. This is relatively easy to do, because whining usually is not continual. Wait for a natural break in the pleading, then praise and reward the dog for silence.

A dog who whines a lot, or in a number of situations, may well be a dog who thinks he is in charge of things. With this dog, you need to assert yourself as leader. Do this by requiring the dog to do something to earn praise and petting. To the dog, this is almost the exact opposite of whining for what he wants. If your dog whines when he is left alone, try to make being alone less stressful for him. (Again, see Preventing Separation Difficulties, page 271, for detailed suggestions.)

WHAT NOT TO DO   Shouting at your dog or isolating him for whining should be avoided, as this will increase the dog's level of anxiety and make him that much more likely to whine or exhibit other undesired behavior to relieve tension.

Major Problems

Aggressive Behavior

Because of the seriousness of all forms of canine aggression, the subject will be discussed separately in chapter 21.

Barking

CAUSES   Barking is one (of many) ways that dogs communicate. Dogs bark when they are anxious, bored, and fearful but also to alert their "packs" that trespassers are approaching and to warn other dogs or people not to come any closer.

RESOLVING THE PROBLEM   In order to resolve a barking problem, you first must determine why, specifically, your dog is barking. The context will generally tell you this. For barking that occurs when you are not home, you may need to rely on neighbors or others who can fill you in. Important clues to why a dog is barking can be found in the dog's body language. For instance, a dog with ears back and tail down is fearful, a dog with ears and tail up and forward is barking aggressively. The steps to resolve barking problems will differ depending on the specific causes:

ANXIOUS BARKING   Dogs bark when they have been left alone, as a way to relieve the anxiety they are feeling (see chapter 19 for a full discussion of separation anxiety). To stop this kind of barking, you have to eliminate the anxiety that feeds it. Probably the most important thing you can do to resolve anxious barking is to teach the dog to be calm and relaxed when you are away. As discussed in chapter 19, do this by setting up mini-separations in which you leave for only a moment or two and then return. Gradually extend the time and distance that you are away, being careful to make sure that your dog remains calm. Should she become fearful, go back to the prior step and stay at that level until you can move on without the dog relapsing into anxiety.

Distract the dog from anxious feelings when you leave by coming up with something novel for her to work on. For example, a toy filled with cheese for her to try to get out may intrigue her just enough to take her mind off your departure during the first few critical moments after you've gone out the door. Experiment with different distractions.

At the same time, work on building up your dog's general confidence level. Run her through some training exercises (refer to chapter 14 for details) so that she can earn praise for performing correctly. End each session on a successful note and make sure your commands and responses are consistent; feeling confidence in you as leader will bolster your dog's sense of security in the social structure.

Try to be very calm when you leave your dog and when you return. Highly emotional departures and reunions only build tension in your dog. What she needs is a sense that coming and going is no big deal.

BORED BARKING   A dog who is barking because he is isolated and has nothing much to do very likely will stop barking if you can remove his sense of isolation. Often dogs are isolated because they have behavior problems. In these cases, the answer is to work on solving the underlying problems so that the dog can be reunited with his family. Dogs who must be alone can be provided with interesting and distracting things to do to relieve boredom and avoid the barking it can cause. Such things include new toys, things to chew on, and fun problems to solve, such as getting inside a container to find a delectable item within. Daily exercise is an important part of relieving boredom, which is actually a unique kind of tension. Hiring a pet-sitter to come by and play with or exercise your dog to break up his day may help. Providing him company in the form of a compatible dog may be the solution. Often just placing the dog in a room that he normally finds very comfortable rather than in a different spot that he associates with waiting and isolation will help.

FEARFUL BARKING   A dog who is barking out of fear, such as the fear of thunder or firecrackers, will not stop barking as long as the feared object or condition is present. To truly solve the problem, the dog must learn not to be afraid of these experiences. This is taught by very slowly and gradually reintroducing the dog to the sound of thunder, for instance, in such tiny steps that she is able to be calm in its presence. For example, a sound recording of a thunderstorm may be played at very low volume to see if the dog can tolerate it. If she can, the sound is then increased in small increments until it is full volume. Something the dog likes to do, such as happy play with a ball, should be made available at the same time so that the dog begins to connect the sound of thunder with something fun. This kind of program needs to be done very carefully and slowly, as moving too fast can make the problem worse. Probably you should seek the help of an animal behaviorist to put such a program in place. Medications that are calming may be prescribed by your veterinarian to use in conjunction with this kind of behavioral modification program.

TERRITORIAL/PROTECTIVE BARKING Almost any owner would welcome the assistance of a good watchdog, that is, a dog who barks loudly whenever a stranger steps onto the property. However, dogs in general have difficulty distinguishing true strangers from people who are not complete strangers but also are not people the dog knows well. Most dogs are automatic watchdogs, but some go completely overboard and/or don't know when to stop. The solution to this problem is to teach such dogs who to bark at, how much to bark, and to stop barking on command.

The first step is to make sure your dog understands what really is your property and what isn't. Male dogs who are allowed to urine-mark territory beyond their own property lines may come to think of all this land as theirs to protect and defend. Discourage this thinking by restricting your dog to your own property. If the dog has not been sterilized, having him neutered should help.

The next step is to teach your dog that delivery people, children walking to school, stray dogs and cats, casual passersby, even the neighbor, are not intruders but friends, and that good things happen to him when these people come onto "his" territory. To do this, enlist the help of people your dog usually barks at. Have someone, your neighbor for instance, walk by your yard but at a distance far enough away so that the dog doesn't bark. Ask your dog to "Sit" or "Down," then reward him with a very special tidbit for being quiet. As the person gradually comes closer, continue to reward quiet behavior. If your dog barks, squirt him with a stream of water and/or use your "correction" voice (see Your Voice, page 205) to discourage this behavior. As soon as he is quiet, reward him with a tidbit. You may need to ask the "intruder" to move farther away again for a while longer. Repeat this process as the person slowly walks closer, until your dog can be quiet with the neighbor nearby. Then ask the neighbor to reward the dog with a tidbit. Have a variety of people play the intruder. As your dog begins to anticipate the person's approach with friendly behavior and the barking decreases, move farther and farther away from your dog. If your dog barks at people outside while he is inside and you are home, call your dog to you, have him obey a "Sit" command, and reward him.

WHAT NOT TO DO   The essence of teaching your dog not to bark is to consistently reward him for being quiet. Punishing barking by shouting (barking back!) or harshly scolding your dog will not be effective because the dog already knows that barking "works" for him. After all, in some cases barking eases anxious feelings, in others it appears to drive off intruders. What you need to do is make *not* barking even more rewarding. At the same time, make sure you don't inadvertently encourage territorial barking by enticing your dog to bark at certain sounds, people, or animals by exaggerating any uneasiness you may be feeling by saying such things as "Who's there, Skippy? Shall we see? Shall we? Shall we?" Whenever you react in an excited or nervous way to such "intruders," you are teaching your dog to do the same.

Chasing

CAUSES   Dogs who leave their property to chase are heeding basic instincts to chase anything that moves quickly and/or to drive trespassers away from what they consider to be "their" territory. In modern times, chase objects include not only dogs, other domestic animals, and wildlife but also joggers, bicycles, delivery vans, and cars.

RESOLVING THE PROBLEM   Since your dog thinks he is defending his territory from intruders, the first step in correcting this behavior is to teach the dog that his territory ends at your property line wherever the "line" may be. For the time being, refrain from walking your dog on streets or roads just beyond your own property line so that he cannot urine-mark these areas and therefore think he has to defend them. You can do this by training your dog to eliminate immediately upon leaving your home (see chapter 12), moving briskly through this adjacent area, encouraging your dog to keep up a steady pace, and not allowing him to stop and sniff along the way. He will soon enough learn what happens where. If your dog has not been neutered, attend to this right away as unneutered males are more likely than other dogs to try to extend their territories.

To encourage your dog to tolerate passersby without barking excessively, teach him the actual boundaries of your property through use of a leash and your voice. (Gorman Bechard and Casey)

Next, sharpen up your leadership role by asking your dog to do something to earn attention or petting from you. For example, ask the dog to sit before you pet him, or put on his lead, or give him his dinner. (Go back to chapter 14 for help with basic training.) You'll know this is working when you see your dog begin to look to you for directions rather than just follow his own inclinations.

The next step is to decide what actual physical boundaries you want your dog to respect (they need not be the legal boundaries of your property, but in no case should they extend beyond your property lines). Examples might be a fence on one side, a row of trees on another, and the edge of the garage on a third. Ideally you should have a fenced yard for your dog. However, a dog with a strong instinct to chase would be at the fence line, endlessly trying to find ways to get over, under, or around it to pursue whatever is passing beyond the wire. Once you've decided on boundaries, proceed to teach them to your dog. Do this by pretending your boundary is an electrified fence that just happens to be invisible.

Begin by putting your dog on-lead and walking purposefully toward the "fence." When your dog is within a few feet of it, stop suddenly and let out a short shout as if you'd gotten a shock, then turn and walk very quickly back to your house. Praise the dog as he "retreats" with you. Repeat this process over and over until your dog has learned all his boundaries and stops himself when he reaches them and looks toward you. What you have done is shrunk the area that your dog feels he must defend so that he will not feel obliged to chase the cars and other trespassers beyond that point.

WHAT NOT TO DO   Avoid any kind of harsh punishment or remote electronic control of your dog for chasing behavior. Even if effective in curbing the behavior, the cause of the problem will not have been eliminated. This sets the stage for other behavior problems to develop out of the dog's frustration of wanting to chase but being afraid to.

Destructive Behavior

CAUSES   Chewing, scratching, tearing up, and generally trashing the environment by adolescent and adult dogs are examples of destructive behavior. The reasons that dogs are destructive vary widely and include separation anxiety, fear, boredom, and frustration. Sometimes a medical condition such as gum disease can cause destructive chewing. Predatory behavior can cause a rampage of scratching and chewing in a dog who senses rats under the floorboards, for example, or a cat on the other side of the wall. All puppies are likely to cause some destruction as they explore everything in reach with their teeth (see Chewing, page 279), but we don't think of this very normal developmental stage as destructive behavior — primarily because puppies will grow out of it with reasonable care.

RESOLVING THE PROBLEM   As with other behavior problems, the "cure" must relate to the cause in each individual case.

SEPARATION ANXIETY   Dogs who are very dependent on their owners may suffer separation anxiety whenever they are separated from them. When left home alone in particular, such dogs can be very destructive as they chew, scratch, and tear up the house in an attempt to relieve their anxious feelings. See chapter 19 for suggestions for resolving this problem.

FEARS AND PHOBIAS Dogs who are terrified of such things as thunder, firecrackers, and gunfire may become destructive during an event that triggers their fear. See Fearful Behavior, page 300, for specific suggestions for managing this problem.

BOREDOM When a dog is isolated for a prolonged period of time without anything much to do, she may become bored and restless. Her attempts to relieve these uncomfortable feelings may easily result in chewing or scratching at nearby objects and surfaces. To correct this behavior, you first must make sure that boredom is the cause.

For example, how do you know your dog is bored rather than suffering from separation anxiety? One way is to think about how the dog behaves when she is with you. Does she follow you from room to room and seem reluctant to let you out of her sight? Does she tend to overdo the greetings when you return after being away? A dog who becomes bored when isolated is not necessarily overly attached to her owner. She may very well be a sociable, outgoing type who just hasn't had much experience being by herself.

The question to ask yourself now is whether or not the dog really needs to be isolated, remembering of course that dogs are highly social beings who almost always prefer to be with their family members. If your dog is put out in the yard or in a pen because she has other behavior problems, then these should be looked at and resolved. If this isn't the reason, you may need to look for more ways to include your dog in daily activities so she won't have to be isolated as much. You may find that if you spend more time with her doing vigorous outdoor activities, particularly before she needs to be isolated, that she'll be tired enough to rest quietly or sleep when left alone rather than look for ways to entertain herself. In the meantime, when she has to be alone, try interesting her in new toys or unique items that it's okay for her to chew. To keep these items "fresh" for her, don't make them available at other times. Finally, if your dog is otherwise well adjusted and you've been thinking about adding another dog to your household, maybe now is a good time to put that plan in action (see chapter 22 for suggestions about managing changes of this sort).

ATTENTION-GETTING Just like small children, dogs will sometimes misbehave just to get our attention. Even the shouting and scolding that we may do when we catch them misbehaving seem to be better than no attention at all. To correct this kind of destructive behavior, make it a point to give praise and positive attention to your dog for doing things you approve of or have taught her to do.

PLAYING AND EXPLORING   The very normal and natural way that dogs play and explore their environment — by chewing and shredding, pawing and shaking, dragging around and carrying — can very easily lead them to damage items that appeal to them, such as shoes, socks, and paper objects. This behavior is most common in puppies and young dogs and eventually tapers off and disappears as the dog matures. In the meantime, why not "proof" your home by removing from the dog's access any items that you would be upset to find destroyed? You can further limit your dog's potential for destruction by supervising her play and exploration and by making sure she has plenty of opportunities to play and explore items that are acceptable and safe.

INAPPROPRIATE PUNISHMENT   Dogs who were punished after the fact for misbehavior that occurred when their owner was absent are likely to feel anxious as the time approaches for the owner to return from being away. To relieve this anxiety, the dog may chew or scratch — which ironically may lead to more punishment. You can interrupt this vicious cycle by ignoring any damage that your dog does in your absence and instituting a new kind of fun activity to begin as soon as you return home. Ideally, it should be something that involves your giving the dog a few commands such as "Sit," "Back," "Wait," and "Catch." Praise the dog for correct responses, and continue to ignore any mistakes that happen when you're not there.

BARRIER FRUSTRATION   Dogs have an instinct to resist anything that restricts their freedom, and barriers do this, particularly closely confining ones such as airline crates or small bathrooms and laundry rooms. Removing the barrier usually resolves the problem. If the dog is being crated because of other behavior problems, such as house-soiling or chewing, these problems must be resolved.

WHAT NOT TO DO   Avoid scolding your dog or meting out any kind of negative correction for what she has done in your absence. Unless correction is applied *as misbehavior is occurring,* the dog cannot make the connection between your actions and hers. Your behavior then can only confuse her and cause her to be wary of you in the future, particularly under similar circumstances. Also, don't make the mistake of assuming your dog is being destructive to get even with you for leaving her alone. Unlike humans, dogs have no capacity to be either spiteful or vengeful.

Escape Behavior

CAUSES Dogs escape from their homes and/or yards in order to get *away* from something they view as negative or to get *to* something they view as positive. Negatives are things they fear, including being alone, and feelings that are uncomfortable, such as restlessness and boredom. Positives include searching for sexual partners, food, or companionship as well as engaging in pleasurable activities such as hunting and fighting.

RESOLVING THE PROBLEM Many owners focus their efforts on preventing escape by erecting a higher fence, a stronger latch, or replacing dirt and grass under the fence with poured concrete. Dedicated escape artists will still find a way to get out. Even if they don't, however, preventing escape does not address the reasons why the dog wants to escape. The first question to ask yourself is "How much time is the dog alone in the yard?" Ideally, the dog should never be outdoors unsupervised. Many dogs, of course, will keep asking to "go out" so that they can keep a close eye on what's going on around their property. Nevertheless, it is not in a dog's nature to spend a lot of time by himself, and sooner or later, the dog in the yard is going to want out of it — either by coming back inside, if that's where his people are, or, if they're away, then over the fence. If the dog's powerful urge to escape is frustrated, he may easily begin to show other behavior problems.

FEARFULNESS If a frightening noise such as thunder occurs, the dog may try to escape the home or yard in order to get away from it. The dog may have a generalized fear of the yard or pen because something frightening happened to him while he was there. In either case, in order to resolve the escape problem, you must find a way to decrease your dog's fearfulness. The technique most often used to help a dog get over his fear of certain loud noises, for instance, is to play a recording of the noise at very low volume and raise it very gradually, over time, until he can tolerate it more easily. At the same time, distract the dog with something that he really enjoys, such as a game of catch or other physical activity. The idea is to teach the dog that good things happen in the presence of the feared noise. If your dog appears to fear the yard itself, you will need to figure out what happened to him there and then use similar techniques to teach him not to fear the event (sight, sound, activity, other animal or person). Be aware, however, that it takes skill and patience to apply this technique successfully. If your theory about the cause — or your timing — is off, you could actually make your dog more fearful. You may want to consult with an animal behaviorist rather than trying to handle this on your own.

SEPARATION ANXIETY   Dogs who become extremely anxious when their owners leave them are strongly motivated to escape their fear by leaving the place where it is occurring. Dogs with separation anxiety often escape the home and/or yard, only to hang around the property or even return to sit on the front porch. Presumably this is because the home is filled with the owner's scent and allows the dog to feel more closely connected — he just didn't realize it until he'd run away. Techniques for resolving separation anxiety are given in chapter 19.

SEXUAL ROAMING   An unsterilized male can detect the presence of a female in season from a long distance away and often shows great cleverness and tenacity in escaping his yard to pursue her. Unsterilized males are often strongly inclined to patrol "their" territory to chase off any competitors. The first order of business is to have your male sterilized so as to lessen or eliminate this reason for roaming. Other suggestions for combating this behavior are given under Chasing, page 293.

BOREDOM   If spending time out of the yard is more fun than staying in it, dogs will continue to escape because such good things happen when they do. Neighbors may take the dog in, play with her, or feed her. While out, she gets to investigate many interesting smells, get lots of exercise, and maybe visit other dogs. In order to keep your dog from escaping, you have to tip the "good times" scale in favor of staying home. Suggestions for making the yard less boring are given under Destructive Behavior, Boredom, above, but you should realize that things your dog can do alone in a yard are going to have a hard time competing with the "adventures" that await on the other side of the fence. Unfortunately, many dangers also await, including the very real danger of being killed on the road.

WHAT NOT TO DO   Punishing a dog after the fact for running away will not teach your dog to stay in the yard; it will teach her not to let you catch her. If you catch your dog at the very moment she is going over or under the fence, scolding her and then praising her for coming back in may help resolve the escaping problem, if you also follow other suggestions. Excessive punishment is never appropriate. It will cause your dog to fear you, which in turn may lead to additional behavior problems. Never punish a dog who escapes your yard due to separation anxiety or fear. Punishment will only make the dog more fearful, not less.

Do not reassure your dog when he is reacting fearfully. (Kathan McCarthy and Wally)

Fearful Behavior

CAUSES We don't really know why dogs are so often frightened, sometimes terrified, of loud cracking noises such as thunder, firecrackers, backfiring automobiles, and gunfire, which come on seemingly without warning. There may be a genetic basis in some cases and in some instances a puppy may have been at a particularly sensitive stage when she heard the sound the first time. More often, though, the fearfulness just seems to develop on its own. It is not unusual for a dog who reacts calmly enough to thunder for a year or two to later on develop a terrible fear of it. In many cases our well-meaning actions to calm or reassure our dogs probably go a long way to actually making the problem worse!

RESOLVING THE PROBLEM If you can recall the first time your dog was frightened by thunder, for instance, think back to how you and the rest of your family reacted. Your behavior at that time, particularly if you held the dog and crooned to her and gave her treats to make her feel better, actually rewarded whatever fearful behavior your dog had shown. If you got excited yourself, running back and forth slamming windows to keep out the rain, you undoubtedly added to your dog's conviction that fear of thunder was very appropriate. Thus a vicious cycle was begun that caused your dog's fear and your attempts to calm her to escalate over time.

To reverse this process and make your dog feel less afraid, try the following:

- Try to create a safe place where she can go when she's afraid, whether you're there or not. This should be a place your dog considers safe, not

Instead, offer your dog a tidbit of a food he really loves. (Kathan McCarthy and Wally)

necessarily one that you would pick. If you've noticed that she tries to get to a particular spot, that means she's already picked out a place. Consider giving her access to it if you possibly can. Usually it will be a small dark place that is shielded as much as possible from the fearful sound. Note: Some dogs want to be moving constantly when they're afraid, and a safe place won't appeal to them.

- When the noise is at its lowest level of intensity, as in a storm, try to distract your dog when she first begins to be watchful. Entice her with something she really likes to do, such as fetch a tennis ball. The more often you do this, the more likely the distraction will work for longer and longer periods of time. However, once your dog begins to be really afraid and lose interest, put the ball away or you could inadvertently reinforce her fearful behavior.

- Consider consulting with an animal behaviorist to set up a behavior modification program to desensitize your dog to the sound she now fears. If this person is also a veterinarian or works with a veterinarian in her practice, she may recommend the use of anti-anxiety medication that will take the edge off your dog's fear so that she can respond more positively to the other parts of the program.

The behavioral consultant will first work with you to identify everything that the dog is afraid of in connection with this particular noise. In the case of thunder, for instance, the dog may also be afraid of wind, lightning, and rain, and possibly even the yard in which she has sometimes been when a storm broke. Next, the consultant will expose your dog to a level of the sound so low that it does not produce fear in her. At the same time she will offer your dog an activity or a tidbit of food that she really loves. This will help the dog begin to associate good things with the fearful sound. Very gradually, the volume of sound will be increased but will continue to be paired with something the dog loves. If the plan is well conceived and carried out with care, in the end your dog will be able to tolerate the sound without reverting to fearful behavior.

WHAT NOT TO DO   Do not reassure your dog when she is behaving fearfully. Stay calm yourself and talk to your dog as quietly as you can. Also, do not scold or punish your dog for being fearful, as this will only make her more afraid. Likewise, forcing your dog to remain close to the source of the sound will increase her fear and could cause her to snap or bite in an attempt to get away. Confining her in a crate to prevent her from being destructive is not recommended. She could easily injure herself in frantic attempts to get out.

House-Soiling

CAUSES   Dogs who have been carefully housetrained sometimes still urinate and/or defecate inside the house. (If you're not sure whether or not your dog really is housetrained, go back to chapter 12 and review the section titled Signs of Success.) Usually you can tell from the circumstances if house-soiling is an accident or something the dog is doing on purpose. The causes of accidents and purposeful acts are different and so are the recommended approaches to resolve them.

An *accident* tends to be a sporadic rather than daily event and seems to occur when certain circumstances are present. These include certain medical conditions, and fear-provoking events like thunderstorms, being left home alone, or being approached by certain people in certain ways — among others. A *purposeful act* just has that look about it. Your dog may hike his leg even if you're standing right there looking at him!

RESOLVING THE PROBLEM Whatever's going on when your dog soils in the house, the first thing you should do is have your veterinarian give him a thorough examination. Medical conditions that could cause a dog to urinate indoors include urinary-tract infections, diabetes, or kidney disease; conditions that might cause in-house defecation are intestinal parasites, impacted anal glands, and diseases of the digestive system. But if your veterinarian finds no medical reason for the behavior, your next step should be to try to figure out what is the reason. Careful observation of all the factors that are involved with each episode may make this easier than you might have imagined.

FEAR-PROVOKING EVENTS If your dog's accidents occur during Fourth of July celebrations, fireworks, hunting season (that is, within earshot of gunfire), and the like, you can be pretty sure the cause is extreme fearfulness. To eliminate house-soiling you must first reduce her fear. See the techniques suggested under Fearful Behavior, above.

SEPARATION ANXIETY House-soiling is a common problem when some dogs are left alone. If on top of that they are scolded or harshly punished for being afraid or for any misbehavior committed while in the home-alone state, they will be more uneasy the next time and therefore even more likely to soil the house. To correct the problem, which really is only a symptom of a problem, think again about what you can do to lessen your dog's dependence on you and build her self-confidence at the same time. See chapter 19 for a full discussion of the problem.

SUBMISSIVE/EXCITEMENT URINATION It is natural for dogs, and especially puppies, who generally mature out of it, to dribble a little urine to show submissiveness to a strong leader figure, whether canine or human. If your dog happens to be very submissive, she may dribble in situations that both are exciting and call for greeting rituals, such as when company arrives. The key to resolving this problem is to build your dog's confidence in herself. One way is through such things as obedience classes, where dogs are helped to succeed. Another is to ignore the dog completely when you first arrive home, but then later on reward her for calm behavior.

TERRITORIAL URINE-MARKING   Unneutered male dogs in particular will come indoors after a walk around the neighborhood and promptly lift their legs to deposit a few drops of urine near the front or rear door. They are heeding the instinct to let other dogs in the neighborhood know that this house is "theirs," and that trespassers should beware. The first thing to do to try to curb this behavior is to have the dog neutered. This should lessen his hormone-driven impulse to mark territory and fight off all challengers. Other techniques are to strengthen your own leadership role within the home by asking your dog to sit or do a small trick to "earn" petting and other good things from you, rather than just have them lavished upon him. If you assume your role more fully, chances are good that your dog won't feel so responsible for patrol and protection duties. While this training is taking place, it may help to use an enzymatic odor remover to deodorize favorite marking areas, since the scent of his own urine will draw him back to the same places again and again. Another technique to try is to place the dog's food bowl as close as possible to a "marking" area, as dogs are loath to soil their eating (and sleeping) areas.

WHAT NOT TO DO   The main thing to avoid in all cases of house-soiling is punishing the dog. If she is soiling indoors out of fear or anxiety, being punished will only make her more fearful. If he is urine-marking, punishment will frustrate him in his attempts to care for his "family." In neither instance will punishment have any lasting positive effect on the behavior.

Mouthing/Nipping

CAUSES   Mouthing and nipping are normal puppy behavior, but if not discouraged at an early age they may lead to biting in an adult dog.

Puppies investigate their world by putting most things they encounter — and particularly things that move quickly — into their mouths. They play-fight and roughhouse with their mother and littermates by nipping at her and one another. When we bring a puppy into our home, he or she automatically transfers the behavior to our feet and hands.

RESOLVING THE PROBLEM   Since it is so normal for puppies to take things in their mouths, attempts to suppress or stop the behavior are unlikely to be successful unless the puppy is provided with an alternative. The goal of working with this behavior is to redirect the puppy's desire to put something into her mouth by giving her acceptable objects and teaching her to be very gentle anytime a hand is in her mouth.

A first step to encourage acceptable behavior is to offer the puppy a small tidbit of food or a rawhide chew toy whenever you pet her. Scratch the puppy under her chin with one hand and offer a chewie or tidbit upon your open palm with the other (alternate hands frequently). This will not only help puppies learn that people and petting are wonderful, but will also keep the puppy's mouth busy while being petted.

At the same time, teach your puppy that nipping has negative consequences for her — it turns off any attention and social interaction with you. Should the puppy nip your hand, look her in the eye, tell her "No" in a firm voice, and ignore her. Either get up and walk away or fold your arms and remain completely immobile without looking at her. At first, your puppy is likely to pester you for more attention. She may jump at you, bark, or pull on parts of your clothes. If you laugh, look at her, or give in, you've only taught her to be even more out-of-control in order to get your attention.

You can also discourage nipping by gently holding on to the puppy's upper or lower jaw after she has taken your hand into her mouth. Wherever her mouth goes, your hand is still in it. She will soon grow tired of this. Be careful not to pull your hand away quickly, as this is likely to result in her pouncing on it and repeating the nipping behavior.

WHAT NOT TO DO Avoid punishment. Tapping, slapping, or hitting a puppy are guaranteed to fail, and may likely make the problem worse. She may become hand-shy and cringe whenever a hand approaches her face. She may become afraid of you and refuse to approach you at all. Or she could respond defensively, attempting to bite you to protect herself. Finally, if your puppy is already nipping, avoid games such as tug-of-war and wrestling, which may tend to cause her to grab at and lunge for you. Some puppies can play these games and some cannot.

The marketplace offers products and procedures to help prevent dogs from doing certain things that their owners don't want them to do. Some products may be used without undue risk and are recommended for people who wish to use them in a limited way or in conjunction with training and behavior modification techniques. Other products and procedures may seem to work, but in reality have only suppressed symptoms or prevented the behavior from being expressed. In such cases, the root causes of the dog/owner/environment problem will not have been addressed, and sometimes the side-effects are additional behavioral problems. These products cannot be recommended.

RECOMMENDED

STERILIZATION Sterilization is recommended as a means of controlling the pet overpopulation problem. In addition, sterilization can help with some behavior problems in some dogs. These include hormone-based behaviors such as escaping to search for sexual partners; barking or howling when separated from females in season; fighting with other dogs of the same gender; urine-marking, including indoors; and sexual mounting. This is universally recommended for all dogs.

NO-BARK COLLAR (CITRONELLA SPRAY) When properly fitted, this collar is activated to produce a spritz of lemon scent whenever a dog barks. Its advantages over the hand-held spritz bottle with a water/lemon juice solution are that it works whether or not you are with your dog, and the dog does not associate you with the correction.

NO-PULL HARNESSES The no-pull harness is a passive-restraint device whose construction causes tightening around your dog's middle whenever he begins to pull. It is humane and effective in preventing the dog from pulling on-lead but does nothing to eliminate his desire to pull. Dominant dogs and very determined pullers may whirl around and try to bite at the harness the first few times they feel it tighten. Recommended for occasional use.

NO-JUMP HARNESSES Similar to the no-pull harness, this device prevents your dog from jumping but does not eliminate his desire to jump. It is recommended for occasional use, such as when company is expected.

HEAD HALTERS (to replace the traditional collar) The head halter allows you gently to lead your dog by the head (where the head goes, the body naturally follows) rather than try to forcibly control him by a collar around his neck. One strap of the halter tightens around the muzzle when the dog pulls or resists being led, which simulates the way a mother dog grasps her puppies to discipline them. Your dog may try to remove the muzzle at first, but most learn to accept it if you are patient but firm. It is recommended as an alternative to the buckle collar and lead. The halter is not suitable for attaching ID tags but highly recommended as a humane and effective training aid.

DRUGS (for anxiety, hyperactivity, hormone-related problems) Drugs that affect behavior can be helpful when prescribed by your veterinarian and used in conjunction with a professionally designed program to modify your dog's behavior, but are not recommended as a sole means of resolving problems.

REPELLENTS (to keep dogs out of gardens and off particular surfaces) A number of products exist that have a smell that dogs don't like. These nontoxic products are effective in keeping most dogs away from surfaces that have been treated with the repellent. The repellent is not effective in all cases and does not cause your dog to become more attuned to your wishes. This is recommended to be used in conjunction with techniques to modify your dog's behavior.

SNAPPING TRAINING DEVICE (to keep dogs off furniture) This device replaces the mousetrap as an effective way to set a booby-trap for your dog. Based on basic mousetrap design, the trainer is triggered when your dog steps on the surface the trainer is resting on, causing a loud snapping noise that startles the dog. Humane and effective in keeping your dog away from or off certain objects, it does not eliminate the dog's desire to go there. The device is recommended for use in conjunction with a behavior modification program.

NOT RECOMMENDED

DEBARKING OPERATION This surgical procedure on the dog's vocal cords changes the dog's bark from a loud, sharp sound to a hoarse, softer one. It does not eliminate the cause of the barking, and thus allows the dog's tensions and frustrations to remain at the same level. It entails the risk of anesthesia and surgery, with no medical benefit to the dog.

NO-BARK COLLARS (shock and high-frequency) Various devices exist that use electrical stimulation or high-frequency sounds to either interrupt or punish what a dog is doing. These devices are not recommended because they do nothing to eliminate the dog's motivation to bark.

REMOTE TRAINERS (to correct various unwanted behaviors) The collars and other electronic devices that are designed to "train" a dog from a distance are not recommended because they contain potential for misuse and abuse if used incorrectly.

UNDERGROUND ELECTRONIC FENCING (to prevent escaping) This boundary training system includes an electrified line that is buried underground and a special collar that the dog must wear. When the dog attempts to cross over the buried wire, a shock is transmitted to the dog through the collar. This device is not recommended because it does not protect your dog from attack or contact by other animals, or from theft or injury by people coming onto your property. Neither does it provide to passersby assurance that your dog is safely confined and unable to approach them.

Aggression **21**

What gives? Our dogs live to be with us, follow us everywhere, want only to please, even give their lives to save ours. Yet they bite. Sometimes they bite the very hand that feeds them. How is this possible?

Dog bites are a serious public health concern in this country, especially where children are involved. The Centers for Disease Control and Prevention estimate that there are more than 4.5 million biting incidents a year, with between fifteen and twenty fatalities. Roughly two out of every one hundred Americans will be bitten by a dog in a given year, with perhaps half being bitten by their own dog or a dog whom they know. On the other hand, 4.5 million dog bites is still only a tiny fraction of the hundreds of millions of human–dog interactions that occur every single day. Overwhelmingly, most dogs do *not* bite, but statistics will offer small comfort if yours is one of the ones who do.

Few things in life can feel more like betrayal than being bitten by your own dog. Loyalty from our dog is taken as a given. We not only expect it, we hold it as an entitlement. The pain of being bitten by your dog is much more than physical.

We have different but equally strong feelings if our dog bites someone else. If she bites one of our children, we are anguished and outraged. If he bites the letter carrier or our next-door neighbor's child, we are horrified, guilty, and fearful of the consequences. It breaks our parental heart if he bites our other dog or our cat. We're stunned if she kills a rabbit and drags its bunny-fluff body home, nauseated beyond belief if she tries to eat it. It's a nightmare: How did our good dog go bad?

Once our initial shock and horror has passed, it's time to ask ourselves some tough questions: Could I have seen this coming before it happened? Did I just get a "bad dog"? Was it the breed that was at fault? Or was there something I could have done to prevent it? These questions will be answered in this chapter. The short answer, however, is that there are two primary ways to avert/prevent aggression: sterilization and socialization. They can't guarantee that no dog will ever display aggressive behaviors under any circumstances, but they can make a very big difference in the kinds of numbers cited above.

What Is Aggression?

Aggression covers lots of different behaviors, which animal behaviorists, incidentally, call "agonistic behaviors" in order to lose the negative value judgments that seem to go along with the label "aggressive." These behaviors include (as is outlined later) dominance, protective behaviors, territoriality, and predation.

All of these behaviors are important to the survival of wild dogs, as they help control who gets access to limited resources such as food, mates, and den sites. In this sense, aggressive behaviors, like all dog behaviors, are natural, not "bad."

In the movies we've all seen aggressive dogs snarling savagely with lips curled back over their teeth. As they pursue the terrified intruder across the yard, snapping at his heels as he flings himself over the chain-link fence, we all agree that these dogs mean business. In our kitchen or backyard, or when walking our own dog down the street, it can be harder to be sure if this or that behavior is aggressive. "He's just grumbling," we may think, or "She's in a bad mood today."

The fact is that aggression is not just biting. It includes anything a dog does to harm or intimidate a person, other dog, or other animal. According to this definition, aggression includes not only snapping and biting, which are obvious, but also behaviors that convey the *threat* of aggression, such as snarling, growling, baring the teeth, and lunging. Far from being an idle threat, such behavior will usually escalate to snapping or biting if the threat is ignored or countered. Note: Although some dogs "attack" vacuum cleaners, lawn mowers, hissing radiators, and children's wind-up toys, there is no evidence that this behavior is a precursor to aggression toward living beings. Nevertheless, such behavior should not be laughed at or otherwise encouraged in a dog who shows any signs of aggressiveness toward people.

Aggression is the one behavior problem in dogs that you really *must* find unacceptable. If your dog has the occasional housetraining accident and that's okay with you, then it's not a problem. Maybe you think it's kind of cute that she drools on your shoes from under the dinner table every night, pawing at your knee if you fall behind in passing down a few tidbits from your plate. If you don't care that your dog rattles the windows with her ferocious barking every time the Q33 bus hisses to a stop across the street, far be it for us to tell you that you have a problem. But aggression is different. The stakes are just too high. Aggression holds dreadful potential for injury to others, to your relationship with your dog, and therefore to your dog as well. So if your dog is showing signs of aggression, you *do* have a problem. The problem may or may not be solvable, but it must not be ignored. Unfortunately, left untreated, aggression problems almost always get worse over time.

Fortunately, most dogs live their whole lives without ever developing an aggression problem. To understand why most are nonaggressive but some are not, it's important to understand where canine aggression comes from and the kinds of factors that influence whether and when a dog will respond aggressively to what goes on around her. Keep the following points in mind as you think about your own dog's aggressive behaviors (he's bound to have some!) and what kinds of actions you may need to take to modify his behavior.

Where Aggression Comes From

In the wolf, aggressive behavior is a very efficient way to settle social conflicts among individuals without compromising the pack as a whole. Wolves tend to use the least amount of force necessary to make their point — often just the threat of aggression will do — and rarely harm one another.

Dogs have inherited aggressive behavior from the wolf. But selective breeding by man — to produce guard dogs, fighting dogs, and various kinds of hunting dogs, for example — has made domestic dogs in general much more aggressive than wolves. As a result, dogs are more likely than wolves to harm people and other dogs, and to kill small animals other than for food. For this reason, any signs of aggression in your dog must be taken very seriously.

Aggression is partly genetic. Breeds and types of dogs that were bred to be aggressive may pass this potential down to their puppies, just as may two aggressive parents of any breed or mixture of breeds.

Although some breed types are more likely to be aggressive than others, levels of aggression vary widely from dog to dog. There are no surefire predictors of which puppies will grow up to be aggressive and under what circumstances. Probably the closest thing to "a sure thing" is the puppy who growls, snarls, and bites from a very early age (under three or four months) despite appropriate corrections. (This is not to be confused with play-fighting with littermates or obliging humans, which is normal. You may want to go back and reread the discussion about Mouthing/Nipping in chapter 20.)

Aggression is partly "environmental." It is affected by a dog's interactions with his owners and his home environment, particularly during the first year of life. In other words, you can unintentionally cause your dog to behave more aggressively than he otherwise might. (By changing your behavior and/or your environment, you can also cause him to become less aggressive again.)

Aggression covers a very wide range. On one end of the spectrum it can mean a single snap or bite under a special set of circumstances, with exemplary behavior at other times. For example, if a dog has suffered a traumatic injury and is in intense pain, or if he is present during a terrifying experience such as an explosion or tornado, he may very well "attack" his owner or a kindly stranger attempting to help him. At the other end of the spectrum is the dog who may show aggressive behavior many times a day, resisting with growls and snaps any and all attempts to be controlled (handled, groomed, challenged, confined, restrained) by you or anyone else.

Factors That Influence Aggressive Behavior

LEVEL OF SOCIALIZATION   Whether or not and how extensively a dog was socialized as a puppy has a great deal to do with how much aggression he or she shows as an adult. Dogs who were exposed at an early age to other dogs, to children, and the elderly, as well as to a wide variety of sights and sounds, are better equipped to cope with whatever comes their way.

STERILIZATION STATUS   Bite statistics show that unsterilized dogs are up to three times more likely to bite than sterilized dogs — another reason why sterilizing your dog is so important.

GENDER   Some forms of aggression are more likely in males than in females. Nonsterilized males in particular are more likely to fight over social status or in defense of territory, while aggression that is motivated by fear or that comes up over food or other prized possessions is as common in females as in males. In general, two dogs of the same gender are more likely to fight with one another than are dogs of opposite genders.

AGE Aggression in puppies under three months of age is rare, although it does sometimes occur. For most dogs, however, aggressive behavior begins to show up around the onset of puberty, at six to eight months of age, and increases rapidly until the dog is roughly a year old, then increases more gradually until maturity, which varies from about two years for small breeds to three to four years for large ones.

BREED As mentioned above, breeds that were bred to be protective, to work as guards of property or livestock, or to hunt are apt to be more aggressive in general than other dogs. Other "fad" dogs, breeds that have become very popular very quickly for a variety of reasons, often are irresponsibly bred by unknowledgeable people who are primarily interested in making money. These dogs often are physically and behaviorally unsound and may show high levels of aggression.

HEALTH AND PAIN STATUS A dog who is ill or in pain may very well behave aggressively. So, too, may dogs who are deaf or blind and therefore cannot "read" the intentions of those around them. This includes dogs with hair covering the eyes, either by tradition or from lack of care and grooming.

LEVEL OF TRAINING A dog who has been humanely trained by his owner(s) to obey certain commands and is routinely required to defer at least some of his wishes to those of the humans he lives with is a dog who is under control. This dog is less likely to show some forms of aggression than a dog who has never been trained. Also, his basic training will provide the framework for helping him overcome whatever aggression problems he may have.

SUPERVISION AND RESTRAINT Dogs who are appropriately restrained and supervised by their owners whenever they come into contact with other dogs, other animals, strangers, and even nonstrangers such as neighbors, regular delivery people, and the veterinarian are less likely to behave aggressively than those who are allowed to roam the neighborhood or who are tethered in the yard or kept behind a fence. Tethering, in particular, whether on a rope, chain, or commercial tie-out, causes many dogs to develop serious aggression problems. A relatively high proportion of fatal dog attacks on humans have occurred when dogs were or had been routinely tethered for long periods at a time.

VICTIM BEHAVIOR Most of us have always believed that dogs don't bite people unless provoked, and from a dog's point of view, this is true. For instance, we could probably all agree that a child who pokes a sleeping dog with a stick is asking for trouble — though many dogs would just get up and walk away from even that. On the other hand, people who intend to be friendly toward a dog, or who may be completely unaware that there's even a dog around, may find out the hard way that the dog viewed their actions as threatening or challenging. Examples include the veterinarian's assistant reaching forward to take the dog's leash from the owner's hand, or the neighbor's child rattling up the driveway on his big-wheel tricycle, or a helpful houseguest trying to retrieve the dog's dish from under the chair.

VICTIM CHARACTERISTICS Thousands of years ago when dogs were still wolves, they learned that they could be most successful on a hunt if they attacked as a group and if they selected the easiest targets: animals who were very young or old, weak, sick, or injured, or isolated. Though it may break our hearts to accept it, this knowledge lives on in our dogs. Most of the people who are bitten by dogs are children or seniors.

Reasons for Aggression

From a human point of view, because we don't see the world the same way dogs do, it's easy enough to conclude that a dog may become aggressive for no reason. On the other hand, some of us like to think that *our* dog could never be aggressive under any circumstances. Neither is true. From a dog's point of view, aggression is *always* for a reason — even if he *is* biting the hand that feeds him — and it's always a possibility, because to a dog aggression is a completely natural response in certain situations.

There are a number of reasons why dogs behave aggressively, and in any given incident, more than one reason may be at work. Regardless of the reason, however, the only effective and humane way to resolve the problem is to reeducate your dog through new experiences in such a way that the events or situations that trigger his aggressive behavior become much less compelling.

What follows are the seven major reasons why dogs are aggressive, together with suggestions for approaching the problem. Note that in most if not all cases of aggression, you will need to seek professional help, and we urge you to do so. The suggestions given below are to get you started and to suggest the kind of program you should expect a professional to recommend. We cannot overemphasize that aggression is never effectively, and never, ever humanely resolved with pain, punishment, or fear.

Dominance Aggression

DESCRIPTION   When a dog has come to see himself as the dominant member in the family hierarchy, he (or less frequently she) will very likely respond aggressively if he feels his status or control is being challenged by another family member. ("Family" of course includes the entire household: the humans, including children, other dogs, and cats.) Male and female dogs, even if spayed or neutered, often establish separate dominance hierarchies within the family, so you may see more intense fighting within than between the sexes for rights to the cozy bed or the food bowl. Female-female squabbles are often the most severe. The tendency to seek dominance depends on the basic temperament of the individual dog, but also on experience — what he or she has been able to get away with.

SIGNS TO LOOK FOR   A "bossy" attitude in general. Examples include a dog who typically pushes ahead of everybody, including you, for food, for going out, for investigating new sights and sounds and a dog who ignores most of what you say, won't come when called, or may nudge your hand to demand petting. You may often find yourself backing down when he resists doing something you want him to do, such as get off the bed or let you examine his ears. He may look right at you and growl, and you have the sense that you better not push him too hard. The dominant dog will present much the same demeanor to dogs he meets on the street, to the veterinarian or groomer who tries to handle him, or to anyone who "bothers" him. When challenged, his body posture tends to be "up," forward and rigid, with ears and tail up and also forward, and with the hair along the back of his neck and between his shoulders standing erect.

TRIGGERS TO AGGRESSION   These include being disturbed while resting; any kind of physical restraint, including being pushed into a crate, being picked up to be bathed, being lifted onto an examination table, or being hugged; being touched unexpectedly, especially on his head, neck, or muzzle; being approached boldly from the front, with a direct stare into his eyes; being leaned over or reached over, as when you extend your hand to take him by the collar or to pet him on the back.

WHAT TO DO   If your dog is already growling at you or other human family members, you should proceed with extreme caution. First, have

A dog can exhibit all three kinds of aggression: fearful, dominant, and predatory, in a single interaction. (Kathy Milani's Bailey)

Encourage your dog to exhibit submissive behavior even if he isn't feeling submissive — tempting him to crawl under a chair for a treat lowers the dog's body position. Be sure to praise him afterward.
(Gorman Bechard and Kilgore)

him examined by your veterinarian for any physical conditions that could be causing the behavior. If he hasn't been neutered, schedule the surgery as soon as possible. If the veterinarian finds no physical illness or injury that might be causing pain, ask him for a referral to a person trained in animal behavior. You need someone who will work with you to custom-design a program to help you gradually reverse roles with your dog, so that you are the leader, other family members come next, and your dog is on the bottom rung of the social ladder. In the meantime, begin by implementing the following techniques, which lay the foundation for change. Note that these techniques call first for changes in *your* behavior, which will cause your dog's behavior to change in turn. Note also that at no time will you be using harsh, frightening, or painful methods of correcting your dog.

- Write down a careful history of the dog's aggressive behavior, including any growling, snarling, and snapping: What does he do, where does he do it, under what circumstances does he do it, when did he begin to act this way, what else is going on at the time, who does he do it to, what have you done up until now to try to correct it, and how has the dog responded. (This information will be essential for an animal behaviorist to have and will also allow you to avoid the kinds of situations that trigger your dog's aggression.)
- Withhold all gratuitous attention and affection from the dog. (Take heart: This is only temporary!)
- Ask the dog to earn any attention, petting, or treats that he gets by executing a simple command such as "Sit," or by doing a simple trick such

as offering a paw for shaking or barking on command. A trainer or animal behaviorist can also help you learn to elicit (not force!) submissive behaviors from your dog by rewarding such behaviors — for example, by having the dog crawl under a chair or roll over to receive a reward.

- Begin training your dog to stay off the beds and furniture (if the dog defends the bed against its rightful human occupants) by using snapping training devices or repellents. (See Quick Fixes, page 306, for details.)
- Feed the dog after the family eats, and ask him to sit before you put down his bowl.
- Use a head halter instead of a collar with your dog's leash (he'll probably try to scrape it off at first); this will allow you to gently control your dog without using physical force that he will resist (also see Quick Fixes, page 306).
- Make as many easy changes in your environment as you can think of to reduce the chances of additional episodes of aggression (for example, if your dog growls when you pass nearby while he is eating, find a new, off-the-beaten-path location for his food bowl); it is far better for you to avoid situations and actions known to trigger your dog's aggressive behavior than it is for you to continue to "back down" and give him his way.

WHAT NOT TO DO   Resist the natural temptation to "prove who's the boss." Avoid physical punishment of any kind, including striking, restraint by tying or chaining, confinement in a crate or small room, or isolation in the yard or other location away from the rest of the family. Using force against a dominantly aggressive dog will more than likely cause the dog to become even more aggressive to retain his dominant position. Do not attempt to control or correct your dominant dog's behavior toward other dogs in the family; instead, support his status with any other dogs by feeding him first, putting on his halter first, and passively allowing him somewhat greater privileges around the home (i.e., don't insist your top dog share his toys with his "brothers and sisters" — this may make sense for human siblings but is completely unnatural in a canine social system).

Fear-Motivated Aggression
DESCRIPTION   A dog who feels threatened by physical harm (whether or not a threat was intended) or is in a fearful state for other reasons will often first try to run away. If unable to do so for any reason, this dog may then bite a person who tries to handle, restrain, help, or comfort her.

SIGNS TO LOOK FOR A fearful dog seems edgy or unnecessarily wary, usually in a variety of situations. Her body may become tense and rigid or tremble, her posture and head low and cringing, ears back and down, tail tucked, eyes rolling.

TRIGGERS TO AGGRESSION
- being approached by strangers or strange dogs, especially if she is cornered
- seeing an arm suddenly raised
- being touched unexpectedly
- being in an unfamiliar place for the first time
- being forced to walk over uneven or unstable surfaces
- being subjected to crowds, loud noises (including thunder and firecrackers, but also loud electrical appliances, rattling windows, and wind)
- being approached by people in strange costumes or outfits or who move in unfamiliar and/or unpredictable ways such as with a staggering or lurching gait

WHAT TO DO If your dog has already threatened to bite out of fear, she probably will do so again if the motivation is strong enough. To avoid being bitten, schedule an appointment with your veterinarian to have the dog examined for any physical condition that might contribute to the dog's fearfulness. Examples are an ear infection or joint pain that you might inadvertently aggravate or a sight or vision problem that limits the dog's ability to sense danger in the normal ways. If the dog's hair hangs over her eyes, obstructing her vision, tie the hair up or keep it cut short.

If physical causes are ruled out, contact an animal behaviorist for help in coming up with a program that will help your dog feel less fearful in general. Prepare for your consultation by writing out a careful history of your dog's fear-aggressive behavior, including as much detail as possible (see suggestions for history-taking under Dominance Aggression, above). If your dog only becomes aggressive in one or two situations, such as at the veterinarian's or when having her nails clipped, the veterinarian might prescribe a tranquilizer to use on those infrequent occasions. If her fearfulness is more general, the veterinarian might prescribe other psychotropic medication to "turn down" her anxiety level just enough that she is able to participate in any training or behavior modification program that is recommended. Medication of this kind usually is prescribed as part of an overall strategy to change the dog's behavior; in and of itself, it is not a solution to the problem.

In general, you will want to try to teach your fearful dog a new and different way of responding to the various stimuli that she now finds threatening. The main technique for doing this is to distract her at the moment she begins to respond with fear and then immediately engage her in something that she really enjoys doing. Eventually she will associate the stimulus with happy times instead of with fear-filled ones.

If you don't already know of something that she loves to do, like catching a ball or retrieving a hard rubber toy, your first task is to find something that fills that bill. Most dogs cannot resist a sharply bouncing ball or a toy that squeaks, although very fearful dogs may shy away from both at first. In these cases, you must go even further back and look for anything, even a treat, that elicits strong interest or excitement. Encourage even the slightest positive (i.e., nonfearful) response, by offering an immediate reward of calm praise or a brief pat.

Make the most of the ball, squeaky toy, or fun game by limiting its use. In other words, bring it out only to train the dog, use it for no more than a minute or two at a time (or even a few seconds at first), and put it away while the dog is still very interested in it. Come up with a name for your "distracter" so you need only say "Squeak Squeak" or "Wanna fetch?" and your dog will start running in circles for you to toss the toy.

Once your dog is predictably responding in a happy way to your distracter, you have a tool powerful enough to take her attention away from a fear-inducing event such as the ringing doorbell. But be prepared for this process to take weeks. Start slowly and spend only as much time per training session as your dog remains happily distracted. You should be able to distract her for longer and longer and in the face of more and more serious fears as time goes on.

WHAT NOT TO DO   Avoid any kind of harsh response or punishment of a dog who is already fearful, as this will only increase her fearfulness. At the same time, resist the impulse to comfort a fearful dog by soothing, consoling, or other sympathetic sounds or gestures; these will actually teach the dog to be fearful in these circumstances. Avoid any and all situations that are currently known to frighten the dog. For instance, if there's something about the foyer by the front door that sets her off, try using the back door for a while. If she always panics when put up on the examining table at the veterinarian's, maybe the veterinarian can examine the dog on the floor or on the bench in the waiting room.

Possessive, Territorial, and Protective Aggression

DESCRIPTION These forms of aggression are similar and often overlap. *Possessive aggression* is when a dog thinks she is defending her food, toys, or other valued objects — such as that sheet of Kleenex stolen from the trash. *Territorial aggression* arises over defense of property, which in the dog's mind is whatever he feels able to defend, not just what you legally own. *Protective aggression* is directed toward people or animals whom a dog perceives as a threat to his family members. These kinds of aggression are fairly easy to distinguish by the circumstances in which they occur.

Possessive Aggression

SIGNS TO LOOK FOR Most dogs have some degree of possessive aggression. Suspect it if you see your dog kind of guard her "stuff." She may drop a toy on the floor and walk off and lie down several feet away, but immediately raise her head or get up if someone else walks too close to it. She may also gobble her food, grumbling a little to herself as she does so, especially if anyone walks nearby.

TRIGGERS TO AGGRESSION Possessive aggression is triggered when a person or other dog tries to take something — or the dog thinks that's the intention — that the dog claims as his own property. For example, the kindly houseguest who tries to help by retrieving the dog's dish from under the chair is likely to become a victim of possessive aggression.

WHAT TO DO Begin by taking your dog to the veterinarian. You want to be sure he isn't malnourished or hungry, which would justify even extreme possessiveness over food. Sharpen up your dog's obedience training so that you can use his response to commands to remind him that you are his leader. Introduce your dog to the head halter and long lead, and get him used to the new sensation for a day or two. When not training the dog, ignore him much of the time in order to increase his attention to you. Ask him to sit or lie down before you feed him or put on his leash.

Next, as in the case of fear-induced aggression (above), spend some time finding your dog's ideal "distracter." Once you have, throw the ball or get your dog moving with the squeaky toy, but make sure that you remain in control of when the game begins and when it ends. Since your dog already has a problem with possessiveness, you want to avoid allowing him to develop those same feelings toward this special toy. From the very beginning, use a firm tone of voice and say, "That's all," to signal the end of the game, then praise the dog for his compliance. Put the toy away until next time; if your dog whines or barks to let you know he wants it back, studiously ignore him.

When all these preliminaries are in place and the dog is attending well to you, begin to train him systematically to feel less possessive of food and other objects by making him come to expect a fun time in the presence of both those coveted objects and someone who might take them away. One way to do this is by setting up learning experiences. Begin by putting a head halter on the dog and attaching a long lead for control in case the dog lunges forward. Next, give the dog an object, let's say a rawhide chew, that you know he likes. Then have another family member or friend make a long-distance move toward the chew. In the instant that the dog notices the friend's movement toward his chew, distract him by squeaking the toy or calling out the name that you've given the game. As soon as you've gotten his attention, immediately toss the toy and spend a fast few minutes acting like loonies together. It's important that this activity involve the two of you. Giving something to the dog and leaving him to his own devices might not be compelling enough.

Repeat these steps many times over a few weeks. Gradually offer the dog objects he feels even more strongly about and have different family members approach more closely. Make sure you keep your distraction powerful by playing the game on a limited basis, always ending before the dog is bored.

Another technique to reeducate a dog who is overly possessive of his food bowl is to make him totally dependent on family members for every morsel. In other words, instead of putting his food in a dish on the floor, begin to feed him dry food by hand for several days. After that, put the food in the bowl but continue to hand-feed the pieces, one or two at a time, making sure that all family members take turns doing this. Gradually move from hand-feeding to feeding in a bowl again but remove the bowl from the floor between meals. The idea is to teach your dog that his humans are providers, not threats, at mealtime.

In time, your dog should lose his possessive feelings toward his food and whatever other objects previously stimulated such feelings, at least around family members. Your dog may or may not extend this feeling to visitors and strangers in your home. It would make sense for you to instruct them in how to approach your dog and to advise them to respect the dog's right to feel possessive about certain things.

Hand-feeding a dog who guards his food bowl at mealtime provides an opportunity for him to learn that the food is yours to dispense, not his to defend. (Deborah Salem and Bonnie)

Territorial Aggression

SIGNS TO LOOK FOR A dog who marks with urine every vertical surface on and around his property is likely going to object if a strange dog or person comes along. This territorially aggressive dog becomes enraged at the sight and sound of the UPS delivery truck or the letter carrier's three-wheeled cart.

TRIGGERS TO AGGRESSION Territorial aggression is triggered by the arrival of visitors, the sound of a car or van in the driveway, strange voices at the door — anything that heralds the appearance of strangers within the borders of the dog's personal territory.

WHAT TO DO   If your dog snarls, growls, or lunges at visitors or delivery people, you are looking at the very real possibility that he will actually bite such a person if he gets the chance. As in all types of aggression, begin with a visit to your veterinarian. Most of the dogs who show this type of aggression are nonsterilized males, so if you haven't already had your male dog neutered for other reasons, this will be the first order of business. Do not, however, expect neutering alone to resolve the problem.

The second order of business, as in other types of aggression, is to write out the history of the problem. This will document what your dog is doing and under what circumstances, just in case there is any doubt about the kind/cause of aggression. The history should also provide lots of specific details that you can then use to help make easy environmental changes to short-circuit your dog's established way of responding to visitors. For example, if a common trigger is the sound of the UPS truck pulling up the drive, ask the driver to park at the curb instead (he should be more than happy to avoid a confrontation with your dog). If the doorbell is a trigger, ask friends to call from the corner and not ring the bell.

In chapter 20 we saw that one of the major reasons for excessive barking, for urine-marking, and for chasing joggers, cyclists, and the UPS truck is the dog's strong mission of territorial defense. You may want your dog to think of himself as being in charge of defending your home, property, and perhaps surrounding areas from real and imagined intruders, but you also want to set limits on his behavior. Naturally enough, your territorial dog will respond to strangers and visitors as adversaries who must be faced down, scared off, and beaten back. The step up from barking and chasing to snapping and biting is not hard to understand, though not all barkers and chasers necessarily take that step. Your dog has to learn that it is his job to alert you to potential problems so that you, as the family leader, can deal with the problem. (Be sure to give your dog the appropriate follow-up instructions, such as "It's okay, Jack. Sit.")

The key to reducing your dog's territorial aggression is to reduce his exaggerated sense of himself and his duty (by enhancing his respect for you as leader while simultaneously shrinking his sense of domain) and to help him discover that really good things happen if he is calm and quiet when visitors come. Review the sections on barking, urine-marking, and chasing in chapter 20 for some specific things you can try to improve your leadership standing in your dog's eyes and to give him happy experiences with visitors that in time may replace the self-reinforcing pleasures of barking and chasing. If

To encourage your dog to tolerate visitors, control his movements and teach him (here, with a hand signal) to stay seated at your command. (Patty Thrift's Toucie)

you do not almost immediately begin to see some improvement, even if very small, contact an animal behaviorist for help.

Protective Aggression

SIGNS TO LOOK FOR   Protective aggression should be suspected in a dog who rarely relaxes completely when there are strangers around his family, or when his special person is up and about and engaged in lively conversation with others. He will usually position himself nearby, may try to place his body between that person and others, and may prowl about nervously as long as there's a lot of talking and laughing going on.

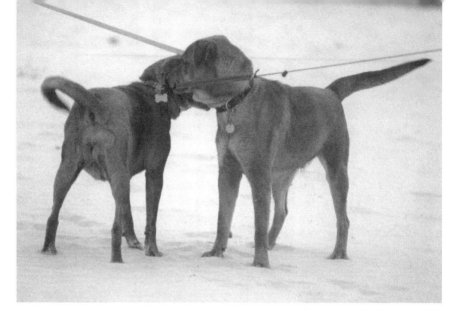

Carefully control the introduction of one strange dog to another by observing the dogs' body language as they slowly approach one another. Be prepared to separate the dogs at the first sign of trouble.

TRIGGERS TO AGGRESSION Protective aggression will be triggered if a stranger begins to grapple with the dog's owner as they're walking down the street. The trigger can be less obvious when the threat is not real, as when two family members get into an argument or even are roughhousing and one pushes or slaps at the other. Typically the dog will run growling in between the two and may bite one or the other if the pushing behavior continues.

WHAT TO DO Certain working breeds, such as German shepherd dogs, Dobermans, rottweilers, and Akitas, are reputed to be strongly protective of their owners, but many others as well as mixed-breeds have this quality too. Some powerful protective dogs are under complete voice control of their owners at all times and will never pose a threat to anyone — as long as the owner is conscious and competent. Others, however, have turned out to be more than the owner can handle. In addition, circumstances in the home, particularly the lack of strong, firm leadership qualities in *all* the humans, can cause the family dog of whatever breed to begin to think that it's his job to take care of everybody else.

Many owners inadvertently encourage their dogs to be overly protective by allowing them to make too many decisions, such as where to stand or sit or lie down, and how to position themselves in relationship to their owner, especially around other people. A common mistake that owners of "protective" breeds make is to limit the dog's interactions with others out of a preconceived idea that the dog is a one-man type and won't like strangers. On the other hand, for a variety of reasons, some owners of protective breeds truly don't want their dog to be friendly to people or to other dogs. This is a dangerous attitude; ironically, it can lead to dangerous behavior.

If your dog is threatening aggression toward others, particularly toward other people, as a means of protecting you or other family members, you will need to consult with an animal behaviorist so that you do not risk endangering others. The situation is a bit more urgent than territorial aggression because it's so difficult to predict when your dog might perceive you to be in danger. If her efforts to protect you were limited to the times when your well-being truly was at stake, the problem might be manageable — assuming your liability insurance covered any damages (see If Your Dog Bites, page 336). But if your dog misgauges the intentions of others, possibly including others in your own family, the situation clearly is a dangerous one. Some dogs actually go on alert if a stranger walks up and stands facing their owner on the street; in dog language, this is a "frontal" approach and represents a challenge. If the stranger were to stand alongside the owner instead, the dog might relax. But would you really want to have to be continually on guard against possible misinterpretations by your dog?

After you've consulted with your veterinarian to determine if your dog is in good health, and you've written down with as much detail as you can the circumstances under which your dog shows aggressive behavior, take the results with you on your first visit to the behavior counselor. The counselor's primary task will be to devise a plan to give your dog a new set of experiences with human beings, starting with you, in order to help her come to a different conclusion about her role in relation to you, both at home and in the wider world. In general terms, this means that you must become a strong leader to your dog, a person who can take care of herself and to whom your dog can look for guidance and protection, instead of the other way around. Exercises to increase your leadership qualities, as discussed under Dominance Aggression, above, and in many other places in this book, will help your dog relax her vigilance around you and turn her attention to the more appropriate pastimes of a dog, such as chasing after a ball or a flying disk that you throw and taking nice long walks with her nose to the ground.

The animal behaviorist's second task will be to observe and carefully supervise interactions among you, your dog, other people, and other dogs. Chances are that your protective dog was not well socialized as a young puppy and adolescent and still needs to learn how to have a good time in the presence of others, not to be on guard duty. The key to teaching the dog this lesson will be to find a distracter that will interrupt the dog's protective feelings and give her a chance to have even a few seconds of fun in those situations where she normally would be growling or threatening to attack in your defense (see Fear-Motivated Aggression, page 318, for a fuller discussion of finding and using the ideal distracter for your dog). After many repetitions, your dog will come to associate your presence and the simultaneous presence of other people and/or other animals with good times; instead of going on red alert, she will become excited about the prospect of play. This will not happen overnight, and care must be taken not to try to move too fast. Protective dogs tend to be more serious than silly, and it may take a while to find something the dog really really enjoys doing. An adult dog who has been protective for a while will need many positive experiences around others to overlay early negative ones or simply the absence of social interactions.

WHAT NOT TO DO Avoid using force, pain, intimidation, or isolation to counter your dog's aggression. Do not, however, avoid the problem, thinking it will go away or get better on its own. Dogs do not grow out of aggressive behavior — they grow into it — and it invariably becomes worse over time. Be careful not to encourage your dog's aggressive tendencies by letting him feel your own tension about how he may act in the presence of strangers or other dogs. For example, holding your dog on a tight leash or pulling him away from others while uttering repetitive phrases such as "No! Be nice!" will be translated by him to mean that there is something wrong with the situation and he will be more, not less, likely to respond aggressively.

Predation

DESCRIPTION Many animal behaviorists believe that predation is not truly a form of aggression, since other aggressive behaviors are intended to drive the target animal or person away from something (food, a mate, a protected area), while the intent of predation is to pursue, kill, and eat prey. However, because this behavior causes injury or death, we are classifying it here as aggression.

Dogs are direct descendants of predators, who historically hunted and still hunt other animals in order to feed themselves and their young. Under certain circumstances the modern dog may still revert to predatory behavior, including attacking and killing other dogs, cats, livestock, small wild or domestic animals and birds, and even people, especially children and the elderly.

SIGNS TO LOOK FOR
- a dog who "alerts" to the sight, sound, smell, or movements of another dog, a cat, a wild or domestic animal, or even a person
- a dog who becomes visibly and intently focused on her intended victim, largely impervious to other sights and sounds, and who may assume a "stalking" posture, even if only for a second or two, before rushing in to attack

Some dogs seem to become caught up in predatory aggression as a result of circumstances, such as when nearby dogs attack a victim, rather than through initiation of an attack on their own.

"Incomplete" predatory behaviors are seen in some of the livestock herding breeds (Shetland sheepdogs, border collies, corgis, some of the shepherds and cattle dog breeds). Many dogs of these breeds still retain strong instincts to herd livestock because they have continued to be bred and trained for this work. Thus a household pet corgi or sheltie may alternately stalk and nip at the heels of children, or valiantly try to direct the movements of the family cat. These behaviors may be worrisome to owners who aren't aware that they are witnessing very typical, highly prized (by ranchers) incomplete predatory behaviors. The behaviors are considered incomplete because humans, through hundreds of years of selective breeding, have modified true predation to a lower but still intense level that allows these dogs to offer great service to humans by helping them move sheep or cattle from field to field without actually harming them.

TRIGGERS TO AGGRESSION   Dogs who have not grown up with cats, small mammals, or birds may be naturally aggressive toward these prey species, pursuing and attacking them on sight; other dogs may be incited to attack an animal who "acts" like prey by running away, especially in an erratic, darting manner and while squealing, screaming, or making other high-pitched sounds of fear or pain. Excited, frenzied play among children can stimulate predatory aggression, as can "moving targets" such as joggers, cyclists, skateboarders, and even cars, vans, and larger vehicles.

WHAT TO DO   As always, begin by taking your dog to the veterinarian for a thorough checkup. Spay or neuter dogs who have not already been sterilized, as sex hormones circulating in the bloodstream cannot help and may actually increase the likelihood of predatory aggressiveness in some dogs.

Prepare your history with care. Which kinds of animals trigger predatory aggression in your dog? When did your dog first meet up with this kind of animal? Was it "bite at first sight"? If not, try to recall the first instance of aggressive behavior toward the animal or animals in question: What preceded it? What did you do or say before, during, or after an attack, if one occurred? What did the dog do then? In answering these questions, you will probably discover two things: that your dog did not get to know this kind of animal as a puppy; and that you or others may have inadvertently encouraged a predatory response by becoming excited about the animal, either positively ("Look, Girl, it's a kitty-cat!") or negatively ("Don't even *think* about it!"), especially while restraining the dog on a tightly held leash and then dragging her away. Subsequent episodes may have involved the dog in barking, lunging, snarling, and chasing these animals, so that by now the mere sight of a cat, for instance, sends her into attack mode.

Resolving the problem of predatory aggression will require that you turn back time and reintroduce your dog to these kinds of animals, including infants and small children, in a such a way that she associates them with fun and games rather than with tension ("There's something wrong with this thing my owner is so excited about") and frustration ("I can't reach it! I can't reach it!"). In the case of infants and children, you must take the precaution of *never, ever* leaving a newborn baby alone with your dog, especially within the first few days of bringing the baby home from the hospital.

Try the following steps to resolve predatory aggression problems:

- Sharpen up your leadership role by withholding all petting, attention, and even conversation from your dog for a few days. Feed her and let her out, but otherwise ignore her completely. You should see her begin to shift her focus onto you (perhaps more strongly than ever before).
- Praise and briefly pet your dog only after she has earned it by carrying out a command or performing a simple trick.
- Spend a few days finding some toy or activity that your dog really loves, then make her love it even more. Do this by deliberately exciting her with the toy, tossing it for her for a minute or so, then removing it before she has a chance to become bored. Keep this special toy out of sight in between training sessions. Come up with a name for the toy or activity and teach it to your dog so that she reliably responds with happy excitement whenever you use it (try to always use the same tone of voice as well; you want to make it virtually impossible for your dog ever to miss this cue).
- Next, set up situations with willing pet owners so that you can begin to reintroduce your dog to her prey of choice. If it's a small dog breed, for example, begin by making sure the other dog's owner has her pet securely leashed and perhaps even behind some kind of sturdy, see-through barrier. Then, at the very moment your dog notices the other dog, distract your dog by calling out the name of the favorite toy. If your dog turns toward you and away from the other dog, you've succeeded. Try to keep your dog happily distracted while the other dog's owner removes her pet from the area.
- Repeat these introductions a few times a day (not one after another) for several days or weeks, until your dog turns to you on her own with happy

anticipation when she sees the other animal and you no longer have to get her attention first. Gradually move the other dog in closer and closer, but always be prepared to increase the distance again if your dog seems to be less than happily distracted by her favorite thing.

WHAT NOT TO DO   There's no way that you can force your dog to "be nice" to other dogs or other animals. Scolding or punishing her for showing aggression toward cats around the neighborhood will only increase the tension that already exists whenever she encounters a cat. Also, be aware that your own demeanor around cats must always be happy, not just when you're in a training session with your dog. In other words, you can't be upbeat and positive in the moment that you're distracting and playing with your dog and then angrily shoo a stray cat out of your flower bed a few hours later. Our dogs take their emotional cues from us.

Redirected Aggression

DESCRIPTION   When an aggressive response is triggered by a person, other dog, or other animal that the dog can't get at, often the dog will redirect his aggressive behavior toward someone or something he can get at, an "innocent bystander." Redirected aggression can seem completely unprovoked.

SIGNS TO LOOK FOR   A dog (or dogs) who is barking or growling at another dog or person but is unable to really confront him or her, as when confined inside the car or behind a fence, or when indoors looking out at the street through a window. The dog may seem completely focused elsewhere and almost unaware of his surroundings. For instance, he may run into a piece of furniture on his way to a different window unless this is a regular routine where he almost has a track run into the floor. The behavior can occur in both multidog and single-dog families. Usually the attack will be directed at someone or something who is also "on edge" rather than at someone who is asleep nearby.

TRIGGERS   The triggers of redirected aggression do not come from the person or animal who is actually attacked, but from the original object of the dog's aggressiveness. Redirected aggression is most likely to arise out of territorial disputes, possession of food or other objects, and predatory aggression.

WHAT TO DO   Take a careful history of any and all episodes of redirected aggression in your dog. You want to try to figure out who or what is the real reason for your dog's aggressive response, because that is what must be reduced or eliminated. When that has been done, the redirected aggression will automatically be resolved as well.

Once you have determined, for instance, that your dog's real beef is with any other male dog who comes within a half-mile of "his" property, you can begin to go to work on reducing your dog's territorial aggressiveness. This will involve the now-familiar steps: neutering your male dog if this hasn't already been done; enhancing your role as leader to reduce your dog's need to protect and defend the domain; requiring your dog to earn attention from you so that he begins to look more to you for guidance rather than going his own way; refraining from walking your dog in the neighborhood around your property, particularly if he's been in the habit of urine-marking far afield; teaching your dog the boundaries you want him to observe (in this case, make sure his boundaries are well inside any areas where he might see other dogs passing by).

At the same time, work at changing your dog's response to canine passersby by distracting him at the moment he sights another dog on the street, then immediately engaging him in some game or activity that he absolutely can't resist. Eventually he will associate happy feelings instead of outrage with passing dogs. In the meantime, if his aggression is usually directed at someone in particular, such as another dog in the family, keep the two separated at the times when redirected aggression is likely to occur.

WHAT NOT TO DO   Avoid any impulse to punish your dog for his behavior. Harsh treatment is always a mistake, but in redirected aggression, which in a sense is aggression once removed, it is even less likely to make any sense at all to your dog or, therefore, to gain the result you're hoping for. What harsh and incomprehensible (to the dog) treatment can do, however, is undermine your relationship with your dog, even to the point where the unthinkable happens and he lashes out at you.

How Likely to Bite?

Aggression is a natural canine behavior, but not all dogs bite. The truth is that dogs differ widely in how likely they are to show aggressive behavior in any given situation. Some respond aggressively with very little stimulation. Others may be subjected to all kinds of threatening stimuli and events and never attempt to bite. The difference is called the dog's "threshold" of aggression, and is influenced by both genetic and environmental factors. If the threshold is lowered, the dog is more likely to bite. If the threshold is raised, he is less likely to do so.

What actually happens when you use the training and behavior modification techniques we've discussed in this book is that you raise your dog's threshold for aggression. There is no such thing as a "cure" for aggression, because aggression is not a disease. It is impossible to say that a particular dog will never bite or will never bite again. How much and how easily a particular dog's threshold for aggression can be raised depends on such things as the dog's age, breed, gender, and general temperament, as well as on whether the whole situation is analyzed correctly and the right techniques are selected. If you have a dog who is potentially aggressive yet you feel strongly committed to trying to modify his or her behavior, you owe it to both of you to enlist the aid of an animal behaviorist. See If Your Dog Bites at the end of this chapter before proceeding.

Can Aggression Be Prevented?

Aggression cannot be prevented under all circumstances and in all dogs, although the chances that it will be expressed can certainly be substantially reduced. Let's look again at the factors that influence aggression, on the table on page 334.

Beyond Your Own Backyard

Dogs who bite, or rather owners who don't take the steps to make sure their dogs don't bite, can make it hard for the rest of us. As lawmakers respond to dog-bite incidents, they often penalize everybody who owns a particular kind of dog or sometimes everybody who owns *any* kind of dog. What can we do to help improve the big picture regarding dog bites in this country? There are several things:

- *Support legislation against dogfighting and the irresponsible use of guard and attack dogs.* As long as these activities exist, dogs will continue to be bred and trained to be aggressive. Not only do these dogs present an unnecessarily high risk to the public, but they are condemned to live short, unhealthy lives outside the warm glow of a loving human family.
- *Avoid pet stores* that obtain their puppies from puppy mills.

- *Advocate at the local and state levels* against laws that target specific breeds as being vicious; instead, lobby for laws that place responsibility and penalties on owners for the actions of their dogs.
- *Encourage public education.* Dog owners need accurate and easily accessed information about keeping dogs safely and humanely. The general public, especially children, need to be taught how to behave around dogs and to approach them safely.

Factor	What to Do
level of socialization to people, especially children	Socialize! Nothing can make as much difference in the dog's ability to accept change and to be flexible with many different people and situations as being exposed to a huge variety of experiences when he is young.
sterilization status	Spay or neuter your dog, the younger the better (any time over eight weeks is medically safe).
gender	Be aware that dogs of the same gender are more likely to fight to establish their own dominance hierarchy than they are to fight with dogs of the opposite sex. If you have any choice in the matter, consider acquiring dogs of the opposite sex. If you do have two females, for instance, do everything you can to support whichever dog seems to be dominant over the other. Insisting on treating them as equals will only intensify the problem.
age	In general, the younger the dog, the more easily you can train her — to be calm, to be tolerant, and to be peaceable.
breed	Be particularly careful in choosing, training, socializing, and handling pit bulls, Akitas, Chow Chows, Dobermans, German shepherd dogs, and rottweilers, or mixes of these breeds. At this time, these breeds have the highest reported bite incidence per the number of them who are found in the overall dog population. However, please remember that dogs are individuals, and by no stretch of the imagination is every dog of these breeds going to be aggressive. At the same time, other breeds such as terriers, cocker spaniels, shelties, border collies, and cattle dogs also nip and may not be the best choices to have around children.

Factor	What to Do
health status	Maintain your dog's optimum health; be especially cautious if you suspect your dog may be in pain.
level of training	Train your dog in order to establish firmly his subordinate role in relation to the humans in his family and to provide him with a strong sense of security in his social system.
supervision and restraint	Do not allow your dog to roam; do not chain him or leave him unattended outdoors.
victim behavior	Don't assume there is little risk as long as no one "bothers" the dog — dogs perceive threats differently than we do and may very well feel bothered even though no one is paying any attention to them.
victim status	Supervise interactions between your dog and children; teach children, elderly people, and high-risk groups (e.g., letter carriers and delivery people who come to your home) techniques that minimize the risks of being bitten.

In the instant that your dog bites you, a family member, or anyone else — sometimes including criminals on your property — your fondest dog dreams become a nightmare. As the dog's owner, here's what you need to be aware of:

- In most states you are legally responsible for any damages caused by your dog, no matter who was at fault or whether or not you knew your dog might bite. In addition, you must take action to prevent a recurrence. In serious dog-bite incidents, this may mean that you have to have your dog destroyed.
- Prevention is key. Learn all the signs of aggression in dogs and immediately take remedial action, preferably with the help of an animal behaviorist. Train and socialize your dog to be friendly or at least tolerant of friends and strangers alike. Avoid frustrating your dog by chains and barriers or by leaving him unattended outdoors. In addition, make sure your dog can't get off your property; post signs to warn others that you have a dog. Keep the dog's license and ID tag on his collar at all times (the sooner your dog is returned to you, the less chance he will have to harm anyone or anything). Keep your dog's vaccinations up-to-date; any dog that bites a person and has no proof that he is up-to-date in vaccination against rabies must be quarantined.
- Damages awarded by courts in cases of severe dog bites can be enormously high. Make sure your dog is covered under your home-owner's liability insurance. You should also consider obtaining a special insurance policy for the dog.
- If you have truly tried everything and your dog is still dangerously aggressive, you owe it to your dog (who, because he *is* aggressive, probably is not living a high-quality life), to yourself, and to society at large to have the dog euthanized. As is true for terminally ill and long-suffering dogs, the aggressive dog deserves to be released from his pain. As his partner, companion, and care-taker, this is your ultimate responsibility to him.
- After you have had your dog euthanized and have given yourself time to grieve his loss, take time to think about your experience of owning a dog. When so many people all around you seem to be able to get it right, it can be particu-larly hard to be one of the few whose dream did end in nightmare. It may help if you can go back and discover any little things along the way that you might have done differently. For instance, what about your initial decision to get a dog? Or what about the kind of dog you chose . . . did you let your heart rule your head? Did you socialize your puppy or young dog? Did you handle him and train him to get along in your world? And what about early signs that

things were going wrong — did you see them? If not, why not? If yes, what did you do about it? Was there something more or different that you could have done? The point of this review is not to break your heart again. It is to learn from what happened and do better the next time. What greater honor to the friend you lost than to dedicate a new relationship to his memory?

22 *Changing Situations*

Change is stressful. It's a well-known fact that illness often follows in the wake of negative lifestyle changes, such as a loved one's dying, getting divorced, being fired, or losing a lot of money in the stock market. What is less well known is that illness is almost as likely to follow positive lifestyle changes, including getting married, being promoted, going on a fabulous vacation, or buying a new home. While some amount of stress stimulates us and actually makes us more resilient, too much stress or stress that is not managed well can have negative effects on the body, mind, and emotions.

The same is true for our dogs. Puppies who are subjected to small amounts of stress through change and variety in their surroundings, routines, and interactions with others (human and other animals) grow up to be more flexible and resilient than puppies who are sheltered and protected from change and upsets of any kind. Even so, virtually all changes in adulthood will be tolerated better if they are introduced gradually. For example, an abrupt change in food or water can cause diarrhea, but if a new diet is introduced gradually over a week or two while the regular food is decreased by the same amount, the changeover usually causes no upset at all. Similarly, a new tennis ball may be rejected if it is suddenly tossed to the dog in place of the familiar old but filthy one. However, if you take the time to build interest in the new ball by gently teasing and tempting the dog with it for a few minutes at a time over a day or so, you should be able to discard the old one successfully.

If sudden changes are potentially stressful to our dogs, abrupt changes to their "social security" (i.e., their home and family) are especially difficult. Behavior changes may result, which if handled inappropriately can lead to problems. This does not mean dogs cannot weather lifestyle changes; they can and mostly do — often more readily than their owners. (Don't forget: It is the dog's ability to adapt to new circumstances that allows shelter animals to fit so successfully into new homes in the first place.) Nevertheless, if you understand the kinds of lifestyle changes that may cause upsets and what you can do to minimize their effects, you'll have a good head start on making sure that you, your canine partner, and your entire household make as painless a transition as possible. The following three steps should help:

Step 1. Anticipate Changes

The first step is to look ahead and anticipate any changes in your life or lifestyle that are on the horizon. Your list should include all events, such as going back to work or even switching from a day job to the night shift, that will change your daily routine and therefore your dog's routine. Also, bear in mind that anything that affects your mood, your time, or your energy level will invariably affect your dog as well. Unlike you, your dog cannot balance his uneasiness about today's change with happy anticipation of future benefits. To your dog, today is as far forward as he can see, and if today isn't pretty much like yesterday, he's likely to be uneasy about it — at least at first. (See Handling Common Changes later in this chapter.)

Step 2. Know How Behavior May Be Affected

A wide variety of behavioral changes may be seen as a result of the stress your dog is feeling. Some of the more common ones are:

- loss of appetite
- restlessness, sleeping less or less soundly than usual
- hypervigilance (seeming constantly alert to sights, sounds, smells)
- pacing, panting, trembling, whining
- digestive upsets (vomiting and/or diarrhea)
- ingesting inedible objects (fabric, dust, wood chips, rocks)
- lack of interest in toys and usual favorite things
- house-soiling problems

- licking/chewing on self
- destructive chewing or scratching
- clinging behavior/separation anxiety
- fearful behavior, including aggression

Step 3. Be Prepared to Help Your Dog Adjust

Tips for handling specific situations are given below. In the meantime, note the following general suggestions that apply to all lifestyle changes and transitions:

- Expect a period of adjustment to be necessary; for maximum peace of mind, consult ahead of time with your veterinarian, an experienced dog trainer, or a behavioral counselor for help in planning appropriate strategies to resolve particular problems if/as they develop.
- Attend to your dog's health; clear up any unresolved medical problems such as internal or external parasites, dental plaque, and minor ear or eye infections.
- Make changes as gradual as possible in order to give your dog time to adjust. (For example, if you plan to convert the den where the dog sleeps into a nursery, begin to introduce your dog to her new sleeping area long before the baby arrives.)
- Postpone or cancel other changes that may be optional. (If you are moving to a new home, consider either putting off your annual vacation or taking your dog along rather than placing him in a boarding kennel at this time.)
- Spend more quality time with your dog; refresh his training and socialization in order to enhance his "flexibility quotient" and feelings of self-confidence.
- To increase your dog's self-assurance in the face of change and upset, encourage all tolerant and calm behavior rather than coddle him when he's behaving fearfully.
- Keep as much the same as possible (familiar routines, furniture placement, diet) while your dog is coping with an unsettling change, but don't hesitate to add pleasurable new items/treats/additional rides in the car, and so on to the dog's usual allotment.
- Involve the dog in the change in whatever ways you can. (For example, rather than allowing departing family members to slip away without saying good-bye, let your dog see the packing and eventual departure, warmly praising all calm behavior.)

- Be patient with inevitable mistakes as your dog adjusts to the change in his life. (Be kind to yourself, too; you are probably under as much stress as your dog, if not more!)

Handling Common Changes

Listed below are some of the most common changes that affect families and households and are likely to upset the family dog. The list is not complete. Add to it any important events that might well present the same kind of challenge to your dog.

Depending on the particular situation, the dog may be challenged in one or more ways. For most dogs, the toughest challenge is the addition of a new pack member, who inevitably upsets the social equilibrium and whom the dog may see as a threat to his own status in the household. Other difficult challenges include changes in the dog's routines, particularly in the amount of time he must spend alone; these changes tend to create anxiety in the dog, resulting in such unacceptable behaviors as house-soiling or destructive chewing, which in turn are likely to lead to even more upsetting events such as being scolded, ignored, and socially isolated.

Along with each common lifestyle change are given some strategies you can try to avoid or minimize problems.

New Baby

Accepting a new baby may be the most important lifestyle change your dog will ever have to master, simply because the baby is here to stay and the change really has to work. It may also be one of the hardest. As an analogy, imagine (or remember!) the kind of resentment an older sibling might feel when her mother comes home from the hospital with a new baby who suddenly gets the love and attention that used to be the older child's exclusively! From the dog's point of view, the new baby is challenging him for a favored position within the family. The baby makes him nervous with her crying, and has a strange scent about her, too. Even so, there's no reason why this situation can't work out if your dog is reasonably well-adjusted to begin with and you take some sensible precautions to avert trouble.

For starters, make sure your goals are realistic. You need your dog to accept the baby without resentment. If your dog learns to love the baby and happily appoints himself nursemaid, consider yourself blessed; it happens often enough, but is not a realistic expectation of any dog or breed of dog.

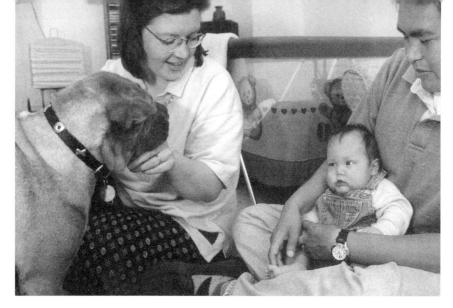

Accepting a new baby may be the most important lifestyle change your dog will ever have to master. (Carlos and Christy Gonzalez, baby Cole, and Randy)

Your attitude is the most important factor. Take any steps you can think of that will help *you* feel comfortable about close encounters between your dog and your baby. You are more likely to be calm about interactions between the two if you have the facts clear in your mind. For instance, if you're not sure whether your dog has any medical problem, such as a skin condition, that could be unhealthy for your baby to be around, check ahead of time with your dog's veterinarian and your baby's pediatrician, and follow their recommendations. If your dog tends to have a few fleas at any given time, you should probably treat the dog, the house, and the yard before the baby arrives.

Make ahead of time, and gradually, whatever changes in the dog's routine (feeding times, playtimes, walks, sleeping arrangements, and so on) that will be necessary when the baby arrives. You don't want your dog to associate the baby's arrival with upsetting changes in the way things are done.

Try to convince your dog that you brought this baby home just for him. Do this by including the dog in the homecoming. It complicates the logistics, but if you can arrange to have the first meeting take place away from the home, it may be well worth the trouble in the long run. Pay more attention to the dog than the baby for the first few hours (the baby won't know the difference) and give your dog more quality time than ever before over the first few weeks.

Your dog takes his cues from you. If you act happy and confident about his interactions with the baby, your dog will be likely to see it your way. Praise him warmly for his curiosity and interest in the baby, and for calm and accepting behavior. If he should show signs of uneasiness or resentment, distract him gaily with a toy or tidbit, again looking for positive responses that you can praise him for. Try to make sure that good things happen to him when the baby is around.

For the first day or two, expect the dog to react with a mixture of curiosity and uneasiness when the baby cries. Guide his response by talking to him in a calm, matter-of-fact manner as you go together to investigate the crying, at which point you may want to train him to sit or lie down quietly while you tend to the baby. (This is not unlike training him to alert you to someone at the door but then to wait quietly while you take charge of the situation.)

Watch your dog carefully during the first week or so to see how he seems to be feeling. Does he appear to be "himself" around the baby? Is he eating normally, sleeping normally, and playing normally, or is he intently interested in where the baby is and what the baby is doing? Does he either steal away when the baby is brought near or constantly hover nearby, almost as if stalking the baby? When your dog begins to wag his tail in a relaxed manner when the baby is brought near, you can be fairly confident that things are going well. Still, you must never forget that dogs are predators by nature, and that the high cries, waving arms, and unsteady gait of your infant or young child are bound to remind your dog of animals his species preyed upon in the dim past. *For this reason, you should never, ever leave the dog and the baby together without the supervision of a responsible adult.* And you should be doubly careful about supervising all interactions between dog and baby within the first few days of bringing an infant home from the hospital. In at least one, horrible, case a sleeping infant was killed by the family dog while the baby slept in the same room as the parents!

As your baby progresses through childhood's various developmental stages (crawling, standing, making different kinds of vocal sounds, eventually walking and running), recognize these as new challenges to your dog and be especially attentive until once again the dog seems to be happy and relaxed around this child with the surprising new behavior. At the inevitable point in time when your child wants to explore your dog's eyes, ears, and nose and to pull his hair and tail, take time to teach the child firmly that she may not do these things. Until you can fully trust your child to understand and heed what you are saying, never allow the dog and child to play unsupervised.

When your child is five or six years old, begin to teach her how to control the dog using the leash, simple commands, and food rewards for desirable responses. Discourage roughhousing and wild play between your dog and child until your child has the physical stature and presence to command respect from the dog.

New Spouse or Partner

A new spouse or partner represents more to your dog than a new pack member; he or she is an additional person who will immediately outrank the dog in the pecking order and to whom the dog must yield in day-to-day situations. Although every situation is different, a female dog will usually accept a male human friend more easily than will a male dog (and vice versa). This is a moot point of course, if you already have your dog, but it may be useful to be aware that these natural affinities/antipathies may exist. It goes without saying that a new household configuration is most likely to be successful if your new friend is someone who feels the same way about dogs as you do and is enthusiastic about having your dog as part of his or her new family.

To give the new situation the best chance of working smoothly, make it a practice to select a place away from home, such as a nearby park, to introduce your dog to any serious romantic prospects in your life. This is particularly important if your dog is a dominant type with strong territorial or protective tendencies, or if it's been just you and the dog for an extended period of time. Ideally, the dog and any new friend should be on good or at least neutral terms before the friend visits your home for the first time. To help this process along, try having your friend toss the dog's ball for him in the park or throw him a disk to retrieve.

When your friend visits you at your home, pay more attention to your dog than ever. Praise him for friendly and/or accepting behavior and distract him happily if he seems either fearful or too intently interested. Depending on how smoothly things are going, encourage your friend to ask the dog to sit for a treat.

Unless your dog is very mellow and already seems quite relaxed with your friend, refrain from any loud or boisterous behavior during your friend's early visits and avoid any kind of physical contact with one another — even dancing — that the dog might construe as confrontational. Expend the time and effort now to help foster friendly feelings between your dog and your friend; it is much easier to prevent problems than to resolve them later on.

As with a new baby, accept that your job is to convince your dog that this new person was acquired just for him. Both you and your friend should work at making sure the dog associates the new person with more fun than ever. At the same time, if any changes need to be made in the dog's feeding and playtimes or in his sleeping quarters, make these changes before your new partner moves in. You don't want your dog to associate your partner with upsetting changes in the usual way things are done.

Even if you will continue to be the primary caretaker of your dog, it's important that your spouse or partner develop the skills to walk, feed, groom, and care for the dog as well. At some point it would be a good idea for your partner to take the dog through a brush-up obedience class and thereafter periodically to use the skills he or she's developed. This will reassure both your spouse or partner and your dog that they know where they stand in relationship to one another.

New Dog

A new dog is an automatic challenge to your resident dog. Suddenly the pack has an additional canine member, who because he is new, probably will become the underdog at first (though this isn't always true). After that, it is very much up in the air where the newcomer will fit in.

Before introducing your new dog to your resident dog, it's recommended that you keep your new dog isolated for a couple weeks in the home to protect against his introducing any parasites and latent diseases to your resident dog. (Also, make sure your resident dog is up-to-date on her shots and in good general health before introducing your new dog.) You can do this by confining your new dog to one room equipped with a crate while allowing your current dog full run of the rest of the house as usual.

Of course, the two dogs will sense each other's presence in the house until they are "formally" introduced, but it's important to take precautions to limit their exposure to one another. For example, select a special area outside where the new dog will urinate and defecate and that your resident dog will not have access to, and be careful about washing your hands in between handling the dogs.

When you're ready for the formal introduction, keep in mind that it's often a good idea for your new dog and your resident dog to meet on neutral territory such as a nearby field or park in order to avoid the complication of home territory defensiveness. Enlist a friend to hold the new dog on a leash while you hold the leash of your resident dog. Keep the dogs some distance apart at first and keep them happily distracted with toys or tidbits so that they do not focus exclusively on one another. This will allow each to begin to associate the other with pleasant experiences.

As long as both dogs remain nonbelligerent, gradually bring them closer together, eventually allowing them to sniff one another briefly while both you and your friend talk to them in a happy, upbeat, and confident way. Don't allow the sniffing to go on and on, as this can trigger an aggressive response in one or both. At the first sign of any trouble (direct stares, stiff posture, growls, or snarls), immediately distract the dogs in a happy voice and increase the distance between them again. Do not reprimand the dogs in any way as this will only increase their tension.

It would be wonderful if one of the dogs were to invite the other to play with the traditional canine "play bow" (rump up in the air, tail wagging, chest and forelegs on the ground). This signals friendly intentions and usually elicits a friendly response. Don't, however, feel discouraged if no such thing happens. Many dogs who live together in perfect harmony never really play with one another. If there is no overtly friendly overture, but no aggressive display either, you and your friend may proceed to walk along together, side by side but perhaps six or more feet apart, allowing the dogs to continue to sniff one another at intervals. Continue to talk happily to both dogs and to offer occasional treats, preferably in response to a simple command. Spend as much time on this introduction as you can. Ideally, both dogs will relax more and more as time passes.

Travel on foot to your home so that the two dogs enter your dog's home territory together. Once at your residence, begin to defer to your resident dog, allowing her to enter the home ahead of the other. Keep both dogs onleash inside the house at first to make sure you are in control of the situation in case hostilities develop in this confined space. Make sure the new dog is not allowed to usurp the resident dog's food or water bowls or any of her favorite places to lie down. Also, make sure you feed, walk, and play with your resident dog at all the usual times. You do not want her to associate the new dog with unsettling changes in her familiar routines.

In time, it will become obvious which of the dogs is dominant over the other. The dogs will work this out between themselves, usually without warfare, based partially on size, age, and gender but also on factors that we humans cannot fathom. Whichever way it goes, you and everyone else in your household needs to support the agreement the dogs have reached. If you do not, your behavior may well instigate fighting that could have been avoided. Remember: Your resident dog will not be unhappy, as you might be, if she moves to a lower rung on the social ladder. All she really needs is to know that you are in charge and that she has a well-defined position in relationship to everyone else.

New Cat

A new cat can present an additional challenge to your dog, particularly if your dog had no opportunity to become socialized to cats as a puppy. It's always a good idea to choose a dog who had early exposure to cats. This may be difficult to know for certain about some shelter dogs, although the shel-

Introduce a new pet other than another dog with great vigilance; a baby gate and leash can help you stay in control during the first encounters. (Jonathan Ragan, Filbert, and cat Hazel)

ter staff will usually be able to determine by the dog's behavior whether or not his feelings toward cats are friendly, neutral, or hostile.

Before introducing your new cat to your resident dog, it's recommended that you keep your new cat isolated for a couple weeks in the home to protect against his introducing any parasites and latent diseases to your resident dog. You can do this by confining your new cat to one room equipped with a litter box, bed, and food bowls. Of course, the dog and the cat will sense each other's presence in the house until they are "formally" introduced, but it's important to take precautions to limit their exposure to one another for a time.

Introduce a new cat to your dog in stages. Allow your dog and the cat to become aware of each other's presence and scent for a day or two before you permit them their first glimpses of one another.

If you can arrange for the dog and cat to see part of one another and let that information sink in before they are exposed to the whole other being, it would be worth the time and trouble. For instance, a door with a largish space beneath it would allow the two to check out one another's feet and noses; opened a crack, the door would permit them glimpses of one another from time to time. A glass door with an opaque curtain hung over it would allow them to see one another but not clearly, and so on. Do the best you can for another day or two. By now you'll probably notice that neither is quite as interested in the other as they were originally.

Next, begin to feed the dog and cat on opposite sides of the door. When both are relaxed enough to eat a more-or-less normal portion of their food with the other so close at hand, congratulate yourself. Things are beginning to fall into place.

When you feel ready to let the two actually meet, enlist the help of a friend. Have the friend sit with the cat on one side of a room, either on her lap if the cat likes to be held, or inside a wire or mesh carrier if the cat doesn't want to be held or your friend feels uncomfortable. Put your dog on-leash and bring her into the room; sit on the side of the room opposite to the cat. What you do next will depend on how both animals react. If they are calm but seem interested in inspecting the other more closely, you may move forward. Be ready to halt at the first signs of uneasiness on the part of either animal. Go back, and proceed more slowly the next time.

At this point, follow the same principles of introduction that apply to a new dog (above). Specifically, make consistent efforts to help your dog associate happy experiences with the cat's arrival by paying him extra attention and finding things you can reward him for when the cat is present and he is able to turn his attention to other things, such as a favorite or new toy, or a treat.

No matter how well things appear to be going, do not leave the cat and dog alone together until you are absolutely certain that the dog has no inclination to harm the cat. And during the first few months, whenever they are in the same room together, make sure the cat has an escape route and someplace to hide if she feels the need.

Loss of Family Member (Human, Canine, or Other)

Loss of any family member is difficult for your dog because her sense of security is completely linked to the established social structure. The most devastating loss would be of the person she sees as family leader (you), but many dogs are deeply affected by the loss of another dog or even of the family cat or bird.

You can minimize the stress of loss by allowing your pet to participate in changes as they are occurring. For example, if your young adult son or daughter is leaving home, or your spouse is moving out permanently — and the dog has no prior negative experience associated with packing and leaving — encourage the departing person to let the dog observe and "help" in the packing process. Ask the person to make a conscious effort to be cheerful and upbeat with the dog rather than mournful and consoling. Have the departing individual avoid emotional good-byes, taking leave of the dog cheerfully and briefly. In the event of divorce, try to cooperate with your spouse in maintaining as much normal behavior in front of the dog as you would in front of the children. At the same time, work very diligently to keep everything else in the dog's life as much the same as possible. If your dog does have negative associations with suitcases and such, and the person who is leaving will be gone permanently or for an extended time, you might be better off having the packing and associated preparations take place out of the dog's sight and hearing.

In the event of illness and impending death, allow nature to prepare the dog. Dogs are extremely sensitive to changes in a person's or other animal's health, and many appear to be able to anticipate death. If you can, let your dog spend as much time as she wants in the presence of an ailing person or animal in the home; she will come to understand in her own way that this family member is dying. Should an elderly family member be moved to an extended-care facility, consider choosing one that allows family pets to visit (this can be extremely beneficial to the ill person as well as to the dog). Should another animal in the family die at home, let your dog investigate the body in order to process this significant change in her life.

After the loss of a family member, for whatever reason, you should expect some amount of upset as your dog adjusts to the new social structure. If you have several dogs and the dominant one has died, you may find that the remaining dogs squabble for a few days while they renegotiate their relative positions in the hierarchy. Be patient with them and be prepared to support whoever emerges as top dog.

Emotional Turmoil

If the people in your home normally shout when they speak and habitually engage in a lot of pushing, shoving, and door-slamming, chances are very good that your dog has learned to accept this as status quo. It is when emotional turmoil is a new situation in the home — whether it be loud and angry, tense and worried, or sad and depressed — that it is likely to be stressful to your dog.

If you are feeling stressed-out about some ongoing, unresolved problem in your own life, no doubt your dog is stressed-out, too. Careful observation of his behavior usually will yield telltale signs.

It doesn't make sense to try to keep your upset from your dog; you probably won't fool him, and the pretense may make you feel even worse. Instead, concentrate on maintaining as much regularity as you can in the dog's diet, as well as his feeding, walking, and play schedules. Your dog's treasured rituals will reassure him as much as anything can. (Don't be surprised if you notice that being scrupulous about taking your dog on his usual two-mile walk in the late evening causes you to feel a little bit calmer yourself!)

Guard against any tendency you may have to shut your dog out during times of emotional stress. However blue you're feeling, your dog would rather be with you than out in the yard where it's sunny. And don't forget that dogs are great therapy in and of themselves! Give yours a chance to lighten your load.

If your dog seems to have all at once forgotten his housetraining, cut him some slack. Once you realize that the "vibes" in your home are contributing to the problem, you should be able to put aside any anger or impatience you may be feeling toward your dog. Seeing the effect that our behavior can have on our dog's state of mind can be a humbling and ultimately inspiring experience.

If your own physical or emotional health is so affected by your problems that you truly can't meet your dog's needs, consider asking a friend whom the dog knows and likes to come in on a regular basis to care for your dog, or think about arranging for the dog to stay with the friend until you're able to take back the responsibility for his care.

New Schedule

Going back to work, changing jobs, or switching from the early shift to the late shift — in fact anything in your life that changes your dog's schedule and the length of time she must be home alone — can challenge your dog.

If possible, help your dog adjust gradually to a new timetable. For example, if you're going to begin working the night shift on Monday, use the weekend or preferably the whole prior week to begin to get your dog used to different mealtimes. Do this in stages; instead of moving her evening meal from 6 P.M. to 10 P.M. in one step, move it by an hour or so at a time. Make sure her walks remain in roughly the same relationship to mealtimes, as her system has undoubtedly been trained to eliminate a certain length of time after eating. Praise her for eliminating as you did when she was being housetrained.

Make the change to a new schedule complete. It will not serve you or your dog well if you follow one schedule during the workweek yet revert to a prior sleeping/waking/eating/exercising schedule on weekends.

Within the new schedule, keep as much unchanged as possible in the dog's routines. If your practice has been to feed her dinner, take her for a long walk, and then brush her while you watch the evening news, continue the sequence of dinner, walk, and grooming — even if "dinner" is at 10 A.M. and the grooming takes place during a morning quiz show. If you want to make changes in some of the old routines, do so gradually, after she's made the major adjustment between day and night.

Try to anticipate any problems that may come up as a result of your new hours. For instance, your dog may be alone now when the sanitation truck clangs and roars underneath the window, and she may feel compelled to bark her head off, waking all your neighbors. Check the situation out ahead of time. If your dog does bark at the sanitation truck, take immediate steps to counter this behavior (refer to the discussion on barking in chapter 20, page 290). Follow the same procedure with any other suspected problems.

If the change in your new schedule will require the dog to be home alone a lot more than she used to be, prepare her for this as carefully as you can. Refresh your memory of separation anxiety and how to resolve any problems that arise (see chapter 19). Pay particular attention to bolstering your dog's overall self-confidence by refreshing her response to commands and teaching her to be calm in your absence. If you can prevent your dog from ever having that first dreadful experience of finding herself alone and chewing up the sofa, whatever uneasiness she does feel may never develop into a full-blown attack of anxiety.

Moving

It matters little whether you are moving from the city to the country, from a large house to a small apartment, or just across town. With a little help, your dog should adjust quickly to cows, to quiet, to a yard of his own instead of the neighborhood dog run. What may turn out to be the more difficult challenge for your dog is suddenly finding himself in territory where he has no standing. You can help your dog most by keeping his self-confidence high.

Any kind of move can cause your dog to feel temporarily insecure, as he suddenly finds himself the new dog on the block, with none of his scent around but plenty from all the other dogs in the neighborhood. Spend time taking your dog on excursions into the neighborhood. (Note: If your dog has shown dominance or territorial aggression in the past, you will want to limit opportunities for him to urine-mark the area right around your property. Review the relevant sections in chapter 21.)

If possible, arrange to have a week or two at home in your new location before you return to work. Use these days to spend time with your dog, not just exploring the neighborhood and trying out the new park, but practicing old training routines and giving your dog things to do to earn rewards and praise. Be careful not to console your dog as you might a child who misses his old chums and the treehouse left behind; coddling behavior will make your dog feel more uneasy, not more self-confident.

As a practical matter, a move to a new home and new neighborhood represents the loss of familiar landmarks (indoors and out). Even if you're getting all new furniture, consider dragging along at least one old piece that the dog particularly likes. You don't have to keep it forever, but it may help ease the transition for your dog. As always, keep as many things unchanged as you can (food bowls, diet, toys, mealtimes). If you're moving to a new water system, take along a supply of water from your old home to mix with the new water and decrease gradually over a period of days.

Be very careful about letting your dog off-leash for the first few weeks at your new location, even in your own backyard. Something in the unfamiliar environment may spook or entice him, and if he runs off, he may not find his way back home. Make sure to have a new ID tag made up ahead of time, as well as recent photos of your dog, just in case he does become lost.

As always, your dog will be at least partially guided by your example. If you approach the new situation in a positive way and show that you expect him (but of course!) to make a rapid good adjustment, he will more likely do so. If you want to concentrate on only one thing, make it being sure that all your dog's early experiences at the new home are happy ones. That will automatically guarantee that neither you nor other family members unthinkingly scold, neglect, ignore, or isolate this creature as he tries to find his place in your new world.

WHEN YOUR DOG MUST TRAVEL

Extended travel (longer than a couple of hours in the car) is stressful for most dogs. It involves two kinds of change: being away from what is familiar, and being subjected all at once to a completely new environment. If your dog must travel for long distances or over an extended period, here are some things you can do to reduce the stress, strain, and real risks involved:

BY CAR

- If the dog isn't already familiar with riding in the car, begin immediately (in very small increments) to familiarize him with it.
- Establish or refresh car routines such as where the dog sits, the use of a crate or seat harness, the presence (or absence) of toys or favorite objects.
- Have your veterinarian examine your dog to make sure he is healthy; ask for a health certificate if you are traveling out of state (this document certifies that your dog has been examined within the past ten days and in the veterinarian's opinion is in good health and free of communicable diseases).
- Be certain that your dog is up-to-date on all vaccinations, especially for rabies, which is a legal requirement in all fifty states; avoid vaccinating within the weeks prior to departure so that your dog's immune system has time to fully recover.
- If your dog is a very nervous traveler, discuss with your veterinarian the advisability of giving the dog a sedative or tranquilizer; administer the medication on a trial basis ahead of time so that your dog's response can be monitored.
- Take along a supply of the dog's usual food and water, but minimize upsets by feeding lightly during the first day or so on the road.
- Try to exercise your dog at the usual times of day and adhere as closely as possible to his usual wake-up and lights-out schedules; have a very firm hand on

the leash whenever your dog is "out" in case he becomes startled and tries to run away; make sure your dog is *always* wearing identification that lists both your permanent and temporary addresses and telephone numbers.

- Do not leave your dog unattended in the car; dangers include overheating in hot, humid weather, becoming too cold in winter weather, becoming overly protective of the car in your absence, possibly being teased by passersby, and being stolen (with or without the car).
- Avoid leaving the dog unattended in temporary lodging while you are traveling, as he may suffer some separation anxiety (review chapter 19 and especially the box "Stress Reducers").

BY AIR

- Consider other options before deciding to travel by air with any but a very small dog who can accompany you in the cabin; only if there is no viable alternative should you ship a dog in the cargo hold or ship him alone, as dogs have died either in-flight or on the ground during delays or transfers, particularly in very hot/humid weather; short-nosed breeds such as bulldogs, Pekingese, and pugs should never be shipped in the cargo hold because they are more vulnerable to overheating than breeds with normal nasal passages.
- Find out ahead of time all the specific requirements of the airline you are flying; choose only an airline-approved shipping kennel that is the right size for your dog, and have your dog's kennel properly tagged and all his paperwork in order; be sure to familiarize your dog with his travel crate in advance of any travel.
- If your dog can fit under your cabin seat, reserve space for him there; if he cannot, follow scrupulously all the recommended procedures for shipping dogs by air.
- Avoid flying in the heat of summer or coldest part of winter; if you must, book early morning flights in hot weather and afternoon flights when the weather is cold.
- Book a nonstop flight if one is available, as changing planes presents more opportunities for foul-ups on the ground.
- Fly on the same flight with your dog, or ensure that the person who is meeting your dog on the other end is in touch with you regarding departure and arrival times.
- Always tell one flight attendant and the pilot that your pet is in the cargo hold;

ask the airline for permission to watch your dog being loaded and unloaded into the cargo hold.

- Tranquilize your dog only on the advice of your dog's own veterinarian (see above); tranquilizers may decrease your pet's breathing and blood circulation once he is in the cargo hold and not being monitored.

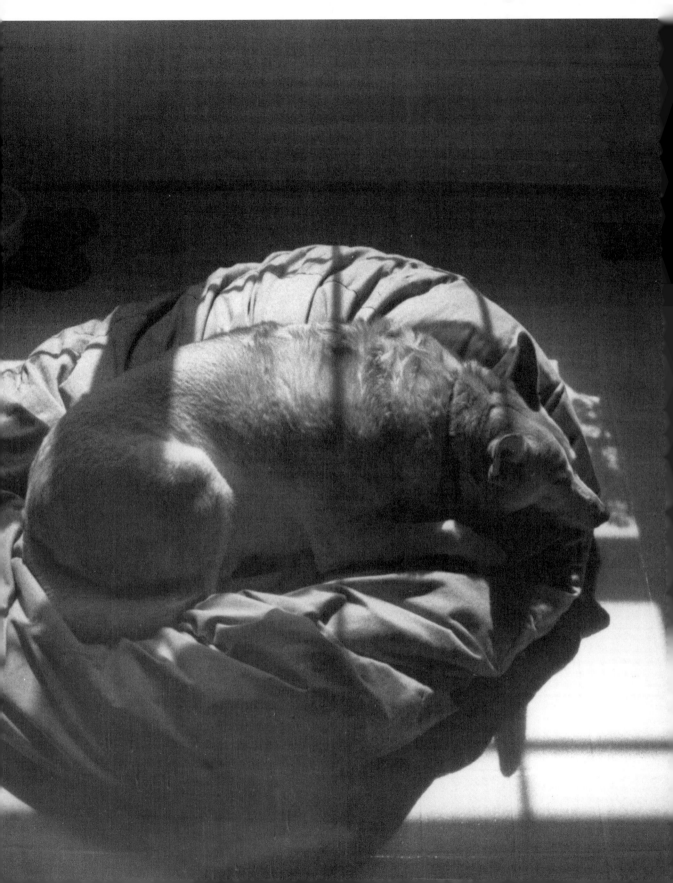

As he approaches the sunset
of life, creature comforts and
reassurance of your continuing
affection can become even
more important to your dog.

Lifelong Partners

Old Friends 23

Dogs live an average of about twelve years. Within that average, however, there is great variability from dog to dog, depending on their breed, genetics, and the kind of care they've received throughout their lives. The notion that one year of human life equals seven years of a dog's life should be considered nothing more than a guideline to remind us that our dogs are on a completely different life line than we are.

In general, large dogs age faster than very small ones. A dog the size of a Great Dane may be quite the senior citizen at eight or nine years, while a small dog weighing under thirty pounds may still seem puppyish at that age. In spite of these differences, however, for most of us, our dog will be born, will enter our life, will become integral to our life, will grow old, and will die, while we live on. As our dogs pass their middle years and slide gracefully into old age, we can commit ourselves to making the most of the time and the life that is left. Here are some things to think about:

Be Aware of Changes to Expect

IN SIGHT Normal changes in the lens of the eye as a dog ages result in a bluish- or grayish-white haze that you can see through the pupil when you look into your dog's eyes. This condition, called nuclear sclerosis, is not cataracts and does not need treatment. Older dogs may see somewhat less well than they did when they were young, much as we do, but since they get the morning news from a nice walk around the neighborhood rather than from the daily paper, these changes are very well accepted in the aging dog. Cataracts, however, the milky-white opaque growths that can develop in the eyes of some old (and young!) dogs, do cause loss of vision and if they occur in both eyes, can eventually result in total blindness. Cataracts *do* need treatment.

IN HEARING   Gradual hearing loss does occur as dogs age. Some of the signs to watch for are what seems to be inattentiveness and/or slowness to respond to your normal tone of voice or to other sounds, such as the clink of the car keys in your hand, which may have always before resulted in an enthusiastic dash for the front door. At the present time there is no effective treatment for hearing loss in dogs.

IN JOINTS   Osteoarthritis, the kind of joint degeneration that affects many humans as they age, also affects many dogs. Typical signs include stiffness and/or lameness upon arising, which seems to improve with activity. There is no way to reverse the joint changes that take place as dogs age, although various methods of relieving pain can make a dramatic difference in your dog's ability to continue to enjoy favorite activities.

IN VITAL ORGANS   As dogs age, vital organs such as the heart, kidneys, and liver become less efficient at their respective jobs. Even without actual heart, kidney, or liver disease, an older dog requires more, not less, attention to his diet and exercise regimen, so that his less-efficient organs don't have to work as hard to digest foods and provide vital nutrients and oxygen to all parts of his body. While gradual degeneration of vital organs is more or less inevitable in older dogs, regular veterinary examinations can detect changes at the earliest possible point in time and allow you to make necessary adjustments in your dog's diet, activity level, and lifestyle to preserve his functional good health for as long as possible.

IN TEETH   A high-quality diet that includes lots of hard foods, regular at-home care of the teeth, annual dental checkups, and professional scaling and polishing of the teeth when necessary can keep your dog's teeth and gums healthy for as long as she lives. Signs that something is amiss in your dog's mouth include bad breath, drooling, unwillingness to pick up and chew hard objects, and reluctance to play games involving the mouth and teeth.

IN SKIN AND COAT   As dogs age, their coats may thin, dry out, and turn gray, and their skin may lose its elasticity and become thin and delicate, like parchment. Older dogs often show greater susceptibility to temperature extremes than they did when they were younger.

You may have to pace yourself during your walks with older dogs. (Howard Edelstein and Stretch, aged fifteen)

IN MENTAL FUNCTION   Many older dogs may begin to show signs of senility, much as many older humans do. Signs include forgetfulness, increased fearfulness, delayed responses to well-known commands, and lapses in training, including housetraining. Many older dogs appear to slow down and become more mellow, while some appear to become more nervous and hyperactive. Fortunately, at least some senility changes can be treated with medication and significantly improved.

In general, an older dog is less able to handle stress than when she was young. Sudden changes in her food, her routines, and her environment are even more likely to "throw" her than before. More than ever, she will want to be surrounded by what's familiar. Ironically, at the age when dogs are more likely to develop medical problems that require periods of hospitalization, the older dog is less likely to do well in a hospital, away from the places and people she knows.

Be Aware of What Doesn't Change

THE SOCIAL BOND   Unlike human children, dogs do not become more independent as they age. On the contrary, they become more and more childlike, seemingly more content to be firmly fixed in orbit around their human leader. At the same time, however, decreased physical activity may cause them to appear to be less attached. Now is when they may begin to favor a quiet place to rest rather than to be in the middle of household hubbub.

NEED FOR STRUCTURE AND ORDER   As she has all her life, your aging dog craves the reassurance of knowing her position in the family pack. It may break *your* heart to see her lose status to a younger dog, or to begin to look up to rather than patiently tolerate your growing children, but the truth is that these are the kinds of changes she was programmed to accept twelve thousand years ago.

NEED FOR ATTENTION, STIMULATION, EXERCISE   Now that he's aging is not the time to exclude your dog from family outings because you think they may be too strenuous. Find new ways to include him, or take up at least some new activities that he can join. It won't be for very long, and you'll be glad you did.

Try to Remain Objective

OBSERVE YOUR OWN DOG   How old is she *really* — not just in years, but in interests, energy, faculties? You don't want to deny that your dog may have diminished capacities at this point in her life, but neither do you want to prematurely label her as "old." There are so many instances of owners giving up too soon on their old dogs, when relatively straightforward treatment could have given them several more years of quality life.

Take vision, for example. If your dog is developing cataracts, this is not necessarily a reason to limit her activities outdoors, and certainly not a reason to conclude she can no longer enjoy her life. For most dogs, vision is not as critical a sense as are hearing and smell. If your own dog lives to catch and retrieve a ball, you may want to discuss the possibility of surgery to remove the cataracts. But if her favorite thing is to dig a cool hole under the back porch and supervise your work in the garden, she may be perfectly content to know you're near and you can avoid the risk that always exists with surgery.

DON'T ANTHROPOMORPHIZE   Your dog is not a human being and you should not ascribe human thoughts and feelings to him. For instance, *you* may feel a twinge every time you lift your old friend into the station wagon, remembering how he used to leap over the tailgate in a single bound, but you can be sure that he's not spending one moment reflecting on what used to be and feeling sorry for himself. As far as anyone knows, dogs are incapable of self-pity or regret.

TAKE YOUR DOG'S "HEART" INTO ACCOUNT   Many dogs, including older dogs who presumably should know better, will exercise far beyond what is wise and prudent, even to the point of exhaustion, injury, or death. If your know your older dog hasn't walked farther than the mailbox all winter long, don't take her out for a fast three miles on the first warm day of spring. She may enjoy it thoroughly at the time, but is bound to pay for it later with stiff, sore muscles and possibly lacerated foot pads.

Make Whatever Adjustments You Can

LET SLEEPING DOGS LIE   Your older dog probably will sleep most of the time, with possibly only a few hours a day of wakefulness. If you or younger family members wish he'd be more active, more "fun" again, try to think back to the days when you wished he'd slow down just a little.

GO EASY ON EXERCISE   Continue to invite your old friend to do the things she used to do, but watch her closely to see what her body really seems capable of. If she seems to lose interest in investigating new scents on her daily walk, probably you're walking her too far. If she hesitates at the foot of a hill, change your route to level ground.

ADJUST YOUR DOG'S DIET   Talk to your veterinarian about your geriatric dog's diet. There are a variety of brand-name and prescription foods for older, less-active dogs and for dogs with a variety of medical problems that frequently accompany old age. If your dog is suffering from stiffness, or even if she isn't, think about buying or building her a feeding station that is elevated off the ground so that she doesn't have to bend over so far to eat and drink.

HAVE SCREENING EXAMS DONE   Many veterinarians offer geriatric screening examinations for dogs when they turn seven or eight. One feature of this examination is a complete blood profile, even on a dog who seems completely well, so that you will have baseline data against which to measure future changes. It's not unlike the midlife mammograms, prostate tests, EKGs, serum cholesterol checks, and other screening exams that are recommended for humans.

GROOM FOR COMFORT   If your dog's hair is the type that has to be cut, clippered, or extensively brushed to stay neat and clean, maybe it's time to think about having the hair cut in a way that requires less fussing. It's hard on old joints to stand for long sessions of clipping and scissoring. Ask your regular groomer about a so-called puppy cut for your dog.

HANDLE WITH CARE   If your older dog no longer hears or sees very well, you may find that you need to adjust the way you approach him, especially when he's sleeping. Dogs who don't hear may startle and even snap if you surprise them by a sudden touch or sound. Make it a habit to announce your presence loudly from a distance away, clap your hands as you approach, or stamp your feet to send vibrations through the floor to dogs who don't hear at all. By all means continue with your weekly whole-body exams, and think about learning how to massage your dog gently to help increase circulation to stiff muscles, especially in dogs with pain and weakness in their hindquarters.

ACCOMMODATE YOUR SENIOR CITIZEN   Elderly dogs are not unlike elderly humans in that they may become less able to tolerate either the heat or the cold. Provide a regulated, draft-free environment if you can, and start using a dog coat or sweater and even dog boots if your dog shivers in the out-of-doors. Soft bedding can ease the discomfort of laying old bones on hard surfaces, and a simple ramp can make it much easier for the dog who is having trouble getting up and down the front steps. If your dog walks quietly on leash, you may want to substitute a harness for her collar, as a harness generally is kinder to the dog's neck and throat than even a flat nylon collar.

Think Twice Before . . .

GETTING ANOTHER PET   It's natural enough to think about adding a new puppy, dog, or other pet to your household as your older dog slows down. Depending on the individual dog, this can be either the best thing that ever happened to him or the worst. One thing is for sure: It is *not* a step to be taken lightly. At the very least, introduce your senior citizen to a friend's puppy or kitten to gauge his response before you commit yourself. In most cases, a new pet is best introduced when the older dog is still in his middle years, when he can see, hear, and get about relatively well, not in his golden ones.

CURTAILING "FAVORITE THINGS"   It isn't always possible to leave it up to your dog to decide for himself when it's time to give up, for instance, the flying disk, or keeping up with the pack at the dog park. Unfortunately, some favorite games can't be played slower or more gently. If it becomes clear to you that your dog is in danger of injuring himself in pursuit of his favorite thing, you may want to try to interest him in something more appropriate to his age and physical condition, then gradually phase out the activity that's no longer safe for him. For instance, it's hard to toss a flying disk slowly, or to prevent your dog from racing out after it and racing back with it in his teeth. What you can do, though, is introduce him to playing with, say, a hard rubber toy that you fill with an irresistible treat. These bouncing toys can be tossed out a short distance so the dog can still chase and grab, if that's what he likes, but will not overtax him with a thirty-yard dash. If yours is like most dogs, he'll become so engrossed in trying to get the treat out of the toy (a bit of cheese spread or peanut butter mixed in with dry dog food is a good choice), that he won't even notice that his flying disk is lying on the ground beside him. It is not recommended, however, that you simply drop his favorite game. Of course he'll get over it, but why not give him a few more months or years of enjoyment?

FOOLING WITH MOTHER NATURE With all the advances in veterinary science and technology, there are now treatment options for animals that rival those available for humans. Many conditions and diseases that afflict older dogs can be helped by one or more of the marvels of modern technology, including cataract surgery or even eyeglasses for dogs who have lost their vision, total hip replacement procedures for dogs with crippling arthritis or other diseases of the hip joints, pacemakers for heart rhythm problems, chemo- and radiation therapy for cancers, and so on. Wonderful as it is to have these choices available, you must not lose sight of the fact that your dog has no way of knowing that all the trips to the doctor, the hospital stays, the injections or by-mouth medications, or the side-effects of treatment are all for his own good, a means to the end of helping him feel better. In almost every case, you will have to weigh the stress and strain of treatment against the condition itself, always trying as best you can to find the balance between quality and quantity of life. Sometimes it may help to ask yourself, "If the choice were *his* to make, what would it be?"

"MADELINE AND TILLIE"

As soon as the morning news is over, I turn off the television set and wash my cup and saucer at the kitchen sink. I glance out the window and there are Madeline and her old dog, Tillie, just coming around the corner, as regular as the clock on the wall.

I admit I'm a creature of habit, but it does my heart good to see Madeline and Tillie, every morning at this same time, taking their "constitutional." I watch them move slowly down the street, the little yellow dog making all her usual stops while Madeline inches along behind her, her long-handled "scooper" always at the ready.

To tell the truth, lately I've been half-afraid they wouldn't show up. A month ago I missed seeing them for five days in a row. Finally I asked one of the neighbors, and he told me that Tillie had been in the Woodhaven Animal Hospital. It seems she'd developed diabetes and the veterinarian had to keep her under observation until he could figure out how much insulin she needed. Can you imagine? Now Madeline gives Tillie an injection twice a day, morning and night. Apparently Tillie doesn't mind at all. I'm just glad to see them back out making their rounds.

Some of the other neighbors think Madeline's gone too far this time. It's true that Tillie has really slowed down the past two years. She used to tear around that corner, practically dragging Madeline along behind her. Now Tillie takes half of forever just getting as far as the mechanical rocking horse in front of Schreiner's Candy Store, where they turn around and go back home, sometimes with Madeline carrying Tillie in her arms. Schreiner's used to be one of the early stops on their journey, so there's no question that Tillie is slowing down. Now diabetes on top of it. No one is about to say a word to Madeline, though. When it comes to that dog, nothing seems to be too much trouble for Madeline.

I'm not a dog person myself, but I must say I think the neighbors are mistaken. Tillie may be slow now, but she still leads the way. It's as clear as the nose on your face that that rocking horse is her destination. After she gives that a good long sniff, she seems willing to be picked up. Sometimes I see her look up and paw at Madeline's leg as if to say she'd like a lift. Other days she walks home under her own steam.

Like I said, my worry is that one of these days Madeline and Tillie won't show up. Over the years they've become part of my day, too. — *A neighbor*

Final Choices

When you acquired your dog, or especially your puppy, the fact that dogs live an average of only twelve years probably didn't faze you in the least. Apartment leases are for one to three years. If you stay at a job for five, you're an old-timer, qualified for the pension plan. Half of all marriages are over in much less than twelve years. Twelve years seemed a long way off, so you didn't worry.

In time, if not now, all that will change. The years, whether more or fewer than twelve, will have run out. Twelve years will not have been a long way off after all, but only the briefest moment, the blinking of an eye. Your dog may have grown old and ill, or just old. If you've been very unlucky, she may have grown ill while still young. Whatever the case, there is no way around the simple fact that death is part of every life, and that one day your dear dog will die.

How can this be borne? With great anguish, we must admit. With worried days and sleepless nights, with torment and tears and grief so profound it may astonish you. If you have allowed yourself truly to love your dog, there is no escaping the pain of losing her. Against the countless hours spent in her good company, there will be a numbing void.

How Dogs Die

Of all the ways that a dog's life can end, probably the rarest is for him to go peacefully to sleep one night and just not wake up the next morning. Much more common is some combination of disease and disability, with discomfort, depression, and distress.

There are as many causes of death in dogs as there are in people. Dogs have the same organ systems that we have, and most of the same diseases. Their hearts fail, their kidneys fail, they get cancer and pneumonia. If you've ever lost a parent or grandparent to old age and illness, you know how long and drawn out a final illness can be, and how undignified. You may have watched helplessly as your loved one suffered, praying for either his recovery or his release from pain and exhaustion. Fortunately, with dogs, we have another option.

What Are the Options?

Basically, when your dog becomes old and ill, you have two humane options. The first is to care for him as you would a human family member, working with his doctor to do anything and everything you can to keep him alive until he dies of natural causes, although without trying to prevent his death by employing extreme technological measures, including extended hospitalization, that in and of themselves may result in pain, suffering, fear, isolation, and a very low quality of life. The second option is to do anything and everything to keep your dog alive as long as there is hope for his recovery and a reasonable quality of life — *but no longer,* so that when the hope of recovery to a reasonable quality of life no longer exists, you may elect to end his suffering, and his life, by what is called euthanasia — the "good death."

Many people lament the option of euthanasia, not wishing to have the power of their dog's life and death in their hands. In truth, though, we have had this power and this responsibility from the very beginning, and we have exercised it every day, perhaps unconsciously, in all the decisions we've made about care and feeding and health and safety — even, most fundamentally, in the decision we made when we selected the specific dog we did to share our lives. It is actually a rare privilege, and our ultimate responsibility to our dog, to be able to bring to an end a life that has become a burden too great to bear. Nevertheless, some dog owners feel uncomfortable with the fact that we urge them to consider their dog a full-fledged family member in so many ways, yet at the same time assure them that euthanasia is a humane option to end that family member's pain and suffering. It is a whole new level of responsibility for most to accept: terrifying and sobering, but empowering in the end.

Planning for the Inevitable

All the decisions that await you regarding your dog's final illness and death are difficult and heart-wrenching. Nevertheless, there are things you can do that may help make this impossibly hard time a little easier on everyone involved. Here are a few suggestions:

TALK THINGS OVER   Probably the most important thing you can do to prepare yourself for the death of your dog is to talk about it in advance with all members of your family. It's natural enough to want to put off this painful discussion for as long as possible. On the other hand, if you talk about your options and preferences *before* your dog is critically ill or a decision about her life or death has to be made, it's more likely that your discussion and decisions can be calm and reasonable rather than hysterical and impulsive. Points that you will want to cover in your talks include the following:

"HOW SHALL OUR DOG DIE?"   Will you allow nature to take its course, no matter what, or will you consider euthanasia? As we've already mentioned, nature's course can be very slow and difficult. In many of the degenerative illnesses of old age, modern veterinary medicine can prolong life with drugs and other treatments, but if you've ever been on heavy medication for a period of time, you know there are often side-effects that can make you miserable in other ways. In considering long-term care for a dog with a terminal illness, think about whether he's up to having a half-dozen or more pills forced down his throat each day or to making frequent trips back to the veterinarian's office to be poked, prodded, and stuck with needles. It may be difficult to separate your needs from your dog's at this point, but you must try. You don't want your old friend to suffer because you can't bear the thought of losing him.

Euthanasia — the injection into a vein of an overdose of anesthetic by your veterinarian — is fast. The only pain is the prick of the needle. Within just a few seconds, the dog will lose consciousness, and a few seconds after that, vital functions will cease. The veterinarian will listen for a heartbeat with her stethoscope. When none is heard, she will pronounce the dog dead.

Although some veterinarians will make home visits for this purpose, a drawback to euthanasia is that it usually is performed in the veterinarian's office — a situation that is stressful to many dogs. Also, a busy veterinary practice may not be able to give you as much time and privacy as you'd like to say your good-byes. Still, euthanasia does allow you to choose the time of your dog's death, so that you can be sure to be present to offer whatever comfort you can and to reassure yourself that your dog's passing was as free of pain and fear as you and his veterinarian were able to make it. If going to the veterinarian's makes your dog very anxious, ask for medication that you can give ahead of time to make the trip less stressful. Some shelters also perform euthanasia, undoubtedly at lower cost, but with the same drawbacks.

"HOW SHALL WE KNOW WHEN IT'S TIME?" If you are considering euthanasia, what criteria will you use to decide that the time has come? Generally, euthanasia is considered appropriate when a dog is suffering and there is no realistic hope that the suffering will abate. It is also appropriate when a dog is terminally ill and has more pain than pleasure in his life. As discussed in chapter 21, euthanasia is the humane and responsible choice in the case of a seriously aggressive dog who seems unable to be rehabilitated, despite the best efforts of his owner, his veterinarian, and an animal behaviorist. Finally, euthanasia may be appropriate when the cost of ongoing care is truly beyond your means, either financially, emotionally, or both.

Euthanasia is not appropriate when recovery from disease or disability is likely or possible, when despite disease or disability a good quality of life can be expected for a reasonable period of time, or when behavior problems stand a reasonable chance of improvement given sufficient time and effort. "Convenience euthanasia," when an owner simply no longer wants his dog, is never appropriate. It goes without saying that it is not appropriate to euthanize a dog simply because he is old.

"WHAT SHALL WE DO WITH OUR DOG'S REMAINS?" You'd be surprised to know how many people never give this important subject a single thought until they are confronted with the question. If you have your dog euthanized by your veterinarian and wish him or her to make the final arrangements for your dog's body, he may be governed by state law as to how that may be done. In New York State, for example, veterinarians have only one option, cremation — either "communal," with other pets, or "private," in which your own dog or cat's ashes are returned to you. In most localities they include *burial,* either on your own property if not prohibited by law or, as is more likely in urban areas, in a nearby pet cemetery; and *cremation,* either private or communal, to be performed by whatever pet cemetery/crematorium you select. Again, if you elect private cremation, your dog's ashes may be returned to you in a tin or urn, buried in the pet cemetery, or scattered on the premises of the cemetery/crematorium. Many pet owners are comforted by having Molly's or Buddy's ashes in a pretty urn over the mantel. Other pet owners have already decided that the small urns shall be buried with them when they themselves pass on.

Other states have different laws governing the kinds of final arrangements a veterinarian may make for your dog's body. These may include mass cremation, mass burial, and shipping to rendering plants, which are factories where bodies, usually of livestock but in some cases also of companion animals, are torn apart (rended) and processed into various products, such as tallow, fertilizer, hides, and even pet foods. Unpleasant as it may be to discuss this subject with your veterinarian, there is peace of mind in knowing exactly what will become of your dog's remains after his death, and making the choice that feels right for you.

"HOW CAN WE EXPRESS OUR FEELINGS FOR OUR DOG?" There are many different ways that you can memorialize your dog, and part of your continuing discussion with family members should be to find out what one another's thoughts are on this subject. Right now, however, it's important just to include the idea of a memorial in your early conversations. Talking about different ways to memorialize the family dog helps everyone understand that *of course* this death will be grieved just like that of any other member of the family, and *of course* you will want to do something to express how much the dog meant to you.

(Note: If you live alone, talk these matters over with close friends and relatives who are also animal lovers and may have also lost a beloved pet. Unfortunately, people who have never had a close and loving relationship with an animal may not be able to share or even comprehend your feelings about losing your dog. Protect yourself from the hurt and disappointment of having your words fall on deaf ears.)

INCLUDE CHILDREN IN YOUR TALKS It is a mistake to try to shield children from the truth about the illness and pending death of the family dog. Very young children should be spared the sight of overwhelming sadness on the part of the adults around them, but even young children should be told the truth, in simple terms that they can understand, and should be given the chance to express their feelings about it.

TALK WITH YOUR VETERINARIAN Don't hesitate to talk frankly with your dog's veterinarian about your dog's condition, about all the options that are available, whether he may recover and, if so, what his quality of life might be. Do not expect your veterinarian to make life-and-death decisions for you, but do ask her any questions you have about euthanasia as well as long-term at-home care so that you can talk intelligently about both options with family members.

TRY TO MAKE SURE MONEY IS AVAILABLE Back in chapter 5 we talked about the wisdom of having money set aside in a "canine bank account" specifically for the purpose of meeting the expenses of your dog's final illness and death. The decisions that you must make at this time are difficult enough without finding yourself unable to afford the option with which you feel most comfortable.

Grieving Your Loss

Deciding about and participating in the death of your dog can be emotionally and financially draining. Depending on how long he is ill, the process may drag on for weeks or even months. In a worst-case scenario, there may be many different tests and courses of treatment, including medicine and surgery, multiple stays in the hospital, even visits to specialists in search of a precise diagnosis, second opinion, alternative treatment, or all three. When an illness is terminal, however, or when euthanasia is elected to bring an end to suffering, eventually the dying will be done. Then the grieving can begin.

Many dog owners are caught completely off-guard by the depth of their feelings following the death of their dogs — feelings not only of sadness, which they expected, but surprising emotions such as anger, or loss of interest in ordinary pleasures. Well-intentioned suggestions from friends and coworkers, even other family members, to the effect that they should get out more to take their mind off their troubles, or should get themselves another dog, only make them feel worse.

Such feelings are completely understandable. They are part of the normal grieving process. Understanding how this process works may help you to accept your own strong feelings. Keep the following points in mind as you struggle to adjust to your loss.

GRIEVING THE DEATH OF YOUR DOG IS COMPLETELY NORMAL It is just as normal and appropriate to grieve the death of your dog as it is to grieve the loss of any other person, place, or thing that you've valued and held dear. It's unfortunate that in our culture, grieving our pet losses is not yet fully accepted. If you already have some notion that your sadness is excessive, the lack of understanding and support from others at this time can reinforce that notion, causing you to conclude there's something "wrong" with you for feeling the way you do. Ideally, we should welcome and embrace our grief, because without grieving, true healing and a healthy recovery cannot occur.

GRIEF NORMALLY CONSISTS OF SEVERAL DISTINCT STAGES Contrary to popular belief, grieving is much more complicated than just feeling sad. The usual stages of grief (you may not necessarily experience all of them or in this order) are guilt, denial, anger, depression, and acceptance.

Guilt may come into play for a number of reasons. Even the most con-scientious owner may wonder if she really did everything possible, or soon enough, or for long enough. Every dog owner, just like every parent, every sibling, every friend, is guilty of some lapses in caring, sensitivity, patience, good judgment. Death, with its awful finality, seems to call to mind every single instance when you might have done better, and feelings of guilt — not just about the death and final illness, but for failures during the dog's lifetime — are the result.

So uncomfortable can the guilty feelings be that the dog owner may move into *denial* as a way of pushing them away. Denial is not so much say-ing, "This didn't happen," as it is saying, "I don't feel this way." The dog owner who sheds no tears and almost immediately is able to talk calmly and fondly about his dog may be denying the pain he is feeling — even to him-self. People who are truly feeling their pain tend at first to dwell on and even obsess about the final days and minutes of the dog's life. People who are in denial are more likely to talk of other things, even to the point of being so-licitous of the feelings of others who are attempting to be of comfort to them!

Anger usually follows guilt and denial in the process of grieving. At this stage, the dog owner, who is as yet unable to look inward and acknowledge how devastated he feels, instead looks outward to find someone or some-thing he can blame for everything that has happened. He may blame the vet-erinarian, for not being able to save his dog's life, or even for being the one to take that life through euthanasia, although the pet owner was the one who first suggested that the time had come. The anger may be directed at other family members, for not caring enough, or even at the dog herself, for not recovering the way that so-and-so's dog had, or for cheating her owner out of the full twelve years she was "supposed" to live.

When anger has run its exhausting course, *depression* may set in. No mat-ter whose fault it was, no matter how badly someone or everyone behaved, the dog is still gone and isn't coming back. In the depression stage, time stands still. It is as if the sun will never shine again, the awful feelings will never go away, no one understands or ever will. Feelings of hopelessness and despair often are present.

Without support — from friends and family or perhaps from a relatively new mental health professional called a "grief counselor"— the grieving process may stall at this stage. In time, to be sure, the intense feelings will fade. This may convince you and others that at last you've "gotten over it." Getting over it, however, is not the same thing as healing. With support, on the other hand, even if it only comes from yourself, you can move on to the final stage of grief: *acceptance*.

Acceptance is feeling your feelings at last. It's standing up for your right to have these particular feelings. It's when you say, even if only to yourself, "This animal was a very important part of my life because . . ." (Your reasons are your own; they may not make sense to anyone else, but they are completely valid for you.) Acceptance is when you say, "I have every right to be crushed by his death. He deserves my sorrow." The act of deciding, almost insisting, on feeling bad for a while is empowering. You will still feel sad, but now it's your decision and it makes sense to you. It's not just an overwhelming sadness that sneaks up and engulfs you. Out of this sense of empowerment, you can begin to take actions to cope with your loss.

(Note: The stages of grief may apply just as well to the period of time just prior to the death of your dog. As you face the difficult decisions involved with his or her final illness, you may find yourself feeling guilty, angry, and generally overwhelmed. It will help you to recognize that these feelings are normal and to just let them happen. In addition, start thinking about and even implementing some of the coping strategies listed below.)

Coping Strategies

Grief counselors recommend the same strategies for coping with the death of a dog as you might use if you lost a human member of your family:

GIVE YOURSELF TIME There is no set timetable for grieving. Your spouse or partner may be feeling much better in a week, while you're still bursting into tears twice a day. That's okay.

SEEK PROFESSIONAL HELP IF YOU NEED IT Although everyone grieves in his own way and at his own pace, do keep one eye open for small increments of progress. It may take you a lot longer than your spouse or partner to feel whole again after the loss of the family dog, but over time you should be able to tell that you're doing better. If not, see if your veterinarian or local humane society can refer you to a pet-loss counselor or support group. Alternatively, contact an organization such as the Delta Society (see chapter 17), which maintains a nationwide directory of persons who can help owners who have lost a pet.

MOURN YOUR DOG'S DEATH When humans die, their families have a wake, a funeral, or other kind of service for the express purpose of saying good-bye in the company of friends, relatives, and members of the community who share in the sense of loss and extend their support and sympathy to those most aggrieved. A similar kind of service, even if on a much smaller scale, would be entirely appropriate upon the loss of your dog.

Probably you will not have a casket and actual graveside service (although you might, if you opt to have your dog buried at a pet cemetery or are allowed under the law to bury her under the apple tree in your backyard). Nevertheless, you can pick a time and place that feels "right" for you and invite to your dog's "funeral" others who knew and had a special relationship with him, such as the children next door who played with him in the yard, or the staff at the veterinarian's office, or your dog's regular groomer or some pals from the dog park. It doesn't have to be a complicated affair — just a chance to say a few words or to make a few meaningful gestures. For instance, if you do bury your dog, perhaps it would be nice to note that you're sending her on her journey with her favorite ball, or wearing the little red collar with the bells that everyone in the neighborhood always noticed. Don't feel that it's selfish of you to ask others to attend. Chances are that they need a chance to mourn and say good-bye too.

Don't be surprised if you receive a note of condolence from your veterinarian's office, as this simple courtesy is more and more often a part of good practice today. Large stationery and card stores also offer a selection of sympathy cards "on the death of a pet." If you've made a practice of supporting your own pet-loving friends in this way, you are more apt to receive such thoughtful notes from them in return. (If there's no such tradition within your circle of acquaintances, why not be the one who starts it?)

CELEBRATE YOUR DOG'S LIFE Offering some kind of tribute or memorial to the life of your dog can be a powerfully healing experience. What you choose to do should reflect your own personal values and style. If you're the creative type, you might want to write a poem or essay about your dog that could actually be published in, say, the newsletter of your local dog owners' association, on your veterinarian's bulletin board, or elsewhere. If photography is more your thing, perhaps you'd like to put together a small memorial album with photos through the years, complete with captions that you and any children you have can write. Depending on the time of year when your pet dies, you might want to select a favorite color photo of the two of you and have it made into your annual card for the holiday season. Or, if you have a high-quality photograph of your dog that you really love, you could commission an animal artist to do a portrait of your dog based on the photograph.

Other ideas include planting in your dog's memory a tree or bed of flowers somewhere "special" — perhaps along a path in the woods where you used to hike. Some pet owners choose to make monetary donations to help support research into the particular disease that claimed the life of their dog. All humane and other animal-protection organizations have special programs that are always in need of financial support, and will publish in their newsletters the names of dogs whose owners have made contributions in their memory. For example, you could be one of the sponsors of your local humane society's annual walk-a-thon to help provide low-cost spay/neuter or lost-and-found services to the community. The possibilities are limitless. The important thing is to choose the kind of memorial that seems especially appropriate as a way of celebrating the dog you have lost.

OPEN YOUR HEART TO LOVING AGAIN   For every dog owner who says "Never again!" many more say "Yes" to another dog to share their lives. It may not (and probably should not) be immediately. But when your own grieving process is completed, the day may come on its own when you start to feel interested in starting over with another dog.

By now, you *know* a new boxer or beagle can't replace the dog you lost. Unfortunately, some people do get the same kind of dog again, as a replacement. It almost never works, because every dog is different from every other, no matter how much they may *look* alike. Replacement, even if intended as a tribute to your former dog, is hardly fair to your new boxer or beagle, who will never understand why he just can't seem to please you.

On the other hand, many people choose the same type of dog again not as a replacement, but because the one they had had suited them so well. Others choose an entirely different type because they've come to realize that a different kind of dog — smaller, larger, calmer, older — may actually have made more sense all along, or because they're simply up for a completely new experience.

There are many different ways to approach the subject of a new dog, and many questions that only you can answer. It wouldn't be a bad thing to go back and review the early chapters of this book to help you sort out your expectations and reassess any changes in your lifestyle. With so much up in the air, there's one thing you can be sure of: In spite of the pain you're just beginning to get over, you'd rather have a dog in your life than not have a dog in your life. This may be the most fitting tribute of all to the dog you loved and lost.

Why not take a ride over to your local shelter next week? Why not find out if they have a dog who's just waiting for you?

Consumer Provisions

Summary

Thirteen states have consumer remedies when purchasing certain animals from a commercial establishment. Eleven are state laws (Arizona, California,* Connecticut, Florida, Maine, Minnesota, New Hampshire, New York, South Carolina, Vermont, and Virginia) and two are by regulation (Massachusetts and New Jersey). All thirteen states cover dogs, twelve cover cats and dogs (California does not cover cats), and one (New Hampshire) includes ferrets.

Thirteen states give between seven and fifteen days for the consumer to have the dog or cat checked for illness. Five states give a year to check for congenital or hereditary disorders (California, Florida, Maine, Minnesota, and Vermont), and two (New Jersey and South Carolina) give six months.

Of the thirteen states, eight allow the purchaser to keep the dog or cat and get a reimbursement of veterinary expenses. Nine of those (Arizona, Connecticut, Florida, Maine, Minnesota, New Jersey, New York, South

---

* References to California apply only to dogs throughout this summary; cats are not included in the consumer remedies portion of the law.

Carolina, and Vermont) reimburse up to the cost of the dog or cat. One (California) allows up to 150 percent of the cost of the dog. The remaining three states (Massachusetts, New Hampshire, and Virginia) do not allow any kind of reimbursement for expenses if you elect to keep the dog or cat.

In all thirteen states, a consumer can exchange the dog or cat for another dog or cat, or get a refund.

In all thirteen states, the pet shop must supply the buyer with written notice of the buyer's rights. And in one state (California), the rights must be given orally as well. Maine law requires the purchaser to sign a form verifying acknowledgment of the notice and all medical information must be given orally.

Summaries of Laws/Regulations

1. ARKANSAS Law contains consumer remedies that allow the dog or cat to be declared unfit for sale within ten days of purchase; the purchaser may keep the dog or cat and be reimbursed for veterinary bills up to the purchase price of the dog or cat, and reimbursement must be made within ten business days. Dealer must supply the buyer with written notice of rights.

2. CALIFORNIA When a consumer purchases from a breeder or a pet store, the consumer has fifteen days after taking possession to have a veterinarian certify the dog as unfit, then the dog may: (1) be returned for a refund or reimbursement of veterinarian fees up to the original purchase price, or (2) be exchanged with the same reimbursement, or (3) be kept and the owner receives up to 150 percent of the purchase price for veterinarian fees to treat the dog. Also, commercial dealers are liable for 75 percent of the purchase price if the dealer fails to provide any promised registration papers within 120 days. Any dogs returned due to illness shall receive proper veterinary care. If the dog will continue to suffer, euthanasia, if necessary. The dealer must supply the buyer with written notice of rights.

3. CONNECTICUT Within fifteen days, the law stipulates that if a dog or cat becomes ill or dies of an illness that existed at the time of the sale, the pet store must either replace the animal or refund in full the purchase price. Additionally, the presentation of a veterinarian's certificate, stating that the dog or cat was ill at the time of the purchase, shall be sufficient proof to claim reimbursement of expenses.

4. FLORIDA Law stipulates that a dog or cat can be declared unfit for purchase due to illness within fourteen days of purchase, and up to one year later for congenital or hereditary disorders. The consumer can get a refund of the purchase price, get an even exchange, or keep the animal and be reimbursed for veterinarian bills up to the purchase price of the dog or cat.

The reimbursement must be received within ten days of purchase. The dealer must supply the buyer with written and oral notice of rights.

5. MAINE   Law stipulates dogs or cats can be declared unfit for sale within ten days or up to one year for hereditary or congenital defects; consumer options include a full refund, exchange for another animal, or retain animal and receive reimbursement of up to one-half of veterinary fees and up to one-half of purchase price. Pet dealers must post rights of consumers; consumer must sign acknowledging rights were given, oral notice must be given of medical problems. Also, consumers must be given written notice that pet registry papers do not assure the health or quality of an animal.

6. MASSACHUSETTS   Regulations stipulate that a dog or cat can be declared unfit for sale within fourteen days. The consumer can then get a refund or make an exchange. The dealer must supply written notice of the buyer's rights.

7. MINNESOTA   Law stipulates that a dog or cat can be declared unfit for sale within ten days, and up to one year later for congenital or hereditary defect. The consumer can then get a refund or make an exchange, and be reimbursed for veterinary expenses.

8. NEW HAMPSHIRE   Within fourteen days of sale, the law states that a purchaser of a dog, cat, or ferret from a pet shop shall have the animal examined by a licensed veterinarian. Within two days of the examination, if the dog, cat, or ferret is deemed unhealthy, the owner shall be entitled to a substitution or a full refund. No dog, cat, or ferret under eight weeks of age may be sold in any pet store.

9. NEW JERSEY   Regulations stipulate a buyer has fourteen days to get a dog or cat declared unfit for sale due to illness and up to six months for congenital or hereditary disorders. Then the owner can get a refund or exchange, or retain the animal and be reimbursed for vet bills up to the cost of the dog or cat. The dealer must supply the buyer with a written notice of rights.

10. NEW YORK   Law gives fourteen days to have a dog or cat declared unfit due to illness. The consumer can get a refund, an exchange, or a reimbursement for veterinary bills up to the cost of the dog or cat. Reimbursement must be made within ten business days. The dealer must supply a written notice to the buyer of rights.

11. SOUTH CAROLINA   Law gives the consumer up to fourteen days to have the dog or cat declared unfit due to illness and up to six months for congenital or hereditary cause or condition. The consumer can obtain a refund, exchange, or reimbursement of the veterinary fees not to exceed 50 percent of the purchase price of the animal.

12. VERMONT   Law gives the consumer up to seven days to have the dog or cat declared unfit due to illness and up to one year for congenital or hereditary disorders. The consumer can obtain a refund, exchange, or reimbursement not to exceed the purchase price. The reimbursement must occur within ten business days, and a written notice of buyer rights must be given by the dealer.

13. VIRGINIA   Law stipulates the purchaser has ten days to have the dog or cat declared unfit due to illness. The consumer can get a refund or an exchange not to exceed purchase price. The reimbursement must occur within ten business days. Written notification of rights must be given to the buyer.

What's Distinctive about an AAHA Hospital Member?

American and Canadian pet owners who take their animals to an AAHA hospital member will find a veterinarian with a unique commitment to the highest standards of veterinary care as well as concern for preventive medicine.

To become an AAHA hospital member, the candidate hospital must meet AAHA's standards for hospital services and facilities in twelve specific areas. A trained AAHA practice consultant periodically visits the hospital to evaluate thoroughly the facility to be sure it complies with these standards. The following areas are covered in the AAHA standards:

- *Orderly and adequate medical records* — These are critical for the pet's welfare and continuity of care. Records are reviewed on-site. There must be an individual record for each pet patient.
- *Complete diagnostic facilities* — This includes the examination room, radiology services, clinical pathology services, and the equipment necessary to provide comprehensive inpatient and outpatient services. The facility must be fully equipped to make prompt, accurate diagnosis and treatment. An on-site library of basic textbooks and current periodicals also is required.

- *Complete pharmacy facilities* — The most frequently used medicines must be available at all times, controlled substances must be monitored, and clients must be adequately informed concerning treatment.
- *Proper anesthetic procedures* — The hospital must conduct a pre-anesthetic examination before surgery and provide a safe, painless, state-of-the-art anesthesia during surgery.
- *Modern surgical facilities* — The hospital must have an aseptic, single-use room for surgery. Proper lighting, sterile equipment and procedures, and easy access to drugs and equipment are required.
- *Nursing care* — This is a vital part of an efficient animal hospital. Skilled veterinary technicians contribute greatly to the professional care pets receive, from diagnosis through recuperation.
- *Properly maintained environment* — Safe and sanitary conditions must be maintained throughout the hospital, from the reception room to the kennel, including the outside premises.
- *Emergency service* — Each AAHA hospital must provide, or have access to, twenty-four-hour emergency service for its clients.
- *Dental service* — Oral hygiene is as important to a pet's health as it is to a person's health. AAHA hospitals routinely perform teeth cleaning, extractions, and gum work.

All AAHA hospital members voluntarily meet or exceed the association's standards for facilities, equipment, and quality procedures. They are regularly evaluated by an AAHA consultant to assure continuing compliance.

In addition, every AAHA veterinarian is encouraged to keep up-to-date on major developments in veterinary medicine. The association offers its thirteen thousand members a wide variety of continuing education opportunities — self-study courses, seminars, lectures, workshops, annual and regional meetings, videotapes, computer education, and publications.

AAHA hospital members are truly distinctive in providing the highest quality care for pets. AAHA standards are recognized around the world as the benchmark for quality care in veterinary medicine.

Choosing a Veterinary Hospital

It's important to choose a veterinary hospital before you need one. Ask family, friends, and neighbors for recommendations. Once you find a hospital, take some time to check it out. Ask for a tour of the facility, and use your eyes and nose to detect cleanliness. Also check if the facility is well-lit. Does it have laboratory equipment? Is there gas anesthesia? If it doesn't meet your expectations, turn around and leave.

In addition to the facility, you'll also want to make sure the veterinarian meets your expectations. It's important that you and your pet are comfortable with the doctor. The veterinarian should be able to communicate with you and make you feel comfortable asking questions. Even if the doctor is highly qualified, if you don't hit it off, you may need to go elsewhere.

Finally, when choosing a veterinary hospital, make sure the office hours and payment policy are convenient for you. Ask for a hospital brochure or welcome letter that explains the hospital policies and procedures.

Hospitals that are accredited by the American Animal Hospital Association (AAHA) meet high veterinary care standards. Each hospital voluntarily completes a detailed evaluation of its services and equipment. Then a trained practice consultant thoroughly inspects the hospital to make sure it meets AAHA's high standards in the areas of

- emergency services
- surgery and anesthesia
- radiology services
- pathology services
- nursing care
- pharmacy
- dentistry
- examination facilities
- pet medical records
- medical library
- housekeeping and maintenance

Less than 14 percent of the small-animal veterinary hospitals in the United States and Canada are accredited AAHA members. For the names of AAHA hospitals in your area, call (800) 883-6301 and ask for the Member Service Center.

The American Animal Hospital Association is an international organization of more than thirteen thousand veterinarians who treat companion animals. Established in 1933, the association is well known among veterinarians for its high standards for hospitals and pet health care.

Reprinted with permission of the American Animal Hospital Association.
To locate an AAHA-accredited animal hospital, contact the American Animal Hospital Association in one of the following ways:

Mail: P. O. Box 150899
      Denver, CO 80215-0899
Telephone: (800) 883-6301
Website: www:\\healthypets.com

Index